Ann Rule is a former Seattle policewoman and the author of eight best-selling books, including *If You Really Loved Me*, a chilling chronicle of a millionaire's murderous secret life; *Everything She Ever Wanted*, the terrifying story of a sociopathic Georgia belle and her fatal allure; *Small Sacrifices*, the horrific account of a woman's homicidal assault on her three young children; *The Stranger Beside Me*, the fascinating tale of Rule's dawning horror as she realised her friend and co-worker, Ted Bundy, was a serial killer; *Possession*, a searing novel of mind control and sexual enslavement on a lonely mountain-top; and three volumes of her unrivalled 'Crime Files': *A Rose for her Grave*, *You Belong to Me* and *A Fever in the Heart*. Many of these are available in paperback from Warner Books.

When she is not attending trials and researching new books, Ann Rule lives near Seattle, Washington.

Also by Ann Rule

BITTER HARVEST
EVERYTHING SHE EVER WANTED
IF YOU REALLY LOVED ME
THE STRANGER BESIDE ME
POSSESSION
SMALL SACRIFICES
AND NEVER LET HER GO

A ROSE FOR HER GRAVE AND OTHER TRUE CASES
(Ann Rule's Crime Files: Vol. 1)
YOU BELONG TO ME AND OTHER TRUE CASES
(Ann Rule's Crime Files: Vol. 2)
A FEVER IN THE HEART AND OTHER TRUE CASES
(Ann Rule's Crime Files: Vol. 3)
IN THE NAME OF LOVE AND OTHER TRUE CASES
(Ann Rule's Crime Files: Vol. 4)
THE END OF THE DREAM AND OTHER TRUE CASES
(Ann Rule's Crime Files: Vol. 5)
A RAGE TO KILL AND OTHER TRUE CASES
(Ann Rule's Crime Files: Vol. 6)

DEAD BY SUNSET

PERFECT HUSBAND, PERFECT KILLER?

Ann Rule

WARNER BOOKS

A *Warner* Book

First published in the United States in 1995
by Simon & Schuster Inc.
First published in Great Britain in 1996
by Little, Brown and Company
This edition published in 1997 by Warner Books
Reprinted 1999, 2001

A CIP catalogue record for this book
is available from the British Library.

*Unless otherwise noted, all photographs
are from the author's collection.*

ISBN: 0 7515 1869 7

Typeset by
Palimpsest Book Production Limited,
Polmont, Stirlingshire
Printed and bound in Great Britain
by Clays Ltd, St Ives plc

Warner Books
A Division of
Little, Brown and Company (UK)
Brettenham House
Lancaster Place
London WC2E 7EN

www.littlebrown.co.uk

to Cheryl Keeton

may your sons know and remember how

very much you loved them

and

to abused women everywhere

in the hope

that they may find freedom and joy

CONTENTS

. . . written laws, which were like spiders' webs, and would catch, it is true, the weak and poor, but [could] easily be broken by the mighty and the rich.

ANACHARSIS, sixth century B.C.

Violence and injury enclose in their net all that do such things, and generally return upon him who began.

LUCRETIUS, 99–55 B.C.

Part I

The Crime

1

September 21, 1986, was a warm and beautiful Sunday in Portland – in the whole state of Oregon, for that matter. With any luck, the winter rains of the Northwest were a safe two months away. The temperature had topped off at sixty-nine degrees about four that afternoon, and even at 9 P.M. it was still a relatively balmy fifty-eight degrees.

Randall Kelly Blighton had traveled west on Highway 26 – the Sunset Highway – earlier that evening, driving his youngsters back to their mother's home in Beaverton after their weekend visitation with him. A handsome, athletic-looking man with dark hair and a mustache, Blighton was in his twenties, a truck salesman. His divorce from his wife was amicable, and he was in a good mood as he headed back toward Portland along the same route.

The Sunset Highway, which is actually a freeway, can often be a commuter's nightmare. It runs northwest from the center of Portland, past the OMSI zoo and through forestlike parks. Somewhere near the crossroads of Sylvan, the Multnomah/Washington county-line sign flashes by almost subliminally. Then the freeway angles toward the Pacific Ocean beaches as it skirts Beaverton and the little town of Hillsboro.

The land drops away past Sylvan, giving the area its name West Slope. Route 8 trails off the Sunset Highway down the curves of the slope, past pleasant neighborhoods, until it runs through a commercial zone indistinguishable from similar zones anywhere in America: pizza parlors, supermarkets, car dealers, strip malls. Approaching Hillsboro, the Washington County seat, Route 8 – the TVA Highway – slices through what was only recently farmland. The Tualatin River valley, once richly agricultural, is now a technological wonderland. Its endless woods are dwindling and the area has become known as the Silicon Forest. There are acres and acres of corporate parks in Washington County now: Intel, Fujitsu, NEC, and Tektronix. Intel is already the largest single employer in Oregon; soon there will be more workers in the computer and electronics industry in Oregon than there are timber employees.

Apparently serenely untroubled by the encroachment of modern technology, the Sisters of Saint Mary have been stationed along the TVA Highway for many years, their nunnery and school on the left, their home for wayward boys on the right.

In an instant Route 8 becomes Tenth Avenue in Hillsboro. A left turn on Main Street leads toward the old city center and the county courthouse. Main Street is idyllically lined with wide lawns, wonderful old houses with gingerbread touches, jack-o'-lanterns at Halloween and spectacular lights during the Christmas season. But it hasn't fared so well commercially since the new Target store and the mall went up south of town; its chief businesses are antique stores and, except for the Copper Stone restaurant and cocktail lounge, the kind of restaurants where ladies linger over tea.

The Washington County Courthouse is surrounded by manicured grounds with magnolias and towering sequoias planted more than a century ago. It *smells* like a courthouse; at least the original structure does: wax, dust, the daily lunchroom special, and old paint baking on radiators. The people employed there are comfortable and at home, bantering with one another as they go about their work; the people who come there on all manner of missions are more often than not angry, worried, grieving, frightened, annoyed, or apprehensive. Some walk away with a sense of justice done, and some don't walk away at all; they are handcuffed and locked up in the jail next door.

Not far from the courthouse, something terrible happened on the Sunset Highway on September 21, 1986, at the Sylvan market, just inside Washington County. And in the end, it would all be settled in this courthouse, as Christmas lights glowed in the branches of a tall fir on the corner of Main and First Streets and icy rain pelted court watchers and witnesses alike.

The end would be a long time coming.

It was about 8:30 on that Sunday night in September, and dark enough so that Randy Blighton needed his headlights to see what lay ahead of him on the curving Sunset Highway. He was startled as he came around one of those curves near Sylvan in the West Slope area and saw that cars a half mile ahead of him were suddenly swerving out of the fast lane into the right-hand lane. It looked as if there might be something in the road ahead that they hadn't been able to see until the last moment. A dead animal perhaps, or maybe a truck tire. Whatever it was, it had to be dangerous; a last-minute lane switch only worked if the right lane was clear.

Blighton traveled another hundred feet and now he could make out the dark hulk of a Toyota van turned crosswise on the freeway. Its lights were off and it was in a perilous position, completely blocking the fast lane. Luckily, the drivers ahead of Blighton had been alert, but it would be only a matter of time before someone came around the curve in the fast lane and smashed into the van. People usually drove the Sunset Highway between fifty-five and sixty-five miles an hour and a crash like that would undoubtedly escalate rapidly into a fatal multicar pileup. Blighton was grateful that, for the moment at least, the freeway was not heavily traveled. And that was only a freak circumstance. At 8:30 on a Sunday night after a weekend of good weather, there had to be hundreds of vehicles heading back to Portland from the coast.

Randy Blighton's first inclination was to swerve around the van; he had things to do at home. 'I was going to go on by too,' he later recalled, 'but then I spotted the silhouette of an infant seat in the van. I couldn't ignore that. I'd just left my own kids, and I could never live with myself if there was a baby or a little kid in that van.'

Blighton's reflexes were good. He tapped his brakes, pulled his car over on the right shoulder, grabbed a couple of flares, and then ran across the freeway toward the van. As he got close to it, he could see that it was perpendicular to the median that separated the eastbound and westbound lanes, its front bumper repeatedly tapping the concrete Jersey barriers. The van's engine was still turning over, and it was in gear, inching forward and then being held back by the barriers.

Blighton knew that he was as much a sitting duck as the Toyota if a car came around the curve, and he hurriedly lit the flares and set them out in the fast lane to warn motorists, in time he hoped, to veer to the right. He had no idea what he might find as he reached for the driver's door handle of the van – possibly someone who had had a stroke or a heart attack. It might even be a driverless vehicle that had slipped its brakes and somehow ended up on the freeway. In 1986, at this point on the Sunset, there were still some neighborhood streets from which cars could enter the freeway as if the Sunset was merely another intersection. Southwest 79th, just to the south of the accident, was one of those streets. Maybe the driver of the van, unfamiliar with the Sunset's eccentricities, had turned far too widely and rammed into the barriers.

Blighton opened the driver's-side door. The van was not empty. He could make out a figure lying on the front seat. The person's legs were near the gearshift console and extended over the driver's seat. The back was on the passenger seat, and the head was tucked into the chest and drooping over toward the floor. He didn't know if it was a man or woman, but he saw a smallish loafer-type shoe on one foot that looked feminine.

There was no time for Blighton to try to figure out who the driver was, or how he – or she – had ended up crosswise on the freeway. He stepped up into the driver's side, pushing the legs out of the way as much as he could. Now he could see that there was a woman's purse jammed between the accelerator and the firewall. That would explain why the van continued to move forward. Blighton felt along the dash to try to find the switch for the emergency flashers but he couldn't locate it; he didn't know that it was overhead.

There was the child's carseat right behind the driver's seat. It was empty, but that didn't make Blighton feel much better; the baby could be on the floor someplace. Counting on the flares to warn other cars to go around, he slid the side passenger door open and patted the floor and seats with his hands. Everything he touched was wet and he realized why it had been so hard to see through the driver's-side window. Something dark splattered the glass. On some level, he knew he was running his hands through pooled blood, but finding the baby that might be there was more important than anything else. When he found nothing, he ran to the back of the van, opened the hatchback, and looked in. No baby. Thank God. No baby.

Instinctively, Blighton wiped his hands down his shirt and pants, wanting to get the wet, iodiney-smelling stuff off them. He shuddered, but he didn't stop to consider how there could be blood if the van had not been hit by another vehicle. He ran back to the driver's door, hopped into the van, expertly shifted into reverse, and backed the van across the freeway and onto the shoulder of 79th where it met the Sunset Highway.

Only when he had assured himself that the Toyota was no longer in danger of being hit by oncoming traffic did Blighton turn to look closely at the person lying across the seat. He *thought* it was a woman. Her hair was short and dark, but he didn't know if she was young or old. She did not respond to his questions, but he still kept asking, 'Are you okay? Are you hurt?'

Blighton ran around to the front passenger door and found it was slightly ajar. He opened it and picked up the woman's hand, feeling for a pulse in her wrist. There was no reassuring beat. He could see blood on her face, and one of her eyes protruded grotesquely, as big as a hard-boiled egg. Even if he had known this woman, he would never have recognized her.

His first thought was that he had to get help for her; maybe she *did* have a pulse but too faint for him to detect. He ran back to the driver's side and reached in, running his hands along the dash, searching frantically again for the emergency flashers switch. He finally saw it overhead and switched them on. They clicked in eerie rhythm, but that was the only sound he heard. The woman wasn't breathing.

Blighton stuck more flares in the gravel along the shoulder of the freeway and traffic in both lanes slowed down as it passed, hundreds of cars whose occupants had no idea how close they had come to being in a massive fatal pileup. Blighton then looked around for a place where he could call for help. He saw lights along S.W. 79th, the street that ran at a right angle onto the Sunset Highway. No one responded to his knock at the first house, even though he could hear voices inside. He pounded on the door of the second house and a young woman opened it.

'There's a bad accident on the freeway,' he gasped. 'Call an ambulance. I'm going back out there.'

It was hard to judge the passage of time, but Blighton estimated that about ten minutes had passed since he first saw the Toyota van angled crazily across the freeway. Cars were inching by in a single lane now, and he caught glimpses of curious faces darting a look at what appeared to be nothing more than a roadside breakdown.

The woman who lay across the seat hadn't moved.

Sirens wailed somewhere in the distance, and soon Blighton could see the flashing red lights of an ambulance.

Thomas Stewart Duffy, Jr – Tom – was on duty at Washington County Fire District Number One, the West Slope station, that Sunday night. The station was just east of the IGA supermarket between Canyon Drive and Canyon Lane at S.W. 78th Street. The alarm bells sounded at 20:44:50 (8:44 P.M. and fifty seconds), and the call came in as a 'probable DOA' on the Sunset Highway. There were a lot of calls from the Sunset, and a fair amount of them were fatals, so Tom Duffy and his partner, Mike Moran, both paramedics, were familiar with the area. Running for their rig, a Chevrolet van, the two men leaped in and headed up Canyon Lane, turned left on West Slope Drive, and then went northbound on 79th toward the Sunset Highway.

It was an older neighborhood with houses on big lots set far off the street and well apart from each other. Huge trees edged the narrow roadway and there were no street lights. The medics' rig lights were on, but they still had trouble seeing until they spotted the flares at the southwest corner of the Sunset and 79th. In a heartbeat, the quiet dark street ended in a usually roaring freeway. That night, they saw cars backed up to the west for miles.

It had taken them two minutes and twenty seconds to reach the site.

Tom Duffy was a former army combat medic who served in Vietnam. He had worked for thirteen years as a paramedic with the Washington County Fire District and Tualatin Valley Fire and Rescue. Altogether, he had over twenty-eight years in the medical field. Very tall and lean, he rarely smiled. He had seen people die in all manner of ways. He had seen scores of fatal accidents, and they always bothered him. He had long since learned to shut his mind to the terrible things he saw during those moments when he fought to save lives, but he never really forgot and he would have almost crystalline recall of that Sunday night.

Duffy and Moran saw a blue Toyota van parked facing north along 79th. A man ran up to them, shouting, 'A lady's in the van. She's hurt really bad!'

'How long has it been since the accident?' Duffy asked.

'I don't know for sure. It took me a while to find a phone. I think about fifteen minutes,' the man answered.

'We saw the van,' Duffy would remember, 'and we assessed the situation quickly. We saw no hazards around it – no power lines down or gas leaking. There was very little damage to the van itself.'

As for the man who had run up to him, Randy Blighton, Duffy didn't know who he was and he had no idea what had happened. Blighton's clothes were streaked with dark stains that could have been blood. The van didn't look wrecked. For all Duffy knew, he and Moran might be walking into trouble.

The three men went over to the van and Blighton opened the passenger door so the paramedics could see the woman inside. 'She's in here,' he said. 'The van was crosswise over there in the fast lane.'

Duffy attempted to find some sign of life in the woman who lay sprawled across the front seat in the shadows of the van. He put a hand on her shoulder and asked, 'Are you all right?'

There was no response.

He exerted more pressure and gave the woman a 'trapezius squeeze' on her shoulder muscle. Someone even semiconscious would have reacted to that force.

There was no response.

Duffy held sensitive fingers to the carotid artery along the side of her neck and felt nothing. 'There was no response at all,' he would remember. 'I could palpate no pulse. No respiration.'

Turning to Mike Moran and three firefighters who had arrived at the scene in a firetruck, he said, 'We need to get her out of this van fast.'

They maneuvered her limp body out of the front seat

with extreme caution, careful not to aggravate any cervical-spinal injuries she might have sustained in the accident. They circled her neck with a bracing collar so that her spinal processes would not be jostled as they took her out of the van. If by some miracle she *was* alive, they didn't want her to be paralyzed. They placed her on the road beside the van and began attempts to resuscitate her, even though they were quite sure it was an exercise in futility.

The gravelly shoulder alongside the Sunset Highway now bristled with people who wanted to help when there was no longer any *way* to help – a Buck Ambulance and its crew, Mike Moran and Tom Duffy, the firefighters and EMTs, and a half dozen state police. In the yellow rays of headlights and flashlights, they could all see that the victim who lay on the ground had suffered massive trauma. The top of her head was, in the blunt words of an observer, 'like mincemeat.' One of the paramedics thought he saw brain matter leaking. There was so much blood – so terribly much blood. It was as thick as curdled sour milk, already beginning to coagulate. Duffy knew that meant that more than five or ten minutes had passed since the woman had last bled freely. Depending on her own particular clotting factor profile, it might have been up to half an hour.

There was no hope of saving her. The dead do not bleed.

'The patient fit into the category of a patient who could not possibly be resuscitated,' he would say later. 'Not at all. She was in cardiopulmonary arrest.' That meant her heart no longer beat; her lungs no longer drew breath. Even without the tremendous loss of blood, the assault to the brain itself would have been fatal. An injured brain responds by swelling, and as it does so, it bulges into centers that control heart rhythm and breathing, effectively shutting down all activity needed to continue life.

By 8:53 P.M., when Oregon State Police Traffic Officer David Fife arrived, the paramedics had given up. There was no hope. The victim lay still, covered partially by a blanket.

Fife walked around the Toyota van and saw it had virtually no damage. But when he lifted the blanket to look at the dead woman, he was appalled at the wounds on her head. How could she have suffered such massive injuries when the van was scarcely marred at all?

Fife moved his patrol unit to the west of the scene and turned on his overheads and emergency lights to warn the drivers who were inching along the Sunset Highway. They weren't going to get to Portland by this route, not for a long time. When his sergeant, James Hinkley, who had been dispatched from the Beaverton substation, arrived, Fife turned the immediate scene over to him and pulled out his camera. He took thirty-six photographs of the victim and the Toyota van, routine for any accident. By this time, Senior Troopers Lloyd Dillon and Ray Veal, along with Washington County Chief Criminal Deputy D.A. Bob Herman, had also arrived to join the group of investigators at the nightmarish scene on the Sunset Highway.

Tom Duffy and his fellow paramedics had quickly reassured themselves that the dead woman had been all alone in the van. Just as with Randy Blighton, breath had caught in their throats when they noticed the child's carseat behind the driver's seat of the van. They knew the woman was beyond their help; they did not know if a baby or a toddler lay somewhere in the darkest spaces of the van or was, perhaps, caught beneath a seat. They steeled themselves to feel with their bare hands all around the inside of the van, running their fingers through the rapidly cooling blood that had spattered, stained, and pooled there. Finally they were satisfied that the child who used that safety seat had not been present in the van when the woman died. The paramedics' hands and arms came away covered with the blood of the female victim.

'There was a lot of blood,' Duffy would recall much later. 'A pool of clotted blood – a big circular pool on the carpet behind the passenger seat. There was blood on the ceiling and on the inside of the windows.' Blood has its own smell, metallic, and that odor clung to the paramedics now.

No one knew who the dead woman was. No one knew what had happened to her. But Tom Duffy was certain of one thing. He had seen literally thousands of car wrecks, and he knew that he was not looking at the aftermath of an automobile accident; he was looking at a crime scene. 'The mechanisms of injury – the damage to this vehicle – could not have produced what we found,' he said later. 'The blood on this person was dried and clotted. There was absolutely no sign of life.'

The Oregon troopers came to a similar conclusion. A slight dent, a few shards of glass from a broken signal light, and a couple of paint chips out by the Jersey barriers that divided the freeway were the only signs that the van had hit anything. The woman hadn't died in an accident. Her injuries had nothing to do with this 'wreck.'

There are always acronyms for official records. Those on the scene at the Sunset Highway used familiar shortcuts now as they filled out forms: DOS – Dead On Scene, MVA – Motor Vehicle Accident, and finally POSS – Possible Homicide. And because this bizarre incident seemed indeed to be a 'POSS,' Oregon State Police Sergeant Hinkley radioed in a request that detectives from the OSP Criminal Division respond to the scene. In Oregon the state police investigate homicides and other felonies as well as traffic accidents.

Detective Jerry Finch wasn't on call that night, but he was the first investigator the dispatcher could raise. Finch ran to his unmarked Ford LTD II and headed for the Cedar Mill home of Detective Jim Ayers. Ayers, in his mid-thirties, had been assigned to the Beaverton OSP station for three years and was just arriving home from an evening out when he heard the crunch of tires on gravel and saw Finch's car turn into his driveway. Finch told Ayers they had a 'call out' to a possible homicide.

Jim Ayers had investigated all manner of felonies in his fourteen-year career with the Oregon State Police. Like most officers who hired on as troopers, he was tall and well muscled. He had thick, wavy hair and a rumbling deep voice. He had worked the road for eight years, investigating accidents. And like Tom Duffy, like all cops and all paramedics, he had seen too much tragedy. But he had also learned what was 'normal' tragedy – if there could be such a thing – and what was 'abnormal' tragedy.

Ayers had become an expert in both arson investigation and psychosexual crimes, and he had investigated innumerable homicides. Jerry Finch had a few years on him, both in age and in experience. Together the two men drove to the scene at 79th and the Sunset, not knowing what to expect. The best detectives are *not* tough; if they were, they would not have the special intuitive sense that enables them to see what laymen cannot. And Jim Ayers was one of the very best. But like his peers, he usually managed to hide his own pain over what one human can do to another behind a veneer of black humor and professional distance.

It was two minutes after 10 P.M. when Finch and Ayers arrived at the scene, and as Ayers gazed down at the slender woman who lay on the freeway shoulder, her face and head disfigured by some tremendous force that had bludgeoned her again and again, he was still the complete detective – curious and contemplative.

The two detectives walked around the blue Toyota van and saw the minor damage to its right front end and where a turn signal lens was broken out. There was a 'buckle' in the roof of the van on the right. That could be explained easily enough; it was unibody construction, and a blow to the front end would ripple back along the side. Randy Blighton was still on the scene and he told Finch and Ayers how he had found the van butting against the median barrier of the freeway. That would have broken the signal light. They found the signal lens itself lying on the freeway in the fast lane. And they also saw the beige purse that had been forcing the accelerator down before Blighton kicked it away. It would have been enough to keep the engine running while the car was in gear.

With flashlights Finch and Ayers looked into the van, playing light over the child's carseat, the blood spatter on the interior roof, the splash of blood on the hump over the transmission, and the pools of blood on the floor behind the front seats. A white plastic produce bag fluttered on the passenger-side floor. It too bore bloodstains.

The van would have to be processed in daylight, but Jim Ayers had already come to a bleak conclusion, based on the physical evidence he saw, and on Blighton's description of how he found the victim and his recollection that the driver's-side window had been rolled partway down. 'I felt the victim had been beaten while she was in the vehicle,' he would say later. 'My conclusion was that whoever had beaten her had intended to send it [the van] across the eastbound lanes of the Sunset Highway so that it would be hit by other vehicles.'

Had that happened, the cars approaching at fifty-five to sixty-five miles an hour would have rounded the curve and smashed into the driver's side of the Toyota van. Even if the van hadn't burst into flames, that would have destroyed every bit of evidence on the woman's body and in the vehicle itself. The massive head injuries she had suffered would have been attributed to the accident. Worse, in all likelihood, she would not have been the only fatality.

State policemen have seen too many chain reaction accidents in which a dozen or more people die. Met by the horrifying sight of another vehicle directly in front of them, drivers cannot stop or even take evasive action. Usually chain reaction pileups happen on foggy nights or when smoke from burning crops drifts across a highway. But this van, deliberately left crosswise in the fast lane of the Sunset, would have been like a brick wall appearing suddenly in the night. Clearly, whoever had bludgeoned the woman to death had not given a thought to how many more might die. All he or she had cared about was that the crime of murder would be covered up in a grinding collision of jagged steel, flying glass shards, and broken bodies.

The dead woman's purse contained her driver's license and other identifying documents – or, rather, it contained *some* woman's identification. This woman, lying beside the road, was so disfigured by her beating that it was impossible to be sure that she was the woman whose picture appeared on the driver's license. However, given the laws of probability, Ayers and Finch were reasonably sure that the purse belonged to the victim. The address on her license was 231 N.E. Scott in Gresham, a suburb about as far east of downtown Portland as the accident scene was west.

Ayers and Finch had just dispatched Senior Trooper Al Carson to the Gresham address to notify the victim's next of kin of her death when Finch carefully lifted a checkbook from her purse. 'Look,' he commented to Ayers. 'These checks are personalized, and the address is different than the one on her registration.'

The checks bore the same name as the driver's license: Cheryl Keeton. However, the address imprinted on the checks was 2400 S.W. 81st, located on the West Slope – only three-tenths of a mile from where they now stood.

The woman lying on the ground was probably Cheryl Keeton, whose date of birth was listed on her driver's license as October 27, 1949. That would make her less than a month away from her thirty-seventh birthday. The height and weight on the license seemed to fit the slender victim. Hair color didn't matter much anymore on a driver's license; women changed their hair shade so often. But it was listed as brown and the victim's hair appeared to be brown, although it was now matted with dried blood.

'I don't think she lived in Gresham,' Finch told Ayers. 'I think that's an old address. You hang in here, and I'll take a run up to the address on Eighty-first.'

Oregon State Police Sergeant Greg Baxter radioed the Portland Police Department dispatcher, who relayed a message to Al Carson, calling him back from Gresham. The next of kin of the victim were no longer there.

Ayers was relieved to let Jerry Finch notify whoever might be waiting at the West Slope address for Cheryl Keeton to come home. Of all the responsibilities of a policeman's profession, that was always the hardest. Sometimes the survivors scream, and sometimes they stare, unbelieving, at the officers who bring them tragic news.

Ayers wanted to be sure that the tow truck driver from Jim Collins Towing understood that the Toyota van was a vital piece of evidence and should be hooked up to the tow rig with extreme care. Collins's own son, Harley, had arrived to remove the van from the edge of the Sunset. 'I told him not to touch it any more than he had to – and not to go inside at all,' Ayers said later. 'Not to strap the steering wheel the way they usually do . . .'

Harley Collins said he would be careful and promised to lock the van behind the cyclone fence of Jim Collins's personal yard so that no one could come near it. Ayers felt better hearing that. Although he didn't know the tow driver, he knew that the tow company's owner was reliable.

All the steps that were post-tragedy protocol had been followed. The investigators at the scene radioed a request for Eugene Jacobus, the Chief Deputy Medical Examiner for Washington County. The body was released to Jacobus at 11:35 P.M. The hands were 'bagged,' and Jacobus was careful to see that the body itself was placed in a fresh plastic 'envelope' inside the heavier body pouch so that any trace evidence would be preserved. He also took possession of the victim's purse and locked it in a drawer in his office on Knox Street.

It was after midnight before the scene alongside the Sunset Highway was cleared, and the many men and women working there with measuring tapes and sketch pads were all gone. This death was not a normal death. Nor was it an accident. It was almost certainly a homicide, one that investigators felt confident would be solved in forty-eight hours – just as Washington County's other homicide that weekend was. A male murder victim had been found stabbed multiple times in western Washington County on Friday, September 19. By six o'clock on Sunday night, police had arrested and charged the suspected killer.

But the investigators on this new homicide were wrong when they expected a quick solution. It was as if they were grasping the end of a thread, expecting to pull it loose. They could not know that the thread was only one infinitesimal piece of a fabric so snarled and tangled that it might well have been woven by a madman.

And, in a certain sense, it had been.

2

The good weather on the weekend of September 19–21, 1986, made little difference to Dr Sara Gordon.* She was working on trauma call at Providence Hospital in Portland and there was no day or night, no sense of the seasons, in the operating rooms. The only sounds were muted voices or the music some surgeons preferred; the only lights were focused on the operating field.

Trauma duty is by its very nature unpredictable. Sara Gordon often worked a full day's shift and all through the night too. She was an anesthesiologist, called in for emergency treatment of accident victims, or for the innumerable surgeries that could not wait, some life-threatening and some more routine.

* The names of some individuals in the book have been changed. Such names are indicated by an asterisk (*) the first time each appears in the narrative.

A beautiful, delicate woman, Sara looked more like a kindergarten teacher than a physician. She had huge blue eyes and dimples, and her figure was slender and petite. In truth, she was a workhorse, a woman whose hand was steady no matter if blood might spray chaotically from a nicked artery in the patient she hovered over, no matter if a heart stopped beating or lungs stopped expanding. She had struggled too many years to win her medical degree to be anything less than professional, and she often worked sixty hours a week, napping in the on-call suite between operations.

Sara Gordon had grown up in McMinnville, Oregon, one of ten children. She and her sister Maren* were identical twins, but mirror image twins. 'I'm right-handed,' Sara would explain. 'My twin is left-handed. We're identical – but opposite. Math and science were always easy for me, and Maren was the creative one. When I graduated from high school with a 4.0 grade point average and she got a 3.8, she felt dumb, but it was only because I had a slight edge in math.'

Looking at Sara and Maren, their teachers could not tell them apart, and they played the usual twin pranks, attending class for each other, fooling their friends. They would always be close, but as adults they would look more like just sisters than twins. Sara was thinner, her blond hair lighter than Maren's, and her face often showed signs of stress, perhaps to be expected in her profession.

All the Gordon children were intelligent. One brother was an attorney. Another was a millionaire who owned thousands of acres of prime Oregon grazing land and as many head of prize cattle. Their grandfather pioneered in the Lake Oswego suburb of Portland, long before it became a suburban paradise. Grandfather Kruse's land turned out to be virtually worth its weight in gold. His old house, barns, and outbuildings remained in Lake Oswego just as they always were, but they were surrounded by posh homes, condos, office buildings, and parkways.

Sara's father was not rich, however, and it was a struggle to raise his large family. He was a dairy farmer, and dairy farmers rarely have the money to finance medical school. Sara's parents had no money even to send her to college, much less medical school, and, like the rest of her siblings, she worked her way through college, graduating from Willamette University in Salem, Oregon, in 1973 with a Bachelor of Science degree. At Willamette she dated a young man who would one day be a deputy district attorney in Washington County, Oregon. She also knew Mike Shinn, who was a football star at Willamette and would become a prominent civil attorney in Portland. She never dated Shinn, and they didn't expect to see each other much after college.

Sara had always wanted to be a doctor. Most of the men who were attracted to her didn't take her ambition seriously; she was too pretty, too diminutive, and she was always so concerned about other people's feelings. Maybe she didn't fit the accepted picture of a physician, but she was completely committed to achieving her goal.

Sara married a young teacher, who convinced her he supported her dream of a career in medicine. He didn't – not really. He wanted a stay-at-home wife. Accepted at Oregon Health Sciences University in 1974, she decided not to go. She tried to be a perfect housewife, but she yearned to continue her education, and after a frustrating year in Astoria on the coast of Oregon, her marriage ended.

Sara also had to convince the University of Oregon's medical school in Portland that she was really serious. Her application was passed over in 1975, but she was finally reaccepted in 1976 and she put herself through medical school by working as a cocktail waitress at a Red Lion Inn in Astoria. The job was far afield from her ultimate ambition, but the tips were good and she had the perfect figure for the abbreviated outfits she had to wear.

Sara's second marriage worked, even though she began medical school in 1976, probably because her husband's job kept him out at sea as much as he was ashore. She wanted very much to prove that she could succeed at marriage, but she also wanted desperately to be a doctor. She was able to juggle the demands of medical school and marriage until 1980, when she received her degree. But when she began a four-year residency in anesthesiology at the same medical school, her second marriage ended too. There was just no time for anything but her career.

Nevertheless, she tried again during her residency – this time with a physician – but her third marriage was as abbreviated as the first two. In 1984, she finally finished her residency and established her own practice as an anesthesiologist. She regretted her three failed marriages, but they had all ended with little acrimony. She still worked with her last ex-husband, Dr Geoff Morrow,* head of the contagious disease department at Providence; theirs was an amicable – if final – divorce.

Perhaps she just wasn't meant to *be* married.

Sara was thirty-three and she had been in school for twenty-eight years of her life. She still had medical school loans to pay back, and she worked every extra shift she could at Providence Hospital. But despite her native intelligence and her sophistication in all things medical, she was a trusting, almost naive woman. Because *she* always told the truth and took great pains never to hurt anyone's feelings, she tended to believe that other people worked under the same moral code. When it came to evaluating men, Sara had made some misjudgments. She had never expected to be divorced even once, much less three times.

Without children, with little trust in the permanency of relationships between men and women, Sara had immersed herself in her career, doubtful that she would ever find true love. There was another obstacle; she earned so much more money than most men that many of the eligible males she was attracted to were scared off. It would take a highly confident and liberated man to feel secure dating a woman who was not only beautiful and extremely intelligent but whose projected income was close to half a million dollars a year. And she certainly didn't want a man who was attracted to her *because* of her money.

In the spring of 1986, Sara was dating Jack Kincaid,* who had a successful advertising agency with several offices on the West Coast. Kincaid was divorced, with two teenage daughters, and he was a confirmed born-again bachelor. He and Sara were not dating exclusively. Kincaid was also seeing a woman in her twenties. If Sara had been completely frank about her feelings, she would have admitted to a smidgen of jealousy about that. But even so, she and Kincaid were good friends, she counted on his being around, and she didn't expect that he would commit either to her or to his other girlfriend, Sandi.*

One night Sara and Jack and her friend Lilya Saarnen,* who was dating one of Sara's fellow doctors, Clay Watson,* were attending a dance at the Multnomah Athletic Club – the 'MAC,' one of Portland's more exclusive clubs. Lilya didn't feel that Jack was good for Sara; he was too much of a playboy. When the men were away from the table, Lilya expressed her feelings and said she knew the perfect man for Sara. She wanted to set her up with a blind date with an old friend of hers. 'His name is Brad Cunningham,' Lilya said.

Sara wasn't looking for anyone else to date and, like almost everyone else, she *hated* blind dates. Men that friends described as 'really fascinating' too often turned out to be anything but. Nevertheless, Lilya persisted. She had once dated Brad Cunningham herself. Now she was happy with Clay Watson, Lilya said, but she and Brad were still friends, he was newly single, and she felt he and Sara would be a perfect fit. She described him as a very special man.

Actually, Lilya went into such graphic detail about how skilled Brad Cunningham was as a lover that Sara was a little embarrassed. She had never heard a woman speak so openly about a man. Indeed, she wondered why – if this Brad was such a marvelous lover – Lilya had let him get away. But she said she had no romantic interest in Cunningham any longer, and she thought Sara would like him.

A little reluctantly, Sara said it would be all right for him to call her. 'He got my phone number from Lilya,' she later recalled. 'He phoned me and we agreed to meet for dinner. I had a date with Jack that week – the last week in March – too, and he had to change the date so I called Brad and we switched days.'

Sara spoke to Lilya early on the day of her blind date. 'She kept talking about the relationship they had had – how she had been in love with him. I *still* thought it was weird that she'd want to introduce me to Brad, but she insisted.' Sara had no intention of meeting Brad Cunningham alone. What would they talk about? She didn't even know him. So she arranged to have her friend Gini Burton,* who worked as an operating room technician at Providence, and Gini's boyfriend, Gil, come to dinner that night too.

'I was in a security building, so I could see Brad on the monitor when he buzzed to get in,' Sara remembered. 'I went down and met him. He was very good looking.' In fact, Brad Cunningham looked as if he wouldn't need someone to fix him up with a blind date. When Sara let him in, she found him tremendously attractive; he was a big, broad-shouldered man with thick dark hair and sloe eyes. He appeared to be a few years older than she was. He dressed impeccably and he had an air of success about him. He was certainly self-assured. *Too* self-assured for Sara's taste. 'I didn't like him on our first date,' she recalled. 'He talked too much about Lilya, and about himself, and he seemed egotistical.'

Brad monopolized the conversation that first night, while Sara, Gini, and Gil listened politely. 'It was very obvious that Brad had once had a lot of money,' Sara remembered. But his conversation about his wealth and his possessions didn't impress her. Besides that, Brad seemed so taken with Lilya Saarnen that Sara wondered why he wasn't still dating her.

'*She* had raved about Brad, and now *Brad* kept going on about her. I really thought that he wouldn't be interested in me because he kept talking about Lilya.'

Easter Sunday was on March 30 that year. Although she had expected him to, Jack Kincaid didn't invite Sara out for Easter brunch. It didn't really bother her; he said he was going to take his daughters out to brunch. 'I told him I'd just leave his Easter basket on his front porch,' Sara said.

Kincaid looked uncomfortable when he said, 'You'd better not do that, Sara. I'm going to be with Sandi.'

Sara didn't take an Easter basket to Jack Kincaid, and she accepted a second date with Brad Cunningham when he called. Even though her three months of dating Kincaid hadn't been an exclusive arrangement, her feelings were a little hurt that he was with Sandi. She undoubtedly said 'yes' to another date with Brad Cunningham more quickly than she ordinarily would have.

She was glad she did. 'On our second date Brad was charming,' she said. 'He asked about *me*.'

Sara figured that he had been just as nervous about their first date as she was. He wasn't really conceited; he had just been hiding his own discomfort and trying too hard to fill the conversational silences. After all, he hadn't known Sara or her friends that first night. The man Sara met for their second date was considerate and concerned, and she found herself extremely drawn to him. Her feelings for Brad were not what she had expected. But there it was. She was surprised at how wrong she had been about him. Every time she saw him, she liked him better. And from the beginning, she had found him physically attractive – not classically handsome, but there was something about him. Maybe it was his eyes.

Bradly Morris Cunningham was not yet forty, but he was a bank executive at Citizens' Savings and Loan. And shortly after he met Sara, he had a new job; he was hired to be part of the top echelon of the Spectrum Corporation, a branch of the U.S. Bank in Portland. He told Sara he would oversee all of their commercial acquisitions. He also told her he had been a real estate entrepreneur involved in a huge project in Houston, Texas, where he had controlled six hundred million dollars. Although that project had gone sour when the oil disaster hit Houston, Brad said he had brought suit against his contractor and the bonding company – litigation that, he said, would eventually net him millions of dollars. And, as if that weren't enough, Brad also had his own company which had diversified interests, some having to do with construction and others in the biotechnology field.

Sara and Brad dated often that spring, going out to dinner and to plays. He invited her to his home, a two-bedroom apartment on the fourteenth floor of the Madison Tower along the Willamette River in downtown Portland. Brad introduced Sara to his fifteen-year-old son, Brent,* who lived with him, a child of his first marriage. He told her he had two daughters, Amy* and Kait,* by former marriages, and three other sons, Jess,* Michael,* and Phillip,* who were, six, four, and two respectively. By the end of April, Sara had also met Brad's younger sons. They were adorable little boys, with their father's dark hair and eyes, polite and endearing children. 'I thought they were *wonderful*,' Sara remembered.

Brad told Sara that he shared custody of his three young boys with his estranged wife. He planned to move to a larger apartment on the eighteenth floor where they would have their own room furnished and decorated especially for them. The little boys were with him as much as they were with their mother.

Sara was touched when she saw how deeply Brad cared for his children; he seemed to build his whole life around them. He confided that their mother was totally unfit, and that he was struggling to gain full custody of the boys. He described his ex-wife to Sara as 'bitchy.' Sara remembered his words. 'He said she would fly off the handle and yell at the kids. He told me she was sexually promiscuous but that he really thought she hated men.'

Sara's heart went out to Brad. He was so worried about his kids that it seemed to color his whole life, and she saw the shadows of pain wash across his face when he thought she wasn't looking. Even so, she found Brad 'fun, bright, and attractive.' She had met very few men in her life who were not intimidated by her intelligence and her income. Not this man. Brad had a remarkably keen mind and Sara found him more and more fascinating. His lifestyle and his interests were different from anything she had ever known. But there was an almost electric energy about him. He was enthusiastic and charismatic and he had risen so high so rapidly in the business world.

Incredibly, just when Sara had pretty much reconciled herself to being alone, Portland's spring of 1986 surprised her. It brought not only its usual profusion of rhododendrons, azaleas, and dogwood blossoms, but also this remarkable man who seemed to be ideal for her. She stopped seeing Jack Kincaid, and Jack dated Sandi exclusively. Sara and Jack were still friendly; it was just that they rarely met any longer.

Brad Cunningham was everything that Sara had ever imagined she would want in a husband, and he had come along just at the time when she believed she would never find anyone. It was funny how life turned out sometimes; that the two of them should ever have met and fallen in love defied the laws of probability. Their backgrounds were so very different. Sara was Dutch; Brad was half Indian, half Celtic. She was small and blond; he was large and dark. They were both, however, determined and ambitious people who could focus on a goal and channel all their energies until they achieved it.

Before April blossomed into May, Brad and Sara were extremely close. 'He waited a long time before he would make love to me,' she recalled. 'And that was thoughtful. He told me that he didn't want to be intimate until he was sure that we were going to stay together . . .'

Brad proved to be both a tender and an exciting lover,

a caring, passionate man. 'He told me over and over again how much he loved me – how beautiful I was,' Sara said. 'He was always telling me what a lucky man he was to be with me, how lucky his boys were.'

Sara had every reason to believe that Brad loved her. 'A nurse friend of mine told me after a party that it was obvious Brad was in love with me,' she remembered. 'She said he never took his eyes off me the whole evening.'

Sara felt just as lucky to have found Brad. It was a transcendently perfect spring for both of them. Brad gave her a friendship ring, which they both knew meant a commitment that far exceeded friendship. He urged her to rent an apartment in the Madison Tower so that they could be closer together.

The three round towers – Madison, Grant, and Lincoln – were *the* place to live in Portland in 1986. Their windows looked out on a renewed riverfront, on all the arching bridges that cross the Willamette River to connect the bisected city, and on the long park blocks that are not unlike Manhattan's Central Park. Brad had moved to a three-bedroom unit on the eighteenth floor where the rent was a thousand dollars a month.

In June, Sara found a unit she liked on the fourteenth floor. It was eight hundred a month. In New York, Chicago, or San Francisco, their apartments would have rented for at least three times as much. The rooms were large and tasteful and there was an outside walkway running around each floor of the soaring towers. Basement parking facilities were available to all tenants. It was, of course, a security building where no one gained entrance to the tower elevators without permission of the guards on duty.

Coincidentally, Brad's former girlfriend Lilya Saarnen – who had been responsible for bringing Brad and Sara together – lived in an apartment on the ground floor of the Madison Tower. That didn't concern Sara. Although Lilya was a very sexy woman, it was apparent that whatever she and Brad had shared was over, and Lilya was in love with her surgeon boyfriend, Dr Clay Watson. He was two decades older than Lilya, but that didn't bother her at all. She was a pragmatic woman, and Watson took wonderful care of her. Like Brad, Lilya had a career in banking, but her health was unpredictable. She needed someone like Watson.

Sara and Lilya were very different types. While Sara was sweetly feminine, Lilya's style was subdued. She chose loose clothing in earth tones, pulled her long hair back in a bun, and wore horn-rimmed glasses. Even so, men seemed to find her almost bland but perfect features spectacularly sensuous. She had a manner about her that suggested a sexuality barely under wraps. She spoke softly, as Sara did, but Lilya had hidden promises in her voice.

Sara was not surprised that Brad had been attracted to Lilya, but now he was completely devoted to her. He had turned her life upside down, and she was gloriously happy that summer. She was so much in love that she never felt fatigued, even though she was working such brutal hours in the trauma unit. It seemed as though everything she had longed for in life was suddenly within her grasp.

Sara adored children although she had never been lucky enough to have any of her own. She had found Brad's three young sons delightful from the moment he introduced them to her. Jess, Michael, and Phillip were as smart as their father, and well behaved. Sara and Brad took the boys sailing on a week's vacation and it was as if they were already a family. Sara hated to say goodbye to them when they went back to their mother. And she worried about them. Brad had come to trust Sara so much that he gradually revealed more and more about what their mother was really like. He confided that she called the children four-letter words and screamed at them continually. The custody of his little boys was desperately important to Brad. All of his business success meant nothing – not if his children were being mistreated.

That summer Brad and his estranged wife wrangled constantly about the boys. It was the one shadow over

Sara's happiness. She heard Brad argue with his wife on the phone, though she never really saw the acrimony between them. She accompanied him sometimes when he went to pick up his sons, but she never spoke to his wife. 'I saw her working in her yard,' Sara recalled. 'Once, we took the boys back and she came running up, holding her arms out for Phillip. But we never talked.'

Sara worried about what effect all this was having on the boys, but she tried to stay out of the arguments. It wasn't her place to interfere, and she was confident that Brad could handle things in the best way for his sons.

Sara continued to pay the rent on her fourteenth-floor apartment in the Madison Tower that summer, but she spent so little time there that it seemed like an empty space with no human energy. 'I kept my clothes in my apartment, but I was basically living in Brad's apartment,' she said. His apartment reflected both his taste and his ability to buy the best. He even had a baby grand piano – although he couldn't play. It was only natural that Sara wanted to spend her few off-duty hours with Brad. 'I was very much in love with him, and I thought he was very much in love with me.'

She had no reason to think otherwise. Brad assured her many times a day of his love. He was always on time to meet her or pick her up, he was always where he said he would be, and their time together was wonderful. In a sense, it was as if they were both recouping the years they had lost in bad relationships. Sara knew that Brad had been married four times and that he had been disappointed in love just as she had. But now, finally, almost serendipitously, they had found each other. They were both under forty and they could plan for so many good years together.

Except for all the hassle that Brad was having with his wife over the custody of Jess, Michael, and Phillip, Sara's and Brad's lives were idyllic. Her practice was well established, his business interests seemed to be booming, they loved each other, and they planned to get married as soon as Brad was divorced. Their days had fallen into a happy pattern. When Sara wasn't working at Providence, she was with Brad. Every other weekend, they planned their time around Jess, Michael, and Phillip. And on the weekends that Sara was on call – as she often was – Brad took the boys to the park blocks or entertained them in his apartment. He had the boys in the middle of the week for a few days too. It seemed that he and his wife had calibrated their joint custody almost down to the minute.

Sara sensed that Brad was often sad, and he finally confessed to her that his wife was continuing to make his life miserable. Sara wondered just what kind of woman she was. *Why* did she have to make everything so difficult? Sara knew that she was a successful attorney, but she certainly sounded like a terrible mother.

Brad needed Sara – and not just because he was having such a bitter struggle to protect his sons. He suffered a wrenching loss in July. Sara was at Providence on an overnight shift when Brad called. He had just learned that his father, Sanford Cunningham, had died of a heart attack at his fishing cabin in Darrington, Washington. 'He was sobbing so hard I could barely understand him,' Sara remembered. 'He needed me, and I managed to find someone to cover for me so I could go home and be with him.'

Sara knew how close Brad had been to his father, and she tried to help him and his stepmother, Mary, too. She went with Brad and the boys to Yakima for Sanford Cunningham's funeral. And afterward she said she would buy a practically new twenty-five-foot Prowler trailer that Mary and Brad's father owned. Mary needed the money, and Sara paid her eight thousand dollars, far more than the book value of the trailer. They left the trailer in Yakima, but Brad drove his dad's Chevy pickup truck back to Portland and kept it in the garage of the Madison Tower. He was grieving hard, but he went back to his job at the U.S. Bank, usually walking to work, although he owned several vehicles and Sara had a Toyota Cressida. He was in top shape and enjoyed the exercise.

All that summer, Brad and his wife continued to butt heads over the little boys. There were trips to child psychologists, endless meetings with their respective attorneys, and more dissension when it was time to register Jess for school. Brad had made arrangements for him to go to Chapman School near the Madison Tower, but on August 13 his wife apparently ignored his wishes completely and enrolled Jess in Bridlemile Elementary near her recently rented home in the West Slope area just outside of Portland.

When Brad found out, he was furious, 'You can't do that, Cheryl,' Sara heard him shout at his estranged wife over the phone. Her name was Cheryl – Cheryl Keeton.

3

Jim Karr, Cheryl Keeton's half brother, had been living with her and her three sons at her rented home on the West Slope for about three months. He had gotten close to his nephews, Jess, Michael, and Phillip. 'I was their "nanny,"' he later remembered. 'I was there to take care of them while Cheryl was at work.'

Jim was fully aware of how acrimonious Cheryl's divorce from Brad Cunningham had become, how they fought over every step in the process. He knew that it made her feel better just to have him living in her home. Although they seldom talked about it, it seemed to Jim that Cheryl lived in a constant state of dread. Brad wanted the boys. Cheryl wanted the boys. And sometimes it seemed that their fierce arguments would never end.

On Sunday, September 21, 1986, Jim Karr spent most

of the day at a girlfriend's house in Gresham and they watched the Seattle Seahawks' football game. He usually felt guilty about leaving Cheryl alone too long, but not on that weekend. It was Brad's weekend to have the boys, and Cheryl wasn't home; she had gone up to Longview, Washington, on Saturday to visit their family and planned to stay overnight. There was no reason for Jim to be around the house. He didn't expect Cheryl to return until sometime Sunday evening. It would, of course, be before seven because that was when Brad was supposed to have the boys back.

Jim called Cheryl about 7:30 P.M. to make sure that the boys had gotten home. He knew she worried if Brad didn't bring them back right on the dot of seven. Cheryl was crying and upset when she answered the phone. 'The boys aren't home yet,' she said. 'Brad had car trouble.'

'Should I come home?' Jim asked.

'No,' she said. 'Not right away. It'll be okay.'

With most divorcing couples, it would have been. But Jim knew that Brad threw a fit if Cheryl didn't have the boys ready when it was his turn to take them, and Cheryl went nuts if they were even five minutes late getting home. But anybody could have car trouble, and evidently Brad had called Cheryl to tell her that he would be late.

Cheryl seemed nervous, Jim thought. True, she always seemed nervous these days; the subtle and not-so-subtle psychological war that Brad was waging against her kept her constantly on edge. She was always afraid that on *some* visitation Brad wasn't going to bring the boys back – that he was just going to disappear and take her sons with him. But lately she seemed convinced that, if things looked bad for Brad in the custody fight, she herself wasn't going to survive. *Literally not survive*. Whether her fears had any basis or not, Jim had caught them the way you catch an infectious disease. Cheryl was so smart and so intuitive, and yet she had become almost stoic when she told Jim that she might die soon – and that it would be his job to find out the truth.

That was nothing like Cheryl's usual behavior. She had always been so strong, so resilient. One thing about his half sister, she had never, ever been passive. So even though Cheryl had told him he didn't have to come home early that Sunday night, Jim was uneasy and he headed for the West Slope house within an hour after he spoke to her on the phone. When he drove up to the house at 9:15, he saw that all the lights were blazing, but Cheryl's van wasn't there.

That scared him.

Once inside the house, Jim noticed that the vacuum cleaner was sitting in the middle of the living-room floor. It looked as if Cheryl had rushed away in the middle of housecleaning. With a hollow feeling in his stomach, Jim walked quickly through the empty rooms. It was very quiet and his heart was beating too loudly. There was a note on the kitchen counter. It was from Cheryl, written on a sheet of paper she had torn from the notebook in which she recorded the content of all of Brad's phone calls.

'I have gone to pick up the boys from Brad at the Mobil station next to the IGA. If I'm not back, please come and find me. . . . COME RIGHT AWAY!'

Cheryl would have written that note between 7:30 and 8:00, Jim thought, and she should have been back with Jess, Michael, and Phillip within fifteen minutes. Now it was almost 9:30. Jim called their mother, Betty, in Longview, an hour's drive north of Portland. Betty picked up the phone before the first ring had even ended. When Jim told her that Cheryl had obviously left the house in a hurry, and then read the note, Betty started to sob. That scared Jim even more. That wasn't like his mother.

'She's dead,' Betty cried. 'She called me. I told her not to meet Brad alone. I know she's dead.'

Jim tried to comfort his mother. He said there had to be a reasonable explanation why Cheryl wasn't back yet. He told her he was heading down to the Mobil station, and he promised to call her as soon as he got back. But Jim knew that the station had been closed down two days earlier, the windows soaped over, the pumps empty. It would be very lonely and dark at night. It was an odd place for Brad to bring the boys for Cheryl to pick up. If he *was* having car trouble, there would be nobody at the Mobil station to work on it.

Still, Jim kept hoping that he would find his sister there, loading up her precious sons, just beginning to start for home. It was a short drive, but his mind went over a dozen possible reasons why Cheryl would be there, safe.

She was not there.

The Mobil station was dark and deserted, just as he had expected. The place was abandoned. It was out of business. Even the IGA supermarket next door was closed for the night. Jim scanned the parking lot there for Cheryl's Toyota van, but he didn't see it. There were only a few cars, probably those of employees who were emptying the cash registers and preparing night bank deposits inside the store.

Jim returned to Cheryl's house and when he stepped out of his car, a figure emerged from the shadows. It was Jerry Finch, who was there to find out what he could about the woman whose body was now on the way to the Medical Examiner's office. He asked Jim Karr to identify himself, and when he learned that Jim was Cheryl Keeton's brother, he drew a deep breath. He had to tell Karr the monstrous truth. It was a truth that somehow Jim already knew.

His sister was dead.

Jim wasn't even very surprised. That was why his mother had sobbed when he called her. Every single one of them in the family had tried to save Cheryl, as if they could somehow build a wall of love and solidarity around her so strong that nothing and no one could harm her. And yet, all the time, they had known it was like trying to stop Mount St Helens from erupting. Something had to blow, something inevitable, and all the love and concern in the world never could have stopped it.

'He did it,' Jim Karr shouted to Jerry Finch. 'That bastard did it!'

He didn't say which bastard.

4

It was a quarter to midnight when a group of law enforcement officers headed to the Madison Tower to inform Brad Cunningham that his estranged wife was dead. Because they had no idea what they might find when they got there, Detectives Jerry Finch and Jim Ayers and Senior Trooper Keith Mechlem from the Oregon State Police had asked for backup from the Portland Police Bureau. Officer Richard Olsen joined them in the parking lot of the new apartment complex.

Together the four men took the elevator to Cunningham's floor. A railed walkway ran around the perimeter and the apartment's main door opened off that. Rick Olsen stood back near the rail as the State Police investigators knocked on the door of Cunningham's apartment, watching silently while Finch and Ayers spoke to the tall dark-haired man who answered the door. Olsen could not hear the conversation, but he could see the face of the man in the doorway and knew that he had just been told his wife was dead. Olsen heard no loud exclamations, and he saw no emotion flicker across the man's face. 'He didn't look surprised or shocked or agitated,' Olsen would later recall.

That didn't necessarily mean anything. Shock does funny things to people. They can hear their whole world end in one sentence and never blink an eye. Not until later. For that matter, there are no rules about how the human mind or the human body will react in any given situation. People have been known to sustain a bullet wound to the heart and run half a block before they drop.

Ordinarily it would not have taken four officers to bring such terrible news to the family of the deceased. But Finch and Ayers were already convinced that Cheryl Keeton had not died in an automobile accident; she had been murdered. At this point in the investigation, they could not say whose powerful hand held the weapon that had struck her repeatedly, could not say who had then maneuvered her van onto the eastbound lanes of the Sunset Highway where it was almost certain to be struck by other vehicles.

Finch had talked with Cheryl's half brother, Jim Karr, who had reacted in a more predictable way to ghastly news. He had shouted, 'He did it. That bastard did it,' and handed over the note Cheryl had left behind. Finch had told Ayers about the note as they drove to the Madison Tower. Even so, they were still only at the embryonic – and dicey – stage of this investigation. They knew who Jim Karr meant by 'that bastard,' but there was a great deal more they needed to know.

When Brad Cunningham came to the door, he was barefoot and wearing a gray University of Washington T-shirt and reddish orange jogging shorts. Ayers noted that he seemed wide awake, not like a man roused from sleep. And when he told Brad quietly that his estranged wife, Cheryl Keeton, had been killed, Brad blurted out, 'Was it in a traffic accident?'

'No.' Ayers offered no more explanation.

'How—?'

Even up close, the Oregon State Police detectives could discern no sign of grief on Cunningham's face. That wasn't too unusual; Cheryl Keeton was apparently his *estranged* wife – not a woman, perhaps, who was still a big part of his life or even a woman he had any fond feelings for. Divorces could be bitter. Ayers had recently gone through one himself. He knew too well how nerves and emotions can be frayed in the wringer of divorce.

'*How?*' Brad Cunningham asked again. 'How was she killed?'

'We haven't determined that yet,' Ayers said. That much was true. There wouldn't be a postmortem examination until the next day. Ayers wasn't about to reveal his own conclusions.

'Should I contact an attorney?' Brad asked next.

Now *that* was a little over the line. They were still in the doorway of this man's apartment, he had just heard that his estranged wife was dead, he hadn't been told how she had died, and he was already asking if he needed a lawyer.

'You could, I suppose,' Ayers said slowly. 'But we're only here to see what your last contact with her was.'

Brad finally opened the door wide enough for the detectives to go inside. Rick Olsen stayed outside on the walkway, Trooper Mechlem waited in the front hallway of the apartment, and Jerry Finch deliberately stayed behind in the living room so Cunningham wouldn't feel that they were 'double-teaming' him. Brad led Ayers into the dining room and gestured for him to take a seat at the table. They began to talk, an edgy and strange conversation. After a while Finch walked into the dining room and sat at the end of the table. Brad was leaning casually on his elbows, looking at Ayers who sat directly across from him.

They would talk for almost two hours. At one point early in their conversation, Brad moved to the back of the apartment to check on his sons. He said that he didn't want them to wake up and find their home full of strangers. Later, Brad would recall leaving his conversation with Ayers because he was so upset that he had to vomit. But Ayers could not locate that violent reaction in his memory. He heard no one vomiting in the apartment that night.

Ayers did not Mirandize Brad Cunningham. There was no reason to – he wasn't a suspect. He was merely one of the bereaved in this tragedy. Ayers only asked Brad when he had last seen Cheryl Keeton.

Brad recalled the weekend just past for Ayers. He hadn't

seen Cheryl, he said, since sometime between 5:30 and 7:00 on Friday evening when he had picked the boys up for their weekend visit with him. He either forgot or chose not to mention that Cheryl had broken their custody agreement by showing up at Jess's soccer game at the Bridlemile playing field on Saturday.

'Today – today . . .' Brad struggled to recall, running his mind back over the previous twenty-four hours, when Ayers asked him to try to give as much detail as he could about that Sunday.

'I took the boys to the park to play.'

'What about earlier this evening?' Ayers asked.

'We went to meet my fiancée, Dr Sara Gordon,' Brad said. 'She was on call at Providence Hospital. We went out for pizza with the boys.' Brad said that Sara had his Chevrolet Suburban and that he was driving her Toyota Cressida. He did not mention why they had switched vehicles.

'You own any other vehicles?' Ayers asked.

Brad nodded. He had a pickup truck and several motorcycles. He said that his father had died in July and he had inherited his pickup truck. It was a tan Chevy, license number HS12936, parked in one of his assigned spaces in the garage of the Madison Tower. Cheryl had possession of their Toyota van, Brad said, although its final disposition was in contention.

Finch and Ayers knew where *that* van was. It had been taken away by Collins Towing and was currently awaiting processing by criminalists from the OSP crime lab.

Finch quietly left the apartment to check the garage for the vehicles Brad had mentioned. He returned some time later and silently shook his head at Ayers. The Chevy pickup and Sara Gordon's Toyota Cressida might be there in the multilevel garage, but he hadn't found them. Ayers kept his face blank of expression. It didn't mean much; Cunningham's vehicles probably were somewhere down in the cavernous garage.

Brad told Ayers that he hadn't actually *seen* his estranged wife that evening, Sunday, but he had spoken with her on the phone.

'I called her around seven – seven-thirty,' he said. 'I told her I was running late and that the boys were watching the last half of *The Sword in the Stone*.'

Cheryl had been 'short' with him, Brad said, and anxious to get off the phone. It had been his impression that she was not alone, that she might even have been drinking. From his demeanor, that didn't seem to be an unusual circumstance to Brad. He said he had called Cheryl back an hour later and she had grudgingly agreed to come over to the Madison Tower to pick up their sons.

She had never shown up.

Ayers nodded noncommittally. If that *had* been Cheryl Keeton's plan, it meant that she could have been driving east on the Sunset Highway somewhere around 8:00 or 8:30 P.M., within the same time frame when Randy Blighton found her dead in her Toyota van. That would jibe, at least partially, with the tragic event that had occurred.

Brad's explanation that he had expected Cheryl to pick up their sons at the Madison Tower didn't seem unusual. Ayers did not know yet how stringent and meticulous the custody transference 'rules' were in the Cunningham-Keeton divorce. But he and Finch had gone over all the facets of the case that they had gleaned in the first hour or so, and Ayers knew that Jim Karr believed fervently that Cheryl had gone to meet Brad Cunningham in her own neighborhood over on the West Slope just before she died. She had left a note that was very explicit about that. The note said nothing at all about plans to drive into Portland.

'Cheryl left a note for her brother that she was meeting you at the Mobil station on the West Slope,' Ayers said to Brad. 'She told her mother that, too, when they talked on the phone this evening.'

'No.' Brad shook his head. 'She was coming *here* to pick up the boys.'

They had been talking for about forty-five minutes, and

Jim Ayers had yet to detect any sign of emotion in the man sitting before him. It was very quiet, high above the city of Portland, in the early hours of a Monday morning, a long time before the city below woke up to begin the business week. Somewhere in that large apartment, three little boys slept, unaware. Brad's older son Brent was also in the apartment, although the detectives didn't yet know that.

'Did you kill Cheryl?' Ayers asked, suddenly blunt.

The question hung heavily in the air. Ayres's dark brown eyes bore into Brad Cunningham's. Brad stared back, unflinching.

'*No.*'

At that time, Ayers saw what he later estimated to be 'fifteen seconds of emotion.' Brad seemed startled and even a little frightened. But those feelings washed over his face like a slight wind rippling a pond, gone as quickly as it blew in, leaving no sign that it had ever been there.

Ayers pulled back. 'When were you in the Toyota van last?'

'March – March, I think.'

March was almost six months ago. Of course, even if they found Brad Cunningham's fingerprints in the Toyota van, they would likely be useless as far as physical evidence went. Mom-and-Pop homicides were tough when it came to physical evidence; both victim and killer had good reason to leave their prints, hair, cigarette butts, semen, urine – you name it – where they lived or had once lived. Fingerprints could be retrieved after decades, and Cunningham's prints could be expected to be found in a van he had often driven. Unless they happened to find his prints in *blood*, they wouldn't necessarily link him to this investigation.

Having sprung his most straightforward question on the man before him and gotten little in the way of response, Ayers excused himself and went out on the walkway to have a cigarette, allowing the events of the evening to sink into Cunningham's mind. Sometimes silence was more intimidating and productive than questions. At this point,

Ayers and Finch knew next to nothing about Cheryl Keeton or her estranged husband, other than that there seemed to have been no love lost between them. The two detectives were akin to researchers just beginning a scientific project. They would weigh any number of variables that might eventually bring them to the truth.

Brad had not spoken of his newly deceased wife in hushed, shocked tones. Whatever love or respect or friendship he might once have felt for Cheryl, it was patently clear he felt it no longer. He was coarse and voluble about the woman who had been his wife for seven years, who had borne him three sons. He told the two detectives that Cheryl had been 'fooling around' with a large number of men – primarily other attorneys with whom she worked at the law firm of Garvey, Schubert and Barer. These men, he said, were all married. 'There are a lot of mad wives,' Brad said a little smugly.

Of course, he admitted with a half grin, half grimace, he had not been exactly celibate himself. Why should he have been faithful, once he found out Cheryl was cheating on him? He told Ayers and Finch that, initially, he had been involved with a woman named Lilya Saarnen who worked with him while he was a bank executive in Salem and then in Lake Oswego. Coincidentally, Brad said, Lilya also lived in the Madison Tower. 'In fact, it was she who introduced me to Dr Gordon, and we started dating.'

Ayers let Brad continue his odd, almost stream-of-consciousness conversation until he eventually wound back around to Cheryl. His description of his dead wife was hardly flattering. He said that she had been a great fan of country music and had often hung out at the Jubitz Truck Stop south of Portland alongside the I-5 freeway, where she went to pick up men.

Finch and Ayers exchanged glances. Why would a woman who was a partner in a prestigious law firm be picking up truck drivers? But then, why not? The OSP detectives had seen all varieties of human sexual peccadillos.

Brad went on to describe Cheryl as 'narcissistic,' a woman who enjoyed going to nude beaches along the Columbia River. 'And she hung nude photographs of herself around the house.' Ayers had, in fact, noted several artistic photographs of a nude female on the walls of Brad's apartment. He couldn't know if they were of Cheryl; at this point, he didn't know what Cheryl Keeton might have looked like in life. She had been so brutally beaten that she was unrecognizable. And the nude's head was cropped from the photographs, revealing only an exquisite torso. They weren't '*Playboy* shots'; they were beautifully done.

The woman Brad was describing sounded as if she had been a wanton creature who might very well have been a set-up for violent murder. Ayers had no way of knowing if he was hearing an accurate description of Cheryl Keeton, but her alleged avocations and preferences certainly sounded bizarre. Maybe she *had* been one woman in the courtroom and another after dark.

Ayers asked again for specific details on Brad's movements during the hours preceding Cheryl's death. Brad seemed calm and confident as he thought back over the evening. After he returned to the Madison Tower from the pizza parlor with his three sons, he said, he had left only once, and that was just long enough to put some things in his car – shoes and work clothes he needed because he had an on-site inspection of some property the next day. 'In fact,' he said, 'I talked to a cop in the garage. He was talking to two people down there, and he nodded at me.'

Ayers made a note to check on that. He asked if it might be possible for him to ask a few questions of the three Cunningham children.

'No,' Brad said firmly. 'Not until I talk to an attorney about it.'

Again the two detectives' eyes met, but they said nothing.

Glancing at the jogging outfit Brad wore, Ayers asked, 'Are you athletic?'

'No. I used to jog, but I haven't for some time.'

'Was Cheryl athletic?'

'Cheryl?' Brad looked surprised. 'No – not at all.'

As Brad became more expansive, seeming to relax slightly, Ayers commented that he himself had been through a divorce and could empathize with the stress and frustration involved. And then he caught Brad up short again by repeating the question he had asked earlier. 'Did you kill your wife?'

The second time was too much. Brad got up from the table and walked to a phone. He called Wayne Palmer, a Portland lawyer, and left a message with his service.

Within a short time, the phone in the apartment rang and Jerry Finch answered. Wayne Palmer, who said he was representing Bradly Cunningham, asked that all questioning of his client stop. He informed Finch that he didn't want the children to be questioned either. 'Don't wake them up.'

So, at close to 2 A.M., the questioning had to end. After Brad denied for the second time that he had killed Cheryl Keeton, and after his attorney demanded that the detectives' questioning stop, there was nothing more for them to do. They had informed Brad of his estranged wife's death and he seemed no more troubled than if they had told him someone had dented the fender of his truck. Now he wanted them out of his apartment.

Whatever had happened to Cheryl Keeton, the answers were not going to come easily. Her almost-ex-husband – now her widower – was most assuredly not devastated to learn that she was dead. He wasn't surprised either, he said – not given the lifestyle she had chosen. But he had assured the detectives that what had happened to Cheryl had nothing to do with him, with his children, or with his activities during Sunday evening, September 21, 1986. His duty now was to protect his children, and he intended to do just that.

5

At 6:30 on Monday morning, September 22, Brad called Sara Gordon at Providence Hospital with news so shocking that she could scarcely believe what he was saying.

'Cheryl's dead. The police came by last night and informed me.'

'*Brad!*' Sara gasped. 'Why didn't you call me?'

'I didn't want to disturb your sleep.'

Disturb her sleep? Didn't he know that her profession disturbed her sleep all the time? Way back when she was an intern, Sara had learned to fall asleep leaning against a wall if she had to. She could wake in an instant, be perfectly alert during delicate surgery, and then immediately fall back asleep. All doctors could. They had to learn to sleep when they had a chance or they wouldn't survive. Sara couldn't understand why Brad hadn't called her the moment he learned the awful news. When his father died only two months before, he had called her at once, begging her to come home and be with him. And she had moved heaven and earth to go to him. Of course, he had loved his father deeply, and he detested his ex-wife, but even so.

Sara and Brad talked for five or six minutes, as she tried to assimilate the fact that Cheryl was dead. Brad said he didn't know how Cheryl had died; the police hadn't been specific but they had said it wasn't in a traffic accident. Finally, he hung up, and Sara's hand trailed down the phone.

She sat, leaden, wondering what on earth could have happened. And then Sara simply had to call Brad back. In some ways she and Brad had had such a strange weekend; they had even had an uncharacteristic squabble on the phone the night before. Earlier, Brad had said something about Cheryl that was almost unbelievable. 'Brad had told me Friday night – when we picked up the boys – that Cheryl and her mother were planning to poison him,' Sara remembered. 'He had told me that before – that he had listened in on their phone conversation while they plotted against him . . .'

Sara had never known Brad to be frightened of anything before – except for the safety of his children. Now she had to find out more. She called Brad back. There was something she had to ask him. She hoped he wouldn't be hurt or angry, but she was aware that the rage between Brad and Cheryl had escalated tremendously over the past few weeks. She had seen his face when he talked to her on the phone.

'Brad,' Sara said quietly, 'do you *swear* that you had nothing to do with Cheryl's death?'

His voice was firm and clear. 'I had nothing to do with it.'

She believed him. She didn't sense a trace of deception in his voice. Reassured, she hung up the phone.

Sara was scheduled to administer anesthesia for two eye surgeries. There was nothing she could do to help Brad at the moment, and so she walked to the operating room.

Dr Karen Gunson, a forensic pathologist and deputy state medical examiner, was a soft-spoken woman with blond hair, high cheekbones, and lovely large eyes usually hidden behind glasses. On Monday afternoon, September 22, she performed a postmortem examination of the body of a young woman who had been found dead the evening before. Dr Gunson had been with the State of Oregon's M.E.'s office for about eight months; to date, in her training and career, she had performed approximately three hundred autopsies. But this one among the hundreds would prove to be memorable for many reasons, one dead woman whose foreshortened life and sudden death she would never forget. Seldom had Dr Gunson seen so many injuries inflicted upon one person. In the end, she would estimate that the victim had been struck approximately two dozen times – twenty-one to twenty-four separate and distinct blows – but some of the injuries' edges merged into others, so she could make only an educated guess.

How long does it take to strike a struggling adult human being twenty-four times?

The yellow band on the victim's right wrist gave a tentative identification and an estimated age – thirty-seven. She was still dressed in the blood-soaked clothing she had worn when she was found: a pullover, a T-shirt, blue jeans (zipped), a white bra, beige bikini panties, black socks and loafers. She wore a gold chain with a pendant containing clear stones around her neck, and a watch on her left wrist. There was a blue cord with a key attached to it wrapped around her other wrist.

Undressed, the dead woman was almost anorexically thin, so thin that her ribs and hip bones glowed through her skin. She was five feet five and one-half inches in height, but she weighed a mere hundred pounds. Only her face was swollen and puffy. There, Dr Gunson saw a mass of injuries – lacerations, contusions, and abrasions. She counted five different shapes of lacerations on the top of the head; some were linear, some were U-shaped, and some were too ragged to label accurately. The facial bones themselves had been fractured, but the skull had not.

Dr Gunson dictated into a tape recorder as she listed the fractures to the left mastoidal area – six in all, 'four horizontal and roughly linear, one oblique, one vertical.' There were bruises on the left upper neck. The cartilage on the top of the left ear was fractured. 'There are a series of lacerations and contusions involving all planes of the face – linear, Y-shaped, triangular, all full thickness lacerations . . . including contours of the upper and lower eyelids . . . lacerations of both cheeks, multiple small and large lacerations around the mouth . . .'

The dead woman had four broken teeth, her upper jaw

was broken, her right lower jaw was broken, and the force of that blow had even displaced her teeth.

Dr Gunson continued the postmortem procedure with an internal examination of the skull. She cut the skin at the back of the dead woman's neck with a scalpel and peeled away the entire scalp like a tight latex mask, up over the top of the skull, and inside out, down over the face. She then sawed away the top of the skull so that the brain itself was exposed. The smell of burned bone, no longer noticeable to experienced pathologists, filled the room.

Dr Gunson found extensive hemorrhaging all over the surface of the brain, but, again, no fracture of the skull itself. Like a thousand other variable characteristics that differentiate one human body from another, thickness of the skull is one. This victim had a rather thick bony calvarium; it had done her no good. Ironically, her strong skull had been an unyielding force that helped to destroy her brain.

Dr Gunson noted the thick subdural hematoma (large blood clot) over the right side of the brain. The dead woman's brain had been literally displaced and squeezed because of traumatic swelling and tremendous bleeding. 'The subject . . . has suffered contra coup injuries. The head was supported on the right, and struck on the left,' Dr Gunson recorded.

A contra coup injury to the brain occurs when the head is hit on one side and the brain is then macerated as it is slammed forcibly against the opposite side; it is an injury seen often, tragically, in battered infants and children, inflicted when they are shaken violently. At the time this victim was struck repeatedly, the right side of her head had probably been trapped against some unyielding object. When her head did not move, her brain had bounced again and again into that side of her skull.

It was obvious that this shockingly slender victim had not gone down easily. Her hands and left arm and shoulder bore defense wounds; even her lower legs and feet were bruised

– injuries that had occurred, perhaps, as she fought her attacker or struggled to get away. There was a peculiar linear abrasion near her waist, a scarlet line where the waist band of her jeans had been.

Dr Gunson knew that detectives would ask how long someone could have lived with the terrible brain injuries this dead woman had suffered. She estimated only minutes. The growing blood clot pushing her brain to one side, compressing it until it could no longer sustain her breathing and her heartbeat, had built up rapidly. She would not have been paralyzed, but she could not have fought back for long. And while she was still alive, the terrible hemorrhage into her brain continued. Paradoxically, the bleeding stopped when she died. The huge hematoma grew no larger, once it no longer mattered.

Although the dead woman had been fully dressed when she was found, that didn't preclude the possibility that she might have been sexually assaulted. Dr Gunson found no vaginal or rectal contusions, but she routinely took swabs from the vaginal vault and the rectum and slipped them into labeled test tubes so that an acid phosphatase test for the presence of semen could be done. If semen was present, the chemical would turn the swabs a bright purplish red.

Criminalist Julia Hinkley of the Oregon State Police Crime Lab stood by during the autopsy and took possession of the evidence Dr Gunson collected. Hinkley also attempted to retrieve fingernail scrapings beneath the dead woman's nails. There was nothing there but her own blood.

Sometimes the contents of the stomach can provide a clue to time of death, to place of death, to a myriad of other questions. Not this time. The victim had only about 100 cc of brown liquid in her stomach, most likely coffee. There was no food. She was so thin that this didn't surprise Dr Gunson. And there was no urine in her bladder.

In further tests that had grown routine at a time when drug use was rampant, Dr Gunson took blood samples and secured them in gray-stoppered tubes. If the dead woman had ingested alcohol, cocaine, barbiturates, amphetamines, psychotropics, or any of an array of drugs, a scanning electron microscope with a laser probe could isolate that. The metabolites of most of the drugs would last for years – even if the test tube was not refrigerated.

Autopsy means, quite literally, 'to see for oneself,' and there is a sad kind of justice in the fact that the body of a murder victim contains secrets that often either convict or free a suspect. But even if Dr Gunson had seen a photograph of the woman who lay before her when she was in life, she could not have said that it was this victim. Her eyelids were blackened and swollen closed and her face was so misshapen. Beneath those closed lids, the dead woman had worn soft contact lens, tiny circles of transparent material that gave her myopic eyes perfect vision. The contacts had either been displaced during the violent beating she had endured or lost in a mass of blood and tissue.

Dr Gunson could only speculate about what kind of weapon had been used to inflict such terrible wounds. Certainly, it would have to have been dense and heavy and something with many sides and varying surfaces. A wrecking bar? A tire iron? A heavy flashlight, maybe? Unless the weapon itself was found, no one would ever know for sure.

When she completed her examination, Dr Gunson knew how this woman had died. She could not know why, or by whose hand. It would not have taken a particularly powerful person to do so much damage, but it certainly would have taken a person so full of rage that he – or, again, she – kept striking and hitting. Again and again and again and again.

Twenty-four times.

6

It had, of course, been too good to last, a love affair too wonderful in a world where nothing perfect ever seems to endure. Sara and Brad would never be able to resume their untroubled, romantic courtship. From the moment he called her at 6:30 A.M. on September 22, Sara knew that everything had to change. And she knew, too, that Brad and his little boys would need her more than they had ever needed her.

Sara couldn't feel any personal sense of loss for Cheryl Keeton, although all human life mattered to her. That was why she was a physician. When she learned that Cheryl had been beaten to death, Sara, long inured to disasters of the flesh, would shudder. The police believed that she had been murdered, and Brad seemed to agree with them. But how could Sara grieve personally for Cheryl? She had never known her; she had never seen her except at a distance. She had never talked to her. The last time she saw Cheryl, it was through a car window, and her voice had been muted by distance and rainy wind and thick glass so that Sara had only seen her mouth moving. Cheryl had seemed angry, harried, and rather desperate on that last Friday night before she was murdered.

From what Brad had told her, Sara knew that Cheryl's life was untidy and full of unsavory characters. She had not been a fit mother for the children; Brad had said that often enough, too. But now Cheryl was gone, and her little boys had loved her, as all children loved their mothers. Sara's heart broke for Jess, Michael, and Phillip, and she vowed to try to be there for them. She wondered what part she would play in their lives now. She loved them, that was certain. Would they be with Brad all the time – or would they go to Cheryl's parents?

Brad had denied having any part at all in Cheryl's murder. He had been at home with the three boys at the time of her death. It was true that his voice had sounded rather flat when he told Sara about Cheryl, but he had probably been in shock. When you lose someone who has been a part of your world for as many years as Cheryl was part of Brad's, shock is natural. And then he had been furious with Cheryl for blocking him at every turn in his efforts to give his children a peaceful home. Sara reasoned that Brad couldn't be expected to mourn the woman who had made his life miserable for so long.

Sara had continued with her scheduled surgeries that Monday morning. Once she was masked and gowned, she had always been able to shut away the outside world. Her only concern was for the patient beneath her hands. She had to monitor pulse, respiration, oxygen content in the patient's blood. For those hours she was in the operating room, she didn't have to think about how Cheryl died.

Brad paged her sometime before ten that morning. He said he had lost the single car key she had given him for her Cressida. He needed to come and pick up his Suburban, which was parked in the hospital lot. Sara arranged to meet him between surgeries.

Carrying two-year-old Phillip, with his two older boys trailing behind, Brad hurried into the hospital cafeteria and told Sara that he had taken the MATS, Portland's rapid transit light rail system, to get to Providence. If he had lost the key to her Cressida, Sara wondered why he hadn't driven his father's pickup truck; it was parked at the Madison Tower. Brad shook his head impatiently. Maybe he hadn't even remembered the pickup. He said he wanted his Suburban. He needed to consult with an attorney.

Sara watched the little boys as they ate breakfast in the cafeteria. They seemed completely normal. They hadn't caught the nervous energy that seemed to vibrate from Brad. When they had finished eating, Sara gave Brad his keys and walked with him and the boys as far as the parking lot.

'Do the kids know – about Cheryl?' Sara asked.

'I told them she was killed in a car accident,' Brad said.

After he drove off, Sara returned to the operating room. She had back-to-back surgeries scheduled until three or four that afternoon, and when she was finally able to come up for air, she realized that she had no way to get home. Her Cressida was at the Madison Tower. She called her sister Margie and asked for a ride there. On the way, she stopped at the Broadway Toyota dealership and arranged to have keys made so that she could drive her car. It had been such a weird, upside-down day. Who could remember keys and cars and details when the specter of Cheryl's death loomed over everything? Sara just wanted to get to Brad and the boys and help them through whatever might lie ahead. Then suddenly, incongruously, she remembered that Michael's birthday was only three days away and asked her sister to turn into the Toys 'Z' Us parking lot to buy him a present.

When she got back to Brad's apartment, to her shock, Sara found him in a state of silent terror. She had never – ever – seen him like that before. He had always been a man totally in control, fully capable of handling whatever came his way. But she could see that something was very wrong, something more than Cheryl's strange death. Brad drew Sara away from the windows and asked her to sit down. He told her softly that he had no choice but to warn her that they might all be in terrible danger. Cheryl's murder was only the beginning, he said, only the 'first shoe' dropped in a massive plot to eliminate him – and everyone connected to him.

'But *who? Why?*' Sara gasped.

'It's too complicated for me to explain. You'll just have to trust me to take care of us.'

Brad showed Sara a loaded handgun he was carrying for protection. Then he led her around his apartment, showing her where he and Brent had tied ropes between interior door handles to prevent anyone who crawled through a window from gaining entrance to the center of the apartment. He and Brent had also arranged pop cans and coffee cans filled with pennies so that they would crash and warn them of any unexpected entry through the main door. Brad had even loaded another gun and given it to his fifteen-year-old son; two guns would be better than one. Even though they were in a security building, he told Sara they couldn't count on protection. The people they were dealing with were far more sophisticated than the rent-a-cop security guards at the Madison Tower.

'*Who?*' Sara asked again, baffled. 'Who would try to hurt us?' But Brad wouldn't tell her whom he feared. It was enough for her to know that they all might be in danger. He said the little boys would sleep in his king-sized bed, and Brent would stay in his own room – where he had a good view of the walkway around the eighteenth floor. If someone could murder Cheryl, Brad said tightly, that meant that none of them was safe.

At 9:15 that night, a loud knock sounded at the door and Brad signaled Sara to be quiet. They peered out a security peephole and saw a uniformed man standing there. He was an extremely big man, probably six feet four or five and solidly built. He looked to Sara like either a Portland policeman or a state trooper. The uniformed man waited, balancing on one foot and then the other.

Brad held a finger to his lips, shushing them, and shook his head. He wouldn't let anyone answer the door.

'*But, Brad, why?*' Sara asked again, appalled.

He sighed and said he guessed he would have to level with her. He told Sara he had every reason to believe that Cheryl's family was going to come after him and that, quite possibly, they meant to murder him. If they didn't come in person, he felt they would hire someone in a cop's uniform to do it.

Sara, who had never led anything but a safe existence, who had never known anyone involved in such James Bond-like intrigue, was frightened. Cheryl was dead and Sara knew absolutely nothing about her family, nothing beyond Brad's conviction that Cheryl and her mother had planned to poison him. She supposed there *could* be people like that. If Brad was scared, then she was scared. Sara wondered if she might be next. And Brad. And maybe even the little boys.

Sergeant James Hinkley walked away from Brad's door, but he came back and knocked again a few minutes later. He was there to serve subpoenas summoning Jess and Michael Cunningham to appear before the grand jury. Senior Trooper Keith Mechlem and a Madison Tower security guard stood behind Hinkley. After a long wait, Brad opened the door a crack. He was holding a gun, which understandably gave Hinkley pause. Hinkley was armed with a steel Smith & Wesson .357 revolver and he recognized the gun in Cunningham's hand as the same kind of weapon. Reluctantly, Brad opened the door wide enough for Hinkley to step inside the apartment.

'For the reasonableness of this situation, I think you can put your gun down,' Hinkley said quietly. 'You can see we're police officers.' Glancing around the apartment, he noticed that the doors were tied shut with white rope that extended from door to door.

'I just wanted to make sure who was out there,' Brad said. 'I'm afraid for my children's lives. I rigged those ropes for their safety – but only the doors facing the walkway.'

'Could you put the gun away?' Hinkley asked again.

Brad set it down on a low bookcase. He called his sons from the master bedroom and Hinkley handed them the subpoenas and left.

Now Sara was more puzzled than ever. Why were the boys being asked to testify? Was Brad suspected of Cheryl's murder? She needed more answers, and Brad insisted that he had been in his apartment with his sons all of Sunday night – except for two short errands. 'Michael and I checked the mail,' he said. 'And then we went down to the garage to put my shoes in your car. I was going to inspect that land this morning—'

'Why did you take Michael with you?' Sara asked.

'You know Michael,' he said. 'He was horsing around and keeping Jess and Phillip from watching the movie.'

'But why did you put your shoes in *my* car?' Sara persisted. 'Weren't you coming over to the hospital to get the Suburban?'

Brad looked at her, distracted. He didn't need this aggravation. He had enough on his mind. 'I'd better not answer any more questions,' he said, putting an end to her worried queries.

There hadn't been a subpoena for her yet, Sara thought, but there probably would be when the police found out how close she was to Brad.

Brad's tension was contagious and Sara spent a restless night. But she had to go to work the next morning, and so she called the Madison Tower security guard to escort her to her car. The little hairs on the back of her neck stood up as she kept close to the guard in the underground garage. She didn't ever want to go back to that apartment.

Beyond the fear that someone was stalking him, Brad had other worries. He knew that the husband of a woman who dies under suspicious circumstances is always the prime suspect. He hadn't liked the way Jim Ayers and Jerry Finch stared at him when they questioned him on Sunday night, or the big state cop showing up with subpoenas for his boys. He had been involved in many civil litigation cases and always believed in hiring the best attorneys for the job. Early Tuesday morning Brad called Sara at the hospital and told her he had retained Phil Margolin, a prominent criminal defense attorney in Portland. Margolin paged Sara at Providence later that morning to ask her questions about the events of Sunday night. 'He told me that he'd talked to Brad, and that he was convinced of his innocence,' she recalled. 'And that reassured me.'

Sara spoke only briefly to Margolin, explaining that she was needed in surgery. But within an hour she was paged again and was shocked to hear that Brad had been brought into the emergency room at Providence by ambulance. *My God!* Had someone gotten to Brad, just as he feared?

Terrified that he had been shot, Sara rushed down to the emergency room and stood by as Brad was wheeled in on a gurney. He hadn't been shot; at least he wasn't wounded. He had apparently suffered a heart attack in Phil Margolin's office. That was something she had never even thought of. Brad was such a strong man, and he was only thirty-seven years old. But her physician's mind told her that didn't mean he couldn't have heart trouble. His father had just died of a massive coronary in July, and he was only sixty-one. And Sanford Cunningham had suffered several heart attacks in the years before his death; it was an ominous cardiac history for Brad.

It was 11:45 A.M. when Dr Steve Rinehart, Sara's friend and a cardiologist on staff, began treating Brad. He complained of chest pains, and he winced when Dr Rinehart touched the left front of his chest. The heart monitor showed that Brad was throwing PVCs – premature ventricular contractions. There was an early extra beat of the ventricles and his heart was contracting out of normal sequence. It was a very common condition – and sometimes it was life-threatening.

Sara understood the potential danger of this particular irregularity of the heart's rhythm. A lot of people under extreme stress throw PACs – premature atrial contractions – and they were not nearly as likely to interfere with life itself. But the ventricles were the largest chambers in the heart and she knew that Brad's heart could go into fibrillation and lose all of its normal rhythm in an instant, becoming just a useless squirming organ unable to pump blood. If that happened, Steve Rinehart would have to put the electrical paddles from the Lifepak on Brad's chest and try to shock his heart back into normal sinus rhythm.

Sara had seen too many patients go sour and die with exactly the same condition that Brad had. She watched, stricken, as Rinehart examined the man she loved. How much emotional pain could she and Brad be expected to take in one day? Their happy time with his laughing little boys at the pizza restaurant on Sunday seemed a million years away, and it had been less than forty-eight hours ago. Now, Brent kept his little brothers occupied in the nurses' lounge while Brad was being treated. Sara couldn't bear to think that they could be orphans in an instant.

To her immense relief, Brad began to come around and his EKG tracings showed he was back in perfectly normal sinus rhythm. Despite Sara's pleading, he refused to be admitted to the hospital. He had too much to do. Dr Rinehart insisted, however, that Brad take a stress test on the treadmill before he would release him. Leads were attached to his chest, arms, and ankles so that his blood pressure and heart rate could be monitored as he walked on the moving belt. Every three minutes, a technician increased the rate and the incline of the treadmill. Brad's heart picked up speed, but it beat as steadily as a clock. At 2:30 that Tuesday afternoon, he was released from the hospital.

Brad took Sara aside and told her that they had to continue to take great precautions to protect themselves. He felt it wasn't safe for them to stay in the Madison Tower. Whoever was stalking them, whoever had killed Cheryl, could trap them there. 'That's exactly where they will expect us to be,' he whispered.

Phil Margolin required a retainer, Brad told Sara. That was standard, she knew. She wrote out a five-thousand-dollar check and assured Brad that she would pay for private investigators – for anything he needed so that he would be adequately represented and they could all be safe. She knew Brad, and she loved him. The world seemed to be closing in on him, and Sara wasn't about to let that happen. He was making almost one hundred thousand dollars a year at U.S. Bank, and he said he had millions coming to him from his suit in Texas, but his assets were not as easy to get to as Sara's were. There was no question in Sara's mind now that they were going to be together – forever – and they would share everything.

Brad explained that it wasn't safe for Brent to stay at his apartment either, and Sara agreed. She wrote a thousand-dollar check for Brent to help him find a hiding place. All this had to be terrible for him, too. He had come home from a camping trip only a few hours before Brad's apartment was invaded by a half dozen police investigators.

Gini Burton, the surgical technician who was Sara's friend and one of the guests on the blind-date evening when she first met Brad, had stopped by the ER to check on him. 'Anything I can do to help, I will,' she told Sara.

'Could we stay at your house tonight?' Sara asked.

'Sure, we'll make room. Come on over.' Gini was too tactful to ask why they couldn't stay in Brad's apartment or even in Sara's. If Sara asked, she must have a good reason.

She did – Brad's conviction that they had to keep moving, that they must never stay more than a night in one place.

Sara was certain that, underneath, Brad had to feel some sadness and regret about Cheryl's death, even though he had been so angry at her. Those emotions had probably contributed to the arrhythmia that brought him into the ER. When a person dies suddenly, leaving so many loose ends, so many quarrels unresolved, the one left living almost always feels guilty.

Sara felt sadness and regret too. It would have been better for their sons if Cheryl and Brad had had a civil relationship. It would have been better if Brad and Sara had been able to find a common meeting ground with Cheryl so they could all work for the boys' best interests. But now Cheryl was no longer in the picture. Sara wished she had known her; maybe if she had, she would be able to understand why someone had wanted her dead.

Brad knew why, and Sara sensed that he was trying to protect her from awful truths, things about Cheryl he had never told her. That was like him; he was strong but he was so gentle with her and the boys. No matter what the police might think, Brad was not a killer. There was no violence in him, of that she was certain, just as certain as she was that she had never loved anyone the way she loved him.

Yet Brad was afraid that he – that *they* – might be murdered, too. That he should be frightened of anyone or anything was the most inexplicable reaction Sara could ever have imagined. But she trusted his instincts, and she would follow his lead. Somehow, he was going to bring them all safely through this nightmare.

7

On Tuesday night, September 23, Sara, Brad, Jess, Michael, Phillip, and Brent all stayed at Gini Burton's two-bedroom apartment in the Mount Tabor district of Portland. Brad got to Gini's place about four that afternoon, just as Gini was arriving home from her shift at Providence Hospital. Sara showed up a short time later in her own car. Brad seemed none the worse for his trip to the emergency room, and he didn't complain of any more chest pains or erratic heartbeats.

Gini didn't ask questions; they all seemed so grateful to be with her in an 'anonymous' location. It took some figuring to find a spot for everyone to sleep, but Gini made a bed for Jess and Michael on the couch, Phillip slept with Sara and Brad in one bedroom, and Brent slept in a sleeping bag on the living-room floor. Gini and her fiancé slept in the other bedroom.

Gini could see that Brad was nervous. 'He seemed bothered, preoccupied,' she would recall. 'He was concerned that someone might take his children away.'

The OSP detectives were concerned with finding the person who had killed Cheryl. In September of 1986, Lieutenant DeBrand Howland was Superintendent of the Oregon State Police Criminal Investigation Division. He was kept updated on the Keeton homicide by Lieutenant Corky Forbes, who commanded the Beaverton office of the OSP, or by OSP Sergeant Greg Baxter, who was the hands-on supervisor of the case. Baxter had chalked up seventeen years on the force and that third week in September had been one of his busiest. With Washington County District Attorney Scott Upham and his staff, Baxter and his investigators had worked almost around the clock on the Friday night murder. Cheryl Keeton's bizarre death had put a strain on both departments. Baxter assigned Jerry Finch and Jim Ayers to carry through as the lead detectives in the Keeton homicide. They would be the most actively involved, but Lieutenant James Boyd Reed, Les Frank, Tom Eleniewski, Robert C. Vance, and Richard McKeirnan would all participate, along with Julia Hinkley and Greg Shenkle from the Oregon State Police crime lab.

In the first week after Cheryl Keeton's body was found on the Sunset Highway, Finch and Ayers had more than enough to do. They had already talked to Brad Cunningham, the victim's estranged husband, into the early hours of the morning after her death. Ayers wanted to know a lot more about Cunningham – but that wasn't going to be easy; they couldn't find him. He wasn't in his apartment, and he hadn't shown up at work at the U.S. Bank either, though he apparently hadn't left town. Ayers and Finch had reports that Brad had been seen here, there, and everywhere. But they were always two steps behind him.

Southwest 79th Street was the likeliest place for the OSP detectives to begin their 'heel-and-toeing' – canvassing the area, asking questions, handing out flyers. The person who had propelled the blue Toyota van onto the freeway could have done it only from 79th. The detectives might get lucky. People living along the street abutting the freeway might have seen that person. Or they might not. It had been almost completely dark when Randy Blighton discovered Cheryl's body. Maybe nobody had seen anything at all.

Jack and Danielle Daniels lived at 2035 79th. Daniels had been playing golf that Sunday and had driven home a little after eight – up Canyon Drive to West Slope and then northbound on 79th. He had seen a van on the east side of the street, facing north, almost directly across from his house, near his mailbox. As he pulled into his driveway, he recalled, the van had gone forward about fifty feet. At that time, he saw two people in the front seat. And he *thought* he saw a child standing in the backseat. But it might have been only the outline of the child's carseat just behind the driver.

Danielle Daniels was watching the Emmy Awards show when her husband got home. She told Jerry Finch that she had heard loud 'banging' noises sometime between 8:00 and 8:40 on Sunday night. She had gone to the window to look out and asked Jack, 'Did you hear something?'

'No,' he had responded. 'Only the dogs barking.'

Once more, Danielle heard something and looked out. She told Finch, 'A man came to our door about twenty minutes later, pounding on the door, and I called my husband.'

That, of course, was Randy Blighton frantically trying to get help for the woman he had found in the Toyota van.

Asked to describe the 'banging' noises and to try to isolate the time she heard them, Danielle said, 'Jack came home at

8:10. I heard the noises ten minutes later. It sounded like a rubber hammer on a car. A few minutes later, I heard the noise again. And it was fifteen or twenty minutes after that when the man came to the door looking for help for the woman.'

Michael Cacy, a freelance illustrator, lived in the 2100 block of S.W. 79th. He told state police detectives that he and his neighbors were used to seeing vehicles with lost and confused drivers on their street. 'We saw a lot of freeway refugees,' he commented wryly. He tried to reconstruct in his mind the evening of September 21.

That Sunday Cacy had a 'rush' project to finish, so he had worked all day in his office in Portland's Old Town district. He went home for a quick dinner around six and then prepared to head back to his studio. 'I expected that I'd have to work all night if I was going to finish.'

Cacy said he had had no particular reason to keep track of time, save for the fact that he wanted to get to Old Town in time to watch the Emmy Awards show at 8 P.M. on the television set in his studio. It was a way for him to fool himself into thinking he wasn't really working around the clock – and on a weekend to boot.

Cacy had been a little impatient as he started back to Old Town and found his way blocked by a small late-model van that was stopped in front of him on S.W. 79th. It was right around 8 P.M. – a little before or a little after – and now he was sure he was going to miss the start of the Emmy show. Although the sun had disappeared into a purpling layer along the horizon, it was light enough for Cacy to see that the van was either a Toyota or a Dodge and probably blue or blue-gray in color.

Cacy was in a hurry and the van's driver didn't seem to know where he was going or have the initiative to get out and ask. The van was aimed at the freeway, but it wasn't moving. A little annoyed, Cacy sighed, backed up, and pulled around. Idly his mind computed that the driver was male. 'If it had been a woman, I would have stopped and offered her some assistance,' he said. It was a fleeting encounter, erased from the surface of Cacy's consciousness almost as soon as he eased onto the Sunset Highway and merged with the steady ribbon of traffic heading for Portland.

When the news of the death on the Sunset had hit the papers, the Beaverton station of the Oregon State Police got the usual number of phone calls from people who offered tips, suggestions, and, in a few cases, sightings of 'suspicious' men. Finch was hurrying out of the office when a clerk handed him a telephone message slip. He read it, he remembered the contents, but somewhere in his travels that day, he lost the slip itself. And with the slip, he lost the name and phone number of the caller – if, indeed, the caller had left either. Anonymous calls tend to be the rule rather than the exception when people call police.

The message was from a couple who had read about the Toyota van on the freeway. They happened to own an identical car, and the news coverage caught their attention. They had been driving in the West Slope area at dusk on Sunday and recalled passing a dark, muscular man, who was jogging near the freeway. It had seemed an odd place to jog. The man had something tucked under his arm as if he was carrying a football. For an instant, their headlights had picked up his face, and then they swept on by, his image as blurred as their memory of the moment.

Human memory is a fascinating and imprecise faculty. In this instance, it didn't matter. Finch could never locate the memo or the people who had called about the man running in the West Slope area that Sunday night. If he had been Cheryl's killer, might he not have stopped behind a bush or in the shadows, removed his outer clothing, rolled it into a ball, and then run from the scene until he found a dumpster or some other spot to throw away possibly bloodstained clothes?

It was a theory that seemed plausible. Michael Cacy had seen only one vehicle on S.W. 79th when he left home within a half hour of the discovery of the homicide on the Sunset. Unless there had been more than one killer involved, whoever had beaten Cheryl to death would have had no way to leave the area except on foot.

Joggers were everywhere; this one might have thought no one would notice him. But someone had. It was one very small chip in a very large mosaic.

The reason that investigators could not locate Brad Cunningham for further questioning in the days following Cheryl Keeton's murder was, of course, that he was on the move constantly, taking Sara and his sons with him, running from whatever enemies and demons pursued him. Thanks to Sara's friends and her relatives, they were welcome at a number of residences. Brad was adamant that it was far too dangerous for them to return to either of their apartments in the Madison Tower.

Brad had Phil Margolin representing him, but Margolin explained that he couldn't represent the children too. When Brad insisted that his sons must have an attorney, Margolin suggested that he retain Susan Svetkey, a lawyer with his firm. Her practice was devoted to children's interests – to making sure that they came before any other agendas. Sara wrote out another check, this one for Susan Svetkey. Susan never talked to Brad, nothing more than saying 'hello.' She was not his lawyer.

Brad wanted his sons protected, and he didn't want police playing with their minds – perhaps trying to force their memories into flawed recollections. He knew that the Washington County grand jury was about to meet, and two of his small sons had been subpoenaed to testify. He didn't want *anyone* talking with his sons – not the police, and certainly not the grand jury. They were little boys, they had lost their mother, and, of course, they were in as much danger as he was.

Brad could not ignore the subpoenas but at least Jess and Michael would have legal representation. Susan Svetkey was a slender, attractive woman with a warm and earnest manner. It didn't matter who hired her; her allegiance was always to the children she represented. She was very concerned about Jess and Michael Cunningham. As a separate matter she wondered about their competency as witnesses. They were so young.

Served at the hospital, Sara responded to her own subpoena and also delivered Jess, Michael, and Brent Cunningham to the Washington County Courthouse on September 24. And shortly before the grand jury hearing into the death of Cheryl Keeton, Susan Svetkey and Jerry Finch talked with Jess and Michael in a conference room in the D.A.'s office. They needed to determine what, if anything, the boys might be able to testify to. If neither child was competent to appear before the grand jury, they needed to know that too. Grand jury hearings are cloaked in secrecy, and attorneys are not permitted to accompany their clients into those sacrosanct chambers.

At six, Jess Keeton Cunningham was an extremely bright little boy. So was Michael Keeton Cunningham, but he was only four and seemed distracted and querulous. Why wouldn't he be? He had just lost his mother.

Finch would ask questions, while Susan Svetkey took notes. It had never even occurred to her that Brad would want his children sequestered from the detectives investigating Cheryl's murder. As far as she knew, he had been home with the youngsters the night their mother was killed. She believed she was with his sons solely to make this process as untraumatic as possible for them.

Finch was a kind man and he began talking quietly to Jess, assuring him that he was not in trouble, not at all. Finch just needed to ask him some questions. When he asked Jess how old he was, Jess said he was six – and that his birthday was on October 25. He also said he liked sports and that he played soccer.

'Did you have a soccer game last weekend?' Finch asked.

'I don't know the days. . . .'

Patiently, Finch drew parallel lines representing the days of the week on a piece of paper and found that Jess was perfectly able to show him which days were his school days and which were soccer days. Jess remembered that his father had picked him up from his mother's house on Friday or Saturday (September 19 or 20) and that they had talked about his soccer game.

'What day was your soccer game?'

Jess pointed to the sixth line (Saturday). 'My team was the Bridlemile Buddies and we played the Bridlemile Blazers. We won six to two!'

Jess remembered that his dad had taken him and his brothers to the doughnut shop after the soccer game. He touched the seventh line (Sunday) as the day he was supposed to go back to his mom's house.

'Why didn't you go back, Jess?' Finch asked.

'I don't know.'

The day after the Saturday line, Jess said he and his dad and brothers had gone to the hospital to have pizza with Sara, and he described the pizza restaurant as being two streets away from the hospital. After they all ate together, Jess said his dad had switched cars with Sara 'from the Suburban to the "short white car" because Dad's car wasn't running right.'

'Do you remember what you did next?' Finch asked.

According to Jess's memory, they had gone back to his father's apartment in the Madison Tower, and they had a sandwich and some popcorn while they watched a movie on the VCR.

'What was the movie?' Finch asked. 'Do you remember?'

Jess nodded. 'It was *The Sword in the Stone*. There was this boy and this magician – Merlin – and they tried to pull the sword from the stone, and whoever pulled it out would become the king of England. Arthur did. Once you did,' Jess confided, 'you always could.'

'Where was your dad?' Finch asked.

Jess said that his dad had gone jogging with Michael while he and Phillip stayed in the apartment and continued to watch the movie. When Finch asked him if he remembered what part of the movie was showing when Brad and Michael left, Jess nodded. 'Merlin and Arthur turned into squirrels and climbed up a tree.'

'When did your dad come home?'

'After it was over.'

'How did you know it was after the movie was over?'

Jess said the screen had gotten all 'fizzed up' and he didn't know how to rewind the tape, so he had just turned the power off. He thought maybe his father had gotten home two or three minutes after the end, but he wasn't sure.

Jess thought for a moment and then remembered that he had left his father's room where he had been watching *The Sword in the Stone* and had gone to his own room where he had a television set too. *Rambo* was playing on one of the local channels and he started watching that movie.

'Your dad came home sometime after you started watching *Rambo?*' Finch asked.

'Yeah. When Rambo was captured by the bad guys and General War Hawk took Rambo into a little cabin.'

Jess had a remarkable memory. He also remembered that when his dad came back from 'jogging' he was wearing an orange and yellow 'hunter's vest.'

'Did you see your father coming through the door?' Finch asked.

'No, he came through the elevator.'

'What did your dad do after he got home?'

'It sounded like he was washing the dishes. I heard water running in the kitchen.'

Jess remembered that Michael had left with his dad, but he couldn't recall seeing Michael come back the first time Brad returned to the apartment. He thought his dad had left again and gone to his car to get Michael.

He didn't know what his father had been wearing when he left to go jogging that Sunday night: 'I didn't see him when he left.' But he remembered that he and both his brothers had slept on the floor of their father's bedroom that night.

Susan Svetkey took twelve pages of notes on Jess's memories of the night his mother was murdered. She took only two on Michael's recall. Michael didn't want to talk about anything, especially the night his mother died. He crawled under the big oak table in the conference room, and he whimpered and turned away when Finch tried to talk to him. It was obvious that Michael was essentially ineffective as a witness. If he remembered anything about the time when he and his father left the Madison Tower apartment on Sunday evening, he didn't want to answer questions about it.

Svetkey and Finch looked at each other. They were not going to push this child. There was no point in questioning Michael further.

Jess, a small, lonely little figure, walked into the grand jury room and was given an oath to tell the truth. There were five grand jurors there that day in the fourth week of September. None of them would ever forget Jess Cunningham. He was very smart. He was very brave. He was without guile.

Jess's feet dangled far from the floor as he sat upright in the witness chair and told the people on the grand jury about the night of September 21. Frank L. Smith, one of the jury members, had worked for the U.S. Post Office for almost seventeen years. He took notes as the little boy talked. Smith would remember this moment for many years to come.

Jess told the grand jury the same things he had told Jerry Finch and Susan Svetkey. He recalled more, however. He testified that he had to unlock the door for his father when he came back. Jess said his father had told him he'd been jogging 'from Sara's hospital,' and that he was wearing red jogging shorts and a yellow and red shirt (probably meaning the vest).

Asked if Brad was sweaty or out of breath when he came back, Jess said, 'No.'

When Brad learned that Susan Svetkey had allowed his children to be questioned by Detective Jerry Finch, he was enraged. 'I was at Juvenile Court on September twenty-sixth,' Svetkey recalled, 'when I received a phone call from Mr Cunningham. He said, "You're fired."'

8

The successful investigation of a homicide is composed of many segments, not unlike bits of colored glass in a kaleidoscope. Detectives have to deal alternately with human emotion, experience, recall, and prejudice – *and* with solid physical evidence. The testimony of human beings has always been mutable; forensic evidence has become more sophisticated and definitive with every year that passes. Fingerprints, blood tests, DNA profiles, hair and fiber identification – there are so many ways to tell if a suspect has been at the scene of a murder at the time the murder occurred.

Did a suspect have means, motive, and opportunity to kill? Did he or she leave something behind and take something away? The answer to that last question is always 'yes.' According to the great-granddaddy of all criminalists, Dr Edmonde Locarde, every felon takes something of the crime scene – no matter how minute – away with him on his person or in his vehicle, and every felon leaves something of himself – no matter how minute – at the crime scene. Locarde's theory does not guarantee, however, that those investigating the crime will *find* the infinitesimal bits of telltale evidence left behind. It is never as easy as it looks in the movies and on television. The death of Cheryl Keeton would be one of the most inexplicable and difficult murders to prove in Oregon criminal history.

The men and women investigating the case were faced with two widely divergent assessments of who Cheryl had been. What kind of woman was she? Was she an amoral slut, as her estranged husband had characterized her – a victim just waiting for a murder to happen? Or was she the brilliant attorney, the devoted mother, the frightened near-divorcée that her family and her associates were describing to detectives?

And just who was Bradly Morris Cunningham? Was he the man of singular accomplishment, the constant father, the compassionate lover that Sara Gordon knew – that his surroundings and possessions confirmed and that he himself claimed to be? Or was it possible that he was not what he seemed, that he was a man who had brutally bludgeoned his wife to death and abandoned her vehicle on a busy freeway, hoping to make her death look like an accident?

More painful to consider was the possibility that *if* Brad had murdered his wife, he had done so in the presence of their four-year-old son, Michael. Six-year-old Jess had told Jerry Finch, Susan Svetkey, and the Washington County grand jury that his father had taken Michael and left the Madison Tower apartment for a considerable length of time that Sunday night. Brad himself said he had only run errands around the building, checking the mailbox, putting boots in Sara's car. The running time of the two movies that Jess was positive he had watched that night would give the investigators parameters to determine the length of time his father had been gone from the apartment. Had there been time enough to commit the crime? Perhaps only young Michael knew. And either he didn't remember what had happened on

Sunday night, or he had buried his memories deep in his subconscious mind.

Under the direction of Oregon State Police Lieutenant James Boyd Reed and Sergeant Greg Baxter, the investigation into Cheryl Keeton's murder proceeded – both the search for physical evidence and the less precise evaluation of the personalities and characters of the victim and the suspects that would emerge. Jerry Finch would continue to be the lead investigator, along with Jim Ayers – with backup from OSP detectives Al Carson, Gus Bradford, and Richard McKeirnan. And in the beginning, the only thing they could do was fan out and try to cover as much territory as possible.

Cheryl Keeton had had so many facets to her existence: her career, her family, her friends, her failing marriage. Each contact the OSP investigators made led to another. But little by little, they added to their store of knowledge of Cheryl's life and of Brad's life too.

Greg Baxter talked to Cheryl's mother, Betty, who was now married to Marv Troseth. She was grief-stricken, but she took a deep breath and tried to reconstruct the last day she had seen her oldest child alive. She remembered the previous weekend all too well. Although Cheryl often visited her hometown of Longview on the weekends when Brad had her three little boys, this visit had been different somehow. It had been almost as if she had known that it would be her last. Betty and all the rest of Cheryl's family knew that she was going through an agonizing divorce and custody battle. But they had been shocked to see that Cheryl, always slender, was bone thin and that her face was drawn with worry and tension.

Cheryl had spent Saturday and most of Sunday visiting relatives, and then had left in the afternoon so she could be at her house on the West Slope before Brad brought Jess, Michael, and Phillip home at seven Sunday night. Every moment of that weekend was etched in the minds of

Betty Troseth, her daughters Julia and Susan, and Cheryl's stepfathers Marv Troseth and Bob McNannay. Theirs was a large and closely knit family and they could scarcely absorb the fact that Cheryl had been murdered. They all adored her.

At only thirty-six, Cheryl Keeton – who had never taken her husband's surname – was already a full partner in the law firm of Garvey, Schubert and Barer. On Monday morning, September 22, the unbelievable rumor that Cheryl was dead had begun to circulate in the Seattle offices of the firm. Cheryl had begun her career with Garvey, Schubert in Seattle, and she had often commuted from Portland to work on unfinished litigations in Washington State.

Greg Dallaire was the managing partner of the Seattle office. When he arrived at work before eight on that Monday, he heard the rumors and Cheryl's face flashed in his mind, an image of a young woman so alive, so vital, so tremendously competent in her work as a litigator for the firm. He could not imagine that she was dead.

Dallaire started calling Portland to see what he could find out. It was a chilling thing to phone law enforcement agencies and morgues searching for a friend. Dallaire really didn't want to confirm the rumors. 'I called the Multnomah County Sheriff's office first,' he said. 'I just assumed she would have been in Portland or in Multnomah County; I didn't know she lived in Washington County. The sheriff's office referred me to the coroner's office.'

Even years later Dallaire still could not speak of that awful morning without pain. 'I called the coroner and I got somebody who worked there. He left the phone for a moment, and then he said, "Yeah, she's here. We have her here." Just like that. It was true. Cheryl *was* dead. It must have been about eight-thirty or nine that morning. The coroner said that she'd been bludgeoned to death.'

Dallaire went around to speak with the Seattle staff.

'There would have been about fifty people with the firm then – lawyers and staff. Everyone was absolutely stunned.'

Several members of the Garvey, Schubert staff attended Cheryl's funeral services in Longview the Thursday after her murder. It was an ordeal she would not have chosen to put anyone through, and it was not the kind of service she would have wanted.

Almost paralyzed with grief and shock, her sister Susan and her mother had made the arrangements. Susan would recall going to Steele's Funeral Home the Monday night after the murder. Eerily, she already knew what her sister had wanted. Cheryl had had a presentiment of doom and she had confided to Susan that she wanted to be cremated. 'They released Cheryl's body to us right after the autopsy that first night,' Susan remembered. 'It sounds terrible, but we were so upset at the funeral home that we got the giggles. I think we were too shocked to cry, and I know Cheryl would have understood. She always used to say, "Buy me flowers when I'm alive," and we were trying to do what she would have wanted. We arranged for the cremation as Cheryl wanted.'

But Cheryl's father's sister – Ida – was horrified when she heard that Cheryl was going to be cremated. 'She told us that "no way" could they permit that,' Susan said. 'They were Southern Baptists and they didn't believe in cremation.' Aunt Ida put up such a fuss about it that Betty, Susan, and Julia didn't have the energy to fight her. 'Cheryl was gone and we were having such a hard time about losing her that we just couldn't deal with all the family stuff,' Susan remembered. 'They went and picked out a coffin. It was an awful bright pink. That wasn't Cheryl. Actually, she would have laughed at the very sight of it.'

At least Cheryl's mother was able to stand firm that there would be no viewing at the funeral. On Wednesday, September 24, both sides of Cheryl's family along with representatives from Garvey, Schubert attended her services. 'It was awful,' Susan recalled. 'Cheryl would have hated that pink coffin so much. It was raining cats and dogs. And even so, Julia got stung by a bumblebee.'

Cheryl was buried in the Bunker Hill Cemetery, several miles north along the Columbia River from Longview. It had been established in 1889, and its gates were guarded by giant cedars. Her grandmother Edna Keeton, whom she had loved so in life, was next to her. Her grandfather Keeton was nearby.

But it was too soon, far too soon for Cheryl to be dead.

Jess, Michael, and Phillip, the sons she had loved more than life itself, were not present at Cheryl's funeral. Nor was her estranged husband Brad. Later he complained that Bunker Hill Cemetery was so out of the way that it was impossible to find, and that no one in Cheryl's family had made the slightest effort to inform him of her funeral arrangements. Some time after Cheryl's funeral, Brad did take their sons to Bunker Hill Cemetery and show them their mother's grave.

A week after the 'pink funeral' in Longview, Cheryl's coworkers from Garvey, Schubert and Barer had a private memorial service for her. They gathered at The Meeting Place at Seattle's historic Pike Place Market. 'We talked about the Cheryl we knew,' Greg Dallaire recalled. 'Even attorneys whom she'd opposed got up and talked about what a fine lawyer and fine person she was. We had a kind of closure.'

Garvey, Schubert was not a criminal law firm. Like everyone else, Cheryl's coworkers expected that the police investigation would come to a successful conclusion, and that someone would be arrested soon and prosecuted.

Cheryl's blue Toyota van remained parked at the Jim Collins Towing yard at 12090 S.W. Cheshire Court in Beaverton. On Tuesday, September 23, 1986, two OSP criminalists – Senior Trooper Greg Shenkle, an expert in fingerprint identification, and Julia Hinkley (who was married to OSP

Sergeant James Hinkley) – processed the death car there. Shenkle also processed Cheryl's purse and its contents.

Fingerprints are, and long have been, one of the most valuable resources for detectives. If Shenkle got lucky and Cheryl's killer had left prints inside the van or on her property, they could identify him, or her, through the AFIS (Automated Fingerprint Identification System) easily. Unless, of course, Brad Cunningham – who had had reasons to want Cheryl out of his life – was her murderer. His fingerprints would have an evidentiary value of zero; they would be expected to be there. He had told Jim Ayers he had driven the van often, the last time six months before.

Shenkle looked through Cheryl's purse and found two phone cards, one for 503–555–3939 and one for 503–555–2637. He also found credit cards: Sears, Nordstrom, American Express, Visa, First Interstate Bankcard, and several gasoline cards. Credit cards are often fertile areas for fingerprints, but only Cheryl's prints were on them.

Using various colored powders and oblique angles of light to highlight latent fingerprints, Shenkle then processed the Toyota van inside and out and lifted several latent prints around the driver's-door window on the exterior and several more inside. He even found one in blood on the outside passenger door handle. A print in blood is the best evidence he could hope to find. Shenkle drove to Olympia, Washington, Brad's home state capital, carrying the fingerprint exemplar he had taken from the door handle. He held his breath as he compared the whorls, loops, and ridges to Brad's known print exemplars. But the print proved instead to be from the right thumb of Randall Blighton, the man who had risked his life to get Cheryl's van off the Sunset Highway. He had already told police that he touched the passenger door when he looked to see if the person inside was all right.

There are some prime spots where fingerprint technicians find useful prints, spots criminals don't usually think of when they wipe a crime scene clean. Shenkle tried them all, including the rearview mirror. He performed his arcane alchemy on items he found in the glove compartment: a Mobil oil receipt, a Texaco gas receipt, a lightbulb, several matchbooks, a map, Cheryl's pen, a glasses case – even a pack of chewing gum.

Many of the prints didn't have enough points to make a match to anyone's fingertips. Not surprisingly, several were Cheryl's. And, as expected, some were Brad's – one on a map in the glove compartment and one on a temporary registration. That meant nothing at all, since Brad and Cheryl were still living together – and both driving the van – until February or March.

Julia Hinkley had been a criminalist with the Oregon State Police for almost two decades. She was an expert in electrophoretic toxicology and crime scene photography as well as in the collection and preservation of evidence. By her own estimate, she had worked on hundreds of homicide investigations. 'I'm there to assist the police, and to collect and preserve evidence,' she said succinctly. She had also attended several hundred postmortem exams and reconstructed 'many, many' crime scenes.

Hinkley had been present at Cheryl's autopsy the day before she processed the Toyota van. It was she who had received the blood samples and the rectal, oral, and vaginal swabs taken from the victim. She had also received the bags from Cheryl's hands, samples of her head and pubic hair, the dark hairs caught in her left hand, and a few stray hairs and fibers found clinging to her shirt.

Cheryl's body had already been transported to Longview for burial when Hinkley joined Shenkle at the tow yard to process the victim's van. Finch and Ayers were there too, and Greg Baxter, all hoping that something might be recovered that would bring a quick solution to this case.

First, Hinkley took photographs of the Toyota van. Then she shone a high intensity light at an oblique angle to try to pick up any trace evidence not visible in direct light. There is an irony in the aftermath of murder. The ambiance is calm and impersonal, as if maniacal violence had never occurred in the now silent, empty crime scene. There is no longer any need for haste.

Quietly, meticulously, Hinkley worked her way around the van inch by inch. She saved a hair from the driver's door and a hair that adhered to dried blood on the steering wheel. She would bag and label every possible shred of evidence. She divided the van into six sections and vacuumed the contents of each section, sealing and labeling the bags. She noted clumps of dark hair, and everywhere she worked there were massive amounts of dried blood. Back at the Oregon State Police crime lab, she would carry out painstaking forensic tests on the items she bagged as she looked for some telltale marker Cheryl's killer had left behind.

•

9

Fear traveled with Brad and Sara wherever they went that first week. Brad warned Sara that they had to be careful not to develop a pattern in their movements. The people who were stalking them would pick up on that instantly. So some nights while Brad and Sara stayed at Gini Burton's, they hid the children at Sara's sister Margie's house.

Jess had testified at the Washington County D.A.'s office for the grand jury, and Brad had fired Susan Svetkey for allowing his son to talk to Jerry Finch. It was all such a nightmare, having a six-year-old who had just lost his mother subpoenaed to testify. Meanwhile Sara was continuing to work, trying to keep them all together emotionally and physically and to keep her own feelings on an even keel. It wasn't easy. Every time she managed to achieve some sort of equanimity about their situation, something happened to throw her off balance.

On Thursday morning, Sara and Brad took a shower together in Gini's bathroom. The warm water splashed over them and it almost seemed as if they could wash away all the tragedy and the ugliness of the past few days. Brad was much taller than Sara. She barely came to his shoulder. That was one of the things she liked about him; his massive size made her feel protected. She turned toward him, looking up at his face, and gasped suddenly. Brad had a huge bruise under his left arm. Her doctor's eye noted clinically that it was dark purple, not yellow yet. She knew that meant it was three or four days old.

'Brad!' she exclaimed. 'Where on earth did you get *that?*'

'What?'

'That bruise under your arm.'

'Oh – that. I was playing on the jungle gym in the park blocks with the kids on Sunday while you were sleeping. I slipped at the top, and caught myself on one of the bars on that arm.'

It was a terrible bruise. And strange. Sara had never before seen a bruise on Brad. Maybe it was his darkish olive complexion, one of the few signs of his American Indian heritage, that made a bruise hard to detect.

That same Thursday, September 25, Brad and Sara spent the night in yet another location. The children were safe with Margie, and they checked into the Sheraton Hotel at the Portland Airport. For the first time since Cheryl's murder, they were by themselves and Sara didn't feel as if some unknown terror was waiting just outside their door. No one but her sister knew where they were. Brad told her a little more about Sunday evening, almost as if he was trying to establish an alibi. After he left her at the hospital, he said, he had taken the boys back to the apartment and waited for Cheryl to pick them up. She never came. And he had left the apartment only to do some errands around the Madison

Tower. He had seen people and they had seen him. 'I saw Lilya outside her apartment on the first floor at eight,' he told Sara. 'And I saw a policeman talking to a couple in the garage at eight-fifteen.'

'Did they see you?' Sara asked.

Brad shook his head sadly. He didn't think so.

Exhausted, they fell asleep to the sound of jets taking off nearby. And it must have been well after midnight when they woke to the sound of someone pounding on the door. Sara ducked into the bathroom and began to dress while Brad went to the door.

Jerry Finch and Jim Ayers stood there, accompanied by uniformed officers. They had been looking for Brad Cunningham for several days. They needed blood, hair, and fingernail scrapings from him, but he had been anything but cooperative with the investigators working on his estranged wife's murder case. Finch and Ayers had located Brad by a fluke. A Multnomah County deputy had been cruising through the parking lots at the airport when he spotted Brad's Suburban and called in the location to the Oregon State Police. The vehicle had been on a 'hot sheet' on the dashboards of every law enforcement agency in the Portland area.

Clearly irritated, Brad got dressed and went with Finch and Ayers to the Multnomah County Sheriff's substation at 92nd and Powell to give them their damn samples. For Sara it was yet another blow. Obviously the police considered Brad a suspect in Cheryl's murder.

In 1986, criminalists did not have the benefit of DNA testing. Julia Hinkley did what forensic tests she could do, given the state of the art. The results were disappointing:

Hair from driver's door: Microscopically similar in class and characteristic to Cheryl K's.

Oral, vaginal, rectal swabs: Negative for semen.

Hair from victim's hand: Microscopically similar in class

and characteristic to Cheryl K's.

Alcohol in victim's blood: None.

Brad had told Jim Ayers that he thought Cheryl had been drinking when he last talked to her on the Sunday evening she died. But the percentage of alcohol in her blood was zero. Death can sometimes *raise* the alcohol reading in blood; it never diminishes it.

The investigators reached an impasse when Hinkley wasn't able to come up with any clues that would lead to Cheryl's killer. The OSP criminalist had Brad's samples, but it was a hollow victory. They didn't find any matches. Whatever their suspicions about Brad, they couldn't arrest him. There was absolutely no physical evidence linking him to the crime. And there were no eyewitnesses who could place him at the scene. He was a free man, free to go to Venezuela if he wanted to – although if he did go, they'd have found that interesting.

But after all the physical evidence was collected, tested, and dismissed as borderline, one idea kept surfacing. The solution to this murder might lie not in blood tests or latent fingerprints. It might lie somewhere in Cheryl Keeton's life, or in Brad Cunningham's past. Maybe recently. Maybe far, far back in time. Generations, perhaps.

Part II

Brad

10

In 1948, Seattle, Washington, had a downtown with lights that were reflected in the night sky, and department stores so big that everyone from miles around came to shop, to eat out at fancy restaurants, to see first-run movies. Always a wondrous city, surrounded by water, shrouded in green foliage, softened by constant rain, and watched over by a beneficent Mount Rainier, Seattle never had slums, only neighborhoods less appealing than others. And eventually, it had suburbs that were a world, rather than miles, away. By 1986, Seattle was struggling to maintain its center. After World War II, young professionals migrated east across Lake Washington to Bellevue. Doctors and lawyers settled on Mercer Island. Probably the most desirable spot to live was Bainbridge Island, a ferryboat ride across Elliott Bay.

South of Seattle, the Boeing Airplane Company is on one side of the Duwamish River, and South Park and the Cheerie Daze tavern are on the other. South Park used to be pastoral. And the Duwamish was once a clear, sweet river. Now, fish caught there are suspect, eaten only by the extremely hungry or the very reckless. Some years ago, a young woman from east of the Cascade Mountains was murdered and thrown into the Duwamish. She was buried in an unmarked grave as a Jane Doe. Her parents had reported a brown-eyed girl missing, and the corpse's eyes had been turned blue by the chemicals in the Duwamish.

As the Duwamish River curls south, it parallels Boeing Field, Seattle's smaller airport, then pulls away from the hamlet of Riverton and edges a golf course in Tukwila. Once the center of fertile truck farms, Tukwila is now the location of Southcenter, a huge shopping mall. Midway through Tukwila, the Duwamish becomes the Green River, site of the discovery of the first five bodies of young prostitutes in America's worst outbreak of serial murders to date, a chain of slaughters that would claim almost fifty similar victims between July 1982 and April 1984. The Green River Killer has never been caught.

Burien, Washington, is a south-end town too, sitting five miles due west of Tukwila by freeway. If possible, Burien is even less distinguished than Tukwila, a prosaic little town located near the flight path into the Seattle-Tacoma International Airport. The south-end Park-and-Ride station is located there. Old Burien is quaint and quiet; the newer downtown has no particular charm. There are a number of small ranch-style homes with carefully groomed yards, numerous antique and second-hand stores, an inordinate number of Asian restaurants, and, down along the banks above Puget Sound, expensive waterfront homes accessible only by private funiculars on steep tracks slicing down through the maples and fir trees.

Although few who met him as a grown man knew his background, Bradly Morris Cunningham grew up in Burien along with his two sisters, his cousins, and scores of friends. His progenitors were from two proud and completely diverse backgrounds. Brad's mother, Rosemary Edwards, was a Colville Indian; his father, Sanford Cunningham, had roots in the British Isles. Rosemary was slender and beautiful with thick dark hair and flashing black eyes. Sanford, often called Stan, was big, blond, and florid, with a strong, almost prognathous jaw. In the early years of their marriage, they loved each other passionately, they had wonderful plans for the future, and they wanted nothing but the best for their children.

If every marriage started fresh with no memories and

nothing from the past, the odds for success would be far better, but each partner inevitably brings along old scars, prejudices, and unrealistic expectations. Stan and Rosie were no different; indeed, they probably carried more baggage than most. Each generation before them had added another stone to the load, and by the time they got together, some patterns were so thoroughly entrenched that one could almost predict that they would continue their destructive erosion through a family begun with love and happy plans.

The Cunningham clan was proud, loyal, and spread out all over western Washington, although its home base was originally on Whidbey Island. That was where they always held their annual summer reunions with huge barbecues and potluck picnics. Sanford and his younger brother Jimmy were born to Dr Paul L. Cunningham and his wife Bertha* in the decade after the First World War – Sanford Morris in 1924 and James Lincoln in 1926. Dr Cunningham had a successful chiropractic practice in North Seattle. He was a handsome man with an aquiline nose, and he was also a talented artist and wood carver, with many of his best pieces on display in the Museum of Art and History at the University of Washington. He carved a scale model of the campus, and he carved a statue that still stands outside the Pullman Library at Washington State University. It is the figure of a man reading a book, and it was cast in bronze.

Except for Dr Paul's belief that it was possible to receive messages from the spirit world, he and Bertha lived a fairly unremarkable life until 1927. When Sanford was three and Jimmy still a babe in arms, Bertha became pregnant with her third child and confessed tearfully to her husband that he was not the father. She had no other choice; her lover was reportedly Hispanic and it was highly unlikely that this baby would resemble her first two fair-skinned, fair-haired sons.

Dr Cunningham was not a man who could forgive, but he was something of a stoic; he could wait for his revenge.

He didn't rail at Bertha, nor did he banish her immediately. Rather, he said she could stay in his home until the baby was born, but then she had to leave. He would not, of course, allow her to take Jimmy and Sanford with her. There would be no discussion about that. She had forfeited her position in the lives of her two little sons.

After several months of silence and frigid distance, Bertha gave birth to her third son in 1927. She named him Marcellus, although nobody in the family ever called him that. He became 'Salie,' and in time 'Uncle Salie.' Bertha then packed her things and left her home, her unforgiving husband, and their little boys, Sanford and Jimmy. Salie, the baby, was raised by his maternal grandmother. Bertha eventually moved to California where she remarried and gave birth to one more child, a daughter called Goldie. According to family lore, Bertha's Mexican lover was later found murdered, and no one was ever arrested for the crime.

As far as Sanford and Jimmy knew, their mother had left them without a backward look. Their father let them believe that, and even embellished occasionally one of his favorite themes, the treachery of women. In their formative years, Sanford and Jimmy probably never encountered a female who made them doubt their father's teachings. They had an utterly miserable childhood after their mother left. Oddly, although he had decreed that Bertha could not have custody of Sanford and Jimmy, Paul Cunningham chose not to keep them either; he farmed them out to relatives and acquaintances where they never felt that they were important members of the family. They were always the odd boys out, and they never again had a mother figure. Not surprisingly, Sanford grew up with a basic distrust of women and with the conviction that women had to be kept in their place because they had infinite power to hurt men if allowed the opportunity.

Even when Paul Cunningham married again, he didn't bring Sanford and Jimmy home to live with him; perhaps they reminded him too much of their mother's betrayal, or it may have simply been that he had long since gotten used to a life without them. So Sanford and Jimmy grew up with no one but each other. Sanford Cunningham would turn to women out of sexual need, and sometimes because he was in love, but after his mother left he never totally trusted females.

Dr Paul and his second wife, Lydia, had two daughters, Mary Alice and Gertrude or 'Trudy.' Mary Alice married and moved to Texas. Trudy, an extraordinarily lovely girl, received Seattle's highest accolade to beauty when she was chosen SeaFair Queen in 1955. Later she married Dr Herman Dreesen, a highly regarded chiropractor with a practice in Lynnwood, north of Seattle.

Sanford and Jimmy stayed tightly bound as they grew up. Their total allegiance – at least until they had sons of their own – was always to each other. Sanford married at least once, briefly, before he wed Rosemary. That wife's name was Norma. There may also have been a second wife before Rosemary; if there was, even her name has been obscured by time. But the true love of Sanford's life was undoubtedly Rosemary Edwards. Their courtship and early marriage was as sweet and loving as the songs played on 'Your Hit Parade' in the forties. Jimmy Cunningham met Rosie's cousin Caroline at the same time. And so the brothers married cousins, and from then on, all of their descendants would be interrelated in complex ways that were virtually impossible to explain.

Rosemary and Caroline were Indian girls as delicately featured and slender as wild columbines. They had the blood of both the Yakima and Colville tribes in their veins, but tribal rule commanded that members choose one tribe or the other. So Rosie was officially deemed a member of the Colvilles and Caroline of the Yakimas.

Sanford and Rosie and Jimmy and Caroline made striking couples, the big, fair, red-cheeked men and their slender, bronze-skinned brides. While Jimmy and Sanford had been almost as close as twins before, they simply enlarged their alliance and drew their new wives in. The foursome lived in Everett, Washington, at first, and then Jimmy joined the merchant marine. There was no question of the brothers living apart, so the two couples moved to California together.

By 1946 they were living in Calwa City, just outside Fresno. Their mother, Bertha, was also living there – the mother they had never known when they were children. Jimmy and Sanford and their brides stayed in the Fresno area because the job situation, while it wasn't great, was better than in Seattle.

Just before Christmas 1946, Rosemary reluctantly left Sanford for a visit to her mother, who lived in the Shalishan Housing Project in Tacoma, Washington. Ethel Edwards was then forty-nine, and a handsome woman. Rosemary's father was Simon Paul Edwards, whose Indian name was Skis-Sislau. He and Ethel had eleven children, although three were stillborn. In her later years Ethel was a nutritionist who worked in Native American hospitals. In retrospect, some of her descendants would feel that Ethel was probably bisexual; she always had a very close female friend in her immediate circle. But no one thought anything of it at the time.

Ethel Edwards had an extremely strong personality. Her husband tried to advance his philosophy that the man should be the center of the home, the master of his family. He never completely succeeded. Not with Ethel. She was bright and inventive and a rebel, and her daughter Rosemary was probably closer to her than to her father, more imbued with the old matriarchal views of the Yakimas and the Colvilles. Rosemary looked delicate, but she had inherited her mother's will of iron. Her children would be raised with full knowledge of their Indian heritage, and she urged them to be proud that they belonged to the Colville tribe.

Sanford Cunningham was twenty-two and Rosie twenty-one when they married. He had been taught that women had to be kept in their place or they would betray him. She had been taught that men would try to hold women down, and that women were really more capable than men and better at making decisions anyway. But they were young, and love was all that mattered. Neither of them could imagine there might come a time when they wouldn't be in love.

When Rosie left to visit her mother, Sanford was desolate from the moment her train pulled out of the Fresno station. He wrote to her almost daily. And a week or so later, he had enough money to take the train north and rejoin his wife. Their first child was undoubtedly conceived during that reunion. Sanford and Rosie's daughter was born in California in September 1947, and she was named for her grandmother Ethel.

There were more separations when Sanford couldn't find a job that would support them. Rosie and the baby had to stay with Ethel in Tacoma while Sanford pounded the streets in Seattle. Finally, he and his brother Jimmy both got jobs. Jimmy and Caroline found a house in one of Seattle's rent-subsidized projects. Predictably, Sanford and Rosie rented one too, and both couples began adding to their families.

Rosie and Sanford had their only son, Bradly Morris Cunningham, in October 1948. Susan, their youngest child, was born in 1953. Jimmy and Caroline had five children, whose ages fit in with their 'double' cousins'. Penny was the oldest, Terry was born in November of 1948, and Gary in December of 1949. Later came Cheryl, and the baby Lynn, who died at the age of two when a milkman ran over her in the family driveway.

All of the Cunningham cousins had Indian blood, although some of them looked far more Indian than others. In actuality, they were between a quarter and a half Indian. According to tribal law, Ethel, Brad, and Susan were half

Colville because that was Rosemary's chosen tribe, while Penny, Terry, Gary, Cheryl, and Lynn were part Yakima through Caroline's official tribal papers.

Both Sanford and Jimmy raised their families in the neighborhood between White Center and Burien. Sanford and Rosemary moved to 203 128th Street just off First Avenue South in Burien in the early 1950s. They bought a good-sized L-shaped house on a large lot. A huge step up from the project, it had an impressive-looking stone facade, and they planted trees as a buffer against the traffic noise on 128th. Jimmy bought a house a few blocks away. And while it was true that Jimmy and Sanford were closer than most brothers, and that they had depended on each other since they were little boys, it didn't mean they weren't competitive. Sanford always seemed to have a newer, more expensive car than Jimmy did, and a nicer house. And he always seemed to have more money.

Through the years, Sanford held a variety of jobs, sometimes as a contractor, sometimes in the glass business, and later with Associated Grocers. 'My dad was a consultant on building projects and landscaping projects,' Susan would remember. 'He traveled most of the time. He was the only really financially successful man in his family. My dad never felt that anyone really liked him, but he thought he could make them like him with money. It seemed as though my father was gone most of my life. He showed his love by buying things for me. When I was older, I was getting a hundred-dollar-a-month allowance. If I said I was interested in skiing, my dad would take me out and buy me skis, boots, the whole outfit.'

Some members of the family, with a bit of envy, would recall that Sanford used credit lavishly, and nobody ever knew whether he *really* made that much more money than Jimmy or if he was paying on everything by the month. Either way, Sanford and Rosie were happier when they were poor.

The Cunningham cousins all went to Cedarhurst Grade

School, Cascade Junior High, and Evergreen High School. They celebrated birthdays and holidays together. They were beautiful children, a happy melding of their Anglo-Saxon and Indian genes. Jimmy's son Gary was the handsomest by far of the boys, and his son Terry – who was Brad's age – was the biggest. But Brad was the natural athlete and unquestionably the smartest. As a child – and later as man – he had uncommon brilliance. He was a leader, a bossy, confrontive boy who could be a bully at times. In every family snapshot he stood out, grinning broadly, dominating each celebration. He mugged for the camera outrageously, pushing his cousins out of the way as if to say, 'Look at *me!* Look at *me!*'

As they got older, many of the Cunningham cousins grew to dislike Brad. Some were afraid of him. 'When Brad showed up to play, I always went home,' one girl cousin remembered. 'I knew that pretty soon somebody would be crying, or maybe that someone was going to get hurt.' And Brad was highly competitive with his cousin Terry. Terry was always larger than Brad – maybe not by a lot, but there was no question that he was the taller. He was a month younger than Brad, and it rankled Brad that Terry outgrew him. His cousin Gary had trouble with reading. He was dyslexic long before the deficit was commonly diagnosed, and Brad teased and tormented him about that. Brad could read anything from an early age and he always had superior report cards. Even after they were adults, Gary didn't care to be around Brad.

No one really knew what went on inside Rosie's and Sanford's house, no one but the family who lived there. There were secrets kept inside those walls. As the years went by, the marriage that had begun with such high expectations right after the Second World War wasn't turning out the way Sanford and Rosie had hoped. While things appeared calm on the surface, the family dynamics were ugly and hurtful and, ultimately explosive.

11

Brad's birth may have been the catalyst for the inexorable disintegration of the Cunningham family. At the very least, his arrival marked the end of Ethel's small place in the sun. He was a man child and Ethel was only a girl. Sanford was delighted to have a son.

As an adult, Brad would recall that he had been told his mother's labor for his birth had been prolonged and arduous, and she had always blamed him because he had such a large head. He *was* a big baby with a disproportionately large and rounded head – a physical characteristic that would stay with him. When Rosemary developed uterine (or perhaps cervical) cancer four years after his birth, Brad said she blamed him for that, too.

When Rosemary became pregnant for the third time, she faced an agonizing decision. She took a gamble with her health to deliver Susan safely. 'My mother was diagnosed with cancer while she was pregnant with me,' Susan recalled. 'She wouldn't have an abortion – she delayed treatment until I was born.' After Susan's birth, Rosemary underwent a complete hysterectomy. She was still in her twenties. 'She had to have chemotherapy and radium treatment,' Susan said. 'Those treatments were in their infancy in the 1950s, and Mom suffered severe internal burns. And she had to take hormones, too, and they didn't work right. Everything went wrong. She even grew a mustache.'

It may have been Rosemary's health that changed her personality. Susan would remember that her mother was a woman of mercurial moods. 'She never disciplined us, though. She kept track of who was supposed to be punished and told my father when he came home. Dad would rather have been anyplace but there. Sometimes we'd all been waiting for four hours to get whipped and we were all terrified.'

The children sensed that Sanford didn't *want* to beat them – that when he came home after a day's work, he would have much preferred to be greeted with something other than a list of his children's misdeeds. But he nodded as Rosemary told him which of the children needed punishing, and he unbuckled his belt. 'He beat us with a strap,' Susan recalled. 'Mostly Ethel and Brad. I was younger. One time, I saw that Ethel had welts all up and down her back and legs. She had to go to school like that, but she wore stockings and clothes that hid the marks.'

Although Sanford dreaded taking his belt to his children, he soon fell into a kind of frenzy. 'He really got into it,' Susan remembered. 'He hit harder and harder. He really lost control.' But, in Susan's recall, it was Ethel who was the psychological whipping girl in their home. Pictures in the family albums show Ethel and Brad when they were toddlers. They were only a year apart and Brad was so large that they looked like twins. Indeed, Rosemary often dressed them in matching sunsuits. But it was definitely Brad who drew most of the positive attention in the family. Other family members would agree that Ethel was left out, but felt that Susan wasn't. 'Their whole house was decorated with Brad and Susan,' one cousin recalled. 'Brad had so many athletic honors and Susan was so pretty that their pictures were all over, but you hardly ever saw any of Ethel.'

As a child, Susan adored her big brother. She saw Brad as a protector and a hero. He took her along with him, and he didn't seem to find her an annoying baby sister. She felt proud to be with him. 'Brad taught me how to catch a football. He built a bicycle for me. Brad was the only one who listened to me. Later, when I dropped out of college for a while, he listened to my reasons and he didn't say I was stupid. He was my idol.'

Rosemary tried to discourage Susan from bonding with her brother. 'When I was little, she told me that Brad was evil,' Susan remembered. 'I didn't know why she said that.' And although Sanford favored his son, Brad still took his lumps along with the other children when Rosemary said he needed punishing.

Both Susan and Ethel recalled that Brad had suffered a concussion from falling down the basement steps. Ethel remembered that when Brad was five or six, he was helping his father move wood from the woodpile. He had tied a rope to a log and was tugging it behind him. But as he tugged, he lost his balance and fell backward about ten feet, down the steps to the basement, landing on his head. Ethel said her parents took Brad to a doctor who told them to watch for 'personality changes such as acts of violence.' But if Brad was only five or six when he landed on his head, Ethel would have been only six or seven and probably the doctor story was apocryphal.

Susan, who would have been little more than a toddler at the time of the 'log on a rope fall,' said she had watched Sanford knock Brad down the basement steps when he was twelve. 'Brad was stunned. He was saying funny things, all garbled up, and he didn't make any sense.' Susan would have been about seven when that happened. But she had quite clear recall of other acts of violence and abuse that bounced off the walls inside the house in Burien.

To the outside world – even to Sanford's brother Jimmy and his wife Caroline – life was normal in Sanford's and Rosie's family. Only the children caught in the love-hate relationship between Sanford and Rosie would witness the venom that Rosie sometimes spewed after the flawed hormone treatment following her hysterectomy. Only the children knew how bad it could get.

Susan would remember being beaten only twice. 'I was about eleven and my father never beat me again because I called the authorities and he was forbidden to touch me. After that, he put me in a dark closet to punish me. It was my safe place to hide from all the fights. I'd sit there on top of my shoes, holding my dog, and feel safe.' She would blame Rosemary for instigating the violence in her family. 'She controlled all of it. . . . My dad was squashed. He did what she said, and he never stopped any of the abuse.'

Rosemary allegedly belittled Brad and tried to break down his aggressive personality. When Sanford was away, she made him do housework. Then something bad happened when Brad was about eleven or twelve, something that alienated him from his mother for the rest of her life. According to Brad, he stayed home from school one day and Rosemary thought he was malingering. To punish him, she made him put on a dress and clean the house. When Sanford came home and found his son dressed that way, he hit the roof. From that moment on, Rosemary had no say whatsoever in Brad's life. When she spoke to him, it was like shouting into the wind. He didn't listen to her. He didn't respect her. He certainly didn't obey her. The family itself was sliced right down the middle. Sanford and Brad were on one side, Rosie and Ethel and Susan were on the other. 'Brad could do anything he wanted,' a relative recalled. 'The girls were out.'

Brad's story about being forced to dress as a girl may have been true; it may also have been a confabulation that he fashioned from articles he had read about the actor James Garner, whose stepmother had done the same thing to him. Brad's rendition was startlingly like the oft-published account of Garner's bitter childhood in which he told of grabbing a broom from his stepmother's hands and chasing her with it. He also recalled that his father was shocked to find out that his stepmother made him dress in girl's clothes, and that she had been banished.

Perhaps Brad's story was true. Perhaps both men had suffered the same humiliation. Perhaps not. But if Brad was frequently knocked around as a child, he was no angel himself. Ethel remembered the time when she was eight and he was seven. He had done something wrong and thought she was going to tattle. 'He came back to my bedroom and punched me in the stomach and he said, "Don't you tell on me!"'

The Cunninghams always had little, barky dogs, and Brad enjoyed grabbing them by the scruffs of their necks and shoving their snouts together to make them fight. Other relatives would remember Brad as a kid with a 'hair-trigger' temper. No one in his family denied that, by the time he was twelve, he went after his mother with a baseball bat. He was a big kid and Rosemary was frightened as she tried in vain to wrestle it away from him. Ethel ran to the phone and called her father and begged him to come home. When Sanford got there, he hit Brad and barked an order, 'Don't you *ever* raise your hand to me or ever hit your mother again!'

Photographs in the Cunningham family album looked as wholesome as any family's: Susan sitting with her mother at a mother-daughter tea, both of them smiling; Brad and Ethel together; Brad sitting on the couch with his arm around his mother; Sanford and Rosie hugging. They were an extremely photogenic family, but photographs can be deceiving.

That is not to say there were no good times in the family. But they seemed to occur only when they were away from home. It was as if there was an energy in the house that kept all their old resentments alive in a time warp, ready to reignite. When they went on vacation, it was like magic. 'We never fought when we went camping. We were a whole different family,' Susan would remember. They all became somehow nicer to each other, less combative than the family that lived at home.

Brad got his love for cars and trucks and trailers and all manner of heavy equipment from his father. Sanford had a king cab International truck to pull his huge camping trailer. The whole family traveled together through Oregon, California, and New Mexico. They went rock hounding and explored caves. 'The camping was so good,' Susan remembered many years after the fact. 'Our parents would sing together, harmonizing, songs from the thirties and the forties. Everything was really great. Nobody hit anybody. Bodies weren't flying.'

If only they could have kept the good feelings they had when they went camping and brought them home. For whatever reason, the pressure was off when they were sailing down the road in the big old International truck, or sitting around a campfire listening to Sanford and Rosie sing. But the closer they got to home, the more the tension built. They were, essentially, a family divided: husband against wife, parents against children, brother against sisters, male against female. They had no loyalty to one another and no connections. There had been too much violence, too much punishment, too much rivalry.

Sanford always believed that money solved everything, and Brad learned that lesson well. And Sanford believed that women were inferior to men. 'Your place is in the bedroom or the kitchen,' he lectured the girls. 'All a woman is good for is to cook and be a whore in bed.'

His daughters would fight to prove him wrong. His son apparently believed him.

12

As Brad entered his teenage years in the early 1960s, Sanford grew even prouder of his son. He rarely punished him now, even when Brad was rude to Rosie – which he often was. Sanford would no longer back Rosie up when she tried to discipline Brad. This was his *son,* after all, the boy who represented his immortality, and Rosie was only a woman.

For all of her life, Rosemary would love her son, despite

the tribulations he caused her, despite her doubts about him. For all of his life, Sanford would be proud that Brad was the smartest and best of the Cunningham clan. Father and son, neither could do wrong in the eyes of the other. Sanford's values were Brad's values, and as Brad grew older, he and his father shared their most intimate secrets.

Ethel left home and married. She had a boy and a girl, and later adopted a Native American boy. And as the years passed and Rosemary and Caroline put on a few pounds, the fragile beauty of their girlhood years blurred. Rosemary fought to keep her slender figure, and she insisted on dressing well. Even so, her husband viewed her more as a mother and a housekeeper than as a lover. The metamorphosis was gradual enough that it was accomplished before Rosemary and Caroline realized the place they had come to. It was hard to look at the fading snapshots in the old albums and remember that they had been those incandescently beautiful girls clinging to Jimmy's and Sanford's muscular arms.

Just as with all families, the years brought losses. First, Caroline's baby girl dead in the driveway. And then in the mid-1960s, Dr Paul Cunningham and his second wife, Lydia, were in a terrible car wreck in Rose Hill. Grandpa Cunningham looked worse to the ambulance crew and they rushed him to the hospital. They didn't expect him to live until morning. But it wasn't Grandpa Cunningham who died; it was Lydia who dropped dead of a stroke, brought on either by the accident itself or by her worry over her husband. Brad's grandfather recovered and lived for many more years.

Jimmy and Caroline would lose another of their five children. Terry, misdiagnosed at a local hospital and told to go home and rest, died suddenly of meningitis. All his life Brad had tried to grow bigger and stronger than Terry, but he never succeeded. Relatives were bemused when Brad proved to be the most hysterical of the mourners at Terry's funeral. As he walked past his cousin's casket, he fell to the floor in a dead faint.

Gary Cunningham grew up to take a job with the Washington State Department of Transportation. But in the middle and late 1960s, Sanford and Rosie's boy, Brad, was still the standout cousin, both athletically and intellectually. Brad had always been smarter than all of them. And he never let them forget it. If he had a flaw in his made-for-success personality, it was that he seemed unable to downplay his accomplishments. He was so successful that sometimes it was hard to like him. When he might have shown a little humility, he crowed.

Although in later years Brad wasn't close to his extended family, he occasionally showed up at the Cunningham reunions on Whidbey Island. He attracted women with ease, and his romantic history was so speckled that no one ever knew which girlfriend – or wife – he might bring with him. One thing was certain, however. When Brad did arrive, he could be counted on to have the classiest vehicle of anyone there. Like his father, it was important to Brad that the family see how well he was doing. 'One year,' a cousin said, 'he came driving up in this "superjeep." He was showing off, but he showed off too much and he got stuck in a ditch. Some guy with a great big semi had to pull him out, and we took pictures. He was mad.'

Brad Cunningham had begun to pull ahead of the pack early on. He was still quite young when he showed great athletic potential. Even in grade school, Brad had begun to lift weights and work on his body. He made high-school coaches salivate. They watched him at Cascade Junior High School and could hardly wait until he moved up to Evergreen High. He was such a strong kid, broad-shouldered and thickly muscled, and yet light on his feet and graceful. He had Sanford's size, but except for his jutting chin, he had Rosemary's coloring and facial features. He was very handsome.

Like Sanford, Brad always had money. From the time he was fourteen, he had some angle to work. His sister Ethel called him the 'local black market kid.' Girls watched Brad, too, and he watched them. Not surprisingly, as a teenager he adopted his father's and his grandfather's philosophy: women were placed on earth to pleasure men. Although he always had his eye on one girl or another, he did not allow himself to become emotionally dependent upon them. It was understood among his peers that if he asked a girl out on a date, he expected sex. Otherwise, he saw no point in dating. Enough girls were willing to play by Brad's rules that he never wanted for dates.

There were family stories about Brad's coming of age sexually. One version held that his first sexual experience was with a prostitute, and when his father – or mother – found out, he was taken to the family doctor, who diagnosed venereal disease. In truth he found no disease. This was to be a lesson to Brad, and the doctor scared him badly and then administered a series of painful shots to 'cure' him. Another story had Brad going to a doctor for a sperm count: he was worried because he had slept with so many girls and none of them had become pregnant.

It is doubtful that either of these stories was true. If anything, Brad would prove remarkably fertile in later years. When he was seventeen, he was dating a senior named Arlene* who became pregnant, but her parents wouldn't even consider her marrying Brad. Theirs had been a stormy relationship. Rosemary and Ethel remembered that Arlene had done something once that made Brad so angry that he painted 'Whore' on her front door in red paint and threw everything she had given him on her front lawn. 'Arlene just disappeared,' Susan remembered. 'Her parents whisked her away from Brad. They were afraid for her, somehow. We don't know if she had the baby or not.'

Arlene was Catholic and she probably did carry Brad's first child to term. If so, Brad was not told.

Everyone who ever went to high school remembers one student who was a shining light, so sought out and sought after that he – or she – seemed to have been blessed by some benevolent gods with luck and beauty and talent. At Evergreen High School in Burien in the years between from 1965 to 1967, that student was Brad Cunningham. He was tremendously popular. He had one ambition, the goal he had worked toward since he was about ten. He wanted to get a scholarship to the University of Washington and play for the Huskies.

Brad quickly moved into the upper echelons at Evergreen High School. He made the varsity squad for the Evergreen Wolverines, and he was elected president of the sophomore class. His sister Ethel remembered that he wanted to join Demolay, but decided not to when he found he would have to swear to respect women. By his senior year in the autumn of 1966, he was captain of the football team, vice president of the Lettermen's Club, and a member of the Wolverine Guard, the Honor Society, and the Modern Language Club. 'Brad was Mr Popular,' a classmate recalled. 'He was Mr Everything.'

Brad was also charmingly outrageous in high school, particularly in his debates in Contemporary Problems class; he was the bane of his teachers but his classmates found him hilarious. He once argued that the crime of rape was an impossibility. And one of his friends echoed that chauvinistic opinion by writing in Brad's yearbook, 'No girl can be raped because girls with their skirts up can run faster than boys with pants down.'

Although he rarely drank as an adult, comments scribbled in Brad's yearbook referred constantly to his drinking exploits. But nothing kept him off the football squad, and everyone who knew him expected that he would one day be an All-American. Brad could think on his feet faster than any student in school, and he could run through opposing blockers just as fast. He was the one kid in high school whom others envied. The Brads of this world sometimes show up at class reunions driving Cadillacs, and sometimes they end up selling used cars. Brad Cunningham, however, was going to make it big.

Everyone who went to Evergreen with him believed that.

As a teenager, Brad was handsome the way jocks are handsome. He had a wide face and a thick neck. His eyes were clear and penetrating under lidded brows, and his body was perfect. Looking back, some who knew him suggested that by the time he went to college he might have been into steroids. His only physical flaws were a wide nose and a slightly lantern jaw. Brad's Colville-Yakima Indian heritage was more readily apparent in those days. In later years, his nose was more aquiline, in all likelihood as the result of cosmetic surgery. Maybe he had plastic surgery to fix a septum deviated by a football injury or maybe it was because he wanted to look less Indian.

Even in high school, Brad had aspirations to a certain kind of life. He was determined to find a place in a world as unlike the one he had been born into as possible. He wanted nothing to do with being part of a racial minority. He hated references to his Indian roots. But that created a problem for him. When he graduated from Evergreen High School in 1967, he had his athletic scholarship to the University of Washington as everyone expected – but he needed more financial help. The Colville tribe offered academic scholarships. Although he had always tried to play down his Indian blood, Brad accepted the Colville tribe's two scholarships eagerly.

In his senior year, Brad also found another pretty young girlfriend. Their relationship was the closest thing to going steady that he had since Arlene vanished from his life. Loni Ann Ericksen* was a sophomore at Evergreen. She had transferred to public high school that year from Holy Names Academy. Her mother was ill with multiple sclerosis; the whole family had to make sacrifices and private school tuition had to go.

Loni Ann was a pixieish girl with dark eyes and hair and a dimple that showed in her left cheek when she smiled. When she was sixteen, she smiled often. 'You know,' a fellow classmate recalled, 'when I think of Loni Ann then, I can never picture her without a smile.'

Brad had noticed her first when she walked past the radiators in the foyer of Evergreen, the vantage point where popular seniors congregated. She was thrilled when he showed up at her locker, although she tried to act blasé. And he quickly became her whole world. Her feelings for Brad were scrawled over two inside covers of the Evergreen Wolverines yearbook in 1967.

'I thought you were nice, but just another senior. . . . I thought you were funny and a little "different." . . . And then one day when I was freezingly walking home, who should pop up in his super red car? *You!!* I wasn't so sure about that at the time, but now I'm sure glad I accepted your offer. It was then that I decided you were really nice and I wanted to get to know you a whole bunches [*sic*] better. Things didn't seem to be in favor of my decision, but time changed that. Well, now I know you better than that day and I'm terribly happy that I do. You're absolutely, positively, one of the mostest [*sic*] wonderful persons I've had the pleasure of getting to know. . . . You know, Brad, it's really strange how things come about. I never really thought you'd ever like me or that I could ever like a guy as much as I like you.'

Loni Ann developed a huge crush on Brad. She was a small girl but she was almost as athletic as he was. When she confided to her girlfriends how she felt about Brad, they quickly apprised her of the 'ground rules' for girls who dated him. It didn't really matter; Loni Ann was so enthralled with him that she would be willing to do whatever he wanted.

Loni Ann wanted desperately to go to 'Telos,' the Evergreen High junior-senior prom, with Brad. He agreed to take her to the dance, held at the Seattle Elks Club on the evening of April 29, 1967. Overhead a mirrored ball turned slowly, its hundreds of facets casting circlets of light over the dancers below. The class of 1968, the juniors, presented Telos in honor of the seniors, and did all the decorating – which consisted mainly of shiny blue Greek columns placed here and there. It would have taken a lot more than that to transform the basically dull decor of the Elks Club. It didn't matter. The dancers were sixteen and seventeen and the future lay ahead without a blemish or a shadow.

All the boys from Evergreen had short hair; they had yet to succumb to the hippie craze for long hair that was sweeping America. The girls' hair was swept up into bouffant styles several inches high, lacquered in place by enough hair spray to keep it immobile in gale force winds. The dance was a milestone in their young lives, a night they would never forget. And encircled by Brad's powerful arms, Loni Ann danced to Elvis Presley's 'Love Me Tender' and fell absolutely, utterly in love. She could not imagine then how she could ever bear to be away from him, even though she knew she might lose him. She was still in high school and Brad was going off to the University of Washington. She tried to sound philosophical about that as she ended her long message in his yearbook.

'. . . All your high school is over. Now, you'll go to college and be a "Big Man" and I'll just be a little junior at Evergreen or Holy Names. I really hope that it won't change anything. If it should, just remember that no matter what there is a crazy little Catholic girl who thinks you're about the most wonderful person in the world. . . .'

13

Longview, Washington, 120 miles south of Burien, was designed to be the perfect city – actually part of a twin city; no one in the Northwest ever refers to either Kelso or Longview singly, but always to 'Kelso-Longview.' From the ridges of rolling hills covered with fir trees on down to the flats along the Columbia River, Kelso-Longview seemed the ideal spot for a metropolis. The great river passes below the twin cities on its way west to the Pacific Ocean. And a high bridge connects Longview to Oregon where that state's far northwest corner pokes into what seems as though it should have been part of Washington State in the first place.

Neither Kelso nor Longview ever lived up to the grand dreams of the pioneer founders. In fact, in May of 1980, it seemed that Kelso-Longview itself might cease to exist at all. When Mount St Helens literally blew its top on May 18, powdery gray ash clogged the Toutle River's banks ten feet deep, and Spirit Lake near the peak of the mountain threatened to cascade down and wash Kelso and Longview out to sea. Only a natural dam formed from debris stopped the torrent. For months afterward, travelers along I-5 tromped on their gas pedals when they approached the twin cities, nervous that a wall of water might still be a threat.

Cheryl Keeton was born in October 1949 and grew up in Longview in a neat, cozy little house on a tree-lined street only a few blocks from Long Park. And in the summer of 1967, like Brad Cunningham, she had graduated from high school and was about to enter the University of

Washington. Slender, beautiful, dark-eyed, and extremely intelligent, she was a small-town girl who seemed to have everything. She had dated Dan Olmstead* since she was fourteen, and although Dan, two years older than Cheryl, had attended Whitman University, he was switching to the University of Washington in Seattle so they could be together.

Cheryl's family life was complicated as she was growing up but she had always coped with change serenely. She was a girl who fixed her eye on a goal and headed straight for it, and it was virtually impossible to distract her. Only later would her relationships become convoluted and interwoven, old strands braided back into new ones so that it almost seemed as if some terrible blueprint was being traced, some irrevocable plan set into motion.

Her mother, Betty, would divorce her father, Floyd Keeton, and remarry twice before Cheryl was grown. Her father would also marry again, and eventually Cheryl had five half brothers and sisters.

Betty Keeton Karr McNannay had always looked years younger than her true age; she was a tall, attractive woman with a good figure and long brown hair. Most Christmases, she got a new fur-trimmed coat, and she always looked like a model as she posed for somebody's Polaroid camera. From the time she was fourteen, Betty had worked in some aspect of the medical field. She began as a nurse's aide and next became a licensed practical nurse and a certified alcohol counselor. Eventually, she would work as a psychiatric security nurse at Western Washington State Hospital in Steilacoom, an institution for the insane.

Betty's first, young marriage was to Floyd Keeton, a tall, well-built man in his twenties with a crew cut. He was a half dozen years older than Betty and she was barely nineteen when Cheryl was born. After an acrimonious divorce from Floyd, Betty married James Karr and gave birth to a second daughter, Julia, and to a son, Jim, who were five and six years younger respectively than Cheryl. Betty divorced Karr when Jim was six. Betty was working as an LPN, and Cheryl walked little Julia and Jim to and from school and looked after them until their mother got home.

Betty met Bob McNannay, her third husband, when she was hired as his secretary at the Port of Longview. McNannay was about a decade older than she was, forty-two, and still a bachelor. He was intelligent and kind and had a great sense of humor. He would spend thirty-seven years working for the Port of Longview, becoming its general manager for the last fourteen years before he retired.

Betty married Bob McNannay in October of 1963 when Cheryl was two days from her fourteenth birthday. Julia was nine and Jim eight. They all got along fine. Cheryl trusted Bob McNannay and valued his opinion. Betty's welcome mat was always out to her children's friends, and their home was full of parties and games and people. There was often an extra place – or two or three – set at Betty's table; her kids grew up happy.

Cheryl had always been a dedicated student, determined to go to college. Bob McNannay admired her ambition and her brains. 'She was my daughter,' he said later, as close to his heart as any natural child could be. McNannay often found Cheryl sound asleep over her studies, and he would wake her up and send her to bed. 'She graduated when she was only seventeen,' he recalled. 'Her mother thought she was too young to go to the University of Washington. I told her Cheryl would be fine – and she was.'

Cheryl was a senior in high school when Betty gave birth to her last child, Susan McNannay. Bob had longed for a child of his own, and he doted on the little girl; the whole family did. Susan was seventeen years younger than Cheryl, who adored her baby sister. She and her boyfriend Dan lugged Susan around with them wherever they went. Sometimes, when they took Susan to the store, they pretended that she was *their* baby. Nobody doubted that they were her parents, even though they seemed very young to have a baby.

Cheryl graduated from high school fifth in her class; she was coeditor of the school paper, *The Lumberjack Log*. She was pretty and brilliant and happy. Susan grew up idolizing her older half sister. Cheryl was always there for her, 'a third parent, really,' she recalled years later. As warm and loving as Cheryl was, Susan always viewed her as the strongest member of her family emotionally. 'Cheryl was always in control, even with our family. She never lost an argument. She always had the last word,' Susan said. But she stressed that Cheryl wasn't bossy; she was just blessed with great common sense and determination.

Cheryl's natural father, Floyd, had moved to Vacaville, California, and remarried. Cheryl remained close to him, her stepmother, Gabriella, and her half sisters Debi and Kim. From the time she was small, she had spent time every year with her father and his family in California. She was especially attached to her grandmother Edna Keeton.

Cheryl wasn't afraid of much; she was self-confident and had every reason to be. She was smart and she was nice, but few people ever won an argument with her. She wanted to be an attorney one day, and no one doubted that she had what it took. But Cheryl was a romantic, too. Her all-time favorite song was 'Send In the Clowns.' Susan, who would grow up to be one of her closest friends, said that Cheryl loved Kurt Weill's *Threepenny Opera*. She played the album over and over again. But 'Mack the Knife,' a song of betrayal and swift bloody murder, was not one of her favorites.

Cheryl began her freshman year at the University of Washington in the fall of 1967, and even though she was more studious than most of her Gamma Phi Beta sorority sisters, she made a lot of friends. There was a warmth and a vivacity about Cheryl that attracted people to her. For all of her life, she would be considered a cherished friend by dozens of people. Many women who are as attractive as Cheryl was *and* smart to boot have difficulty initiating friendships with other women. Not Cheryl. Everyone liked her.

Cheryl majored in economics, continued to go steady with Dan Olmstead, and worked so hard in college that she probably didn't have much time to attend football games. During her years at the University of Washington, it was unlikely that she had any idea who Brad Cunningham was. He was a jock and she was a scholar. Brad had pledged Theta Chi, the fraternity whose chapter house was next to the Gamma Phi house. Occasionally the two houses had exchanges, casual social evenings. And many years later, Brad would claim that he and Cheryl had dated once while they were in college. It is impossible to prove or disprove that. She was going steady with Dan and it would have been unlike her to date someone else. More probably, Brad and Cheryl had only passed each other as they walked to class, their heads bent against the relentless Seattle rain.

Cheryl's life had been pretty much charted since she was in junior high school, and a big, cocky football player had no place in her plans. Brad Cunningham was not her style.

Not then.

14

Brad's lifetime dream had been to play football for the University of Washington Huskies. And he had made it. He pledged Theta Chi, and Burien and Evergreen High School seemed far away, although he continued to date Loni Ann Ericksen all through his freshman and sophomore years. Then in February 1969, Loni Ann missed her period. She was a senior at Evergreen by that time and she was thrilled to be going steady with Brad; being with him was the pinnacle of all her dreams and hopes. Sleeping with him had, of course, always been a prerequisite for any girl who wanted to date him, but like the other girls who had yearned for Brad, Loni Ann hadn't minded. She loved him. More than that, she idealized him. If she *should* be pregnant, she told herself, it wouldn't be the end of the world. Even though pregnancy without marriage was not socially acceptable in 1969, it was not nearly as disgraceful as it had been a few decades earlier.

Loni Ann, stuck back in high school, had been petrified that she would lose Brad to some college girl. Now she was almost relieved to think she might be pregnant. It would mean that she and Brad would get married. At least, she hoped they would. She already felt like part of his family; she baby-sat often for Brad's sister Ethel, and she was always welcome at Sanford and Rosemary's house.

With the passage of a few more weeks, there was no doubt that Loni Ann *was* pregnant, due in October 1969. When she told Brad, he didn't seem upset. They agreed to get married in March, and they chose the United Methodist Church for the ceremony. It was right on Ambaum Boulevard in Burien, only blocks from the house where Brad grew up. He was twenty and Loni Ann seventeen. They made a great-looking couple. He was so big and handsome, and she was slender and pretty.

Already a perfectionist, Brad took charge of the wedding and had every detail planned ahead of time. He wanted his wedding and reception to go like clockwork. And it almost did. Brad and Loni Ann knew that their friends would tie balloons, crepe paper, and cans on their car, but Brad wasn't about to drive down the street making a spectacle of himself. He was too conscious of his image. He would not be looked down upon, and he would not be laughed at. So he had stashed a motorized golf cart in back of the church and he and Loni Ann were prepared to zoom right out of the reception in the church basement to a *non*-decorated car. Brad had figured out how to escape the ignominious pelting of rice and chorus of raucous comments.

Loni Ann embarrassed Brad, however, before they even made their getaway. When she tossed her wedding bouquet to a group of squealing bridesmaids and single girls, she miscalculated and threw it too high, and it got caught on a low-hanging telephone wire. It was only a small flaw in Brad's perfect plan, but he was furious. With one clumsy throw, Loni Ann had ruined his smoothly choreographed wedding and reception. The damn bouquet teetered on the wire while everyone tried to poke it and shake it down. Loni Ann didn't know why it made such a difference to Brad, but it did. She apologized a dozen times, and finally he told her to forget it. They would not let her bad aim ruin their honeymoon.

Loni Ann looked forward to a wonderful life with her new husband, and with the baby she carried. They rented a small unit at the Mark Manor apartments midway between Burien and White Center, and both of them worked hard. Although Brad had his three scholarships, that income wasn't enough for the way he wanted them to live. He did construction work when the Washington Huskies weren't in training or playing.

The young Cunninghams' first summer, 1969, was a memorable one for its cataclysmic and extraordinary events. Astronaut Neil Armstrong took man's first steps on the moon on July 20. Eight days later, Mary Jo Kopechne drowned in Senator Ted Kennedy's car when it plunged off a bridge on Chappaquiddick Island. And on August 9, Charles Manson's followers carried out his grotesque orders to kill and turned Roman Polanski's home into an abattoir.

Most memorable of all, perhaps, was the Woodstock Music and Arts Fair, which began on August 15. Almost half a million young people gathered on a dairy farm in Bethel, New York, to listen to The Grateful Dead, Jefferson Airplane, Crosby, Stills, Nash and Young, Janis Joplin, Jimi Hendrix, and dozens of other musical groups and performers. But while much of America's youthful population was caught up in peace and love and, most particularly, Woodstock that summer, Brad Cunningham had other things on his mind. He didn't want to dress like a hippie or camp out in a muddy field listening to rock stars in the rain. He was more comfortable in a three-piece suit.

Brad had always been a young man in a hurry and he didn't act like a college boy. He could not have cared less about peace and love and the end of all war, and he had far more important interests than whether the Washington Huskies won the game on Saturday. He still liked football well enough, and he took pride in keeping his huge body toned, but his ambitions had changed and football was no longer his main focus. Brad hadn't made football history at Washington. He was a little fish in a big pond and there were dozens like him.

Twenty-five years later, a man who had played for the Huskies was asked about Brad. He searched his mind and finally a memory dawned slowly. 'Yeah, I remember him,' he said. 'He was "the crook."' He didn't explain his cryptic remark further. But Brad had always been a braggart, and in college he liked to refer to the 'big boys' he worked for. He was still attending the University of Washington, but his scholarships were a mere pittance compared to what he was making at Gals Galore,* a topless tavern that was a major draw in the north end of Seattle. It was rumored to be run by organized crime interests. Perhaps it was, or perhaps that was only one of Brad's exaggerations. While Seattle has never been a big mob town, there have been some 'families' whose business interests were suspect.

Brad began at Gals Galore as a bouncer, but a month later he was promoted to business manager. He was smart, and he was a quick study, but Loni Ann wondered about his rapid rise in the girlie tavern. He was certainly making a lot more money than he had working construction during vacation. And when he dropped off the squad, he told Loni Ann that the coach told him he was making too much money at his outside job to keep his scholarship. Maybe that was true.

Besides that, Brad's personality made it impossible for him to be a team player. College football was only a stepping-stone for him, a way to pay for his education. And he didn't need that any longer. He had his future all planned, and he and Loni Ann were not going to be living in a crummy apartment for long, not if things worked out the way he believed they would.

When she looked back, Loni Ann recalled that the first six months of her marriage to Brad were quite happy. She had always realized that Brad was a little self-involved, that he wanted his own way, but it wasn't that big a deal to her. She had won the boy – the *man* – she loved and she was determined to be the perfect wife. To supplement their income, Brad and Loni Ann served as assistant managers of the apartment house where they lived. She cleaned apartments after tenants moved out, and he handled the books and the landscaping.

Kait Ann Cunningham was born in October of 1969,

the month that her father turned twenty-one. She was an exquisite dark-eyed baby girl. Brad showed her off proudly to his family and friends. Loni Ann was surprised and delighted to see what a proprietary attitude he took with his first child.

But something began to go wrong in the young Cunningham marriage in the first month after Kait's birth. Brad had sometimes gotten impatient and short-tempered with Loni Ann during the two years they had dated, and over the first six months of their marriage, but he had never hurt her physically. It had never even occurred to her that he might. She was a strong, athletic girl – but she was no match for a man who could block a 250-pound guard and drop him where he stood.

The first hairline cracks in the structure of their marriage appeared that fall. Brad seemed to delight in degrading and embarrassing Loni Ann. He told her repeatedly that she was 'really stupid.' He said he could not understand how he could have married someone as stupid as she was. Loni Ann was bewildered. She had believed that Brad loved her. *She* hadn't changed, except to become a mother. But Brad's behavior toward her was suddenly and inexplicably cruel.

He insisted that she dress in a way that demeaned her. He bought her tiny little minidresses and push-up bras. She looked like a hooker. She was a young mother and she could hardly bend over to pick up Kait without showing her underwear. When Rosemary remarked about how inappropriate her clothes were, Loni Ann blushed. 'I hate the way I look,' she said, 'but this is all that Brad buys me to wear.'

Brad was consumed with Gals Galore. Loni Ann knew only what he told her about the place and that frightened her. He referred to 'orders coming down from Reno and Vegas.' 'Brad said that was why they went topless,' she said. 'Those were the orders from Nevada.'

When Brad gave up his football scholarships, Loni Ann was shocked. How could he walk away from his lifetime dream? Now he was working with people who cared only about money. Brad was away from home every day from two in the afternoon until daylight. She had no idea what he did while he was gone, but he would come home 'really pumped' because the 'big shots' from Vegas had been up for a confab. And sometimes Brad brought home television sets and furniture. She didn't know where he got them.

Kait's birth had marked the beginning of the disintegration of their marriage, and Brad's verbal abuse escalated into physical violence. The first time he pushed her, Loni Ann was shocked, but she explained it away. The second time he used force on her it wasn't so easy to deal with. But with every passing month Brad's physical assaults grew in intensity and frequency. 'He would hit me,' Loni Ann recalled many years later. 'He would grab me by the arms and bang me against the wall – throw me to the floor, kick me, bang my head into the floor. He hit me across the face with his forearm . . . split my lip.'

She could never determine just what it was she was doing wrong. She finally came to believe that it was just who she was. Certainly, Brad was growing beyond her in sophistication and in education. He was out in the world, becoming more and more competent in dealing with people. He was so smart and she was an eighteen-year-old girl with a new baby, who helped support them by cleaning toilets and scrubbing floors. She knew she was probably boring to Brad. At the same time Loni Ann was puzzled at how possessive he had become. He wanted to know where she was every moment of the day. That was kind of silly since she had neither the inclination nor the opportunity to be with any man but Brad. And when Loni Ann had the temerity to ask if she might attend some college classes, he laughed. '*That* would be a real waste of money – you're too stupid to learn.'

Brad was doing so well in his job managing the tavern that he concluded it was ridiculous for him to continue at the University of Washington. He was going to college to prepare for a career where he could make money, but he was already making money. He dropped out of school, although he would eventually return and gain his degree in Business Administration in 1978 when he realized that a degree meant money in the bank. Brad was on his way to be the success he had always envisioned.

Loni Ann was afraid when Brad was working for Gals Galore. One time she could see that he was really worried about something. He wouldn't discuss tavern business with her, but he instructed her, 'Don't open the door – not for anyone.' He was gone into the wee hours of the morning and that made her more afraid.

Loni Ann was relieved when Brad went to work for a life insurance company and then started his own business as a real estate entrepreneur in the early 1970s. He called his fledgling corporation 'B.M.C. and Associates.' Brad had not turned out to be the Big Man on Campus everyone expected, but B.M.C. and Associates took off. He proved to be a natural. People responded positively to him. He had such an easy way about him, making everyone he met believe that he sincerely liked them and that knowing him would improve their lives and fortunes immeasurably. He exuded charm and capability at the same time. It was a talent, a genuine talent. It didn't matter that his office was only a little hole in the wall. Brad had a million-dollar personality.

They were still living at the Mark Manor apartments in 1970 when Loni Ann found she was pregnant again. It was not an easy pregnancy, and Brad was far less entranced with the idea of being a father than he had been with their first baby. After a long, difficult labor, Loni Ann gave birth to Brad's second child and his first son on December 9, 1970. Brent Morris* was only thirteen months younger than Kait. Loni Ann had come very close to dying during her exhausting labor, and she was too weak to take care of her new son. Brad's sister Ethel looked after the red-headed baby until Loni Ann was strong enough to take over.

Gradually but inexorably, invisible walls rose higher around Loni Ann. There came a time when she had no freedom at all. She had to account to Brad for every minute of her life. Their apartment was midway between Burien and White Center, and since Brad always had the car, Loni Ann had to walk several blocks either way to reach a grocery store. Brad ordered her to let him know whenever she would be gone from the apartment and for precisely how long. With a one-year-old and a newborn to carry along on all her errands, it was difficult for Loni Ann to *know* how long it was going to take her to get groceries and walk home. She often found herself running in a panic toward their apartment in a futile effort to meet Brad's immutable schedule.

Brad's power over Loni Ann eventually expanded to the point where she was not allowed to take the babies outside to play, or to go to the playground, without notifying him. He instructed her that she must call either him or his receptionist and leave a message to tell him where she was going. If she went to get the mail from the box downstairs and he called twice without reaching her, Brad left work and came home. He punished Loni Ann for such grievous misconduct and he did it physically. Brad would backhand her and she would stagger across the room and crumple to the floor.

Loni Ann didn't tell anyone. Brad was nice to everybody but her. 'I was embarrassed and ashamed that my own husband would treat me so poorly,' she confessed.

It got worse. After they had been married three years, Loni Ann was the object of Brad's beatings two or three times a month. Still, she didn't tell anyone. Once when she had tried to argue back, Brad had looked at her and said quietly, 'You know, I could have things done to you if I wanted to. . . .'

This was the man she had loved since she was fifteen. This was the man she had believed was 'absolutely, positively, one of the mostest wonderful persons I've had the pleasure of getting to know.' Loni Ann realized, far too late, that she no longer knew her husband at all. Perhaps she had never really known Brad. All she knew was that he was ashamed of her, and that she and the babies seemed to mean nothing to him. And after a while, Loni Ann couldn't understand why Brad wouldn't just let her go. He didn't want her. He had convinced her that no one would want her. They had both been very young when they got married, and they had married because Loni Ann was pregnant. Maybe they never really had a chance at a lasting relationship. Still, they stayed together, working at cross-purposes perhaps, but together.

15

Loni Ann had no idea at all where she was. She had come to this dark place in a car with Brad. She remembered that much; that part was not a dream. She knew she had wakened slowly from a nauseous, drunken stupor as they hurtled through the night. It was totally out of character for her to get drunk. Her life had become such a tenuous balancing act that she needed, always, to watch and be ready. She never drank, nothing more than a beer or two; that was probably why the drinks at the party had hit her like truth serum, loosening her tongue. Then she had thrown up until her insides felt sprained and bruised, but it was too late. The alcohol was already in her bloodstream. She didn't weigh that much in the first place. Loni Ann had passed out from the combination of alcohol and humiliation.

She could not really remember leaving the party. She had a blurred recollection of Brad dragging her out of the house and away from the others. Her arms hurt where his fingers had left deep indentations. She was used to it now. Brad was knocking her around regularly, but he was always careful that the marks he left could be covered up by a longsleeved, high-necked blouse. That was the only time he let her wear modest clothes. He didn't want anyone to know he was hitting her. They were supposed to be the perfect couple, and Loni Ann knew that perfect wives don't anger perfect husbands to the point that those wives must be punished. Brad was a stickler about appearances. No one outside their marriage had any hint that they were anything but 'the ideal, happy couple.' Brad wanted it that way. He was a young business prodigy on his way up.

It was Memorial Day 1971, and they had been married two years. Loni Ann had snapped and she had broken a number of Brad's rules. The party was a going-away party for one of Loni Ann's friends, a woman she had come to depend on. The fact that one of her few close friends was moving away was a blow to her. Although she had never told anyone about Brad's beatings, her friends were still important to her. She hated to lose even one. Maybe that was why she had had too much to drink. Brad was incredulous that she could embarrass him that way. But then she had committed an even more terrible offense.

Before she passed out, Loni Ann had crossed another invisible, forbidden line. She blurted out secrets too long pent up. She told about Brad's brutality. Even as her alcohol-loosened tongue babbled on about how awful things were in her marriage, she knew somewhere deep inside that Brad would never in this world forgive her. Never.

And then she had became violently ill.

Her girlfriends led Loni Ann into the bathroom and one of them held her head while she vomited. She was neither the first nor the last wife who drank too much, told secrets, and thoroughly embarrassed her husband. But Brad was capable of a singular kind of rage, an emotion so inherent and dominant in his nature that it defied opposition. Loni

Ann had seen it. His mother, Rosemary, had glimpsed it. And his father had to be aware of his compulsion to control, though Sanford accepted whatever Brad did; Brad was his son and not unlike himself.

Even with all the beatings she had gone through, Loni Ann had never seen Brad as angry as he was at the party. He had pounded on the door of the bathroom and demanded to be let in. Her friends saw that she was terrified and refused to open the door. Brad simply broke in and grabbed Loni Ann by the arm, half pulling, half dragging her to their car. She didn't remember that part; she had passed out.

When she awoke, they were on a dark road. 'I was sick. I was very tired,' she remembered. 'When he stopped the car, he walked me a few feet away from the road and told me, "Just stay here."' Loni Ann was still too drunk to walk and frightened half out of her wits. Brad propped her up at the edge of the road and drove off, leaving her surrounded by absolute pitch-black night.

She stayed. The ground seemed to undulate beneath her, and she struggled to keep upright. Finally she began to crawl, reaching out in the darkness, trying to find the road. She could feel nothing in front of her, so she turned around. Then she saw lights in the distance, lights that would prove to be miles away. In a daze she made her way to an all-night gas station where she called the police. She knew they didn't quite believe her; she knew she smelled like vomit and alcohol, but she was too tired to explain any further. They took her home, but Brad wouldn't come to the door and so they left her at Sanford and Rosemary's house.

Because Loni Ann was only rarely allowed to drive their car, she had to wait five months before she could retrace the route to the dark place Brad had taken her. The night after the Memorial Day party haunted her. She had a sense of where she had been, the general area, because she had actually been relatively close to home. But there was another feeling that gripped her when she tried to remember. It was terror, and she didn't know why. She had already been punished for her behavior at the party, and Brad had apparently smoothed over her revelations as the ravings of a woman who couldn't hold her liquor. What she felt wasn't fear of reprisal or humiliation, it was a compelling need to know. If she didn't find out where she had been, she feared she might go back there one night and never return.

It was a sunny October day when Loni Ann was finally able to get their car for the afternoon. Unerringly, almost instinctively, she retraced the road she had crawled along to reach the gas station and she found the place where Brad had left her; the same smell she had detected that night wafted in the air. The leaves of the trees were gold and russet now instead of the bright green they were in May. That night she had seen nothing but black, but she now knew where she had been.

Loni Ann suddenly felt nauseated again, sicker than the alcohol had made her. Her own husband had pulled her out of their car, pushed her to this strip beside the road, and told her to stay there. Her back had been to the road. But only steps in front of her, in the place where she had reached out her hands and touched nothing, she could now see why. Brad had left her inches away from a sharp drop-off above the Duwamish River. If she had gone forward instead of back, she would have plunged thirty feet down onto the rocks or into the river, and almost certainly drowned.

'I looked down and I felt sick,' she said a long time later. 'I realized how close I came to walking off that cliff. . . .'

Loni Ann drove home, the taste and smell of death in her mouth. If he ever found out where she had been, Brad would probably finish what she was quite sure he had meant to do that night. She thought back to when Brad had picked her up at his parents' house the morning after he left her by the river. She wondered if he was only waiting for another day, another opportunity. How odd it was that things had gone on between them as they always had. He had to know what he'd done, but never spoke of it. And she cared for the apartment house and for Kait and Brent, and acceded to whatever Brad asked of her.

She had loved him so much; now Loni Ann found it hard to remember love at all. Sex continued, but it was all for Brad. 'He forced me to do whatever he wanted whenever he wanted it,' she said. When she finally gathered up enough courage to ask for a divorce, Brad listened coldly and then told her she would never be allowed to keep their children. He reminded her of that every time she repeated her request. 'You'll come crawling back to me,' he jeered.

She could not leave her babies behind, and so she stayed, all the while trying to think of a way for the three of them to escape. Although Brad seemed to find Kait and Brent a nuisance and spent little time with them, he always reminded Loni Ann that they were *his* – that he would never let something that belonged to him go.

Still, on the surface, everything appeared to be normal. No one knew how bad things were between them. Brad occasionally allowed Loni Ann to play softball with a local girls' team, they took fishing trips to the ocean, and Loni Ann invited Brad's father and sisters over for dinner.

Perhaps inevitably, there were also dark undercurrents in Sanford and Rosemary's marriage. Brad and his father were now such close confidants that he was fully aware that Sanford had begun an affair with a woman named Mary. He reportedly told his son that he was tired of Rosemary. And that may well have been true. 'My mom was really out of hand,' their daughter Susan recalled. 'She lost her temper and was hard to deal with.'

Sanford traveled a great deal, all over Washington, Oregon, Idaho, and Montana. 'You know,' Susan later said, 'I never really did know what my dad did. I know that he designed storefronts; he was always bringing home blueprints to work on, and he was always gone, but to tell you precisely *which* stores – or where – I can't remember.'

To read Sanford's letters to Rosemary and to hear of the gifts he gave her in 1972, it would have been hard to believe there was trouble in their marriage. He may have been devious, he may have felt guilty, or both. 'My father bought my mother a new wedding ring, and it was loaded with diamonds,' Susan recalled. 'And that was just before he left her.'

When Rosemary visited her mother that summer at the Kanakanak Native Hospital in Dillingham, Alaska, where Ethel Edwards was working as a nutritionist, Sanford wrote letters to her that were almost as full of longing as those he had sent when he was a lovesick bridegroom in Fresno in 1946. He wrote her a stack of long letters, and all the time he was in love with another woman and trying to figure out a way to leave Rosemary and go to Mary. On July 22, Sanford wrote to her from their cabin in Darrington:

> Hi Sweetheart!
> . . . Sunday, Susan and I stood at the window in the airport waiting for you to look out of the plane but you didn't. . . .

The letter went on to tell of meals at Ethel's, visits from Susan and Brad and Loni Ann.

> Brad and Loni Ann and their kids are sleeping out in the front yard in their new tent they bought. . . . Your nasturshims [*sic*] are all in bloom and are quite pretty. The hummingbirds were sure complaining about their feeder being empty, so I whipped up a batch and filled the jars. . . . Boy, it sure is lonesome around here. The cabin is so quiet. I'll be glad when you get home. . . . Well, Mama, it's 12:30 in the morning and I'm tired. . . . So good night, sweet dreams, and I love you. . . . Your Old Man

In other letters Sanford wrote about pets, family, cooking, gardening, and how much he missed his wife. He kidded her that their living room looked like a warehouse for Luzier – the cosmetic line that Rosemary sold. If his plan was to reassure her that everything was normal at home, his letters were masterpieces of deceit. The only thing that seemed to trouble Sanford was his father. At the age of forty-eight, he still had a prickly relationship with Dr Paul Cunningham. He wrote about it to Rosie.

> Friday, I came up to the cabin but my Dad had to complicate things for me. He called me at the office and wanted to have me drop off the air compressor for him. I told him I was going straight to the cabin after work. This didn't faze him at all. He wanted to use that compressor so I had to go back home and help him load it on his pickup. I sure was unhappy about that.

Paul Cunningham was the father who had kicked his first wife out of the house and farmed their sons Sanford and Jimmy out for their whole childhood, and Sanford, at least, had never quite forgiven him. Otherwise, Sanford's letters were full of love and plans for a future with Rosie.

'I know it's hard to understand how my father could do that – write such nice letters when he was planning to leave my mother,' Susan said later. 'But you have to understand that my father always prided himself on his letter writing. He *always* wrote long letters full of news. But, most of all, the way he did it was the *only* way he could have left my mother. If she'd known – she would have feigned illness, she would have screamed and made scenes.'

For the two weeks in July and August of 1972 that Rosemary was in Alaska, Sanford wrote every third day or so. She had no inkling that her husband was not as lonely as he sounded. 'I haven't seen anyone or called anyone. . . . But there again,' Sanford wrote, 'you're the only one I want to talk to anyway. Or at least be around. I really miss you honey. I didn't think it would be this lonesome. I guess I love you so much and you're so much of my life . . . I really am anxious for you to get home again so I can hold you in my arms and squeeze you till you holler.'

Rosemary came home from Alaska to a husband who was, apparently, devoted to her. But sometime later that year, Sanford told Brad that what he really wanted was to live with Mary. Brad thought that was a reasonable plan and offered to help his father defect from his marriage with a minimal loss of assets. Brad was twenty-two when he learned that his father was involved with another woman. He hated his mother so much that it probably gave him pleasure to know that his father was cheating on her. The two men talked over Rosemary's head, using double entendres and winking. And she didn't have a clue.

Although her marriage had been far from perfect, Rosie loved her husband. She was touched and amazed when Sanford bought her a new car, a Pontiac GTO. To top that off, he and Brad urged her to consider taking another vacation. She looked from one to the other in surprise. She had no idea that either her son or her husband cared whether she needed a vacation.

'You've worked so hard, Mom,' Brad said. 'We think you deserve a vacation.'

'Why don't you fly down and visit your sister Jewel in California?' Sanford urged.

After a lot of coaxing, Rosemary agreed that it would be wonderful if she could take a trip like that. Her husband and son helped her pack and waved goodbye.

She was gone for two weeks. And as soon as she had left, Sanford called his children and said, 'You gotta come help me move.' Susan would acknowledge that she helped pack. Her father was in such a panic to get out without a scene. It seemed the only way. She knew how bitterly her parents fought; they were never going to stay together.

When Rosemary returned two weeks later, she was rested and anxious to get back to Sanford. But her homecoming was anything but happy. When she opened the front door of their house on 128th Street, she thought at first they had been robbed. Everything of any value was gone. The place had been ransacked, almost totally cleaned out. About the only objects left behind were her 'Indian' things – stools with deer legs, old photos, 'Dream catchers,' a few linens, and some furniture that was almost worn out.

That brutal trick was the way Rosemary found out about Sanford's new woman. Her husband had left her and taken everything they had bought for their home. And Brad, her own son, had helped him do it. Susan's part in the deception was minuscule, and Rosemary may not have known that she helped at all.

Rosemary had not been the perfect wife and, certainly, she was not a perfect mother. But the fact that Brad had plotted against her probably hurt her as much as losing her husband to another woman. The men in her life, the ones she had loved and looked to for protection, had betrayed her. She turned now to her nephew Gary, Jimmy's son.

In her despair, Rosemary visited her nephew Gary and his wife for hours every day and wept and wailed about Sanford's infidelity. She begged Gary to spy on him and his new girlfriend. Maybe he could find out something she could use to get her husband back. Gary held her hand and commiserated with her, but he wasn't about to become a private eye. He knew that the break was final.

'Brad *introduced* that woman to Sanford,' Rosemary sobbed, almost unbelieving. 'That woman worked with Associated Grocers in Yakima and I didn't know one thing about it.'

Sanford moved in with Mary and in time they were married. He helped raise her daughter. In their divorce settlement, Sanford got the house on 128th Street and Rosemary held title to their cabin in Darrington. She never planted nasturtiums there again, and eventually she transferred it back to Sanford.

After that, it was a long, long time before Rosemary trusted anyone. And in the end all the members of the Cunningham family would be completely estranged from one another. Some would be dead. Others would not speak. And if Brad was full of guile and cruelty in his marriage to Loni Ann, he had an expert mentor in his father.

16

Much to Brad's disgust, Loni Ann had always maintained her friendship with his older sister Ethel. An assertive woman, somewhat garrulous, and surprisingly strong given the experiences of her childhood, Ethel was one of the few women in Brad's life who were not afraid of him. In desperation, Loni Ann went to Ethel in September 1972 and confided that she had begged Brad for a divorce but that at first he would not even consider it. Then he had told her, 'Fine, you want a divorce? Go for it. You'll never keep these kids. I'll get them. How dare you try to get away from me?'

'Brad laid out a scenario for me,' Loni Ann would say later. 'He told me what would happen to me if I left him. He said that I was a slut. He said he could kill me in our apartment and make it look like a rape killing, and that no one would ever suspect him.'

'I believed her,' Ethel would confirm. 'We moved her and the kids out of her apartment that night.'

'You have to understand,' Loni Ann said, 'that I got to a point with the relationship that I believed nothing worse could happen to me by going than by staying. . . . I had become "punch happy." I could never tell when he was going to be Dr Jekyll and when he was going to be Mr Hyde.'

Loni Ann had no friends who were in a position to help her, and there were no women's shelters to go to in the early 1970s. She was totally dependent on Brad, and he had always been the one who kept track of whatever money they had and who paid the bills. 'I had no survival knowledge to exist on my own – but I had to,' Loni Ann said.

Surprisingly, Brad didn't put up much of a fight when she finally left him. He was finished with her anyway. Their divorce was final in May 1973, awarded to Loni Ann on her filing of 'cruel and unusual treatment.' Initially they had an agreement to share custody of Kait and Brent, although the children would live with their mother.

Loni Ann moved to Oregon to attend college. She hoped eventually to graduate from Washington State and then go on to graduate school so that she could support herself and her children. At the moment, they had virtually no resources beyond what Brad was willing to send her. And even that she could never really count on.

In 1974, however, Brad told her that he had changed his mind about letting her have Kait and Brent. She had been accepted at Washington State University in Pullman that summer, and Brad had shown no concern that she and the children would be moving three hundred miles east of Seattle. 'He waited until within four weeks of my scheduled move before trying for the court order,' Loni Ann recalled. 'He contended that he was not interfering with my attending the university. . . . If I wanted to attend school . . . fine – the children could live with him. The court order was denied. Then he field for custody a second time.'

Actually, Brad had never intended that Loni Ann should have Kait and Brent. He just needed some time to build a life in which he felt he would have a better chance of having the children awarded to him. When he had done that, he initiated legal action to gain full custody of his children. Even his own parents were never quite sure why. Loni Ann was a good mother, and Brad could be an impatient, punishing father. But Brad wanted his children, and the struggle to possess them – actually to *re*possess them – was, in Loni Ann's recall, 'desperate . . . emotional.'

Brad had warned her any number of times that if she ever left him, he would take the children from her. Still, he had let them go with her and she had begun to hope cautiously that Brad's threat to fight her for the children had been empty. Now she realized he had only been biding his time. There was nothing he could do to her that would hurt her more than taking her children and he knew it.

Brad had married again. Rapidly. He told associates that he felt he would have a much better chance of gaining full custody of Kait and Brent if he was a married man. Because he knew mothers were awarded custody more often than single fathers, Brad's second trip to the altar was probably nothing more than a marriage of convenience. His second wife, Cynthia Marrasco,* was fifteen years older than he was and as different from Loni Ann as she could possibly be. A teacher, divorced after a long marriage to a wealthy attorney, Cynthia lived in a luxurious six-bedroom estatelike home in an upscale suburb of Seattle. She was a striking woman with black hair. One of Brad's sisters thought Cynthia resembled their mother, Rosemary, a great deal.

Cynthia was over forty and Brad was only twenty-five, but he seemed older because his presence was larger than life and he was tremendously self-confident. At first glance, they did not appear to be the mismatched couple that they were. She was very attractive and looked younger, and he could have passed for a man in his thirties. Cynthia had three sons, of whom the youngest, Nicholas,* was in grade school when she met Brad through their mutual interest in real estate ventures. Because she was so devoted to her own boys, she could empathize with Brad's passion to get his children back. He seemed utterly bereft without them.

Brad told Cynthia he was worried sick about Loni Ann's complete disregard for Kait's and Brent's well-being. He said he had seen some small children playing alone in a park and had walked over to see if they were okay. 'They were my *own* children,' Brad moaned. 'And Loni Ann's out there on the highway *hitchhiking* with them. Can you imagine the danger that puts them in?' Cynthia was appalled. She already had the perfect home for raising children, and Brad had the prospects, she believed, for a splendid future in the business world. Together they could make a team that would help Brad regain custody of his children, and he would help her raise her three boys. Beyond that, she felt they would work well together in business. Beginning in March 1973, Cynthia lent Brad money every two or three months – to help pay his child support and for investments. By January of 1974, he owed her almost fifteen thousand dollars.

There are few women facing their forties alone who would not have been dazzled by the attention Brad paid to Cynthia Marrasco. After their wedding ceremony on June 4, 1974, which was legal if not lavish, Brad moved into Cynthia's lovely home. But the idyllic melding of families that Cynthia had pictured never materialized. Almost from the beginning, her own sons were resentful of this young man in his twenties who suddenly appeared in their lives, moved into their home, and started ordering them around. Brad wasn't that much older than Cynthia's oldest son and he certainly wasn't a tactful, considerate father figure; he was impatient and mercurial.

Cynthia did her best to make the marriage work. Brad had often talked about how much he liked to camp out and about his love for the Yakima area. Cynthia bought a Volkswagen camper and all the gear needed for outdoor trips. The few good times they had together were their camping trips. Unconsciously, perhaps, Brad was emulating the family he had grown up in. Rosie and Sanford's home life was marked by argument and punishment – but their times out camping were always happy and without strife.

Now, when Brad appeared in custody hearings for Kait and Brent, he would have the advantage of being a married man living with his wife and three stepsons, while Loni Ann was a divorced woman and a student who lived in low-rent apartments, usually with another young woman so that she could make ends meet. And it *was* true that she had hitchhiked with her toddlers. Someone had poured sugar into her gas tank so she couldn't drive her car and she had no choice but to hitchhike.

Loni Ann could not afford an attorney for the custody battle, so she was represented by a lawyer from Legal Aid. Brad had his own attorney and clearly felt he would win. He had lined up his new wife, his father, and other witnesses prepared to give such cogent testimony against Loni Ann that he was sure it would convince the judge that he was the more competent parent. He was apparently doing very well in business, and he certainly dressed the part of a successful man.

Rosemary Cunningham agonized over how she was going to testify. She loved her grandchildren, and she had been witness to Brad's vicious discipline of them when he brought them to family reunions. 'When the children didn't want to eat something on their plates,' she recalled privately, if not in court, 'he would force them to eat it until they threw up on their plates.' In the end, thinking of the children and pushing down her own fear of what Brad might do to her, Rosemary testified for her former daughter-in-law, saying she thought that Kait and Brent should be with Loni Ann.

Sanford Cunningham equivocated; he said that he thought it was six of one and a half dozen of the other. He didn't think it mattered *which* parent had custody.

Brad had lost one good witness he wanted, Susan, his younger sister. 'I moved away from home when I was sixteen, and I hadn't even seen Brad for more than five years,' she said. 'I moved because we all always had to take sides against each other, and I refused to take sides.' Now her father and brother wanted twenty-year-old Susan to take sides once more. 'Brad and Dad approached me and asked me to testify against my mother in Loni Ann's custody hearing. They wanted me to say that my mother was a homosexual.'

That, Brad and Sanford figured, would undermine Rosemary's testimony. Her father and brother had spent a whole day with Susan, saying how happy they were to see her, buying her lunch. But Susan knew what they wanted; they wanted her to help them destroy Loni Ann and her own mother in one fell swoop.

Susan refused. 'I testified instead about the time that Brad beat Mom,' Susan said, 'and I was out of the family from then on.' When she chose to help Loni Ann, she ended, in essence, her own connection to the males in her family. Her father had always felt that 'money meant there was a reason' to do something, and he apparently believed that money could also entice – or punish. He used money for revenge against Susan for her betrayal. 'I was out of his will,' she said. 'So was Ethel. He left us each a hundred dollars, and everything else went to Brad.'

Loni Ann presented a very effective case. Despite Brad's continual attempts to convince her that she was 'stupid garbage' who would be insane to think about going to college, she testified that she was doing quite well in her classes where she was studying physical education. She wanted to be a teacher or a coach. She admitted on the stand that it was difficult to get by; she had very little money. Yes, she usually had to split her rent with another woman or a family.

Loni Ann had learned that Brad had tried to get to her housemates and have them testify against her. Her first roommate told her that Brad had offered to pay her to lie about Loni Ann during the custody hearing. She had refused. 'I wanted you to know what he was planning,' the woman said.

Another woman with whom Loni Ann had lived just prior to the hearing moved out abruptly one day while Loni Ann was at school in Portland. She turned up again as a surprise witness for Brad in the custody hearing and she wouldn't meet Loni Ann's eyes. But her testimony did not mesh with the written affidavit she had given earlier, and she waffled under cross-examination. During a recess, an officer of the court overheard Brad berate Loni Ann's ex-roommate, 'You didn't say what you agreed to say.' The woman later admitted on the stand that she had lied about Loni Ann's competency as a mother.

Suddenly, for the first time in a long time, the tide turned in Loni Ann's favor. And to Brad's utter amazement, she won their latest court skirmish.

When the judge awarded custody of the children to Loni Ann, she glanced fearfully at Brad, wondering what he would do. She saw his face darken, the veins stand out on his neck, and a pulse beat fiercely at his temples. He was in the blackest rage she had ever seen, and she had seen many. After the judge left the bench and disappeared into his chambers, Brad toppled to the floor like a felled tree. It seemed at first that he had had a heart attack or a stroke. But he got to his feet in a few moments, apparently fully recovered. It may have been that he was so angry he had blacked out. Brad had never lost before. Nor would he soon lose again.

After Loni Ann won custody again in court, the original reason for Brad's marriage to Cynthia dissolved. He seemed totally uninterested in her now. She had also discovered that Loni Ann was nothing like the neglectful, promiscuous woman Brad had described to her. At that point, Cynthia just wanted out of her marriage, and she had to find a way to do it with as few repercussions as possible.

Cynthia had finally come to the realization that her main attraction for Brad had been her house, her money, her stability. If she stayed with him, she might lose all three. Yet even though she could now see him in the clear light of day, she would always soft-pedal how bad things got. There were arguments – over her boys, over money, over almost everything, it seemed. Brad broke Cynthia's collarbone, although many years later, Cynthia would downplay the violence in their marriage. 'It wasn't his fault, it was mine. I pushed him and he reacted.'

They separated on September 17, 1975, and Cynthia filed for divorce on November 26. Brad moved into an apartment in Bellevue and Cynthia didn't expect to see him again. But she would learn, unhappily, that no woman simply walked away from Brad Cunningham.

In their divorce settlement, the division of property should have been simple. They had signed prenuptial agreements specifying that they would retain their individual assets as they were when they went into the marriage. Among other things Cynthia had owned a yellow 1973 Volvo, which she had financed through a credit union. Of course, she had also paid for the 1973 Volkswagen camper. According to the prenuptial contract, they reverted to her. She also wanted him to repay the money she had lent him, plus accrued interest.

By May of 1975, Brad and Cynthia were living apart, and she was again using the name Marrasco. She had gone into the marriage with few stars in her eyes, hoping that love might grow with familiarity. She knew the marriage might not last, but she had never dreamed that she would be caught in a spider's web where she would come to fear Brad, with his .38 Colt 'Detective's Special' and his awesome temper.

All Cynthia wanted was to have her serenity back and to keep what she'd had before the marriage. She and her now teenage son Nicholas were going on with their lives. The older boys were grown and out of her home. She had her master's degree and she could still teach school. But Cynthia would learn – just as Loni Ann had learned – that Brad was a man who felt betrayed if someone tried to rob him of what he considered his. Furthermore, he would prove to be a tremendously sore loser.

Some time after their separation, Cynthia and Nicholas had moved from the big house she once owned and were living in a luxurious apartment overlooking a private golf course when Brad slipped back into their lives. In an oddly childish show of power, he stole Cynthia's vehicles twice in one day.

Cynthia had an appointment with her attorney on May 22, 1975, at his Bellevue office. At 6:45 that morning, she found that her Volvo was missing. She had no choice but to drive the Volkswagen camper. But when she left her lawyer's office, she found that the camper had disappeared too. She was pretty sure that her vehicles had not been random targets and she thought she knew who had taken them.

Brad.

Cars were almost as important as children to Brad; once he had them in his possession, he didn't like to let them go. Later, when he was much richer, he would own whole stables of Mercedes cars and usually some 'macho' vehicle like a Unimag or a Humvee, plus a couple of motorcycles.

In this case Brad neither owned nor needed them, but he knew Cynthia would be terribly inconvenienced without the Volvo and the camper. In her police report, Cynthia named 'Bradly Cunningham, my estranged husband,' as a possible suspect. She warned the King County Police officers who took the report that Brad routinely carried a Colt .38.

'All I want is to have my vehicles back,' Cynthia said quietly. 'I don't want to file charges.'

The officers saw that she was obviously afraid of her ex-husband. Informed that she was setting the judicial process in motion by filing a complaint, Cynthia finally acquiesced. She had precious little choice. If she didn't file the complaint, she feared she would never see the Volvo or the Volkswagen again.

Later that May afternoon, Brad himself walked into the King County Police's south precinct to report that his .38 pistol had been stolen. He was surprised and outraged when he was arrested and booked on two charges of 'Grand Larceny – Auto.' Faced with the very real probability of spending at least one night – and maybe more – in the King County jail, Brad admitted that he had taken Cynthia's vehicles. It was a divorce thing, he explained, just the bad feelings and reprisals that happened in a lot of marriages. He was certainly no criminal, he said with a grin, and he would be glad to tell the officers where the 'stolen' car and camper were.

He said the Volvo was over in Bellevue a half block from Cynthia's attorney's office. The Volkswagen camper was on the sixth floor of the parking garage of the Pacific Building where his office was located. Detective Gary Trent of the Bellevue Police Department checked for the yellow Volvo and found it just where Brad said it would be. It was in perfect shape. Seattle Police detectives went to the Pacific Building parking garage. The Volkswagen camper was parked there. However, the steering wheel was immobilized with a chain and lock. Brad had the key to the Volvo and the key to the locked steering wheel in his possession. He surrendered them easily enough, and the two vehicles were returned to Cynthia.

The police looked upon the double 'auto theft' more as a symptom of post-marital rancor than as felonies. They were annoyed that Brad Cunningham had made thoughtless, childish abuse of their time, but since neither vehicle had been damaged and Cynthia didn't want to push prosecution, the matter was apparently settled amicably. But the day was not over. At five that evening, Nicholas looked out the window of his apartment and saw his stepfather walk up to his mother's Volvo, unlock the driver's door, jump in, and drive the car away.

Once again, Cynthia called the police. And once again, she stressed that she didn't want to irritate Brad by pressing charges. She just wanted her Volvo back. Police located it at Brad's apartment, but it wouldn't start. He had removed both the coil and distributor cap wires. The officers drove Cynthia to a garage to buy the parts she needed to get her car going. It was annoying, certainly, but police had seen divorcing couples play far worse 'tricks' on each other. One Washington State man had been so furious when his wife was awarded their home that he rented a bulldozer and systematically leveled the house and everything in it. In comparison, a day's spree of car hiding didn't seem that pathological.

Human behavior rarely reveals itself all at once. Most people grow stronger in one area, weaker in others, perhaps more compulsive in still others. An old adage says that 'what we are when we are old is only a progression of what we have always been.' If you were a mean kid, you will probably be a mean old man. Brad Cunningham had always had tremendous charm, intelligence and business acumen. But long before he was thirty, he had demonstrated decidedly negative aspects of his personality – particularly when it came to his relationships with women. Two tries at matrimony revealed that he required an inordinate amount of control in a marriage, and that he did not give up those things that he felt *belonged* to him easily.

At his center, moreover, he seemed to have a mean streak, snaking through everything he did and everything he was. He had tormented his cousins and smaller children from the time he was a boy. He had charmed, seduced, and walked away from teenage girls who idolized him. He had always appeared to consider women lesser humans, mere lowly females put on earth to help him achieve what he wanted – whether it was to climb higher in business or to become a father; whether he needed sexual satisfaction or, in the worst of circumstances, a punching bag.

He was, of course, only twenty-six, and there was the possibility that he was simply immature, given to temper tantrums and petty revenge. His mother hoped so. Despite the physical harm he had done to her, despite the way he had sided with his father and helped to betray her, Rosemary Cunningham still loved Brad.

He was her only son.

* * *

Loni Ann continued going to college and in 1978 graduated with a bachelor's degree in physical education. Brad paid child support for Kait and Brent only sporadically. By 1983 he ceased any contact at all with his children. There were no phone calls, no birthday cards, no Christmas presents. Nor were there any child support payments. Loni Ann was going on with her life, but emotionally Brad had almost destroyed her. She would gladly have traded his support money for peace of mind. She never knew when Brad might turn up again and try to take her children, or just what revenge he might have in mind.

Cynthia received her final divorce decree from Brad on February 9, 1977 and the property settlement agreement was signed on March 6. Brad offered her six thousand dollars in cash. He said he was unemployed and his yearly income was only five hundred dollars – but that his father had agreed to lend him the money to pay Cynthia. He said he planned to go to school in Colorado.

Cynthia agreed to the settlement, with the proviso that if it turned out that he had lied about his assets, she could have the agreement set aside.

Cynthia Marrasco had self-esteem going into her marriage with Brad, and she soon found it again when he was finally out of her life. She remarried, this time with great happiness.

She never saw Brad again.

Part III

Cheryl

17

Brad was a marrying man. There were to be five women who became Mrs Brad Cunningham before he reached his thirty-eighth birthday. And for each he was – in the beginning – the perfect man. Except for his second engagement, which was by its very nature expedient and hurried, his courtships were exquisitely planned. He was a prince, the kind of husband many women long for. He was handsome, charismatic, ambitious, and more and more successful each year. He still had the biceps of a college football player, but he was smoother, more urbane and cosmopolitan. He drove the best cars, he knew the best restaurants, and many women who were intimate with him remember him as a superb lover, attentive and intuitive, patient when he needed to be, wildly passionate later.

Moreover, what woman's heart wouldn't go out to a father crying for his lost children? None of Brad's new fiancées ever considered talking with his former wives to learn more about him. Why on earth would they? When Brad described the women who had come before them, he made his ex-wives sound so despicable and immoral that they all wondered how he could have been so stoic and long suffering. He had stayed in the marriages, he assured them, 'for the children.' His exwives had been 'alcoholic,' 'drug addicts,' 'bisexual,' 'tramps,' and 'lousy mothers.'

Lauren Kathleen Swanson* was a gorgeous, willowy woman, the prettiest of all Brad's women to date. Born in January 1949, she grew up in Redmond, a once rural suburb east of Seattle, and went on to enter the University of Washington in the same freshman class as Cheryl Keeton and Brad Cunningham. Along with Cheryl, Lauren pledged Gamma Phi Beta. Indeed, she and Cheryl were great friends as well as sorority sisters. Lauren majored in education, and when she graduated in 1971, she began a teaching career.

Lauren's and Cheryl's friendship grew during their four years in college together until they were very close, probably *best* friends. Lauren knew Dan Olmstead too; she had met him when he came to pick up Cheryl at the Gamma Phi house. After they all graduated, Cheryl married Dan and the Olmsteads became part of Lauren's immediate social circle. Although Lauren was still single, she often joined Cheryl and Dan and several other young couples for parties, dinners, and boating trips. Cheryl and Dan had a sailboat they dubbed the *SummerFun,* and they and their friends had many great times sailing on Puget Sound.

At first Lauren shared rent with a number of friends from her sorority in one of the big old houses that abound near the university. Later she had her own apartment on Eastlake Avenue a few miles away. She had met Brad Cunningham at the University of Washington and talked with him from time to time since his fraternity, Theta Chi, was next door to the Gamma Phi house. After his sophomore year, Brad didn't live in the fraternity house, of course. He was married to Loni Ann and a father, and working at Gals Galore. Lauren had always rather liked Brad and found him attractive. Sometimes she wondered how his life had turned out. Then in 1976, five years after she graduated, she met Brad again.

In the mid-1970s, the Madison Park area of Seattle was in transition. Located on the west shore of Lake Washington, it was crisscrossed with some of Seattle's most expensive streets, but it ran out of high-end real estate as Madison Street headed west up the long hill toward downtown Seattle. There the neighborhood decayed into time-battered wooden houses, small ethnic grocery stores, and taverns.

For decades it had been a question of which ambiance would prevail. But by the seventies, Madison Park had begun its climb to utter desirability. Singles were flocking to the funky taverns and trendy restaurants that were popping up close by the shores of Lake Washington at the east end of Madison Street.

Lauren and Brad ran into each other there one night at the Red Onion, a popular tavern. Balancing drinks, they swiveled through a laughing crowd to find a booth where they could hear each other talk. Brad told her that he was divorcing his second wife, who, he said wryly, had turned out to be a major disappointment. He didn't go into detail, but Lauren noted how sad and moody he seemed about his bad luck in love.

Like almost all women, Lauren found Brad fascinating. He was even better looking than he had been in college and he sounded as though he was doing wonderfully well in the business world. She was delighted when he asked her out. They were soon dating steadily, and in a whirlwind courtship they were engaged just a few months later. Lauren introduced Brad to her circle of friends, and so it was that he met Cheryl and Dan Olmstead for the first time. The two couples rapidly became very good friends and socialized often. Brad was fun and he was obviously a real mover and shaker in business.

After Cheryl Keeton had graduated Phil Beta Kappa from the University of Washington and married Dan Olmstead, he began law school while she took a job doing actuarial work for an insurance firm. She would follow Dan to law school as soon as they could afford it. It was what they had always planned to do; Cheryl had never foreseen anything different in her life. She and Dan would get started in their careers, and at some point they hoped to have a family.

In the meantime, Cheryl remained close to her family in Longview and continued to play second mother to her half sister, Susan McNannay. Betty and Bob McNannay had separated and were in the process of divorce. Cheryl adored Bob – she always had – and she was impatient with her mother for leaving him. Susan, who was Bob's only child, was eight or nine then, and she was the light of Bob McNannay's life. She stayed in the ranch house in Longview with her father.

Susan spent any number of weekends with Cheryl, doing 'girl things.' Bob would put her on the train that ran up from Portland, and Cheryl would pick her little sister up at the King Street station in Seattle. In the years that followed, Betty would marry two more times, but she would always remain friends with Bob McNannay. And Cheryl would look upon him as a father figure until the day she died.

Susan would remember that Cheryl's marriage was happy and comfortable. Dan adored her and she had really never known any other man. But she married so young and when she walked out of the church in September 1971, Susan recalled, her sister had 'cried and cried.'

Cheryl had a degree in economics. When she worked at Unigard Insurance as a financial analyst, she met another would-be law student who would become one of her most devoted friends – a very tall, dark-haired man named John Burke. Cheryl and John were never more than friends, but she could not have had a better friend.

'Cheryl and Dan lived in a little studio basement apartment just outside the University District at first,' Susan remembered, 'and later they bought a house on North Forty-fifth.' But with the wisdom that came when she herself was a grown woman, Susan realized in retrospect that Cheryl had worried that her marriage wasn't strong enough for her to have children. She put off thinking about it, concentrating instead on her career. She and Dan had been sweethearts all through high school and college, and she wanted their marriage to work. 'The women in our family don't have a great track record in our marital history,' Susan observed. 'But Cheryl's marriage to Dan just kind of collapsed on its own. I think Cheryl had doubts from the beginning, but they had dated for so long. . . .'

Lauren Swanson was amazed at how far Brad had come by the age of twenty-seven. He was a real estate developer and had contracts to do projects with well-known Seattle architects and contractors. Lauren loved her job teaching elementary students, but Brad suggested that she might consider becoming involved in his projects – at least part-time. That way, they could work together and she could learn some of the intricacies of his profession. Lauren was both flattered and excited. By this time, she hoped to become involved in every part of Brad's life.

She was in love.

Lauren still knew next to nothing about the details of Brad's two divorces. She had never met either Loni Ann or Cynthia; she had no reason to. But she did know that Brad was distraught about losing the custody battle for his children. He worried about them continually. 'He said that Loni Ann led a vagabond and often promiscuous lifestyle, and that it wasn't healthy for his children,' Lauren said later. 'He wanted to raise them – they were being exposed to situations that he did not approve of. . . . A lot of men visited, a lot of moving from one location to another.'

Lauren loved children so much herself and she felt sorry for Brad. She thought it must have been hell for him to have to walk away from his children, to always wonder if they were safe and cared for. It touched her heart to see how much Brad's kids meant to him. It made her love him even more.

Their wedding in March of 1977 was very simple. The wedding party included only Lauren's immediate family, Brad's father and his second wife, and Brad's children, Kait and Brent. Kait was almost seven and Brent was five. Loni Ann had won custody of her children, but she acceded to Brad's requests to have them visit him from time to time. At this point, Brad was still paying his court-ordered child support and Loni Ann wanted to keep things between them as peaceful as possible.

Although Lauren and Brad's wedding was a quiet ceremony at her parents' home, the couple threw a wonderful party to celebrate their marriage and, of course, Cheryl and Dan Olmstead were there. The two couples continued to spend many evenings and most weekends together.

Lauren was very happy in the spring of 1977. She and Brad rented a spacious condominium and she kept her job teaching a third-grade class. She also helped Brad with his construction projects. His career was in high gear and he was working hard to achieve the success he had always visualized. To their many friends, including Cheryl and Dan, they seemed perfectly matched.

Just as he had with Cynthia, Brad took Lauren to Yakima often. They headed over the Snoqualmie Pass to eastern Washington to visit Sanford and Mary. Brad's father had sold the Burien house and moved to Tampico, a tiny hamlet near Yakima. Lauren could see how close Brad and his father were. But she found it a little odd that he had nothing at all to do with his mother. When she asked him about it, he told her his mother had always blamed him for something he could not help. 'I was an unusually large baby,' he said. 'I guess that was why she had such a difficult delivery. Later, my mother got some kind of female cancer – and she always blamed me.'

'But that wasn't *your* fault!' Lauren said.

Brad shrugged. He really didn't want to talk about his mother. He said that his father had suffered through years of an unhappy marriage with her, and hadn't been able to leave until he was grown.

The woman Brad described to Lauren sounded like a cruel harridan. Rosemary had made his life miserable when he was a little boy, according to Brad, both with her sharp tongue and with physical punishment. He told Lauren about the day his mother had made him dress up like a girl and clean the house. He had been humiliated, he said, embellishing his story of child abuse. When his father came home and found his son in girls' clothes, he had been outraged. And from that moment on, his mother was virtually banished from Brad's life. His father had told him that he didn't have to pay any attention to her at all. That, Brad explained, was the end of his relationship with his mother as far as he was concerned.

Brad also said there were episodes of physical abuse until he had finally grown big enough to defend himself. 'When I was fourteen or thereabouts, she came after me one day with a vacuum hose and I took her wrist and bent it back. I told her, "Don't ever come after me again."' He didn't tell Lauren about how he and his father had tricked his mother to leave on 'a vacation.' He just said he had sided with his father when he divorced Rosemary. 'My sisters went with my mother.' His sisters, Ethel and Susan, according to Brad, were 'petty and not very bright.'

The only member of his mother's family that Brad seemed to care about was his maternal grandfather. He always spoke of Simon Edwards fondly to Lauren. He said he himself was part Colville Indian through his grandfather's lineage. Lauren knew that Brad received small checks periodically from timber sales on the Indian land.

Brad didn't tell Lauren, and she had no way of knowing, that his mother had remarried. She had gone to college and done rather well. Her name was Rosemary Kinney now, and she was also living in the Yakima area, where she was employed as a caseworker in a social service agency on the Colville Reservation.

Knowing how splintered Brad's family was, feeling sad for him that he didn't have Kait and Brent with him all the time, Lauren was thrilled when she discovered she was pregnant in the summer of 1977. Together, she and Brad would build a solid new family to make up for all that he had lost. Brad seemed as happy as she was when she told him about her pregnancy.

Brad rented office space in the building on Eastlake

Avenue in Seattle where architect Felix Campanella was headquartered. He incorporated his newest business – he would always be a firm believer in the sheltering aspects of corporations – and began to teach Lauren how to present his real estate projects at meetings he was too busy to attend. Lauren felt that she basically played only a supportive role. She represented Brad in a couple of meetings and he was pleased with her, but she was never given any decision-making tasks. That was fine with her; she was a neophyte in real estate development. She would have years to learn the more intricate details of buying land, financing, leveraging, and land use studies. Brad was a walking encyclopedia on everything and anything to do with commercial real estate.

One of the projects Lauren participated in was an apartment building surrounded by trees in Kirkland, at the far north end of Lake Washington. When it was finished, they named it Sylvan Habitat and all the apartments were rented immediately. It seemed that everything Brad touched was making money.

Lauren knew he was doing well, and she was proud of him. Still, she was almost embarrassed by the way he flaunted his wealth. He bought a more expensive car every time he moved another step up in his career. In only two years, Brad owned twelve different vehicles – both cars and trucks. They usually had three at a time. Soon the only make of car that suited Brad was a Mercedes.

He always seemed to have the money to make the payments, but sometimes Lauren wondered what her family and friends thought when she and Brad showed up in yet another, higher ticket, car. It was difficult for her to realize that she had been living on the salary of a third-grade teacher only a year earlier, and now she was riding around in plush cars whose motors were so smooth you couldn't even hear them with the windows closed.

Although Cynthia Marrasco had reported to police a few years earlier that Brad always carried a Colt .38, as far as Lauren knew, the only gun he owned was a hunting rifle. Lauren hated hunting. Much to her revulsion, Brad insisted that she come with him deer hunting that fall on the Colville Indian Reservation. Killing animals was totally against Lauren's nature, but she was in love, and whatever Brad wanted to do she would go along with.

The trip across the Cascade Mountains was glorious as the vine maples glowed coral orange against the sky and the tamaracks and quaking aspens turned bright gold. It was too bad the purpose of their trip was to look for animals to kill. But Brad told Lauren that everyone in his family hunted.

That was certainly true. However, one of the reasons his cousin Gary avoided Brad was the memory of an earlier hunting trip he had taken with him. Brad had shot a deer, but it wasn't a clean kill and the deer was thrashing around in pain. Gary asked Brad to shoot it again to put it out of its misery. Brad followed the deer into the brush but Gary didn't hear the crack of a rifle shot. Investigating, he found Brad beating the helpless animal to death with the butt of his rifle. It made Gary sick; he hunted, but he and his family followed the rules of sportsmanship and they used the game meat for food. 'Stop it, Brad!' Gary shouted. 'There's a house right there. They can see you.' Even that warning didn't work and Brad continued striking the deer long after it was dead. He was filled with an almost inexplicable rage; he literally broke a chunk out of the rifle butt.

Lauren didn't know one gun from another and they all scared her. 'Fortunately,' she recalled of their trip the autumn after their marriage, 'we didn't see any deer.'

Brad and Lauren continued to see Cheryl and Dan often. If the foursome weren't having dinner at the Olmsteads' apartment, they were probably at the Cunninghams' condo. They all got along, they had fun and laughed a lot.

Cheryl had started law school, as she and Dan always planned. Although Dan was already in practice, their budget was a little lean. Brad suggested one night that Cheryl might like to work for him. It seemed like a good solution for everyone; Cheryl and Dan could use the money and Brad's projects needed someone with Cheryl's legal knowledge and flair for detail.

'Yes!' Cheryl laughed. 'Yes, I want the job!'

It was only a part-time job. Cheryl still spent most of her time at law school. But they began working together in the fall of 1977, and Cheryl found Brad as bright and charming as a business associate as he was a friend.

One night in November of that year, Brad and Lauren gave a pre-Thanksgiving party for a number of friends. Lauren was five months pregnant and still working, but Brad had convinced her that she should give up teaching and be a full-time mother. She wouldn't be going back to school after Christmas vacation.

Lauren would remember every detail of that party. As she was refilling hors d'oeuvre trays in the kitchen, Dan walked in and shut the door behind him. Lauren turned to him with a smile, and her hands froze on the tray she held. The look on Dan's face was indescribable. It was as if he had come to tell her that someone had died. And in a sense, someone had. Dan had seen what Lauren had not even imagined. He told Lauren that his marriage – and hers – were in trouble. Although he had tried to deny his suspicions at first, he was convinced that something was going on between Cheryl and Brad, and he thought Lauren should know.

Lauren was stunned, staring at him as if he had had too much to drink. But Dan never drank too much. Still, what he was saying couldn't be possible. She was carrying Brad's baby; they were still practically newly-weds. Brad was her husband and Cheryl was her sorority sister, her friend for so many years. Yes, Cheryl worked with Brad now, but that was only business. If Brad was having an affair, Lauren was sure she would know. There would have been signs, and there had been nothing.

The rest of the evening was a blur. Lauren got through the party with a smile frozen on her face, her stomach churning, until the last guests left. As soon as they were alone, she came right out and asked Brad if there was anything between him and Cheryl beyond friendship. Was he having an affair with Cheryl?

Brad denied it, half laughing. She was being ridiculous. She was overemotional because she was pregnant. She was seeing shadows where there were none. Dan was a troublemaker. Brad hugged Lauren and she tried to feel comfort in his arms, but something had changed. Her world had shifted off its axis and was no longer spinning smoothly.

Nothing more was said about Dan's suspicions. But seeds of doubt took root in Lauren's mind. Even as her child kicked beneath her heart, she couldn't forget what Dan had said. She tried to recall if she had seen some intimate look pass between her friend and her husband and couldn't think of a single instance. It wasn't that Brad didn't have ample freedom to have an affair. Lauren never really knew where he was – his business demanded that he be here, there, and everywhere. That had never bothered her, but now she wondered.

Whenever Lauren got the panicky feeling that Dan might be right, she reminded herself that she and Brad were going ahead with their plans to buy their own condominium. Brad wouldn't do that if he were going to leave her, would he? The new condo was much smaller than the one they were living in, but it would be theirs. The mortgage payments would be four hundred dollars a month.

With Brad's urging, Lauren resigned from her teaching position. She said goodbye to her third graders as Christmas approached. She thanked them for all the presents they brought for her new baby and hugged them. She would miss them, but in three months she would have her own baby.

It should have been such a happy time for her. But it wasn't. Cheryl and Dan had separated. Dan had been right about that part of his disclosure at the party. He and Cheryl *had* been having trouble. And it had all come to a head when they went to Longview for Thanksgiving 1977. There Cheryl told Susan that she and Dan were splitting up. 'She took me out for a drive,' Susan said. 'She told me that she was young – that she'd made a mistake. She even tried to smoke a cigarette – she was so nervous – but she didn't know how to smoke. Cheryl took the train home from Longview that Thanksgiving, and Dan stayed, and he talked with me too. It was very sad.'

Cheryl and Dan were both well under thirty when their marriage ended. Cheryl was still on the path to her dream of becoming an attorney, but she had met someone else, someone who absolutely dazzled her, a man so charismatic and seemingly perfect for her that there was no question but that she would go to him. She was completely spellbound, surprised at the depth of her own emotion. She had always been the one who kept her head. She had never felt passion that made her teeth chatter and her skin burn.

Now she did.

In December, Brad and Lauren were packing boxes in the process of moving out of their rented condominium. Without warning, he turned to her and hit her with paralyzing – stupefying – news. He said that everything Dan had told her was true. He *was* having an affair with Cheryl. 'I don't love you anymore,' he said. When Lauren didn't say anything, he repeated his words. 'Did you hear me? I said I don't love you anymore.'

As Lauren stood with her arms crossed over her belly, unconsciously protecting her unborn child, Brad told her quite calmly that his relationship with Cheryl was deeply satisfying, and that Dan's suspicions had been well founded. He wanted to be free; he loved Cheryl now. 'I'm not moving with you,' he said. 'You're moving into your new condo alone.'

Lauren knew that Cheryl had left Dan and was living in an apartment in Madison Park. Her mind raced as she realized that all her fears had come true. Brad was still talking. He told her that he would be moving in with

Cheryl. And Lauren, now six months pregnant, would be living by herself in the condo that she and Brad had agreed to buy. Brad's instructions were as crisp and deliberate as if he were pointing out the floor-plan for an apartment house. It wasn't just hard for Lauren to believe, it was impossible. Couples didn't get married, plan for a new baby and their first home, and get divorced – all in less than a year. Men didn't walk away and leave their wives pregnant and alone. But Brad was going to do just that. He was resolute. This was the way it was going to be.

'It was an immediate separation,' Lauren recalled, her pain blunted by the passing of years, 'in that he basically never moved his belongings from the [old] condominium to the new condominium in the University District.' It was a nightmare for her. It was incomprehensible. 'I had given up my teaching contract and was saying goodbye to my third-grade class, so that when Brad finally notified me that he was going to be moving in with Cheryl, I was basically unemployed, six months pregnant, and living in a condominium that cost four hundred dollars a month with no way to pay.'

Had Lauren had any early warning from Brad that their marriage was over, she would never have resigned from her job. Under the Teachers' Credit Union benefits, she would have been eligible for maternity leave with full pay and medical benefits. She would have had a secure job waiting for her return, a career that would help her support her child. Brad knew all that and yet he had sat back and watched her cut herself off without so much as a word. Worse, he had *urged* her to resign.

'He left me financially stranded,' Lauren remembered. 'I ended up going to the bank that held the mortgage on the condominium where I was living. Actually I went in when I was eight months pregnant and sat down with the vice president and described the situation. I said that I was confident that I would get some sort of settlement from the divorce. Unbelievably, the bank carried me through the divorce and let me stay in the condominium.'

Over that lonely Christmas of 1977 and into the first months of 1978, Lauren was furious with Cheryl. She was probably angrier at her old friend than she was at the husband who had walked out on her. There was another cruelty that had been inflicted on her. 'When Cheryl separated from Dan – and I am confident that she and Brad were then involved in an intimate relationship,' Lauren said, 'Brad and I were the ones that helped her move into her new apartment and carried her furniture in . . . just some memories that are sort of hard to stomach.'

Lauren hoped never to see or talk to Cheryl again. What good would words or explanations do? What had happened had happened. But a few weeks after Lauren found herself alone, she did see Cheryl again. Even as she still carried his unborn child, Brad had begun divorce proceedings against her, and Cheryl came with Brad to the tiny condo where Lauren now lived. 'She was the person to hand me the divorce documents,' Lauren said. 'That was salt in the wound.'

After seeing Brad's smug face as he watched Cheryl present her with divorce papers, Lauren realized that Brad had really left her, that he wasn't just going through a temporary lapse. He loved Cheryl and not her. That loss was bad enough. The loss of Cheryl's friendship was difficult too. Her behavior was totally alien to the person Lauren had known for almost a decade. It was as if she were hypnotized. She had never known Cheryl to do – or even *say* – an unkind thing before.

Lauren could not have imagined that the day would come when she would forgive Cheryl, when she would begin to understand why Cheryl had changed so completely from her sorority sister and confidante and dear friend into the woman who had stolen her husband and wrecked her life. There would even come a day when Lauren would feel sorry for Cheryl.

18

If Lauren assumed that Brad was completely out of her life – that he had abandoned all interest in her – she was woefully mistaken. Brad was not finished with her. She still had things he wanted. Lauren had legal claim to some of his real estate holdings. But more than that, more than anything, she was carrying his child. Brad was still fighting Loni Ann to win back Kait and Brent, and he wanted this child too. He was a 'child keeper,' a man obsessed with *owning* all the children he had sired.

Even before Lauren gave birth, Brad filed for custody of the baby. And although she was hugely pregnant and struggling to survive financially, he began to fight her in one court hearing after another for property he considered rightly his. She met him in court or in their attorneys' offices for almost a dozen hearings and depositions.

Lauren had naively hired an attorney who would have been perfectly adequate for a simple divorce, but Brad had never had a simple divorce. Lauren's attorney asked her if there were any marital assets that she might still be able to claim, and she remembered that she and Brad had a joint bank account that had twelve thousand dollars in it. The attorney took Lauren at once to the bank so she could withdraw the money; with that done, he was confident that she would now have something to live on. Brad was livid when he found the twelve thousand dollars missing. He filed to freeze money in Lauren's account – successfully – and she could use none of the twelve thousand dollars to take care of herself as she drew closer and closer to giving birth.

Brad battled with Lauren over everything. She had an oriental rug – a rug that had been in her family for years before they passed it on to her at her wedding. Now Brad claimed that it belonged to him. He even deposed Lauren's mother in his efforts to get it away from Lauren.

Lauren's original attorney saw that she was in for a terrible courtroom struggle. 'Within a couple of weeks,' she recalled, 'he told me that I needed a "big gun."' She hired another attorney, one known for digging in and fighting. But by the time she was nine months pregnant, the war had just begun and she was learning that the charming, wonderfully sensitive man she had married had an entirely different side. She would remember that he 'was extremely litigious and seemed anxious to do whatever he could do to make things uncomfortable and difficult in the course of our divorce proceedings.'

Lauren's due date was during the week of March 26, which included the Easter weekend, a three-day holiday. Since she now lived alone, she would have to depend on her telephone to call for help when she went into labor. She was appalled one night during that long weekend when she picked up her phone to make a call and heard only dead air. She discovered that Brad had had her phone disconnected. 'I went through some frantic time,' Lauren said, 'to get the phone hooked up because I was alone.'

When she *did* go into labor, Lauren had to count on her family and friends to get her to the hospital. She went through her labor alone, delivering her baby on a soft spring night. She might as well have been an unwed mother. In truth, she would have been better off.

Amy Cunningham, a beautiful little girl, made up for a lot of the pain her mother had gone through in the months before her birth. But the pain was not yet over. The phone in Lauren's hospital room rang the day after Amy was born. It was Brad.

'I understand that we have a daughter,' he said flatly, and

before Lauren could reply, he went on, 'I wanted to let you know that I have had your car repossessed.'

Lauren wasn't even very surprised. This was the Brad she had come, bitterly, to know all too well. He didn't seem thrilled or even moderately happy about the baby. Even so, Lauren knew that Amy would be used as a pawn in Brad's war against her, and she felt a chill.

When she had left for the hospital, Lauren's car was parked, she thought safely, in an underground garage at the University Towers where she lived. She learned later that Brad had talked the property manager into letting him into the parking area. The car was gone when she returned from the hospital. 'I don't know how he did it,' Lauren said. 'He probably had keys.' She never got her car back.

Even before Lauren regained her strength after childbirth, the legal fight with Brad accelerated. She was asking for full custody of Amy, while Brad requested joint custody. Their divorce trial was held before Superior Court Judge Stanley Soderland, who had just been voted the most respected judge in King County, Washington. 'My attorney was not hopeful about my efforts to basically erase Brad from my life,' Lauren recalled, 'but he said, "You are hiring me, and if this is what you want to go for, this is what I will ask for."'

Lauren had requested that Brad undergo psychiatric testing – and he, of course, countered with a request that she be tested too. In the end, the results were a wash. According to the doctors who evaluated the test results, neither Lauren nor Brad showed any emotional pathology.

Ultimately, Lauren put her faith in pure common sense. She was the abandoned spouse, and she figured that when Brad deserted her, he had walked away from Amy too. 'My point was that Brad had relinquished his paternal rights when he walked out before she was born. And the judge said, "You are wrong." He said, "He is the biological father."' Judge Soderland awarded Lauren sole custody of Amy but he said he could not prevent her father from seeing her. Soderland set up very rigid visitation schedules for the first four years of Amy's life, commenting that he hoped that Lauren and Brad could work out their own custody arrangements after Amy was four.

Amy's visits with her father began when she was a month old. Lauren was ordered by the court to take her to the King County Courthouse and give her new baby to Brad for hour-long visits. 'I had to turn her over to him, and he took her into another room for an hour,' Lauren remembered. 'It was torture for me. . . . I was scared to death that he was going to leave with her. . . . I was awarded sole custody, which is not what he wanted. It just made me very, very nervous.'

Possibly only a new mother can empathize with the terror in Lauren's heart as she carried her month-old daughter onto the creaky elevators of the King County Courthouse and then walked through the marble-lined halls to meet Brad. Every courtroom and chamber in the venerable building has at least two exits; every floor can be reached by stairways as well as elevators. One courthouse door exits onto Third Avenue and another onto Fourth Avenue, while tunnels run from the courthouse's first floor and basement to two entirely separate buildings. Had Brad wanted to take Amy away, it would have been so easy. But at the end of each hour's visit, he returned the tiny baby girl to her mother.

Lauren had no idea what he did while he had the baby. Did he talk to Amy, rock her, walk around with her? Or did he simply put her on a chair and look at his watch until his time was up, relishing Lauren's anguish as she waited beyond the thick oak door? Once Lauren had believed she knew everything there was to know about Brad; now she realized that he had revealed only an infinitesimal portion of his personality to her.

If Lauren had hoped to 'erase' Brad from her life, she had failed miserably. The next step of the visitation schedule with Amy as outlined by Judge Soderland was that Brad would come to Lauren's home. He could stay with Amy for up to two hours, but he was not allowed to take her off the premises. 'By the time she was two,' Lauren remembered, 'he could take her for a couple of hours in his car somewhere, and that would gradually increase – when she was three, he could take her for a day and a half, and so forth.'

For those first two years, Brad visited regularly. The divorce proceedings and property settlement were finally resolved and Lauren was given some interest in Sylvan Habitat, although she never did find out what had become of her missing car. Brad paid her $250 a month in child support. After a while, Lauren no longer felt the absolute terror she had gone through when her little girl was a baby, but she was still uneasy whenever Brad visited Amy. She always had a lingering concern that he might take her away.

Lauren knew that Brad had married Cheryl, and that she was pregnant. She herself had begun to date the man she would eventually marry, Dr Ian Stoneham,* a psychiatrist. Soon after their wedding when Amy was two, she and her new husband planned to take a sabbatical to New Zealand. As they prepared to leave for the other side of the world, they discussed how – or *whether* – they would inform Brad of their departure. Lauren talked with her attorney, who pointed out that there was nothing in her divorce decree that specifically prevented her from taking a sabbatical. 'We both know how litigious Brad is,' he said. 'My advice to you is to put a letter in the mailbox at the airport saying he can exercise his visitation in New Zealand, and tell him your address there.'

That was exactly what Lauren did. And Brad was, predictably, very angry. He went before a judge and obtained a court order that stipulated he had the legal right to go to New Zealand and take Amy away from Lauren. He arranged with his father to accompany him.

Sanford bragged to everyone that his son was treating him to a wonderful trip to New Zealand. He didn't mention the purpose of the trip.

The nightmare was beginning again for Lauren. On Mother's Day 1980, Brad arrived in New Zealand and phoned her. She was taken completely by surprise. 'I am on my way down,' Brad said. 'Tell me where to meet you. I have a court order in my hand that says I can take Amy.'

'Take her *where*?' Lauren asked, horrified.

'Back to the United States.'

Lauren suspected that Brad had deliberately timed his trip so that he would arrive on Mother's Day, giving his demands an extra sadistic twist. Because Amy had always visited with her father for just an hour or two at a time, she really didn't know him. And once again Lauren lived in fear of having her child spirited away. She didn't think that Brad truly cared about Amy, but Amy *belonged* to him, and Brad didn't let his possessions go easily whether he really wanted them or not. He was the most aggressive man Lauren had ever encountered. Years later she would describe his dominant characteristics. 'He is very used to getting what he wants and having things the way he wants them. And he gets very frustrated when somebody tries to get in his way.'

There are few forces stronger than maternal love, that visceral protective stance that grips mothers within minutes of their giving birth. There was no way Lauren could let Brad take Amy. 'I called my attorney and he appealed the court order and managed to have it overturned, but there was a period of time in New Zealand when I was once again extremely anxious about leaving Amy in the room alone at night, for fear Brad would come and try to take her . . . I think it was an intuitive sense.'

Lauren and her husband soon returned to the United States, and as the years passed Brad continued his child support, but his payments became erratic and Lauren and Amy saw less and less of him. He had other interests, and he had begun a third family. By the time Amy was five or six, Brad gave Lauren one large check a year, and after a while he sent no money at all.

Rather pathetically, although Lauren had never actually met Rosemary, Brad's mother stayed in contact with Amy by mail and always remembered her granddaughter at Christmas and on her birthday. She and Lauren corresponded, and Rosemary had Amy's name added to the roster of the Colville Indians. That way, she too would be eligible for tribal benefits. It was through Rosemary that Lauren learned that Brad was not a quarter Colville Indian, as he had told her; he was actually half Indian. His Indian heritage was something he apparently had tried to minimize.

As was the existence of his mother.

19

Cheryl never really got over her guilt about what she and Brad had done to Lauren. Betraying a friend was completely atypical of her. Her natural inclination had always been to be there for her friends, to help them, and certainly never to destroy them. That she could have been a party to Brad's desertion of Lauren when she was pregnant was almost unbelievable. But Cheryl had never felt as powerful an emotion as the love and commitment she felt for Brad.

Her half sister Susan was only eleven or twelve when Cheryl met Brad, but even she had sensed that Cheryl's marriage to Dan Olmstead was in trouble. 'I remember I was in Seattle in October 1977, because my uncle had brain surgery,' Susan said. 'Cheryl was working for Brad at the Austen Company, and he took us out to lunch in his Mercedes. Brad's jaws were wired because he'd had plastic surgery on them. I remember that, and I remember that I knew somehow that Cheryl and Brad were having an affair.'

It seemed impossible, because Cheryl and Dan had been together so long that their names were practically hyphenated when the family referred to them. Susan couldn't remember a Christmas when Dan hadn't been there. He was part of their family. And he remained part of the family, but now he came to visit alone. When Cheryl took Susan for a drive that Thanksgiving and told her she was getting a divorce, Susan knew who had caused that divorce. It was the man with the Mercedes who had taken them out to lunch a month before – the man with the wires in his jaws. Brad Cunningham. Susan was not surprised, and yet she was surprised. 'Cheryl was so *dignified*. Things had to have a certain order. She had been so disgusted when Mom left Dad, but . . .'

There were other changes that Susan noticed. Cheryl had always been so confident, so in charge, so confrontive. But now, when she was with Brad, Susan saw that she was different than she had ever been. She had become passive; she deferred to Brad on any and every subject. She adored him, she respected him, she loved him passionately, but Susan wondered sometimes if Cheryl might not also be a little afraid of Brad.

After living together for a little over a year, Cheryl and Brad were married in March of 1979, a year after Lauren had given birth to Amy. Cheryl was two months pregnant at the time of her marriage, and she was eagerly looking forward to becoming a mother. Cheryl and Brad said their vows in a simple service at the home of friends, and Cheryl's family was not invited. Like all of Brad's weddings, save his first formal ceremony with Loni Ann, it was a legal ceremony but it certainly wasn't romantic or sentimental.

In retrospect, Susan could recall no 'honeymoon period' at all in her sister's second marriage. Cheryl seemed happy, yes, but Brad was not the lovey-dovey groom, not even for the first month or so. It seemed almost that Cheryl was part of some plan Brad had, and now that he had accomplished the business of marrying her, there was no point in wasting time on romance. Of course, it was Brad's fourth marriage in ten years; perhaps he had no energy for all the typical stages of married life. He had a tiger by the tail in his real estate endeavors. He hinted that he was on the verge of making millions of dollars in a new project in Houston, Texas. And Cheryl had her law degree. She graduated from law school with a shopping list of honors; she was in the top ten percent of her class and received the 'Order of the Coif.' She was a beautiful young woman and he was a handsome man. If ever there was a couple slated for success, it was Brad Cunningham and Cheryl Keeton.

And it *was* Cheryl Keeton: she may have been subservient around Brad, but she insisted on keeping her own name. She had fought hard for her law degree and it mattered to her that she be a lawyer under her own name. That was the one stand she took with Brad. Otherwise – even in areas where Cheryl had a great deal of expertise – she invariably deferred to Brad's decisions, from large issues to relatively small things.

Cheryl and Dan had owned the *SummerFun*, and Cheryl was an excellent sailor. She had taken classes and she knew the Coast Guard rules. Brad had owned sailboats too, but she was the more competent sailor. Still, it was Brad who captained the thirty-six-foot sailboats he often rented.

Susan remembered accompanying Brad and Cheryl on one sailing trip to the San Juan Islands in the late 1970s, before they were married. They intended to moor at Friday Harbor on San Juan for the night, but they arrived late and found the harbor already jam-packed with boats. While Cheryl and Susan were craning their necks, looking for an empty slip where they might tie up, Brad suddenly dropped anchor right in the middle of the shipping lanes.

At first Cheryl was bewildered. It was such a dumb and

dangerous thing to do. Then she showed a flash of her old spirit and demanded that Brad pull up the anchor and get them out of there. But Brad only turned on her and said, 'Shut up! This is where we're going to stay.'

Susan expected to see the Cheryl she had always known, the one who would fight for what she knew was the right thing to do. Instead, she was shocked to see her sister break into tears. 'I was scared myself,' she remembered. 'You couldn't drop anchor in the shipping lanes. We could have gotten killed.'

Implacably, Brad went about dropping the sails and acted as though he was going to stay right there all night. Susan was as frightened by her sister's helpless sobs as she was by the thought that their sailboat was probably going to be sliced in two when darkness settled over the harbor. At length, when he was sure that he had made his point, Brad grudgingly raised the sails, hauled up the anchor, and moved on to safer moorage.

This nightmare sailing trip was only the first of scores of frightening incidents that Susan witnessed with the man who had taken over Cheryl's life. She wondered why her sister stayed with Brad, why she married him. Yes, she was pregnant with his child, but that wasn't really forbidden in 1979. Yes, he was handsome, and it seemed as though he was going to be very rich – Cheryl had never lived in homes as nice as those she shared with Brad – but he was so mean sometimes. Susan was, of course, only thirteen and couldn't really understand the relationship between her sister and Brad.

Cheryl had always loved Seattle, from the very moment she arrived at the University of Washington. If it had been up to her, she would have lived in Seattle forever. In 1979 her law practice was embryonic, but she had great confidence that it would grow. She was happy about the baby she carried, too, and was sure she could manage both motherhood and a career if she planned her time well. And she had always been remarkably good about planning her time. She was due to deliver in the fall of 1979.

Brad was nothing if not fertile. All of his wives – except Cynthia, who was in her forties when they married – had conceived almost at the beginning of their sexual intimacy, and he was always proud. Brad seemed pleased that Cheryl was pregnant.

Cheryl may have worried a little that summer and fall. Only two years before, she had watched Brad become disenchanted with Lauren and desert her when *she* was pregnant. Cheryl had given up everything to be with Brad then, and had gone against even her own moral code. She had let herself be swept away from her first marriage; she had been a willing partner in deceiving her husband and her friend. If Brad could betray Lauren, could he not betray her?

It was a fleeting fear, washing over her from time to time and then departing. Brad had a terrible temper and insisted on having his own way, but he was under a lot of pressure getting his growing real estate empire together. Cheryl continually made excuses for his behavior. And from the very beginning of their marriage, she always believed that things would get better. She deferred to Brad in all things and had faith in their future together. She had given up so much to be with him that it was crucial for her serenity to believe that theirs was a true love match that would last forever.

Brad took Cheryl to a Cunningham family reunion on Whidbey Island that summer. His relatives found her pleasant and pretty, but quite shy. It was a description that would have baffled her own family who knew Cheryl as strong and assertive, even take-charge. But with Brad, it was almost as if Cheryl 'knew her place.' 'One time Brad brought Cheryl to the reunion,' a Cunningham cousin recalled, 'and she kind of stood on the sidelines. When I found out later that she was a lawyer, I was amazed. She didn't say one word about what she did for a living. She was just a quiet, pleasant woman.'

Cheryl had gloried in her pregnancy. She didn't mind at all that her usually slim, perfect figure was temporarily swollen. She proudly wore a tight one-piece bathing suit and posed for pictures when she was over seven months pregnant. She smiled for another camera as she balanced a wineglass full of milk on the top of her gravid belly.

Jess Cunningham was born in October of 1979. A handsome dark-haired baby boy, he was the image of his father from the start. Cheryl was thrilled to be a mother. It was difficult for her to think about leaving Jess during the day while she went to work. But after ten weeks of maternity leave, Cheryl had to go back to her law practice on January 2, 1980. They needed her salary.

Jess went to stay with Sharon McCulloch, a day-care provider who had once been a first-grade teacher. Her husband was a teacher too. Cheryl and Sharon had already become good friends when Sharon had occasionally taken care of Jess in the first months after his birth. Cheryl felt secure that Jess was in good hands. But she missed him during the hours she was at work.

'Jess was always happy,' Sharon remembered. 'So was Cheryl. Cheryl laughed a lot when I first knew her. I've raised forty children, but Jess was always special to me. I first started taking care of him when he was two weeks old, and I had him with me more than a year.'

At this time, Brad and Cheryl were living in Laurelhurst, a long-established upper-middle-class neighborhood near the University of Washington. They had bought the house before they were married, with Cheryl owning 29 percent and Brad 71 percent. Set above a terrace of shrubs, the house was white with a big bay window and a wide porch under a sloping roof. Cheryl loved that house, but Brad wanted to live on Bainbridge Island, a half-hour ferry ride across Elliott Bay from Seattle. Cheryl argued that the commute from Bainbridge to her office would add at least two hours to her day and would mean that much more time away from Jess. Still, Brad loved the automatic cachet of living on Bainbridge Island. And if that was where he wanted to live, that was where they would live.

Occasionally Brad picked Jess up from Sharon McCulloch's. Somehow Sharon could not bring herself to like him, although he was quite handsome and exuded sexual energy and charm when he wanted to. 'He had compelling eyes. He had this whole *stud* image,' Sharon remembered. But she found him remote and imperious, and he treated Jess like his property. She noticed that he never called the baby by name. 'It was always, "Is *my son* ready to go?" He struck me as extremely possessive, and I was always under scrutiny.' Cheryl explained to Sharon that Brad was very particular about Jess, and that he insisted on being informed about any changes in Jess's schedule and in his diet. 'If I even fed him cereal without Brad's permission, Cheryl had to justify it to Brad,' Sharon said.

Susan McNannay continued to visit her sister after Cheryl married Brad and although she was only in junior high school, she was a very intelligent and observant girl. She wondered a little bit about her new brother-in-law when she found a stash of magazines under Brad and Cheryl's bed. 'They were porno magazines with pictures of young girls in them,' she recalled. 'That Christmas, Brad wrapped up a *Playboy* and put his name on the card and put it under the tree. It embarrassed Cheryl when he opened it. I don't know why he did that, but holidays never meant anything to Brad.'

Brad ignored Cheryl's family when they visited. 'He sometimes didn't even speak to us when we were in his home,' Susan said. 'He respected my father, though.' And Brad put up with Susan, possibly because Cheryl insisted, possibly because Susan became a handy baby-sitter. She went along on trips to Palm Springs and she often went with Cheryl when she visited her natural father in Vacaville, California. Susan had been a big part of Cheryl's life from the moment she was born, and she would continue to be.

Brad seemed so confident and strong, but Susan noticed

that he was absolutely terrified of natural disasters – earthquakes, floods, hurricanes. 'When Mount St Helens erupted in May of 1980, Brad freaked out,' she remembered. 'He made Cheryl take Jess and go to Canada until he thought it would be safe to come home.' Brad was a man who needed to control everything and everyone in his life. Natural disasters were among the few forces over which he had no control at all.

Sharon McCulloch had seen Brad's need to control both his son and his wife all too often. In March 1981, a few days before Cheryl and Brad moved from the Laurelhurst house to Bainbridge Island, Cheryl asked Sharon if she could keep Jess a few hours later that evening. They wouldn't be moved out of the house until at least 9 P.M. and then Cheryl had to clean it for the new owners. Sharon said she would be glad to keep him all night – Jess was sleeping peacefully and wouldn't know the difference. Cheryl was grateful. That way she would be free to clean and they wouldn't have to wake the baby up and haul him out into the chill night air.

At midnight, however, Sharon woke to a knock on the door. It was Cheryl and she was crying. 'Brad's in the car,' Cheryl said. 'He says I have to take Jess home right now.'

'But he's been asleep for four hours,' Sharon said.

'I'm so sorry,' Cheryl said. 'But I have no choice.'

The Cunninghams didn't live on Bainbridge Island long – only a matter of months. Brad had been negotiating with executives at the Seattle Trust and Savings Bank for a substantial loan that would allow him to work with them as a partner in commercial construction in another state. By the second year of his marriage to Cheryl, he had begun a pattern of traveling most of the time. He had done market studies in Colorado, Alaska, and Texas to determine where there was the most need for apartment and office complexes.

'I went to Denver, to Alaska, and to Houston. I did a complete market study in Houston,' he said years later.

'This is what I *do*. . . . Actually the bank approached us. Seattle real estate wasn't viable. Cheryl and I had a million dollars in the bank already – in cash and CDs [Certificates of Deposit]. The bank offered us a full construction loan – and then they would take fifty percent of the profits.'

During the first half of 1981, Brad drove rental cars slowly through cities that looked ripe for building projects. 'I had a little tie device that was always activated for me to dictate into. I took pictures. I estimated rental density.' He returned again and again to Houston, exploring the empty lots and acreage of that green and humid Texas city. The demand for office space in the Houston area was voracious. Tall buildings with mirrored glass windows were springing up like mushrooms, shining obelisks and domes and towers against the Texas horizon, more every month, and still there weren't enough. Brad could almost see his own reflection in those mirrored windows. Houston it would be.

Armed with his market study, Brad conferred with Seattle Trust officers and went away with a million-dollar start-up loan. Brad and Cheryl both signed the loan, but it didn't matter. Washington is a community property state and his debts were her debts. Brad hired the firm of Baker and Boggs to help him get a license to do business in the State of Texas. He was exhilarated. 'I like the State of Texas!'

Eventually, Brad would engage a huge construction firm in Houston. His company was about to build massive office buildings in Houston, and Brad bragged that he would control six hundred million dollars.

Cheryl was pregnant with her second child, due to deliver in late September. She wanted very much to stay in Washington for the birth, to have her own obstetrician, but Brad insisted that the time was ripe for them to move to Houston. They had the loan, he was negotiating on property, and he had bought a house for them, a very expensive house that was already under construction. It all seemed too fast for Cheryl but, as always, she went along with Brad's plans. Everything they owned was packed into a moving van.

Cheryl went into labor less than a week after they arrived in Houston. Brad was with her for part of her labor and he insisted on taking pictures of her while she was in the transition state. She asked him not to; she didn't look her best, and she was in pain. Cheryl later told her friend Sharon McCulloch that she thought Brad was 'a ghoul' and that she was embarrassed by the camera's intrusion. Michael Keeton Cunningham was born on September 26, 1981, and after his birth Brad activated the time-release shutter on his camera and posed happily with Cheryl, Jess, and their new baby. Brad didn't visit the hospital again until she was ready to come home.

Cheryl later confided to Sharon that that period in September in Houston was 'the worst in my life.' Her mother, now Betty Troseth, flew down to help out, and Cheryl was glad to have her there, but Brad didn't care for Betty and he treated her rudely.

With two babies now, Cheryl agreed that she would stay home and care for Jess and Michael. At some point she would certainly resume practicing law but, for the time being, it was Brad's career that was the more important. It had been hard on Cheryl to move to Houston. But there was no question that she would follow Brad wherever he wanted to go. 'I've got to go,' she had said to Susan. 'My child is going and that's my family.'

Houston was nothing at all like the Northwest, and Cheryl longed for Seattle with its clear, clean air. Houston was hot and humid, day and night. In Seattle there was always a coolness at night, even if it had been ninety degrees during the day. In Houston the air was like a soaking hot blanket. There were bugs and critters that Cheryl had never seen. The music on the radio was different – mostly country. Restaurants featured chicken-fried steak and hot Mexican food instead of salmon, clams, and crab legs. Houston was a different world.

However, they weren't there for more than a few weeks before everything started to slide. The move to Houston had cost ten thousand dollars, they had put thirty-four thousand dollars down on their new home, and Cheryl had quit her law practice. They hadn't even unpacked when Seattle Trust and Savings bank executives called Brad with stupefying news. They had changed their mind about the million-dollar loan. 'It was only a few days after Michael was born,' Brad would recall. 'They said they had new management and didn't want a project that far away.'

Brad had assured Cheryl that the Texas move was a good thing, a vital step on their way to financial independence. Now the balloon had burst and they were still committed to buying a billion-dollar property. Moreover, Brad's boast of a million dollars in the bank was undoubtedly inflated. In reality he had credit lines of ten or fifteen thousand dollars. He vowed to sue Seattle Trust and Savings, and Cheryl drew up a letter of 'Detrimental Reliance,' formally charging the bank with leaving them in such a tenuous position.

'We had to get a new loan,' Brad recalled. And he did. Few entrepreneurs could be as convincing as he was. Even with his back to the wall, he was able to persuade a Texas bank to grant him an open-ended $4.4 million loan. He was back in business and, in Brad's mind, the huge commercial complex he visualized – Parkwood Plaza – was as good as finished.

While Brad busied himself putting the project together, Cheryl was delighted to be raising Jess and Michael, and she was proud of Brad. Their two little boys were as different from each other as they could be. Jess was very bright and active. He looked just like Brad. Michael was just as intelligent, but he was a calmer, sweeter baby. Or maybe it was because second babies just *seem* easier. 'Mikey' looked like his mother.

Brad Cunningham would have a dozen excuses for the financial disaster that Parkwood Plaza became. His huge loan had built-in dangers; it had to be repaid whether his project was finished or not. And many years later, Brad would blame the construction companies he hired, the bonding company, and the grim outlook for the Texas economy. He took no personal responsibility for failure whatsoever; if it had been up to him, Parkwood Plaza would be, today, a booming concern.

'The Parkwood Plaza project started out fine in February 1982,' he would later testify. 'It was under construction and bonded by March. The architect started recommending "withholds" from construction draws; the construction company hadn't done the work. We had problems by May or June.' He said that he himself discovered flagrant violations – such as high-voltage power lines buried much too shallowly under the concrete floors. 'The contractor put 440-volt lines eight inches underground when they should be *two feet* under. . . . I'm going to go ahead and tell you the truth. I was leaving one day for the airport and I saw workers unloading pipe on concrete, *breaking* the pipe. I told the contractor not to install the pipe. When I came back, I crawled under and saw broken pipes installed. I took a camera. I didn't trust the contractor. . . .

'When the buildings didn't meet plans or specs, it gave the permanent lender a way to back out. Around June fifteenth or twentieth, the construction company fired all the architects. *I* hired 3-D International myself, one of the largest construction companies in the United States. The contractor kept working and I withheld a million dollars because it was defective. He had ten days to fix it. . . . The contractor didn't. I had a bond. By October 1982 I fired the contractor and tried to complete it myself. I had to correct the code violations.'

To listen to Brad explain his maneuvers to build Parkwood Plaza was to move into a world where disbelief had to be suspended. He was a superman – financing, bulldozing, building, laying electrical conduit, lifting whole walls. Seemingly all by himself. 'I was working equipment, hiring crews, on site, paving – it's called "mitigating your damages." I finished Building D, and I opened a secretarial service. I hired out nine offices. I worked on A and tried to sell the other buildings. . . . The bonding company basically said, "Sue me."'

In reality, Brad had coaxed Cheryl away from Seattle and her thriving law practice into a monetary sinkhole. Despite Brad's confident promises, it was apparent that they had just missed the boat. Houston was rapidly becoming – not just for Brad but for all but the most solidly grounded builders – a wasteland. Suddenly, in early 1982, the bottom of the Texas economy had sprung a leak, a leak through which first oil, and then all good things, would eventually escape. The oil boom that had promised to be endless had begun to lose momentum and a world oil glut caused gasoline prices to plummet.

Houston's real estate dreams of glory began to evaporate. Jobs were drying up and nobody needed, or could afford, expensive office space. Newly finished buildings stood empty and construction stopped on halfbuilt units. Mirrored windows soon reflected only the end of an era and Brad was left with mostly never-started or half-finished buildings, and a mountain of debt.

He had gambled, made promises with money that depended on filling Parkwood Plaza. He was in trouble. Brad blamed construction delays. He insisted that if the buildings had gone up according to his scheduling, they would have been finished and all the offices rented. What had happened, he argued, was not his fault. There had been enough money there but the construction company had let it trickle away. Now it was drying up fast, and Brad was a man who had always liked to live high. He was not about to go backward when he had long since become accustomed to fine cars, gourmet restaurants, and the best of everything. The Cunninghams could no longer afford such a life. Things looked bad for Brad and, of course, for Cheryl, too.

They discussed their predicament. He didn't want to leave

Houston if there was a chance he could salvage what he had there, but they needed an income to keep him going. Cheryl was an attorney, and she was good. Brad suggested that they separate for a while, but only so they could rebuild their financial base. Regretfully, Cheryl agreed to his plan for her to move back to Seattle and practice law. She would take Jess and Michael with her, and Brad would remain in Houston to try to hold back, or at least slow down, financial disaster.

In September of 1982, Cheryl took her two little boys and moved to Seattle. She was relieved to be out of the Houston climate and back home, but she missed Brad and she worried that Michael and Jess would forget their father. She put a map up on the wall and stuck colored pins in it, painstakingly explaining to three-year-old Jess and one-year-old Michael, who didn't really understand, where their daddy was. She talked about Brad constantly so that the boys would not think of him as some shadowy figure. He was their daddy, and one day they would all be together again.

Cheryl started work with Garvey, Schubert and Barer, moved into a house on Bainbridge Island, placed both Jess and Michael in Sharon McCulloch's day-care center, and set out to help Brad financially. She did well. Cheryl, so cowed in her marriage, was an absolutely spectacular litigator. She had all the raw material to become a successful attorney – and more. She was a natural debater. She had the drive, and she had the staying power. She could be as fierce as any bulldog, holding on until she made her point. Senior partners at Garvey, Schubert noticed her right away. She made enough money to support herself and the boys and to send more to Brad in Houston. If she worried that Brad might be continuing his penchant for extramarital sex, she didn't say so aloud. She may or may not have had reason to worry; Brad and the woman who worked as his secretary were extremely close during his time in Houston. He had never been a man who could exist long without the intimate company of a woman.

Brad traveled to Seattle every once in a while. He spent more time in Yakima, where he and his father were involved in new business projects. At one point, he hired two men from Yakima to fly down to Houston and transport vehicles and equipment from the job site in Texas up to the Tampico property. Despite his grim financial situation, Brad continued to drive Mercedes cars. He usually picked them up when they were imported through Los Angeles. Cheryl went with him on some of those trips, and on one occasion they were in a near-fatal automobile accident. Though they survived, the Mercedes-Benz didn't. Cheryl's family never learned all the details of the crash.

Occasionally, Brad caught up with his other children. He visited with his third child, Amy, and explained to Lauren why he was behind in his support payments. He told her he planned to sue the construction company responsible for his financial troubles and said he was confident that he would win back everything he had lost and more. A major Houston law firm was interested in his case, and he expected them to take the suit on a contingency basis.

Brad also kept track of Loni Ann and his first two children, Kait and Brent, although Loni Ann had done her best to hide their whereabouts from him. Brad learned that Kait was living temporarily with her maternal grandparents in Seattle. He would check into that; he was always alert to any failures in parenting that Loni Ann might demonstrate. Despite the three children he had fathered since Loni Ann won custody of Kait and Brent, he never forgot the ignominy of having her beat him in court.

During one of his visits home, Brad and Cheryl took their boys to a Cunningham family reunion. Cheryl put Jess and Michael to sleep in a tent while the adults visited and the teenagers fooled around with fireworks.

Brad's presence at the Cunningham reunions never went unnoticed. He was a kind of lightning rod who needed to be the center of attention. 'He was always like that,' one of Brad's cousins remembered. 'A long time ago, he called a bunch of us over – he was just a young guy then – and he said he was going to show us something, but we were never supposed to tell. He opened the trunk of his car, and he had all these automatic weapons in there.'

During the reunion in 1983, one of the rockets from the fireworks went awry and zoomed into the side of the tent where Jess and Michael napped. Smoke circled up, and Cheryl screamed. Brad, his cousin recalled, 'just sat there as if nothing had happened. I remember he only said, "Hey, that's a flame-retardant tent. I paid five hundred dollars for it; it had better not burn." Everyone but Brad ran toward the fire, but it was Cheryl who got the babies out of the burning tent. Brad acted like nothing happened at all. He wasn't worried. He was just mad that the tent didn't live up to its guarantee.'

20

In 1982 Kait Cunningham, Brad's oldest child, was twelve, a tall, slender girl with thick dark hair like her father's. She was also exceptionally lovely. Kait had not lived with her father, of course, since she was a toddler, and her memories of him were confusing and somewhat fearful. He was so very big and his reasoning seemed to change with the wind. 'When we were little,' Kait would remember, 'my father always told us to tell him the truth. He would say, "I won't spank you if you tell the truth." And so we would tell him the truth, and he would spank us anyway. That didn't make sense.'

When they were eight and seven and spent time with

their father, Brad played Frisbee with Kait and her younger brother Brent, paying them a quarter for every one they caught. Kait was better at that because she was older, and that angered Brad. He wanted his *son* to be the athlete, not his female child. 'He kicked Brent in the rump all the way to the car to punish him for being clumsy,' Kait recalled.

Brent took after his mother in appearance; he was a cute little kid with red hair cut in the 'bowl cut' popular at the time. He looked nothing at all like his father – and he never would. Even so, Kait sensed that she had always been Brad's least favorite child. Cloaking his words in a thin veneer of humor, he would tell Brent, 'God! Your sister has no brains. Don't be like your sister; she has no common sense.'

'We'd be on vacation or something and I wouldn't be allowed to swim,' Kait said. 'I'd have to take care of the towels because of something I'd done. I was nine or ten. Maybe I told stories or I would exaggerate, and that made him mad.' Brent felt sorry for her and tried to help. Later, when her father was married to Cheryl, Cheryl too felt sorry for Kait. She was always being confined to her room for something she had done to displease Brad. It was Cheryl who would let her out, and tell her to come to dinner with the rest of them.

But Kait Cunningham had a resilience about her; she was a strong-minded girl. She would need that strength.

Brad remained in Houston in late 1982 and through the spring of 1983, while Cheryl tried to keep his face alive in the minds of Jess and Michael and make him a part of their family even though he was so often far away. When Brad returned to Seattle, Loni Ann and Lauren were forced by law to permit visitation with their children. They both longed to have Brad out of their lives, but he insisted on contact with his offspring. If his visits were sporadic, *he* wanted it that way. When Brad claimed Kait or Brent or Amy, he behaved with them as he did with Jess and Michael. They were his. They belonged to him. The women who had given them birth and cared for them were only convenient vessels, and quite dispensable.

On one of his visits to Seattle, after he had learned that Kait was living with her grandparents, Brad picked her up one evening to take her out to dinner with Jess and Michael. But when he headed back toward her grandparents' after dinner, he drove right past the turnoff to their street. 'Are you going to be living with us on Bainbidge?' Jess asked Kait excitedly.

'No,' Kait said.

'Yes, you are,' Brad said, and Kait realized that he must have already announced that to her little half brothers.

Kait didn't know what to say. She wanted to live with her mother, and she had only been visiting her grandparents. She didn't want to live with her father. 'I went to court and got an order to have you live with me legally. I'm now taking custody of you,' her father told her, adding that Loni Ann was not a fit mother. He said that Loni Ann couldn't deal with her any longer, and that Kait would now be living with him.

When her father said something, it was so definite, Kait didn't even consider protesting. From the time she could remember, she had sensed that her mother was afraid of her father. She had seen that her mother always backed down, capitulated, struggling to maintain peace.

Kait did not live on Bainbridge Island long. When Brad returned to Houston, he took her with him. She would never understand why. Maybe he wanted company. Maybe he simply wanted a whipping boy (or, in her case, a kicking girl). Everything she did seemed to annoy him, and he apparently had little use for anything female. It was to be the beginning of a horrendous ordeal for Kait. It was also, perhaps, a period that would demonstrate for the first time what a tremendously strong girl she was. She may well have inherited the best of her father's traits – his self-confidence, his refusal to give up in spite of great odds, and a hard pride. She would need all of that armor to survive so far away from her mother, her brother, and her grandparents.

Brad enrolled Kait in junior high school in Houston and she tried, tentatively, to make friends. She was graceful and athletic, as both her parents were. She won a medal in track and brought it home to show her father. Instead of being proud of her, Brad was annoyed. 'He took it away from me,' Kait recalled. 'I don't really know why. He told me I wasn't to leave my room – that I was being punished – but I didn't know why. . . . I won several ribbons and other awards. [He took those too.] I never got them back from him.'

Kait was continually confused. She wasn't sure why she was in Houston in the first place, and she never knew what was going to make her father angry. Her punishments were usually the removal of privileges or of the belongings that meant the most to her. 'He did that frequently,' she recalled. 'I wouldn't know exactly what I did. He would take my clothes away – the things you would wear out normally – and he made me wear clothes that you would use to paint the house, you know, your ripped-up, bummy clothes. I was obliged to wear those. I wasn't allowed to do any preparation for school – like curling my hair – the things you did when you were young. . . . Sometimes, I could earn back my clothes, and I'd have them for a while, and then he'd take them away again, and I could never understand why. I got to the point where I'd go into school early and get ready in the bathroom.

'After the after-school activities, before I'd go home, I'd get my hair all wet and take all the makeup off. I wasn't allowed to wear that. Basically, he'd take away all my privileges. It was embarrassing for me to go into school with my hair all over the place and my bummy clothes. That didn't feel good. Everyone in school wasn't doing that and you had that peer pressure. I got to the point where I'd get ready in the morning, even if I had to miss a class to do it. He didn't know I was doing that.'

Loni Ann knew that Kait was with her father in Texas,

but she had no way to bring her back; she could only try to comfort her daughter when Kait was able to sneak away to a phone booth and call. It was agony for Loni Ann to hear her sob on the phone and not be able to help her. For Kait, the only semblance of a normal family life occurred when Brad brought the little boys down for a visit and Kait baby-sat them. Sometimes Cheryl could get away too for a short time and visit Brad. He had assured Cheryl that living with him was the best thing for Kait; her mother wasn't capable of taking care of her.

Brad spent a good deal of his time at his office; he had to. He was still fighting desperately to save the real estate empire that had been burgeoning only a year earlier. He ran a 'secretarial service,' although the details of that business enterprise were vague. Apparently he was using office space in the one building he had completed before Parkwood Plaza faltered.

Just like her mother a dozen years earlier, Kait was required to let Brad know where she was at all times. And she soon became the target for her father's rage and frustration. Eventually she had to go to a counselor because she had begun to break under the abuse. In her sessions, or whenever they were around other people, her father jokingly – even fondly – turned away her accusations: 'Stop lying, Kait. . . . Why are you doing that? Knock it off. Be a good girl.'

'He sounded very genuine,' Kait marveled years later. 'You almost felt like you *were* crazy because there wasn't a hint of maliciousness. . . . It was as if I was a liar or something, and it almost made it worse.'

Was she somehow to blame? No. He was the one who told her over and over that she was nothing more than garbage. He was the one who told her that her mother was a bad mother who had mistreated Kait and Brent, who had kept a filthy house, who had done terrible things. He had explained to her through gritted teeth that all women were liars. All women were garbage.

'He said I was going to be like my mother,' Kait recalled. 'He said I was going to be pregnant by the time I was eighteen.' But Kait knew what Loni Ann was really like. She had chosen, always, to live with her mother. 'She was sensitive. She was human. I could talk to her about things. I could come to her when I had a problem. She was a very good person.'

All of Brad's abuse took place behind the locked and alarmed door of his apartment. No one knew that he was anything but a concerned, long-suffering single parent. Brad would occasionally tell Kait that they were going for a drive. 'Then,' she related, 'he would pull over and scream at me and tell me I was garbage and stupid and ugly, and I was no good and I would never amount to anything. That I was crazy . . . those things sort of stick with you after a while.'

Kait was like a little mouse trapped in a cage, constantly beset with different signals. Sometimes, when her father raved on and on about how terrible her mother was, she would break into sobs. And then, as they were about to go out into the world that saw Brad as a suave executive and a concerned father, he would change instantly and become that person. 'Come give your father a hug. I love you.'

'I *wouldn't* hug him and he'd say, "Oh, hug your father." And I'd go to school so screwed up. I didn't have friends because people thought I was weird.'

There was little point in Kait trying to have friends anyway. Brad insisted on having a timetable of exactly where she would be, and with whom, and pertinent telephone numbers. It wasn't worth the effort to have friends. She was in junior high and none of the other kids had to account for every second of every day.

Brad was especially suspicious of boys. Once, Kait got off at the wrong bus stop and called Brad's office to ask him to come pick her up. He said he would be right there. But one of the boys in her class happened to live a few houses away and he invited her to come and see his dog's new puppies.

While she was looking at the puppies, Brad arrived to pick her up, and when he didn't find her at the bus stop, he drove off. When she called the house, he was angry and accusing.

'You'd better get here in fifteen minutes or you're grounded.'

She was two miles from home and she knew she couldn't run that fast. 'I tried – but I didn't make it.'

Brad accused Kait of having sex with the twelve-year-old boy. 'It was ridiculous,' she recalled. 'He was the class nerd. . . . I was only five minutes late to meet my father. He went on about how women are like that, and he'd tell me all about his sexual experiences – which I didn't want to hear. He told me what I was going to be like when I was older, how I'd be around men. He was saying all it would take would be some man saying "I love you" and "you're going to let them screw you. . . ." He said I was fooling around with this boy and that's why I wasn't there. Which wasn't true – but he wouldn't listen to me.'

Brad continually isolated Kait and tried to destroy any vestige of ego she might have left. He didn't want her to have any confidantes. He told her that none of the secretaries at his office really liked her. 'You're just the boss's daughter.'

Kait called Loni Ann every day from school and cried. It seemed to her that she was never going to get away from her father. She was afraid to show it on the outside, but Kait was angry. She was also a gutsy little girl, and she began to formulate an escape plan. She squirreled away every bit of money her father gave her, going without lunch and any of the movies or other treats she might have bought. She hid her money in her closet, counting it carefully as it grew closer to the amount she would need for a one-way plane ticket.

Brad kept the alarm system on whenever they were home, so Kait could not open any door without setting it off, but she knew where the keys were and she finally figured out how to disarm it. If she actually made it onto a plane, Kait knew that her father would check the airline rosters out of Houston. She planned to book flights on her departure day on every airline under her own name. On one of the flights, she would use a false name. That would be the plane that would carry her far away from Houston.

But Kait, as smart as she was, was only twelve. Brad had asked one of his women friends to befriend her and Kait trusted her. 'I told her about my plan, and she told him. And I went on restriction again.'

By the spring of 1983, Brad's grip on his Texas fortune was loosening. But he apparently had a plan. As a grown woman she could no longer recall the details, but Kait remembered how Brad laughed as he told her how he was going to beat the bankruptcy courts. Kait recalled that he showed her a page he had typed, listing his assets. She was impressed, and baffled when he filed for bankruptcy in June. 'He used his credit cards because he didn't have to pay the bills. When I came back and told my mother, she didn't believe me because she said, "No one does that," but *he* did.'

Verbal abuse from her father had long since become an almost everyday thing for Kait, but there was one incident so frightening that she would remember it years later as clearly as if it had just happened. She had almost finished the school year in Houston; she was in her last week in the eighth grade when some gaffe of hers set Brad off into the most violent episode she had yet endured. 'He had told me to come straight with him about everything – meaning any single secret or lie I could have ever possibly had. At this moment, I was supposed to tell him. I told him everything, except there was just one thing that I wanted to keep secret to me. I felt it was my "secret garden," that it didn't hurt anyone and it wasn't any of his business.'

Brad had had to make a trip to Seattle, but he wanted to be sure that Kait remained in Houston, and he had arranged to have her stay with the family of an employee.

This man – who worked in one of Brad's warehouses – had casually mentioned some facet of Kait's life that Brad didn't know about. Certainly nothing big. But Brad's overweening possessiveness was akin to his need to know the most minute information about his children, right down to what kind of cereal Jess had been given. That someone other than himself would know *anything* about Kait that he didn't know was anathema.

When Kait got home from school that day, Brad was talking on the phone with the man whose family had cared for her while he was away. She saw that her father was coldly angry, but she had no idea why.

It began as sadistic teasing. Brad took a pen and ran it up and down Kait's nose. She pushed it away and he asked in a puzzled tone, 'You don't like that?'

'No.'

'Oh, that's too bad,' he said sarcastically.

He kept running the pen along the bridge of her nose, and Kait, annoyed and a little frightened, backed away from him, around and around the room, around the coffee table. 'I would back up, going out of my room into the living room. He was trying to push me down. I'd lose my footing and take two or three steps back. . . . That's when he was screaming at me. I didn't even know him at that point. It was like he was a different person. There was a whole different fire in his eye and he scared me.'

Brad ordered Kait to take off her clothes; they were, he said, his because he had bought them. 'You didn't come straight with me,' he yelled, and he grabbed armfuls of her clothes out of her closet until it was empty except for a few 'bummy' garments. Then he threw a large pre-folded cardboard packing box at Kait as if he were throwing a Frisbee, hitting her in the mouth with a sharp corner and bruising her face. He ordered her to put it together.

'I started to really get scared and I was shaking,' Kait remembered. 'And he told me I'd better put it together and that I'd better catch this tape he was throwing at me, or I'd be in really big trouble. I started to really freak out.'

Kait managed finally to fit the complicated tab-and-fold box together and Brad tossed her clothes inside. Then he walked to the kitchen and grabbed the garbage and poured it in the box on top of her clothes. 'He was screaming at me,' she recalled years later, her voice betraying the damage done. 'He told me that I was no longer part of this family, that my little brothers would grow up not knowing I existed.'

Brad grabbed Kait and drew his mammoth fist back and told her 'that he would just love to hit me. But he knew I would tell – that I had a big mouth and I would tell everybody. But he said one day he was going to do it, and how bad he wanted to hit me.'

Brad ordered Kait to carry the box down the stairs of the apartment building. It was terribly heavy for a slight twelve-year-old girl. She was tall for her age – about five feet five – but she didn't weigh very much, and the only way she could hold the box was to bend her knees, balance it on the front of her thighs, and take the steps one at a time.

'He tried to kick me in the butt, which was something he liked to do to my brother and me when he wanted to be ornery,' Kait said. 'And so I tried to dodge him while I was carrying this thing. Then he told me to go put it in this big garbage bin. I was crying because these were all my belongings. . . . This man had come over, and I was crying and I asked him to help me get my clothes into the garbage, because I couldn't reach, and my father came over and said, "Hey! Get away from her!" I finally got it in the garbage.'

When Kait went back to their apartment, Brad ordered her into her room and told her that he was putting something on the door, and it would go off if she tried to open the door and he would know. At this point, Kait was terrified. Her father had pushed and knocked her around before; he had told her how much he wanted to hit her. She crept into her closet and began to pray.

But Brad would not permit it. He followed her and peered into the closet, demanding to know what she was doing.

'I'm praying,' she said quietly.

'You don't do that in there!' he said and grabbed at her. He lifted her in one muscled arm and held her above him with her back pressing the ceiling. He threw her down on the bed and kicked her. Then he ordered her to stay out of her closet and warned her not to cause trouble.

Kait stayed quietly in her room. She believed every word her father had told her, and she was sure he had booby-trapped her door. Frantically her mind raced, thinking of ways to escape. She thought she might be able to go out the window. She might go to the police and tell them about her father. 'I'd told him once that I was going to turn him in for emotional abuse, and he laughed at me. He said, "Who's going to believe you? You're a little kid. All I'd have to do is tell them you're just a little liar – you're just garbage. They're not going to believe you."'

Kait remembered that and figured there was no point in trying to escape her father. No one *would* believe her.

Brad had allowed Kait to go to the rehearsal for the graduation ceremonies from the eighth grade, and she longed to graduate with her class. She had been in Houston over six months by now, and she wanted to finish the school year. It would be some contact with normalcy, some way to prove to herself that all those months had not been a complete waste. But Kait never went back after her father ruined her clothes with garbage and forced her to throw away everything that mattered to her. How *could* she go to school? She had no clothes.

Kait never knew what she had done to set her father off, to turn him into a raving, frothing stranger. She didn't realize, of course, that she had lived out the same scenario as her aunt Susan. When Sanford Cunningham was angry, Susan had hidden in her closet too, clutching her dog close to her. Even Brad, who seemed so all-powerful at the age of thirty-four, had cowered in terror when he was a little boy, waiting for his father to come home and mete out the beatings his mother decreed.

Kait's mother couldn't help her. Her father barely looked at her. She wasn't sure how to find her other relatives; everyone was far away in Washington State. And then, finally, she learned she was going home.

She could scarcely breathe for fear her father would change his mind. But when he left Houston, Kait was, thank God, in the car. 'He drove me to Yakima,' she said.

After that, Brad never showed any interest in having Kait with him. She saw her father a few times when she was fifteen or sixteen, and never again thereafter – not until she had a memorable confrontation with him in 1995.

21

June 1983 may well have been the turning point of Brad's life. Ever since he was a little boy, he had hustled, always looking upward at the next step on the ladder of success. Financial success. Personal success. And, yes, sexual success. His older sister Ethel had referred to him in a derogatory fashion as the 'local black market kid,' commenting that he was always looking for a way to make a fast dollar. His father Sanford had been the same way and was undoubtedly a model for his only son. According to his youngest daughter, Susan, Sanford had won approval from his father and uncles by being quick with his checkbook. He had always wanted a better house and a better truck than anyone in his family.

Eventually Sanford had wanted a better wife, and Brad seemed to want a better wife often. He had been married to Cheryl longer than anyone so far. He stayed three and a half years with Loni Ann, six months with Cynthia, seven months with Lauren. Cheryl was determined to make her marriage work, sure that everything was going to be better soon.

Sanford Cunningham's 'best house' was only a middle-class rambler on a busy street in a workingman's suburb. His son wanted much more. Unlike his father, Brad had Indian blood in his veins, but it was a heritage that he was ashamed of. As he grew to be a man, he had distanced himself from his roots as quickly as he could. Even so, no worldly possession and no woman had ever yet lived up to his perception of what he felt he needed to enhance the persona he presented to the world.

No woman until Cheryl. She was beautiful and brilliant and perfect. She loved Brad completely and single-mindedly, and she had bent to his will early in their relationship. She had given him two fine sons and she was once again earning a very comfortable living.

Brad was not. His rise as a real estate entrepreneur had been almost meteoric, but when his soaring star faltered, it faltered badly. In June 1983 it plunged straight down to earth. He surely saw it coming. His abuse of Kait that spring in Houston may have indicated something more than pure meanness; Brad was more likely a man walking on the sharp edge of career disaster who defused his own anxiety by berating the only person around who was no threat to him. His behavior was hardly admirable, but if it was a reaction to the crumbling of his dreams, it was easier to understand than cruelty for its own sake.

Brad had kept up his public facade, going each day to his fine office in his shiny Mercedes. If Kait's perception of her father's financial picture, her memory of his boasting about hidden assets and freewheeling charges on credit cards he would never have to pay, was accurate, Brad did not go down without a plan. Perhaps he did have money no one knew about and perhaps he did not disclose all his assets to the bankruptcy court. He had always lived an opulent lifestyle, a few steps beyond what he could really afford.

He was probably grasping everything he could on his way down. But with the Parkwood Plaza project irrevocably gone, he was a man starting over.

Meanwhile, Cheryl was working hard at Garvey, Schubert, where she had made many friends. Her early promise as a litigator had blossomed. She was good. She was more than good; she was partnership material. One of the partners in the firm recalled the first time he realized that Cheryl was a woman to be reckoned with. 'We were at a partners' meeting in Seattle and Cheryl was conducting a deposition. We stood outside the conference room and heard her chewing out two senior members of the bar. We all thought, wow, she's feisty, . . . we've really got a great litigator. She was creative, very bright, tenacious – and the clients loved her.'

Brock Adams was a partner in Garvey, Schubert until his election to the U.S. Senate. The law firm that began in Seattle in 1979 had had any number of top litigators but Cheryl Keeton would be remembered as 'one of the best in the history of our law firm' and 'top notch!' She was a woman for all seasons. Her future seemed to be limitless.

Cheryl had kept the home fires burning for Brad. She was still living on Bainbridge Island and she depended on her sister Susan, her cousin Katannah King, or Sally Nelson,* a baby-sitter, to take care of Jess and Michael while she was at work. Sally worked for Cheryl for only four months. She said later that she was nervous because Brad had so many guns, and because she saw that he was irrationally jealous of Cheryl. He hinted that she was probably cheating on him with other men while he was in Texas. But Cheryl would have needed superhuman energy to find the time and/or the enthusiasm to carry on an affair. She left the house early in the morning to catch the ferry to Seattle, worked a long day, and headed home often after dark. What free time she had, she spent with Jess and Michael and, if he was in town, with Brad.

Besides, Cheryl was carrying another child. She was

pregnant for the third time in four years and expected to give birth around Thanksgiving 1983. With the workload she was handling at her law firm, and with all the responsibility of caring for Jess and Michael while Brad was gone, she was exhausted most of the time. It was, of course, not the most propitious time for her to be pregnant, but she was happy about it nonetheless.

As she always had, Cheryl continued to believe that things were going to get better in her marriage. It was terrible for Brad to lose his Houston project, but she believed at least that meant he would be home and they would be living together as a family again. When Brad was away, it was easy for Cheryl to think like that. But when he was home, all the warm good things she had planned just seemed to slip away.

She tried. She tried very hard. She and Brad socialized with Sharon McCulloch and her husband, and sometimes Brad could be charming. Even Sharon had changed her mind about him. She liked him a lot better now than in the days when she first cared for newborn Jess. If Cheryl and Brad needed a baby-sitter, the McCullochs allowed their teenage daughter to take the ferry to Bainbridge – with the understanding that Brad would be picking her up.

When Brad wanted to be, he was the best person in the world to be around. But when he turned on someone, he was another person, the most formidable of opponents. He was so intelligent, and he had an uncanny knack at spotting a person's most vulnerable area. Then he would go for the jugular. Sharon soon saw that she had been right about Brad in the first place. 'This is a man who was so smooth. It's hard to understand. I trusted him. And then everything fell apart. He was so cunning and so persuasive. It was just chilling. It was diabolical. It was eerie. He turned on me a couple of times and frightened me too. . . .'

After Brad moved back to Washington from Houston, he was often moody and angry and hard to please. Not hard – *impossible* to please. Jess and Michael had been so anxious for their daddy to be home with them, but when he was around, he ignored them. He wasn't working, but he continued to spend money as if he were. When Cheryl demurred, he turned on her, enraged. It didn't matter that she was supporting him and carrying his child. He would brook no interference with his preferred lifestyle.

Cheryl's sister Susan saw it too. Despite all the covering up Cheryl tried to do, she was a woman clearly miserable. Worse, she was afraid. Susan had been a child when Cheryl started seeing Brad, and even then, she knew that something was wrong. Now Susan was a very mature seventeen and had become more of a confidante to her sister. She had also become a close-up observer to the steady disintegration of Cheryl's marriage.

It might be expected that a man who had seen his multimillion-dollar project evaporate would be morose, particularly when his wife's career was soaring. Despite his boast that he would win his suit against the construction company, Brad's financial picture was grim. He had had it all. He had lost it all. His temperament, never predictable, became even more mercurial. Cheryl had done everything she could to support him – both financially and emotionally – and yet he seemed to blame *her* for his troubles.

Then, inexplicably, Brad suddenly moved out of their house on Bainbridge Island. 'Cheryl would come home from work and "Brad's furniture" would be gone,' Susan recalled. 'There wouldn't be anything left that was really valuable – the rolltop desk, the leather chairs, the T.V. [were gone]. He would leave their bed and the kids' stuff.'

Cheryl was constantly off balance.

Brad was home.

Brad had moved out.

Brad was traveling.

Brad was back.

As far as she could determine, he wasn't working, and he certainly didn't seem to be earning any money. He had filed for Chapter 11 bankruptcy. He blamed the bonding and construction companies for that. Brad warned Cheryl that his legal action had unleashed sinister forces that would have no compunction about destroying him, her, and the boys.

With Brad, there was so much to be afraid of. First, there was his own anger if anyone broke his rules. Second, there were malignant entities that he said waited in the background to destroy him and all he stood for – and he was ultimately convincing when he spoke of unseen danger. He had not married a naive and gullible woman. None of his wives had been dumb. Cheryl was, in fact, an extremely brilliant woman. But Brad could convince almost anyone of anything, and that included attorneys and big business executives.

For Cheryl life became a constant walk through erratic situations; one misstep and the calmness she had always sought evaporated. In only a few years everything had changed so radically. At work, she was still totally in control, efficient and effective. At home, she no longer knew what Brad would do or, worse, what the people who were after him might do.

Still, if it was true that they were all in danger, Cheryl wondered why Brad didn't stay home with her and the little boys to protect them. When she came home to find him and his possessions gone the first time, she feared he had been abducted, even murdered. Only later would she find out that he had left of his own volition – and for his own reasons.

Cheryl never really understood what made Brad move out or where he had gone. She was afraid to be alone on the island, but she was more afraid that Brad – or someone – would come back during the day and take more things out of the house. She asked Susan to move in with her and help her take care of Jess and Michael. 'But I knew she wanted someone there too while she was at work,' Susan sighed, remembering. 'Someone to guard the house. She was very upset and she was pregnant.'

Susan loved looking after her two young nephews. 'They were both smart,' she said. 'But Jess was more introspective, and Michael was all high energy with a short attention span.' Michael was still a toddler then, and Jess was three. 'He was brilliant,' Susan recalled. 'He asked me once, "Where does glass come from?" and then he went into one of his meditative states. Later, he popped up with "*Sand!* Glass is made out of *sand!*" Jess always had phenomenal knowledge and concentration, even when he was a really little kid.'

While Cheryl worried about their finances, Brad continued to drive a Mercedes. Not just one, but several. Susan, a typical teenager, thought at first that his cars were 'kind of neat.' He had the mammoth Unimag. He had two four-door Mercedes sedans, a Mercedes station wagon, *and* a classic red two-seater Mercedes convertible. Susan was sure that Brad had to have money secreted somewhere.

'Well, I just don't know where it is,' Cheryl said wearily. 'It doesn't do me any good.'

A woman who had always been in control, who thought precisely and rationally, Cheryl was now often scattered and distraught. She consulted a psychologist in 1983, hoping that she could find a way to run her life as smoothly as she ran her law practice and took care of her sons.

Sharon McCulloch was still Cheryl's day-care provider and continued to be a close friend. Sharon admired Cheryl tremendously. 'She was Super Mom. I've taught school, I've taken care of over forty kids, and I've never known a mom in my life as committed to her kids. . . . She could be so busy, and if I called and said Jess had a little fever and asked her if I should have the doctor look at his ears, she would be there in twenty minutes. Every birthday, she gave a party. . . . Her kids were her life. She was the highest-energy person I've ever met in my life. She was a perfectionist – about herself. It's a little thing, but one time her bra strap slipped down, and it was just pristine white. That was the way she was. Her house was spotless. . . . She was good at everything she did.'

Sharon called Cheryl 'the mother of the world.' She had to be. Jess was three and a half, Michael was twenty-one months old, she was four months pregnant, and now Brad was talking about how he might just go to live in Yakima 150 miles away for a while. He had some interest left in tribal land over there. He was thinking of starting a car wash and a laundromat. There was some acreage he thought they should buy.

Cheryl just stared at him, appalled.

She decided she had to move. It was too difficult and too expensive for her to stay on Bainbridge Island. She needed to be closer to her work and to her doctor. She rented a house in Somerset, an upper-middle-class neighborhood near Bellevue on the east side of King County. Now she would no longer have to depend on the ferry service to get to work, although the commute over the floating bridge could sometimes be frustrating.

Brad moved with his family to Somerset, but then he left for Yakima. Cheryl pinned up the big map again, to show Jess and Michael where their daddy was. Despite everything, she was still fighting to hold the image of the perfect little family together. The boys were probably too young to understand, but she felt it vital that she keep talking about Brad, letting them know that they did have a father.

If Cheryl was beginning to be afraid *for* Brad, she was also often afraid *of* Brad. Even so, she clung to her hope that somehow things were going to get better. Sometimes her sister and her friends wanted to shake her and tell her to wake up and smell the coffee. One day Sharon McCulloch and her daughter Mary visited Cheryl in the Somerset house. 'I remember that there was this *huge* stuffed animal there, and I said something to Cheryl about it,' Sharon recalled. 'She said, "Brad bought it, and I'm going to be paying for it for a long time."' As they left, they walked through the garage to get to their car. Sharon was stunned to see the number of guns in the garage. She was more shocked to see an elongated woven basket; it looked exactly like a coffin – an Indian child's coffin. Her jaw dropped, and she turned toward Cheryl to ask what it was.

'Oh,' Cheryl said, embarrassed. 'That's Brad's idea of discipline – keeping that in the garage for the boys.' When they were naughty, she said uncomfortably, Brad took them out and showed them the coffin. 'He . . . tells them that . . . well, that's where bad boys end up.'

'Brad was into killing things – death,' Sharon remembered. 'He would take the boys to Yakima and they'd come home with boxes of things they had killed. Squirrels and rabbits and snakes. Prairie dogs. *They* weren't killing anything; they were just tiny boys, but that's what Brad brought back for souvenirs of their trip. It used to just make Cheryl crazy.'

On one of the trips in August 1983, Brad sent back a postcard to Cheryl. It was addressed, 'Wife Cunningham,' and the message was one word, written in huge letters: 'SEX.' A card from Jess – but written by Brad – said, 'I'm really getting bigger. I take care of Michael almost all the time, especially at night so Dad and Shaun can go out drinkin' and dancin'. Dad said I did real good.'

It was, of course, a joke. Jess was only three. In October, Brad wrote a letter to Jess for his fourth birthday, apologizing for not being there. He sent three gifts. The first was a 'tooth' from Brad's backhoe that had broken off when he was digging a waterline to a house he was renovating on property he and Cheryl had purchased in Tampico. 'You can keep this on your shelve [*sic*] downstairs to remind you of our backhoe.' The second present was shell casings. 'These are spent bullets from one of Dad's rifles. A pack of wild dogs came into Tampico last week and started raising havoc. . . . Daddy shot two of these wild dogs near your house, and these are the "bullets" from my gun. . . .

'I hope you had a nice and happy birthday. I love you very, very, very much and promise to see you again some day when things are better.

'Love,

'Dad'

Cheryl was all alone with the little boys for week after week. Nevertheless, she continued to make excuses for Brad. When he missed one of the boys' birthdays, she said, 'Daddy can't be here because he's making money,' or 'Daddy can't call you because he doesn't have a phone.' If Brad was making money, Cheryl saw none of it. And as 1983 waned, so did her hopes for a happy ending. If she sometimes felt she was being punished for taking away another woman's husband, no one could blame her. She was living at the edges of hell with a man who had become a stranger. Instead of things getting better, they were growing immeasurably worse.

Cheryl knew Sharon well enough by this time that she no longer tried to mask her true emotions. She was afraid. On November 18, 1983, the Friday night before Cheryl's third son was born, the two women met for dinner at Bellevue Square. Sharon could see how miserable and terrified Cheryl was. They sat in a quiet booth while Cheryl poured out her fears. She was as pregnant as a woman could be – nine full months – and she trembled and cried softly as she tried to tell Sharon how bad things were in her marriage. A no-nonsense person herself, Sharon could not understand why Cheryl clung to a marriage that seemed more like a prison sentence.

'How can you *live* like this?' she asked Cheryl.

'I don't have a choice.'

'You always have a choice. You don't have to live like this.'

Cheryl tried to explain. 'No, you don't understand. If I leave, he'll kill me.'

'Cheryl—'

'No, really. He has always threatened that if I ever left him, he would kill me.'

'Cheryl, you're an attorney. Those kinds of things just don't happen. You could stop him.'

'No. If I ever tried to get custody of the boys,' Cheryl said, her voice choked with tears, 'he would kill me. The only thing I could do, Sharon, if I ever got custody of the boys, is to leave the country and change my name. I'm between a rock and a hard place. If I don't get them away from him, their lives are in danger. They're not safe – he has enemies everywhere. They won't live to be adults. And if I try to get custody, he'll kill *me* probably.'

Sharon didn't like Brad any longer; he was as abrasive and supercilious as anyone she had ever met. She had come to think of him as evil. But what kind of intrigue was he into where someone wanted to kill him and his sons? There was no doubt in Sharon's mind that Cheryl believed he had enemies. But was it really true? And was it true that he might kill her if she tried to get custody of the boys?

On the Monday following Cheryl's tearful unburdening to her good friend, she presented Brad with another son: Phillip. He now had six children by three wives.

Brad's first two children, Kait and Brent, were, for the moment, safely out of his reach. Their mother, Loni Ann, had her bachelor's degree in physical education; she was teaching in high school and working on her master's in kinestheo-therapy. For a woman who had truly begun to believe that she was irretrievably stupid, she was doing remarkably well in college. Her course work involved memorizing all the muscles and tendons of the body and how they worked, and she had no trouble at all doing that. Loni Ann was smarter than anyone had realized. No matter what Brad had done to destroy all traces of self-worth in his first wife, she had survived and had even begun to thrive. Her goal was to work with patients with sports injuries and in general rehabilitative medicine.

Loni Ann's other goal was to get as far away from the

Northwest and Brad as possible. She was grateful to have her daughter back after the nightmare months Kait had spent with Brad in Houston. She was going to need counseling. They were *both* going to need counseling, untold years of therapy, so they would no longer be afraid and would no longer feel like 'garbage.'

When Phillip was born, Brad came over from Yakima and visited Cheryl briefly. Mary Hilfer, one of her friends, recalled that he bought a new puppy for the boys. 'That was the last thing Cheryl needed with a new baby – a puppy to look after too!'

Now that Brad was the father of three more boys, all under one roof, he didn't seem nearly as obsessed with keeping his other children under his thumb. Lauren Stoneham was vastly relieved when he didn't exercise his visitation rights with Amy in anything more than a sporadic fashion. But her relationship with Brad was no longer overtly adversarial, and he sometimes called and talked to her as if they were close friends. Lauren was certainly not going to bring up the past and Brad seemed to have forgotten the agony he had put her through. He filled her in with more details about his high-stakes court battle in Texas, blaming the officers of the construction company, the architect, and the bonding company for the delays that had thrown him into bankruptcy. In his usual convincing manner, he told Lauren that if they had listened to him and met their commitments in getting the buildings done, his current financial disaster would never have happened.

Brad explained that he had filed for Chapter 11 protection because he still had all of his assets; he just had to find a different way to tap into them. But if he did recoup any money, Lauren didn't hear about it. After 1983 Brad never paid her any more child support for Amy. That was fine with Lauren; they didn't need it. And it was a relief to know that Brad was no longer pushing for his parental rights.

22

Cheryl was the primary parent to Jess, Michael, and the newborn Phillip. As her friend Sharon later said, 'Cheryl parented those boys essentially alone.' She was also the primary breadwinner in her marriage. Brad was always gone – to Yakima, to Texas, to Canada, and to any number of other places. He had mysterious missions connected with the financial fiasco in Houston, he was setting up a business for his father in Yakima, but, beyond that, Cheryl was never really sure why he had to be away so often. The map on the wall bristled with pins, as she patiently showed her little boys 'where Daddy is.'

Nineteen eighty-four was a year of separations and strained reunions, a year of despair and even of occasional hope. Cheryl *was* afraid of Brad and of the truth she acknowledged in moments of solitary – but searing – evaluation of her marriage. She realized at last that he was fully capable of killing her if she crossed him. She knew that all of the energy and brilliance and charm that had once bewitched her could just as easily be turned against her. And it wasn't only Brad. He had warned her that there were mysterious forces stalking not only him but his whole family. He could handle himself, but he didn't want his sons to pay a tragic price.

Brad kept Cheryl continually off balance, constantly afraid. And yet part of her still loved him. Only a woman who has been battered either physically or emotionally can understand why. The bad alternated with the good. And when things were good, they were tremendously good. There is no creature on earth more persuasive than a contrite wife abuser, and no woman who wants to believe more than the abused wife.

Cheryl was a woman with superior intellectual strength, but she was also a woman with a tender and romantic heart who detested the idea of a second divorce. Brad had swept her away from her first marriage. If she divorced him, she feared revealing herself as a woman who could not give what marriage demanded. Worse, this time a divorce would mean that her three little boys would lose either their father or their mother. She had grave doubts that Brad would let her keep Jess, Michael, and Phillip – he had told her otherwise often enough – and she could not bear the thought of losing them. If Brad did accede to her having custody, they would probably never see him again. He had threatened to walk completely out of their lives. There would be no need to put pins in a map, because their daddy wouldn't be coming home and it wouldn't matter where he was. She probably wouldn't even know.

Cheryl was stubborn and focused as a litigator and she was just as stubborn in hanging on to her marriage. But she was not stupid. She no longer believed that her marriage would one day miraculously metamorphose into one filled with joy and security. She adjusted her sights lower and somehow she was able to quiet the hysteria she had felt just before Phillip was born, able to relegate the fear to her subconscious – although it still lay in wait like a cancer, ready to burst forth and grow.

Cheryl had always made friends wherever she went, both female and male, and more than ever now, they helped her maintain her equilibrium. John Burke, her old friend from the Unigard Insurance office before either of them went to law school, was still in touch. She rarely saw him, but they wrote and talked on the phone. Burke was married; so was Cheryl. They were platonic friends who admired each other a great deal.

Eric Lindenauer was another good friend. When he had graduated from Willamette University Law School in Salem,

Oregon, in 1983, the firm of Garvey, Schubert was anxious to hire him. He wanted to work in commercial litigation and he specifically searched for a law firm where he would have a mentor, 'someone to teach me the fine points of litigation – the things you can't learn in law school.' Garvey, Schubert assured Lindenauer they would find him a skilled litigator to guide him in his fledgling years. That mentor was Cheryl Keeton.

At thirty-four, Cheryl was a good decade older than Lindenauer, yet they became good friends as well as mentor and student. She took him under her wing and taught him the subtle nuances that separate an outstanding litigator from an adequate one. He was amazed at her professional ability and grateful that she was so generous in sharing her experience.

In the beginning, Lindenauer knew very little about Cheryl's personal life, nothing beyond the fact that her husband had business interests that required him to travel a lot. She was a private person and a very proud woman. No one really knew what Cheryl's life was like. However, the people who worked in Brad and Cheryl's home could not help but notice that theirs was a strange, edgy marriage.

Lee Mauldin* baby-sat for them Monday through Friday in the summer of 1984. She joined a parade of baby-sitters who would go on record to say that they did not care for *Mr* Cunningham. In a statement she gave six years later, Lee remembered Brad's violence and his temper. She recalled that he once removed the tires from Cheryl's car so she couldn't drive. During one of his many precipitous abandonments, Cheryl had changed the locks on the Somerset house, but Brad broke in, shouting threats. Lee Mauldin heard it all and was appalled.

Fortuitously perhaps, Brad continued to stay away from home for most of 1984, spending a lot of time in Yakima with his father. He bought Sanford a gas station in Tampico. Even though Cheryl was the only one working, nothing was ever too good for Brad's father. The business was doomed to failure almost from the start, and it soon went belly-up. Brad was confident, however, that his plan for a laundromat and car wash would be more successful.

He had also moved a lot of heavy equipment onto the property that he and Cheryl owned in Tampico. Cheryl was not sure where the equipment had come from, or how he was paying for it. There were tractors, backhoes, bulldozers, a crawler loader, and a number of trucks and trailers. Brad was bankrupt, but he never stopped acquiring things, and Cheryl knew she too was liable for his debts. She worried about it, staying awake nights.

In late 1984, Cheryl received an offer that seemed to be a lifeline she could grab onto. Garvey, Schubert was growing and prospering, and the firm credited her for a good deal of its success. There were now forty attorneys in the Seattle office, a smaller number in Washington, D.C., and a new branch in Portland, Oregon. Would Cheryl be interested in transferring to Portland? It would mean a full partnership for her. Of course, she would still be returning often to Seattle to work on her cases in progress, and she knew almost all of the Garvey, Schubert staff who were already in Portland. Eric Lindenauer had moved down there a few months before and they often worked on cases together.

Careerwise, it was a wonderful opportunity for Cheryl. Personally, it could be either a chance to separate from Brad or – in the best of all possible worlds – a fresh start for them in a new city. A geographical solution, perhaps, to the doubts and recriminations that had well nigh crippled their marriage.

Although Cheryl hated to leave Seattle, it wouldn't be the cultural and climate shock it had been to move to Houston. Portland and Seattle both have beautiful summers and rainy winters. Seattle has Mount Rainier and Portland has Mount Hood, snowy mountain peaks to gaze at, and both cities are built around water. In one way, Portland seemed an even better place for Cheryl to live; it was an hour closer to her old hometown of Longview, old friends, and her family.

Tentatively, she broached the subject to Brad. To her surprise, he agreed that a move to Portland might be a good idea. While he still didn't have a regular job, he was confident he could find something that suited him just as well in Oregon as he could in Washington. And so, in January 1985, they moved into a rental house in Gresham. It was not a lavish home, but pleasant and roomy. The rent was something over nine hundred dollars a month, and Cheryl paid it, just as she paid all the household bills.

Garvey, Schubert's Portland offices were state of the art, very plush, with thick carpets, lovely paintings, and expensive furnishings. Even the lighting was computerized so that each office's lights went on when someone walked through the door. Cheryl would have her own paralegal assistant and her own secretary, and she herself would continue to mentor young attorneys fresh from law school. She was finally at a place in her legal career that she had always dreamed of.

Maybe, somehow, things would be all right after all.

Since Brad would be job-hunting, he and Cheryl hired a baby-sitter, nineteen-year-old Marnie O'Connor.* She was a very pretty girl and the little Cunningham boys liked her right away. Cheryl was glad to see that, and she was reassured by how dependable Marnie seemed to be. That was important, because she expected to be shuttling between Portland and Seattle over the next year or more. She would be working on a huge ongoing medical malpractice litigation until it was settled, and when she was in the Portland offices of Garvey, Schubert, she knew she might sometimes have to work seven days a week. Brad was the furthest thing from a househusband anyone could imagine. Even when he was unemployed, Cheryl couldn't count on him to stay with the boys. She had to have Marnie there or she would never have a moment's peace while she was away from her children.

Brad found a job in Oregon in the spring of 1985, and it was a position with no little prestige. He was hired to head the income property loan department of the Citizens' Savings and Loan Bank in Salem. He would have a private office, and three employees would report to him. Oregon's capital city is forty-seven miles south of Portland, a fairly easy commute along the I-5 freeway. Besides that, Brad would be going in the opposite direction from most commuters, so he could expect less than an hour's drive each way as he cruised along in one or the other Mercedes.

Citizens' Savings and Loan had hired a most impressive department manager. Brad dressed like a *GQ* model, his smile was wide and confident, and his résumé showed more than fifteen years of experience in one aspect of real estate or another. The Houston credits alone were imposing. He clearly knew income property, and he presented himself extremely well in his interviews. (Whether Brad mentioned his ongoing litigation in Texas or his bankruptcy filing is not known.)

The employees at Citizens' who reported directly to Brad were female. Even though he made no secret of the fact that he was a married man, it was obvious that he thoroughly enjoyed the company of women, and he was a pleasure to work for. He was compelling and dynamic, he drove fantastic cars, and he had an air of wealth about him – almost as if he didn't need to work at all but could have chosen to remain in the leisure class he had been born into. No one would ever have guessed the truth about the modest home where Sanford and Rosemary had raised Brad and his two sisters. No one would ever have suspected his Indian heritage.

Through plastic surgery, education, a certain natural savvy, and the liberal use of Cheryl's income, Brad had completely re-created himself. None of his coworkers at Citizens' knew, of course, that his cars, clothes, and money came not from his own labors but from his wife's. Cheryl worked harder and harder, but however much money she made, Brad always managed to spend more. 'If he brought home a pizza now and then,' Cheryl's sister recalled, 'he thought he was doing his part.'

Cheryl hoped that Brad's new job would help rebuild their financial base. After so many years when his only 'job' had been his dogged attention to the suit he had filed against the Texas construction company, they were both making good salaries. Understandably, Cheryl earned a great deal more than Brad, but had they pulled together, they would have rapidly been in good financial shape.

In truth, Brad's salary made no dent at all in their debts. He continued to overspend, buying whatever he wanted. Cheryl had paid all the household bills since 1983 – the rent, the utilities, the boys' baby-sitters and schools, the groceries – although she deferred to Brad's insistence that the accounts be listed in his name; he was, after all, the man of the family. He didn't want people to know that he was living off Cheryl.

Sometimes it seemed as if Brad spent money just to spend money, and Cheryl despaired of ever catching up, telling her sister Susan, 'Look at all this stuff,' gesturing toward the piles of 'toys' that Brad had bought and then left to gather dust. 'And I can't pay all the bills . . .'

'She resigned herself to debt,' Susan remembered. 'The garage in the Gresham house had four-wheelers, three-wheelers, water skis, jet skis, Brad's clothes, Brad's shoes. One time – and this makes me so sad now to remember it – Cheryl really needed some new underwear. Just some simple, plain underwear, and she didn't have enough money to buy it.'

It was ludicrous that she should be so laden down with debt. Due to transfers of other partners, when she moved to the Garvey, Schubert office in Portland, Cheryl became not only the most senior partner in that city but also an 'owner' of the firm, eligible for salary, profit sharing, and benefits. In 1986 her base salary was fifty thousand dollars. She was also awarded a merit bonus of forty-five hundred dollars, and on top of that she received benefits worth another 15 percent of her salary. She had been picked for the Portland office because of her leadership ability and because litigators traditionally bring more money into a firm, and Cheryl brought in more than her share. 'Cheryl was a business developer,' another partner commented. 'She represented Weyerhauser, for instance.'

In 1984 senior partner Gary Strauss attended a product liability trial involving formaldehyde ingestion. Cheryl gave her closing arguments after the others had all spoken. Strauss found her 'brilliant, poignant, awesome in a roomful of attorneys. The jury told her that afterward . . . that was the way a closing argument should be.' This pleased Strauss; he knew how embarrassed Cheryl had been about Brad's filing for bankruptcy and his constant litigation. 'She wasn't very happy about all the lawyers battling each other in Brad's suits,' he remembered. 'She had been hesitant even about accepting a partnership because of that.'

Even though Cheryl made Brad's standard of living possible, he complained when she had to stay in Seattle overnight – insinuating, as always, that she was sleeping with other men. Brad himself was seldom without female company. From puberty he had had his choice of women, and they always played by his rules. Now, living in Gresham, working in Salem, with Cheryl often gone overnight, Brad essentially lived the life of a single man.

It would be impossible to pinpoint whether he began his affair with the Cunningham baby-sister, nineteen-year-old Marnie O'Connor, or his liaison with Lilya Saarnen first. It would be a moot point anyway; Brad had always been adept at balancing a marriage and two – or more – affairs. There was no reason that Marnie and Lilya should ever meet.

Cheryl had no hint that Brad was sleeping with either of them.

Lilya Saarnen had worked at Citizens' Savings for four years when Brad took over as her supervisor. She found him tremendously attractive and very understanding. Lilya knew he was married, but that didn't bother her. Apparently his wife was so caught up in her career that she had little time for Brad. Although Lilya dressed like the complete career woman, Brad hadn't missed the long slow looks she gave him, or the way she 'accidentally' brushed against him as they were going over loan applications. He saw that Lilya was spectacularly attractive behind her horn-rimmed glasses and her loose clothes. She had perfectly aligned delicate features and long silky ash blond hair.

Careful not to be too obvious in the bank's offices, Brad and Lilya began a physical affair in the late summer of 1985. They would have an oddly connected relationship that lasted for a long time. While Lilya knew about his wife, she did not know he was also sleeping with his baby-sitter. Whether she had any long-term plans for Brad is questionable. Lilya was intelligent and pragmatic, and of all Brad's women, she may have seen beyond his complex and contrived facade early enough to steel her own emotional response. It is even possible that Lilya used Brad almost as much as he used most of the women in his life.

Lilya believed that Brad was very wealthy. She had every reason to. He seemed not only quite rich but munificent with his money. 'He was not overly generous,' she would say one day, with her usual understatement, 'but he was very supportive of the sad situation I was in.' And, indeed, there would come a time when Lilya needed more than flowers, fancy dinners, and lingerie. Although she was a young woman, her health was not good, and it deteriorated further shortly after she and Brad became intimate.

Nineteen eighty-five was an almost schizophrenic year for Cheryl. She loved her career, she adored her little boys, and she was finding wonderfully loyal friends in the Portland office of Garvey, Schubert. Along with her extended family, Cheryl's friends kept her going. Her marriage was little more than a sham. All the Pollyanna philosophizing in the world wasn't going to turn the home she and Brad had rented in

Gresham into anything more than an armed camp. Cheryl sometimes wondered why Brad stayed with her and the boys, but she must have suspected it was because she had become his 'cash cow.'

Cheryl could count on nothing; she walked through her days awaiting the next assault, teetering emotionally on the edge of some precipice from which she might never escape. Brad still pulled his 'move furniture out, move furniture in' games, but by the fall of 1985 he didn't take just 'his' furniture, he took Cheryl's too. There was something ultimately demoralizing about coming home to a house emptied of its furniture, to see the dents in the carpet where couches and chairs and televisions should have been, to watch dust bunnies drifting lazily across bare floors when a door was opened.

By mutual agreement, Brad and Cheryl had enrolled Jess and Michael in the Franciscan Montessori Earth School, administered by Mother Francene Cardeux. It was an excellent and much sought-after school in Portland, with a philosophy that nurtured and encouraged creativity and independence in children. Exceptionally intelligent children like the Cunningham boys thrived in the Montessori atmosphere.

Mother Francene was a serene presence, but in no way a cloistered nun; in her many years of experience in running the Montessori school she had seen all manner of problems with parents and children and dealt with them competently and tactfully. She had, however, seen nothing like the bitterness between Brad and Cheryl. Every encounter with them was unpleasant.

Early in the 1985–86 school year, Mother Francene was informed of an altercation in the hallway; the Cunninghams were arguing loudly outside the secretary's office. She was grateful their children didn't observe that fight, but Mother Francene was appalled at one volatile argument that did take place in front of Jess and Michael. The boys had been waiting for someone to pick them up after school, two lonely little figures clinging together as they watched the other children leave the school one by one until they were the last ones left. 'Day-care children were to be picked up by six-fifteen P.M.,' Mother Francene recalled, and the school set a dollar-a-minute penalty for late pickups, more to protect the children than to add to the school's budget. One day 'no one came for the Cunningham boys.'

Eventually, both Brad and Cheryl showed up, and each blamed the other for failing to pick up Jess and Michael on time. 'He was very angry. She was quieter, saying to him, "You were responsible,"' Mother Francene said with a shudder. 'I just remember I didn't want to be there. I was embarrassed. The *boys* were embarrassed – and agitated. They wanted their parents to leave.'

More and more Jess, Michael, and to a lesser extent Phillip were pulled in two directions like stretchy Silly Putty figures. Their mother wanted desperately to protect them and give them a secure world; their father used them to harass their mother. And the boys were the most vulnerable part of Cheryl's life. She could face anything – *anything* – but losing them.

The product liability cases that drew Cheryl back to Seattle on an almost weekly basis had begun in the late spring of 1985. Garvey, Schubert represented a company that had manufactured an artificial heart valve. The attorney Cheryl faced in litigating sessions, who represented patients whose heart valves had allegedly malfunctioned, was Jim Griswold, onetime president of the Oregon Trial Lawyers' Association.

Griswold described such litigation as 'a very difficult kind of case.' Cheryl and her co-counsel, John Allison, practically had to take a course in cardiovascular surgery in order to defend their clients. Griswold had come up against hundreds of defense litigators: he had been in practice for four decades. When he was later asked to describe Cheryl Keeton, he paused, searching for words.

'Excellent. Outstanding wouldn't cover it. She was intense, professional. She always knew what she was doing. She always knew where she was going. . . . She was never thrown off.' At one time, Griswold was on a committee to compile a list of attorneys to be recommended to the Oregon governor for judgeships. Cheryl was on that list, termed 'highly qualified.'

Cheryl opposed Griswold in the artificial heart valve litigation for a year and a half, and as far as he could see, she was never less than an extremely competent lawyer. Whatever emotions might have been churning inside, Cheryl kept them there. Later, Griswold would be amazed to learn what her private life had been like. Cheryl always managed to keep her personal and professional life separated. Drawing on some deep inner strength, she was holding herself together with brains, guts, hope, and her love for her three sons. But with every passing day, her situation was becoming more and more unbearable.

23

In the fall of 1985 Cheryl's sister Susan was living in Seattle, working toward a degree in sociology at the University of Washington. Her apartment there was always available to Cheryl when she had to be in Seattle on business for Garvey, Schubert. She had her own key, and she averaged one visit a month. Occasionally she could even prevail upon Brad to bring the boys up so they could all be together. She missed them so much.

Sometimes Susan was there; sometimes the apartment was empty. Since Susan's fiancé, Dave Keegan, was in Longview and she often went to see him, Cheryl was occasionally alone in Susan's apartment. But more often they were there together. They were both grown women now and were friends as well as sisters.

That fall of 1985 was the first time Brad explicitly accused Cheryl of having extramarital affairs, and once he had begun, he continually railed at her about her alleged infidelity. It is an all too common ploy for a man who is cheating to defuse suspicion by accusing his wife of what he himself is doing. And it is quite possible that Cheryl did have one or two fleeting relationships with other men late in 1985 and early in 1986. Who could have blamed her? 'The police asked me about it later,' Susan recalled, 'and I told them I didn't know if Cheryl was seeing other men or not, but I told them I hoped she was. She needed someone in her life who made her happy, someone who cared about her. . . . She knew that Brad was cheating on her; she'd known it for a long time, but I think she tried to look away from that. She tried not to think about it.'

Cheryl was a beautiful woman, only thirty-five, and she still drew attention from men. Her years with Brad had well nigh obliterated her self-esteem. When the men she worked with occasionally complimented her, she almost looked around to see whom they were talking about. The experience of having a man actually treat her well, tell her positive things, even hold her with tenderness, was something she had forgotten.

Cheryl was a vulnerable woman and terribly sad. All of her successes in courtrooms and in boardrooms faded when she realized how alone she was. She was married, but her husband didn't love her. Beyond her value as a wage earner, she had become a mere convenience, an irritant. If she had an affair or two, they were brief and born of desperate loneliness rather than passion.

If she had an affair, Susan didn't know about it. She smiled as she remembered a time in the late summer of 1985. 'Cheryl was in Seattle and stayed with me. We went to the Red Robin [a popular upmarket Seattle hamburger restaurant] and we both ordered margaritas. We were having fun. I was in college by then. Then we went to the Red Onion, down by Madison Park. These two guys came over to our table, and they were coming on to us. Cheryl just winked at me. All of a sudden, one of the guys looked close at Cheryl and he said, "You're wearing married lipstick."

'Cheryl laughed and said, "Well, I guess that's it. I'm not changing shades anytime soon."'

Cheryl hadn't taken the men seriously, and Susan knew it. 'Cheryl was responsible. Brad was the first dangerous thing she ever did. She was embarrassed that she was pregnant when she married him. She didn't tell anyone in the family that she was pregnant until she was five months.'

Brad saw accusations of infidelity as a way to harass and humiliate his wife. Smugly, armed with the names of two men he believed Cheryl had been intimate with, he embarked on a tell-all campaign that he felt sure would ruin Cheryl's career.

He first called the wife of a senior partner at Garvey, Schubert and told her that Cheryl had slept with her husband. It may have been true; it may not. Either way, the wife's reaction was not what Brad had expected. She was not hysterical nor was she grateful to Brad for his report. With impeccable class, she called Cheryl and asked her to convey a message to her husband. 'Just tell him that I don't care to talk to him for several days. He'll understand.' Mortified – and puzzled – Cheryl passed on the message.

Annoyed that his sabotage hadn't worked, Brad went a step further. He contacted Stuart Hennessey, who had worked with Cheryl in Seattle, and invited him out for a drink in the bar at the Alexis Hotel near the Garvey, Schubert offices. Hennessey would remember the encounter as a 'weird experience.' Brad told him that he and Cheryl were separated and quickly went on to give Hennessey offensive details about Cheryl's supposed promiscuity. Hennessey stared back at him, disbelieving and disgusted.

'Then he asked how the firm was doing,' Hennessey recalled. 'And he asked how much money I made.'

What Brad really wanted to know, of course, was how much money Cheryl was making and how much her retirement fund was worth. Hennessey stood up to leave and told Brad he didn't want to discuss it – that was private information. He left Brad sitting with two untouched drinks while he went back to his office, shaking his head in shock at Brad's gall and crudeness. Hennessey called Cheryl to alert her to what Brad was saying. 'Cheryl was a strong person,' he said, 'but she was crying. She said, "Stu, he's trying to ruin me."' Hennessey didn't know how to help her, beyond telling her that her friends were behind her and wouldn't believe Brad's lies.

Neither reaction was what Brad had expected, and for the moment he was thrown off stride. He resented Cheryl's independence and success. He had hoped to humiliate her and ruin her career. She was humiliated, but her job was never in danger. She was also puzzled. If Brad had succeeded in getting her fired, who did he think was going to support them? It was her salary that kept them afloat. She had seen him do this before – act out of rage, and spite himself in the process. Cheryl was horribly embarrassed by Brad's vicious lies, but she held her head up and her career never missed a beat.

Even so, Susan could see that the enmity in Cheryl's relationship with Brad was intensifying. And as it did, she saw, too, that the essence that was Cheryl had begun, finally, to disintegrate. As water eventually erodes stone after an eon of continual dripping, Brad's relentless siege against Cheryl was working its devastation. She had been so strong for so long. But now she was growing thinner and thinner, toying with her food and only pretending to eat. Still, through sheer force of will, she was able to compartmentalize her life so that she could concentrate on her work and take care of her boys.

24

Brad's affair with Lilya Saarnen had continued, even as he pointed accusing fingers at Cheryl. In late fall Lilya was told that she needed a kidney transplant. Brad was tremendously solicitous, so much so that he offered to pay her medical bills. He gave her four thousand dollars. She had the transplant operation on November 28, 1985, and testifying in a legal hearing some time later, Lilya had difficulty remembering if Brad had actually paid for her surgery. Staring into Brad's dark eyes from her position on the witness chair, she equivocated. She *thought* that their affair had lasted somewhere between six months and a year. She couldn't really remember.

Lilya did remember that Brad had paid the rent on her apartment in the Madison Tower for some time. Although her ground-floor unit wasn't as expensive as the eighteenth-floor apartment he would soon rent, it wasn't cheap either. But if Brad proved to be a friend in need, his passion for Lilya faded after her surgery. The immunosuppressant medicine she had to take had side effects that repulsed Brad. 'She grew facial hair and that turned me off,' he said later.

And so Lilya had gone on to her relationship with Dr Clay Watson, the surgeon at Providence, although she remained in her apartment at the Madison Tower until late fall of 1986. Earlier that year she had introduced Brad to Dr Sara Gordon, and apparently there were no hard feelings. Lilya and Brad were like dancers who changed partners when the song changed. Lilya did seem a little chagrined, however, when she later learned that Brad was having an affair with Marnie, his teenage baby-sitter, at the same time he was sleeping with her.

Lilya had first known Brad in Salem when he was hired by Citizens' Savings. And then Brad, Lilya, a secretary, and a young lawyer named Karen Aaborg* were transferred to the Lake Oswego branch of the bank. Karen would later testify that federal bank examiners had questioned the Lake Oswego books; the branch's president and most of its directors had been summarily fired, and Brad was elevated to a position of extreme trust as he and his three female assistants evaluated the extent of the damage. They soon suspected that they would only be tidying up loose ends and closing the branch down. It was doubtful that the commercial loan division in Lake Oswego was going to survive. But as long as the branch was still open, Brad was the boss.

He was also a sultan with his own little harem. Brad had scarcely ended his affair with Lilya when he became very close to Karen Aaborg. Another man might have felt ill at ease working in the same small office as two of his girlfriends, but it didn't bother Brad. Lilya was aware that her ex-lover was engaged in daily disputes with his wife. Karen was not – at least for a time. When she first went to work for Brad, she knew almost nothing about his personal life.

Brad had hired Karen to work for him in Salem in the summer of 1985. She was very young, barely out of law school, and she was Brad's type: small, attractive, slender, smart. He liked blond or light brown hair and pretty, small-featured faces. At the bank her title was 'Loan Closer,' and later Brad chose her to go with him and Lilya to close the Lake Oswego branch. To Karen's somewhat naive eye, Brad seemed happily married when she first went to work for him. 'It seemed to change rather rapidly,' she recalled. It wasn't long before Karen suspected that Brad and Lilya had had a physical relationship, but she wasn't positive. It was just something in the way they exchanged glances, and the sentences they left unfinished when she walked into an office where they were. She found out later that she had been right.

Brad told Karen even more about his personal life. Although he had not told Lilya, he was quite open with Karen about his affair with his sons' baby-sitter. 'Cheryl doesn't know,' he said, grinning. 'We did it at my house when the kids were napping and Cheryl was at work.' But he lied to Karen when he said his liaison with his nineteen-year-old baby-sitter was not a long-running affair. 'Cheryl was working, and I wasn't. That was before I came to Citizens'.'

Karen soon saw – or rather heard – that the Cunninghams' marriage was not a happy one. Cheryl often called the Lake Oswego branch of Citizens' and Karen could tell from Brad's reaction that he was 'pretty upset. . . . He would slam the phone down . . . there was a lot of anger.' Indeed, there was more rage surfacing in Brad than Karen could ever remember seeing. In his business world he was always in control, completely charming and affable. Whatever he and his wife were fighting over, Karen was shocked by the violence involved. Brad seemed to truly hate Cheryl, and although Karen couldn't hear the other end of the conversation, she appeared to hate him too.

Nevertheless, the phone scenes she overheard didn't diminish Brad's charisma for the young attorney. It was easier for her to feel a little sorry for him; his wife seemed to be a ranting shrew. Except in his phone conversations with Cheryl, Brad always struck Karen as such a nice guy.

Karen sometimes went to a Portland tavern called Goose Hollow and one evening she ran into Brad there. They played Scrabble, apparently a passion for him, and then he took her back to her apartment. In his version of their affair, he would recall that they had sex there for the first time. She would insist, however, that she was never actually intimate with Brad until after he left the bank they both worked for. And even then, she estimated that their affair had lasted only three or four months. Their friendship, however, continued.

It was odd. Brad's wives all eventually came to hate his guts; his mistresses remained in his stable of friends. Estranged and former wives became prey and stalking targets; mistresses were allowed to walk away.

Brad never let up on his campaign to destroy Cheryl. Along with his other accusations in late 1985 and early 1986, he complained that he had contracted chlamydia from her. Technically at least, chlamydia is a venereal disease, an infection usually transmitted through sexual intercourse. Righteously indignant, Brad obtained two prescriptions to treat himself.

Why Brad insisted that Cheryl was the source of his infection is anyone's guess, given the fact that he was having sexual intercourse with a number of other women. But then, Brad now blamed Cheryl for all bad things that happened to him. He no longer wanted her by 1985, but he would not simply let her go. He accused her continually of being unfaithful, but he didn't tell her about his sexually transmitted infection, whatever its origin, and give her a chance to seek treatment. Indeed, it wasn't until February 3, 1986, when Cheryl began to suffer symptoms herself, that she went to see her own doctor. She learned that she had contracted vaginitis.

A painful infection of the vaginal tissues, vaginitis has many causes. It can be transmitted through sexual contact, but it can occur just as often when a woman is treated for flu or a sore throat with antibiotics which tend to kill the protective bacteria always present in the vagina. A virgin can contract vaginitis. Both men and women can carry the infection and show no overt symptoms at all. Cheryl also tested positively for chlamydia. If she had, in fact, been the source of Brad's infection, she apparently went many weeks without symptoms after Brad had sought medical treatment.

* * *

In those first months of 1986 Susan sensed that something in her sister's marriage was going to explode. Maybe Cheryl could hide her growing anxiety from her fellow attorneys, but she couldn't hide it from Susan, who noticed that she jumped every time the phone rang in her Seattle apartment.

Susan couldn't hear Brad's side of their conversations, but she could tell he was always furious about something from the stricken look on Cheryl's pale face. Although it had been more than eight years since Susan had accompanied Brad and Cheryl on the frightening sailing trip to the San Juans, she again felt the same sense of dread. This wasn't the Cheryl she knew. The woman who could be instantly reduced to hysterical tears by a telephone call was not the real Cheryl, the Cheryl who never gave up, who never lost her confidence.

Except with Brad. And now Brad had hostages: he had Jess, Michael, and Phillip. And Cheryl had a new fear. She confided to Susan that she was afraid that one day she would go home and find not just her furniture missing but her children too.

Susan had seen the way Brad disciplined his sons, despite Cheryl's desperate attempts to stop him. If they were out for dinner and one of the boys did something Brad considered inappropriate – like not eating all his food, or sulking, or crying – he would only say ominously that he'd take care of it. 'Cheryl would try to protect the kids,' Susan said. 'She'd say, "He's tired" or "He's hungry" or "He just woke up from a nap," but Brad wouldn't listen to her. The boys knew that they would get "swats" when they got home. Very matter-of-factly, he'd tote up the swats. Jess would get two because he was the oldest. They knew they were going to get hit.

'Brad created an atmosphere of fear. They were obedient to the point that it was unnatural. They called him "Dad" – never "Daddy." Those kids were his possessions. Brad gets whatever he wants. He wanted children and he wanted boys. Those boys were like another Mercedes to him.'

Cheryl's struggles became so difficult that Susan began keeping a diary. On February 1, 1986, she noted that Cheryl had had to be in Seattle overnight many times in a three- or four-week period during January. She got so lonely for Jess, Michael, and Phillip that she asked her law firm for permission to bring her family up. They agreed and, somewhat uncharacteristically, so did Brad. He came up on the train with the boys. Susan offered to baby-sit on Saturday night, and Brad and Cheryl went out for dinner.

Things seemed to be calm enough when Brad left for home on Sunday night, even though he was clearly annoyed that Cheryl had to stay in Seattle until the following Wednesday. But in reality the situation had not been defused at all. Brad started calling Cheryl almost from the moment he arrived in Gresham, as if he had been quietly fuming on the four-hour train ride home. Susan remembered seven or eight calls. 'Cheryl was very upset. She was crying and yelling – trying to speak, and she couldn't. She cried so hard that she couldn't speak. It was so out of character for her. I begged her not to answer the phone when it rang – and he called all night – but she answered.'

Brad could destroy Cheryl even over the phone. As Susan listened, Cheryl began to scream and shout hysterically. 'No! That's not true! No! I didn't do that. I didn't do that. . . . You're lying to me.'

'Are you okay?' Susan whispered.

'Everything's going to be all right,' Cheryl replied, covering the phone with her hand. But Susan saw she didn't believe her own words. She wrote in her diary on February 3, 1986, 'All hell broke loose last night and this morning. Brad and Cheryl fought, and I mean at the top of their lungs. . . . It's very clear what she needs to do.' What Cheryl had to do was get out of her marriage before she lost her equilibrium, her sanity, her self.

One afternoon Cheryl got a letter from Brad marked

CONFIDENTIAL. She read it without comment and set it down, but when she left the room, Susan's curiosity got the better of her. 'The letter said that yes, Brad had had an affair with their former baby-sitter – but Marnie O'Connor didn't want him to tell anyone because her boyfriend and her mother might find out about it.'

Susan wasn't surprised. 'The guest-room bed was always mussed up in that Gresham house. And Brad had a dead-bolt lock put on that door. He was always saying, "Marnie likes to take naps during the day." He didn't even try to hide what was going on from Cheryl.' Cheryl wasn't surprised by Brad's 'confidential letter' either. It didn't matter any longer.

On Tuesday, February 5, Cheryl seemed strangely calm and resolute. She didn't tell Susan about her visit to the doctor in Bellevue, where she had learned she was suffering from vaginal infections. She was humiliated. That diagnosis may have been the final straw. She told Susan only, 'Everything's settled today. I'm going back to Portland.'

'I was relieved,' Susan admitted. 'My neighbors within a two-block radius could have heard their phone conversations. I was relieved she was gone.' Later, of course, she would rue her feelings.

Cheryl found an empty house when she arrived in Gresham. Brad had moved all the furniture out again and, at first, Cheryl was exasperated with Rose,* their current baby-sitter. But Susan reminded her when she called, 'You know that Rose couldn't stop him. No one can stop Brad when he has his mind set on doing something.'

A few days after Cheryl left Susan's apartment, she called to say she had finally acknowledged there was no hope at all for her marriage. She wanted only to have Brad completely out of her life, although she didn't want her three boys to lose their father. There had to be some way for her and Brad to share custody. She could bear to see him that much, she supposed, just long enough for him to pick up the boys or deliver them back to her.

* * *

In Seattle and Portland that February of 1986, there were breaks in the winter rains, the pussy willows budded out, and crocuses sprang from an earth no longer chained by winter. It was a season of hope and starting over, and it almost seemed as if Brad and Cheryl could separate without rancor. If they could somehow share Jess, Michael, and Phillip, they had nothing left to fight over.

'I was glad,' Susan recalled, 'that she was going to get a divorce. She just wasn't Cheryl anymore. For her own health and well-being, I was glad they were splitting up. . . . Their marriage started out relatively normal on the surface, but somehow people were always uncomfortable around them as a couple.'

When Cheryl asked Brad to move out, he went – uncharacteristically without a fight. He found himself an expensive apartment on the fourteenth floor of the Madison Tower, then moved to an even more expensive one on the eighteenth floor. That didn't surprise Cheryl. Even though the place cost almost twice as much as the house their whole family had rented, she knew Brad; he always wanted the best for himself. She didn't care if he rented the Taj Mahal as long as he was gone.

25

Cheryl had hoped that having Brad out of her home would bring some modicum of peace into her life. And it was true that when he finally moved out, he stopped playing 'musical chairs' with the furniture. But Cheryl was still saddled with all his debts.

Just before their separation Brad had bought himself a huge, exotic, and expensive motorcycle, a Huskvarna. It was a racing bike, absolutely 'top of the line.' Brad wasn't a motorcycle racer, and he kept the Huskvarna in the garage, unused. Cheryl begged him to sell it, along with other costly 'toys' he had purchased and never used. She was desperately worried about money. Each week she felt she was deeper in debt.

Cheryl called Susan on February 28, and Susan could hear new panic in her voice. 'Brad's not going to be reasonable about sharing custody after all,' Cheryl said. 'He told me he's going to fight me for the kids. He's been telling everyone I'm a nymphomaniac – he's trying to tear me apart. I need you to stand up for me.'

Susan assured Cheryl that she would be there for her, and tried to tell her not to worry about Brad's threats and lies. Brad had always been that way; nothing had really changed. But that was the problem. Even though they were now separated, he still had the power to send Cheryl into an emotional tailspin. It took every ounce of her strength to keep him at bay, and every time she felt a little thrill of hope, something happened to dash it. She and Brad made an uneasy truce in March and worked out a tentative agreement about their children. Brad would have their little boys from 7 P.M. on Friday until 7 P.M. on Sunday. The divorce itself lay ahead.

Brad, who always fortified himself with lawyers, had already consulted his own attorney of the moment, Jake Tanzer, who would be only the first of three lawyers he hired and dismissed during his divorce proceedings. Tanzer was a highly respected Oregon attorney who had been at various times a deputy D.A. in Multnomah County, a Court of Appeals judge, the Solicitor General of Oregon, and an Oregon Supreme Court justice. He was in private practice in 1986, but he was not a divorce attorney. He told Brad that he could find himself an attorney who was fully versed in divorce litigation, and at less than half the price. But Brad wanted Jake Tanzer. Brad's charm and convincing ways extended even to lawyers, and there would be many who were chagrined that they had ever met him. Few were ever paid.

Cheryl knew that getting out of her marriage wasn't going to be easy. And she was fully aware that gaining custody of Jess, Michael, and Phillip would be even harder. Every time there was a period of relative calm between her and Brad, she kept waiting for the other shoe to drop. For years she had had fear systematically implanted in her mind like tiny grains of radioactive material, so many little glowing seeds that being frightened was almost normal for her. Cheryl was afraid of the 'enemies' that Brad talked about, of the assassins who were out to get him and his family since he brought his suits against the Houston firms he blamed for his financial downfall. But now, finally, she feared Brad himself more. She had never seen the invisible killers; she *had* seen Brad in a rage.

Things began to happen, small but ominous things. In March, Cheryl was convinced that someone had tinkered with her Toyota van. She was almost afraid to drive it. The brakes seemed mushy, and it had suddenly begun to die in traffic for no reason at all. She got it to a garage where a mechanic said someone had messed up her carburetor so that the mixture of gas and air was way off. She asked Brad for all of the Toyota keys, but he never gave them back to her.

Brad had the tires for her van; he had stored them when he put snow tires on the van the previous fall. In Oregon, studded snow tires have to be replaced with regular tires by April 1. That date was rapidly approaching and she needed her almost-new tires back. She didn't have the four hundred dollars it would take to replace them. And she didn't have the money to pay the fine she would get if she kept driving on snow tires after the cutoff date. She called Brad several times, asking that he bring back her tires. Brad returned her calls and spoke with her secretary or her legal assistant, and he was more than charming. But when Cheryl came on the line, his voice changed to a venomous pitch. He was much too busy to bother with her tires and would she get off his back?

Ironically for a lawyer, Cheryl had scarcely any money for legal help in her divorce. In the early spring she retained the best – on the understanding that she would obtain her divorce 'on a shoestring budget': Cheryl herself would do as much of the legwork as she could. The woman she retained was one of the finest family-law attorneys in Portland, Elizabeth Welch.

'Betsy' Welch had graduated from the University of Chicago Law School and worked for the American Bar Association for some years after graduation. When she moved to Portland, she became a deputy district attorney in the Multnomah County Juvenile Court, specializing in child neglect and abuse and in the termination of parental rights. She worked for five years as the administrative assistant to Neil Goldschmidt, the mayor of Portland. Then she was appointed a Circuit Court judge. When she lost an election, she returned to private practice where she specialized, as always, in children – the rights of children, and the untangling of the traumatic situations in which husbands, wives, and children often found themselves. By 1991 she would once again be a judge – a District Court judge in Multnomah County.

Elizabeth Welch was the perfect lawyer for Cheryl: she was kind, she was smart, and she was a fighter. She also had a wonderful sense of humor, but that was not something she would be called upon to use. The early days after Brad moved out had been, as Cheryl feared, only deceptively calm. He was now gathering a head of steam and was preparing to roll over her, just as he had flattened every one of his other wives. From this point on, every issue, every procedure, every hearing, every order was marked by delay, fights, and tugs-of-war.

The divorce should not have been that difficult. The only issue to be decided was child custody. There was no money to fight over: Brad had his ongoing bankruptcy action in

Seattle, and Cheryl could barely keep her head above water financially. No, they were fighting over Jess, Michael, and Phillip. And Brad knew full well this was the one area where he could terrorize Cheryl.

'This case was at the upper end of the acrimony scale,' Betsy Welch would recall, 'probably as high as any I have ever been involved in. Both of the people were very bright . . . very strong-minded. . . . Nothing ever went through easily. *Nothing*. . . . Every single issue was disputed . . . nothing could be resolved amicably.'

Welch tried to count up the number of court appearances in the divorce and had difficulty doing so. Whatever the judge decided, the orders always had to be redone over and over. Brad fought Cheryl over day-care, schools, support payments, everything she wanted and needed for the boys.

It was ugly.

During that awful spring of 1986, Brad waged a relentless paper war against Cheryl. He flooded her with letters, typed in perfect business form:

Dear Cheryl,

Enclosed is a photocopy of my recent statement from Texaco. I have paid this bill in full. I would appreciate your reimbursing me $40.91 for your personal and business use. Together with the Mobil card use, you owe me $107.85. . . .

Dear Cheryl,

Please accept this letter as my written request to have you return to me all my framed photographs from your office that were mine prior to our marriage. If you insist on keeping these, you may purchase them from me for $210.00. Please advise. . . .

Dear Cheryl,

. . . after the court order I returned to you each and every item I had (the keys to our Toyota van, the house keys.) I

> thought I had the garage door control, in fact I thought it was last seen in Phillip's diaper bag. I said I would replace the control if you could not find it. I will not pay to have the garage door control unit reprogrammed. Further, in the event you are planning to have the house door locks re-keyed, do not plan on me paying for that either. . . .
>
> Dear Cheryl, . . . I will attempt to work with you on getting the regular tires on the van. However, I would appreciate your returning my snow tires as soon as possible.

Brad's letters to Cheryl were quite civil on the surface, but the veneer was thin. They piled into her home, sometimes several a day. There were scores of them. He signed them 'Cordially,' or 'Thank You,' or 'Sincerely.'

Brad fought desperately to wrest whatever he could from Cheryl. He attempted to get the thousand-dollar damage deposit for the Gresham rental. He insisted that he had paid the deposit from 'my separate funds.' Since Cheryl had been supporting the family for two years at that point, that claim was questionable. The landlords finally wrote to Brad's attorney and said they were writing a one-thousand-dollar check to *both* Brad and Cheryl. 'If one tries to cash it without the other, then a crime has been committed!'

Cheryl asked again for the return of 'the four standard tires with rims for Toyota Van so I can replace the studded tires on the van by April 1.' Then one day her assistant said cheerfully, 'Your husband called and said you didn't have to worry about your tires anymore – he said he took care of them.' Cheryl was relieved – until she went down to the parking area of Garvey, Schubert and found all four of the studded tires on her van had been slashed. They had, indeed, been 'taken care of.'

Within a very few days after Cheryl hired Betsy Welch and even before Welch could file the necessary documents for her divorce, Cheryl called her, very upset, and said that Brad had announced he would be moving back in with her

– at his attorney's suggestion. As a general rule, that was good advice, and Welch knew it. There is no rule or law that says a spouse who has moved out of the home cannot move back in. In child custody cases, the parent who moves out acknowledges that the parent left behind with the children is providing acceptable care. In a disputed custody, this gives the parent who remains the upper hand.

Brad had lost too many custody battles. Even Loni Ann, whom he had seen as the weakest link in his chain of women, had prevailed in court and had been awarded Kait and Brent. Lauren had controlled his visits with Amy. He had let his first three children go, finally, because he had Jess, Michael, and Phillip – three bright, handsome sons who looked so much like himself. He was not about to let Cheryl have them. They were his trophies, his prizes. They reflected his boundless ego, miniature versions of himself who would validate his manhood, his potency, and his power.

Betsy Welch immediately called Brad's current lawyer and explained why she felt it would be a fruitless and emotionally damaging move for Brad to return to Cheryl's Gresham house. But Brad did exactly what he had threatened to do. When Cheryl got home from work on the Friday evening of a long holiday weekend, she found him in her bedroom. She was horrified, and she was angry, but she was helpless to get him out. Betsy Welch could not go into court until Tuesday morning to ask for an order to remove Brad. Cheryl knew he wasn't there for anything more than to reestablish his legal beachhead. 'It was a very long, confrontive, unpleasant weekend,' Welch recalled.

Cheryl asked him to go, but Brad refused to budge. At one point, he took Jess with him and locked them both in the master bedroom for hours. He would not allow Cheryl in to get her clothes, her makeup, or anything else she needed. The boys were frantic, Cheryl was frantic, but Brad stayed put, as if he had never left his 'home' at all. Although the house had six bedrooms, Cheryl slept on the couch in the recreation room so that she could watch the stairs from the master bedroom; she was afraid Brad might leave with the boys.

It was a ghastly three days, and Cheryl wondered hopelessly if Brad actually intended to take up their sham of a marriage. He acted as if he was home again for good, and the thought was almost more than she could bear. Knowing that he would listen in to all her phone calls on the bedroom extension, she nevertheless called her mother. Trapped in the house with Brad, she had to have someone to talk to. As they discussed the situation, Betty made a bad joke about ways to get rid of Brad. 'Maybe we should just poison him,' she said. 'I think I read someplace that a woman did that to an abusive husband, and they let her go . . .'

Neither mother nor daughter realized what a devastating impact their conversation would have on Brad. He looked at everything from his own point of view – the point of view of a man who had virtually no sense of humor, who believed that the end (his end) justified the means (any means), and who considered women spawn of the devil.

26

Even though Brad had told her that he had to spend the weekend with his sons, Dr Sara Gordon was blissfully happy, delighted with the new man in her life. She had no idea of the hell Cheryl Keeton was living in. Brad seemed to Sara to be very kind, very honest, and quite remarkable. Often she marveled at her good fortune in finding such a man. Within weeks of their meeting, she was as anxious as he to have his divorce finalized. She was just as concerned as he was about his poor children who had to spend so much time with the woman Brad had described to her as a slut and an incompetent mother. She knew that Brad was only doing what he had to do to save his sons.

Of course, Brad had never intended to leave Sara or the comforts of his new apartment permanently. Once he had proven that he could move back in anytime he pleased, he left Cheryl's house and returned to the Madison Tower.

Both of them aware of the inflammatory possibilities in the divorce action they were handling, Jake Tanzer and Betsy Welch worked together to find the best solution not only for Cheryl and Brad but especially for Jess, Michael, and Phillip. Apparently, each of the parents loved the boys, and the opposing attorneys hoped that a psychologist could help establish which of the dueling parents – if either, and if not both – should have custody of their sons. They needed to know who was the 'primary' parent. Where would the little boys fare better? With their mother? With their father?

Tanzer suggested to Betsy Welch that they contact an expert who was not under the aegis of the family court to be sure they had the most unbiased evaluation possible. Dr Russell Sardo, quite probably the leading clinical psychologist in the family counseling field in the Portland area in the mid-eighties, agreed to consult. He would attempt to establish whether Brad or Cheryl was the primary parent. Dr Sardo would talk to each of them separately, administer the MMPI (the Minnesota Multiphasic Personality Inventory) to both, and then visit with Jess, Michael, and Phillip and hope to get a fix on the family dynamics. After extensive testing and multiple interviews, Sardo would then deliver copies of his report to Jake Tanzer and Betsy Welch.

Dr Sardo spoke first with Brad, on March 23, 1986, and found him very verbal and quite comfortable in communicating. His body posture was relaxed – as if he were a man whose career had been full of high-powered meetings, as, indeed, it had been. Brad explained to Dr Sardo that he and

Cheryl had been married for six years and separated for one month.

'I am the children's primary parent – I always have been,' Brad said with assurance. 'My wife loves the children very much, but I don't think she *likes* them. She is not a natural parent; the children were *my* idea.' Brad stressed that he had been the one who longed to have children in their home, while Cheryl had always seen her legal career as her main goal in life. Although he assumed that Cheryl's profession would equip her to be a superior litigator and make her a trained negotiator, Dr Sardo wondered if he might not be speaking to the 'skilled negotiator' of this family.

Brad was very glib and dynamic. And his description of Cheryl's parenting abilities was devastating. He told Sardo that she was not a nurturer, she had no patience, she was 'overreactive and loses control,' and she was critical and condemning when dealing with her small sons. He said that Cheryl often yelled at the boys, calling them 'fuckers' and 'little assholes.'

Cheryl's career took precedence over everything else in her life, according to Brad. She was always gone and it was his perception that Cheryl found it very difficult even to be around the children – unless, of course, she had someone to help her care for them. Brad sighed as he told Sardo that Cheryl just didn't have the inclination or the skills to cope with the complete care of Jess, Michael, and Phillip.

'Perhaps "hedonistic" would describe Cheryl,' Brad said. And he went on to describe her as 'a very sexual person' who had been 'promiscuous.' Dr Sardo listened quietly now as the man sitting in his office tried to wipe out his wife with words. The Cheryl Keeton that Brad sketched sounded, indeed, like a selfish, dissolute woman who wouldn't be a good mother for any child. But Sardo had listened to a thousand couples argue over their children, and he had long ago learned to reserve judgment until he had heard both principals out.

Smiling expansively, Brad went on to say that he, on the

other hand, had been absolutely faithful in his marriage. As remote as such a possibility might be, he said he actually hoped for a reconciliation. He wanted nothing more than to be back with Cheryl and his children in a solid family unit. It had always been Cheryl who wanted the divorce. He felt, further, that she was seeking custody of their three boys not because she wanted them, but 'because she is combative.'

Sardo was a little bemused by Brad. He was, at the very least, a very complicated man. Sardo found him quite intelligent and sophisticated, and yet he caught inconsistencies in Brad's statements, jarring discrepancies that a man of his obvious brilliance should have noted and censored before they ever passed his lips. Although Brad had stressed early in the interview how scrupulously faithful he had been throughout his marriage, he suddenly reversed himself and described a period when he and Cheryl had had an 'open marriage.' During this time, Brad admitted, he had had an affair with their nineteen-year-old baby-sitter. It hadn't lasted too long, and he had told Cheryl about it.

'And how did she react?'

'We still kept her as our baby-sitter for months after that,' Brad replied.

Sardo's expression betrayed none of his private thoughts, gave no hint of the weighing and evaluating of information that was going on in his mind. Brad plunged ahead, figuratively tearing Cheryl apart so that she seemed to be a woman with no virtues whatsoever – beyond intelligence and a vigorous work ethic.

Early on, Brad had described himself as the 'primary parent.' But now he recalled that he had begun that role only after his business reverses. 'My bankruptcy changed me – almost destroyed me. . . . I concluded that a career and money are just not that important and that my primary commitment to the children [takes precedence]. . . . I will not work more than forty hours a week now.'

So, Sardo realized, Brad had *not* been the primary parent until the last year or so – if at all. His subject continued to talk volubly. A few moments later, Brad reversed himself again and said he had a job offer from U.S. Bank that he intended to accept, although he would also keep his current job. Sardo noted that Brad seemed unaware that a second job would mean he would be working far more than forty hours a week, and that there would be little, if any, time left for his sons. How, then, could Brad be the primary parent? Sardo didn't ask the question aloud. And Brad still hadn't recognized the rampant inconsistencies in his statements.

Brad had, of course, fathered a number of children, and he listed his offspring from his three previous marriages. Brent, who was fifteen, was currently living with him. With intense feeling in his voice, Brad recalled his deep concern about Brent and Kait when they were young. He said he had begged their mother to change her 'hippie' lifestyle – for the children's sake. He had been upset at the idea of his two little children being raised in the laissez-faire ambiance of 'a commune.'

Brad admitted he had married his second wife only because he needed to be married so he could fight for custody of Brent and Kait. He always had done, and always would do, whatever he had to to make sure his children were in the safest environment possible. When the judge in his first custody hearing ruled against him, he had quickly ended his marriage of convenience.

Sardo mentally counted on his fingers. Neither of Brad's first two marriages had come about because he loved his brides. Loni Ann Ericksen had been pregnant and Cynthia Marrasco had been used as a means to an end, an end not achieved. There were also some glaring gaps in Brad's review of his life as a parent. Although he claimed to have loved his third wife, Lauren, he didn't explain to Sardo why he had left her when she was pregnant with his child – except to hint that Cheryl had seduced him. He said that he had, naturally, taken care of that little girl, Amy, who was born after he left Lauren for Cheryl.

When Brad walked out of Dr Sardo's office, he was as

confident as when he walked in, and quite secure in his belief that he had made a good impression. He had been calm – and yet he had shown his profound feelings for his sons appropriately. Cheryl would be nervous; she would not come off well. She was too intense, too scattered, and far too frantic in her fear that he was going to take Jess, Michael, and Phillip away from her.

On March 24 Cheryl presented herself to be tested and it was immediately obvious that she was nothing like the foul-mouthed shrew, the sex-driven huntress, that Brad had described. If she *was* that woman, she certainly hid it well. Dr Sardo found Cheryl's demeanor much different from her husband's. She was very intelligent and verbal – just as he had found Brad to be; no surprises there. However, Cheryl was far more responsive to his questions. Unlike Brad, she did not immediately launch into her side of the case, but rather let Sardo phrase questions for her to answer.

Cheryl said that she felt that their temporary custody truce was working 'fairly well.' But she agreed with Brad that all negotiations in the past to seek a permanent order had been utterly fruitless. These two areas were the only ones where Cheryl's perceptions matched Brad's. And although Brad had smiled and told Sardo that he and Cheryl could work out custody without any outside counseling, Cheryl shook her head in alarm. They could not. They had tried and it wasn't working. It wasn't working at all; it never could. She was insistent that they had to have someone mediate.

Brad, Cheryl said, had become extremely difficult to deal with; even the most minor issues would spark yet another huge fight between them. In a sense, she had been surprised by Brad's stubborn and violent response to her custody requests. 'In the past, when we discussed divorce,' she said, 'Brad sometimes said he wouldn't even *see* the boys, and I couldn't deal with that.'

As unhappy as she had become in her marriage, she could

not rob her sons of their father. But currently that was not a concern. Brad was resisting every one of her suggestions about the boys, wanting to be part of the most minuscule decisions about their lives – so much so that they seemed unable to reach *any* resolution of their children's future.

Cheryl told Sardo that she had no problem any longer in accepting that her marriage was over. She was at peace with her decision to divorce. Her marriage was completely dead. There was nothing in the world that could revive the love she had believed she and Brad felt for each other, and she was anxious to get on with her life.

As for the 'primary parent' question, Cheryl recalled for Sardo all the times Brad had left her and the boys. She had always been the parent who stayed with the children. She told him that it was *she* who had been alone with her sons most of the time since October 1982, when she returned to Seattle from Houston to resume her law practice to help fund Brad's business in Texas. Until they had moved to Portland in early 1985, Brad had lived away from them, except for short visits.

When Sardo asked her to describe Brad, Cheryl said that he was very demanding, very harsh, and used physical discipline – including beatings with a belt – on the boys. Pondering his parenting stance, she finally characterized it as 'militaristic.' The father Cheryl described was like a Marine D.I., expecting his sons to obey instantly and without question. In his testimony, Sardo didn't mention the child's coffin in their garage, or the dead animal 'trophies' Brad had the boys bring back from their trips to Yakima. Perhaps Cheryl worried about what Dr Sardo might think of her for having allowed such things to go on.

Cheryl told Sardo that *she* was the caregiver, *she* was the nurturer, although she had always tried not to say anything negative about Brad to the boys. He was their father, and she had wanted them to know him and respect him – even when he was always gone. Little boys needed to believe in their father.

But even when Brad was unemployed, Cheryl said, he had never stayed home to care for the boys. He was always leaving on trips – to Yakima, to Houston, to California, to wherever – always working on some mysterious projects. She had had to hire baby-sitters. Brad was simply not a man who would submit to being tied down with regular child care.

In the weeks to come, in sessions with Cheryl and Brad together, Dr Sardo would observe the interaction between them. When Cheryl was in the same room with Brad, she seemed to shrink and become very quiet. Sardo was surprised. Although Cheryl was the attorney, it was obviously Brad who had a 'very intrusive style' in transacting. Sardo noted that Brad applied pressure in a great many different areas at different times, controlling the conversation as floodgates control the ebb and flow of a river. If he had not known better, he would have thought that Brad, not Cheryl, was the experienced trial attorney.

Sardo also saw that Cheryl was actually a 'little intimidated' by her husband. She made no attempt at all to negotiate with Brad alone. He ran the show. Very occasionally, Cheryl stood up to him on issues that were vitally important to her. There were certain lines that she had drawn in her mind and she would not let Brad cross over. Even so, Cheryl was always the one on the defensive. It was she who sat braced for Brad's next verbal assault.

In the Minnesota Multiphasic Personality Inventory tests that Sardo administered – tests consisting of more than five hundred carefully worded questions to be answered 'yes' or 'no' – Brad's and Cheryl's personalities emerged clearly, like mountain peaks thrusting through clouds. The MMPI test has many deliberate 'lie' questions which appear several times. Anyone who tries to 'fool' the test tends to answer the way he believes the test designers want him to, and that 'desire to please' is transparently clear to those who chart test results.

Dr Sardo's evaluation of Brad's MMPI test results was

that he 'presented himself as an individual who was very much in control, very selective about the information he was providing, and very concerned with trying to provide an appropriate picture. The picture he tried to put forth was one of sensitivity and tenderness.' But Sardo also detected other traits in Brad's MMPI scores. The test revealed that he was a 'very guarded individual, who does not allow intimacy with others, and who has little genuine insight.'

Sardo noted that Brad had a strong tendency to 'project' onto someone else undesirable traits he himself might have. Either he had virtually no awareness of his own personality, or he contrived to slough off negative traits and attribute them to others. Moreover, Brad Cunningham, whose facade was that of an extremely strong – even macho – male, scored much higher than normal in feminine traits.

Brad thought that he had aced the MMPI, that he had snowed Sardo completely and succeeded in convincing him that Cheryl was a temperamental bitch who cared more for her career and her sex life than she did for her sons.

Sardo had seen an entirely different woman.

Cheryl's MMPI test scores supported the statements she had given in her earlier interviews with Dr Sardo. Although she jousted very successfully with males in a profession where females were still in the minority, the test revealed that Cheryl identified with a 'very traditional female role.' She was far less guarded and defensive than Brad in her answers. She showed herself to be a person with a great deal of energy, and also as someone who could be impulsive. And most interesting to Dr Sardo, given the reason for the MMPI tests, Cheryl's answers disclosed who she was at her very center. Despite her very high-profile and assertive career, she was at heart a mother, a wife, a nurturer.

Weighing what he knew about Brad and Cheryl, Dr Sardo next visited with their sons. Jess was six, Michael four, and Phillip two. And it was clear that *someone* had taken very good care of them. Remarkably untouched by the custody squabbles that swarmed around them like angry bees, they were active and playful little boys. When Dr Sardo asked them who they lived with, Jess said, 'Mom.' Michael said, 'Mom – and Dad.' When he asked them which parent was more fun, Michael instantly said, 'Mom!' Jess said, 'Mostly Mom,' and then quickly said, 'Mostly Dad.'

Sardo found the Cunningham children spontaneous, alert, curious, and extremely intelligent. The two older boys said they could play chess and did so with both of their parents. In fact, the boys seemed so well adjusted that Sardo could only conclude that both Brad and Cheryl must be concerned with their children's well-being – just as each of them claimed. Despite the struggle he had observed between Brad and Cheryl, he could not find that either parent's behavior had been detrimental to the boys; they certainly seemed to be unstressed and happy little kids.

In the couple's joint sessions with Dr Sardo, Cheryl kept hoping that she and Brad could reach a reasonable custody agreement, but Brad would not give an inch. Time after time, Sardo watched Brad flare up and stride toward the door, saying flatly, 'I'll see you in court.' Why did Brad have to make this process so much worse than it needed to be? he wondered.

Dr Sardo's decision wasn't easy. It never was, but this couple was more difficult to evaluate than most. In good conscience, he could not say one parent was a monster and the other a saint. He couldn't even say that one parent would be harmful to the children. It was just that the odds were that Cheryl had been the more consistent parent, and he recommended that the children would probably be better off with their mother.

As to reaching a rational and equitable division of the parents' time with Jess, Michael, and Phillip, Sardo realized that was never going to happen. In the end, although both Cheryl and Brad had said they were seeking a way to achieve joint custody of the boys, Sardo was unable to effect any happy resolution at all. He had to decide, then, which parent would be deemed *the* parent.

Dr Sardo determined that Cheryl had always been the major caregiver. She had been more reliable, and showed fewer inconsistencies in her statements. And she had been all alone with her children for long periods while Brad had pursued his business interests. Much of that time, Brad had been more than a thousand miles away, and it was hard to picture him as the key parent. Moreover, Sardo suspected that Brad's sense of competition over the boys was a major factor in this bitter and ongoing dispute. He was quite clearly a man who wanted to win any battle he was engaged in.

He did not win this battle. Cheryl was deemed the primary parent of Jess, Michael, and Phillip Cunningham. The question now was whether Brad would let go. He wanted his three boys. He wanted to shut their mother completely out of their lives if he could, and he was still determined to accomplish that.

27

Cheryl had married Brad – as Johnny Cash and June Carter sang in their country song – 'in a fever.' She had stayed with him years longer than most women would have, almost blindly determined to make their marriage last. At first, his life before he came into hers hadn't mattered. And later, she was quite probably afraid to go poking around into Brad's business, too wary to search for the secrets she was sure existed. But now, as she met Brad on the battlefield of divorce, she set about turning over the rocks of her estranged husband's past.

Until the summer of 1986, Cheryl had known only one of Brad's previous three wives – her onetime sorority sister and former friend Lauren Swanson. After what she and

Brad had done to Lauren, Cheryl could hardly expect to go to her now and ask for help. Brad had made Lauren sound like the next thing to an ax murderess. Belatedly Cheryl understood that she had been duped into believing what Brad wanted her to believe. He had lied about Lauren, just as he was lying about her now. No, Lauren had just been another of Brad's wife-victims. And Cheryl wondered how many more there might be. How many women *had* Brad victimized in the past? More important, how many would talk about it?

Cheryl had never really had a reason – or an excuse – to contact Loni Ann Cunningham before. Both Kait and Brent had visited in Cheryl's various homes, but Brad had allowed Cheryl precious little say about their care. They were not *her* children, they were his. Cheryl hadn't known about Kait's terror during her months with her father in Houston. Had she known, she would have tried to rescue the little girl – but Kait's ordeal in Houston was only one more of Brad's secrets.

During this bitter summer of 1986, Cheryl knew that Brent was in Portland and living with Brad in the Madison Tower. Cheryl feared for him. He was a nice young man, not even sixteen yet. He didn't have Brad's aggressive, superconfident personality – nothing like it. He could be so easily crushed by the sheer force of his father.

Loni Ann Cunningham wasn't easy to locate; Cheryl discovered that Brad's first wife had done her best to hide from him for more than two decades. Her address was not listed in public records. It took weeks for Cheryl to find Loni Ann in Brooklyn, New York, where she was working as a kinesiology therapist. Cheryl called to warn her that Brad's apartment was not the best place for Brent to be living. Although Loni Ann was worried, there was little she could do. Brent had gone to school in Brooklyn until his freshman year in high school. With his red hair and blue eyes, he had stuck out like a sore thumb, the only fair-haired student in a school where every other student had brown eyes and black hair. 'They walk around me as if I spoke a foreign language,' he told his mother, and he begged to go back to the Northwest to live.

Loni Ann had hoped that Brent was faring well with his father. He *was* a son, and Brad had always treated his sons better than his daughters. Although Loni Ann was still afraid, she did give Cheryl some details about her own life with Brad. She recounted the bitter custody hearings for Brent and Kait. Cheryl was even able to get a half-promise from Loni Ann that she might give a deposition to help in her own custody struggle.

Slowly, very slowly, after all her years with Brad, Cheryl began to uncover the real truth about the man she had married, and to learn the almost unbelievable story of the years before he came into her life. Brad had never allowed her to know his mother or his sisters. True, he had taken Cheryl to some of the Cunningham family reunions, but his mother, Rosemary, had never been there – she had long since been banished. Brad had never wanted to talk about his mother and instantly quashed any mention of her. And he preferred that Cheryl maintain a very low profile at the family celebrations, and not mention her career. So she had said scarcely anything, just engaged in woman-talk about babies and recipes. The men had seemed to dictate the way the reunions would go. The women brought the food and stayed in their place.

Cheryl knew almost nothing about Brad's sisters, Ethel and Susan. He had said they weren't worth knowing. He had cared about his father, and he had suffered the presence of his father's wife Mary because Sanford wanted her with him. The rest of his family hadn't really existed for Brad. It was the same with his Indian roots. Brad didn't want to talk about them and he never wanted Cheryl to ask questions about his relatives.

In her legal cases, Cheryl had always been so meticulous in her research that she was prepared for any eventuality. In her personal life, she had chosen to believe what Brad told her about his childhood, his family, his mother, his sisters, his ex-wives. At first she hadn't questioned him because she loved him. Later she was cautious about making waves. But now she jotted down notes and the names of people who might testify in her divorce case. If it got nasty – and she was quite sure it would – she would have a list of potentially devastating witnesses who could recall the days when Brad Cunningham was part of their lives.

Cheryl was determined to work her way back through Brad's past. She was going to find Rosemary and Ethel and Susan. She would try to get Loni Ann and Cynthia and Lauren to testify for her. She did not yet know the details of all of Brad's previous marriages, divorces, and child custody cases, but she had reason to suspect they had been much like hers, and she was going to validate her suspicions. She was a woman on fire, prepared to ignore her own terror and throw herself into what seemed – at least to her – a life-and-death struggle.

Cheryl was adamant that *she* would handle the witness list for her divorce trial – so adamant, in fact, that Betsy Welch was a bit put off. After all, Cheryl had hired her, yet sometimes it seemed she wanted to run her own case, and any attorney knows that 'he who represents himself has a fool for a client.' But Cheryl was so caught up in this divorce and custody action that she had forgotten. 'Don't worry about the witnesses,' she told Welch. 'I'll have the witnesses.'

Cheryl's decision to open up Brad's past to scrutiny may have been a fatal move. But she didn't care. She was a tigress, obsessed with protecting her young. She was no longer cowed. She was no longer afraid. She feared no humiliation. She had become the worst enemy that Brad Cunningham had ever known. And the most dangerous.

28

Brad was angry when Dr Russell Sardo declared that Cheryl was the primary parent of their children. More than most men, he considered himself an exceptional father, and he was sincerely dumbfounded when Dr Sardo didn't understand. He had pulled out all the stops when he talked with Sardo, certain he had won him over. Now he doubted Sardo's competence as a psychologist.

Under ordinary circumstances, Brad might have raged more at Cheryl over Sardo's decision than he did. But it was during the week following his sessions with Sardo that he met Sara Gordon. And she seemed to be everything that Cheryl no longer was to Brad. She was as beautiful as Cheryl, but she was daintier, more delicate, and seemingly more pliant. True, their first date had been a little stilted, but then Brad turned on the charm and Sara responded. And he had quickly determined she had a handsome income, several times as much as Cheryl's.

Brad plunged into an intense relationship with Sara almost immediately and was soon courting her with his experienced and well-honed romantic fervor. As far as Sara knew – and all her information came from Brad's lips – Cheryl was a monstrous mother, a faithless wife, and a morally loose woman. Brad would make sure that his about-to-be-ex-wife and his new love did not meet face-to-face. His relationship with Sara had nothing whatsoever to do with his determination to gain custody of his sons. Sara was the next step up for him; Cheryl was old – but very pressing – business.

Even so, when his efforts to get custody of Jess, Michael,

and Phillip were met by Cheryl's inflexible stance and her temporary victory, it didn't send Brad into one of his customary rages. He was still angry at Cheryl, but he had Sara to talk to now. She was on his side. Quite probably, their love affair made the summer of 1986 far more serene for everyone concerned than it otherwise would have been. Cheryl was still uneasy. When you have been living in a war zone and the shelling suddenly stops, the ensuing silence is eerie. She didn't trust the quiet, didn't believe for a moment that Brad had given up. He had moved back in with her once; she had no guarantee that he wouldn't move in again.

In June, to forestall such an eventuality, Cheryl invited her half brother, Jim Karr, to share her home with her and the boys. She could no longer afford the Gresham house and she looked for a rental more within her means. Her law career was just as remunerative as it had always been – even more so – but she would have to put away funds to pay for the legal fight she knew lay ahead. And so she made arrangements to rent a house on 81st Street in the West Slope area west of Portland just beyond the zoo. The public schools there were good. It would be another fresh start. And this time, she prayed, it would be a lasting one.

There was no way she could keep her new address secret from Brad – he had to know where his sons were living – but she could move to a place where bleak and frightening memories didn't mark every room. Cheryl wouldn't be any farther away from Brad; actually his apartment at the Madison Tower was equidistant from Gresham and the West Slope. Nothing would change the fact that Brad still had dominion over Jess, Michael, and Phillip for nearly half of each week.

Having her half brother live with her would make Cheryl feel safer. It wasn't that Jim was a muscular hunk – actually, he was a slender young man whom Brad could easily have broken in two – but he would be another adult there in the house with her. That meant a lot to Cheryl, having somebody to talk to, someone who loved her, and a link to a time in her past when life was much simpler and much safer. But even the seemingly innocuous move of inviting Jim to move in with her set off another skirmish. Brad doubted that Karr was capable of caring for his three sons. He demanded that he have psychological testing to determine if he was suited for child care. Cheryl had warned Jim that Brad was prone to off-the-wall demands, so he shrugged and agreed to be tested. Jim met with Dr Sardo for forty-five minutes in July of 1986, and Sardo reported that he would do just fine with Jess, Michael, and Phillip. Grudgingly, Brad agreed to the arrangement.

Jim Karr was a journeyman carpenter and he had enough free time to help his half sister out. He and Cheryl would be able to mesh their schedules so that one or the other of them was always with the boys. The arrangement was symbiotic. Cheryl would give Jim fifty dollars a week, room and board, and gasoline and other necessities.

That summer Cheryl and Brad continued to alternate time with the boys, pending the outcome of their divorce. July and August were almost spookily tranquil. When Brad asked to take his sons on vacation, Cheryl acquiesced without arguing. Even though the fear that he would simply disappear and take her children with him walked with her always, Cheryl knew about Brad's relationship with Sara Gordon. She was reassured when Brad told her Sara was going along on their vacation. Sara had a practice to come back to and a solid reputation. Cheryl didn't know Sara, but the boys liked her. It hardly seemed probable that she would help Brad hide the children from their mother. Her intuition was right. Brad brought the boys back on time. And Cheryl could breathe again.

Meanwhile, she continued her investigation of Brad as if she were preparing for the biggest trial of her life – as, indeed, she was. She kept meticulous notes of every encounter she had with him. Brad was unaware that all of his phone conversations with Cheryl were written down and marked with date and time.

Cheryl confided in Eric Lindenauer. She had been his mentor when he was a fledgling lawyer at Garvey, Schubert and now Eric attempted to be her protector and her confidant. Cheryl needed someone to talk to, someone with whom she could explore her doubts, her suspicions, and her fears. Eric was more than a decade younger than she was, and they had never had anything other than the most platonic of relationships, but he loved her as a brother would love her.

Although Cheryl had not been actively involved in Brad's business dealings during their marriage, common law made her a partner. Sometimes her signature had been required on documents; more often, she didn't have to sign to be equally responsible: she was Brad's wife. She had become aware of irregularities that troubled her. She told Eric that Brad hadn't filed returns on his business income for the past three years. Before that, she said he had put false information on the returns he had filed. Cheryl had seen vast amounts of money pass through his hands; she had never been sure where it came from or where it went. She knew that Brad had owned heavy equipment worth hundreds of thousands of dollars – equipment that should have been listed when he filed for bankruptcy. All assets remaining in a bankrupt estate are legally supposed to be marshaled to pay creditors, and a trustee appointed to see that that happened. 'Brad's got construction equipment that's never been accounted for,' Cheryl told Eric. 'I'm sure he's hidden it over near Yakima someplace. He's driving brand-new vehicles. Nobody who's bankrupt could have so much.'

Brad was still living at the Madison Tower like a man who had money to burn. Before his job with Citizens' ended in mid-April, a professional 'headhunter' had placed him in his top position with U.S. Bank. The bank had purchased his personal vehicle, a Volkswagen Cabriolet, and given it back to him to use. His new job paid close to one hundred thousand dollars a year and came with perks too numerous to list. He was basically in charge of all the commercial property loans in the Spectrum division of U.S. Bank. He hadn't exaggerated to Sara when he told her about his position. He *was* at the top of the heap. There was the possibility of a multimillion-dollar award in his pending suit. But he didn't have it yet, and the Houston law firm handling the case would undoubtedly take a large chunk of any payoff. Cheryl was concerned that Brad was spending a tremendous amount of money to maintain his upmarket lifestyle, more money than even he made.

Eric Lindenauer could see that Cheryl was on the offensive; she was through looking the other way and she would never make an excuse for Brad again. He, of all people, had seen Cheryl in action in the courtroom, and her offensive was tough. She confided that Brad had paid virtually nothing toward their household expenses for years. Even when he had worked for Citizens' Savings as an upper-echelon executive, Cheryl had paid all the bills. 'Maybe he'd buy pizza once in a while,' she said bitterly.

Eric considered Brad 'a major jerk – he was not a nice person.' He felt sorry for Cheryl, and he was amazed that a man like Brad could ever have attracted a woman like her in the first place. She was one of the most brilliant lawyers he had ever encountered. 'Cheryl was fearless in court – one of the fastest people on her feet I've ever seen,' Eric commented. 'Brad Cunningham was the only one to intimidate her. . . . She was the easiest person to like. Besides Brad, she had no other enemies.'

Brad had quite clearly become an enemy. But that went both ways. Cheryl's intimate knowledge of Brad's machinations made her a threat to him. If he was only a blowhard, full of sound and fury and veiled threats, Brad couldn't do physical harm to Cheryl. He had her on the ropes; but she was fighting back now, and she could be a formidable opponent.

In August, when the time neared for Jess and Michael to

be enrolled in school, the long, deceptively cool summer began to heat up. Brad's phone calls had a new, more menacing undertone. And Cheryl continued to write down every word, every phrase. She often showed her notes to her brother Jim. '. . . Called my mother a lying slut on the phone when he called back.' 'Won't give me keys to get tires myself. If not resolved, he will dispose of tires.' Jim occasionally drove the van. He used her keys that she kept on a round leather key ring – car keys and house keys. She had separate office keys.

Cheryl's life was a paradox that summer. One part of her lived in the world of the devoted mother and successful young attorney. There were men who found her attractive, men who called and wanted to date her. Occasionally – *very* occasionally – she went out, but she always seemed to be listening, always waiting for something to happen. She was never completely with anyone, because another role she had assumed was that of quarry. There was no mystery about whom she feared. It was Brad. She had come to a place where she constantly watched her back.

Eric knew that there was nothing he – or anyone – could do legally to protect Cheryl from Brad. It is one of the necessary incongruities of the law that one cannot call the police and report a crime *about* to happen. If that were possible, police dispatchers could never find enough officers to respond. Most of the frightening threats made in anger – or in drunkenness – are never carried out. True, restraining orders can be obtained, but they are only paper. Enraged stalkers are rarely put off by the words on a legal document.

Brad obviously didn't love Cheryl anymore, but he had a new woman and Eric certainly didn't think he might physically assault Cheryl. He never had before, no matter how angry he was with her. The police would probably have dismissed such a notion, too. These were two professional people with too much to lose for them to engage in physical encounters. Eric tried to keep that thought in mind. Cheryl's sister Susan agreed. She would recall saying, 'I'm not afraid of Brad, Cheryl. He's not going to hurt you – he's not that dumb.'

On August 13 Cheryl enrolled Jess in Bridlemile Grade School on the West Slope. Eric went along with her because she was afraid Brad might show up and make trouble. He didn't, and she was relieved.

Brad and Cheryl divided their three sons' time as precisely as if King Solomon himself had shaved the days of the week with a fine-edged sword. He had the little boys Tuesday and Wednesday and every other weekend from precisely 7 P.M. on Friday to precisely 7 P.M. on Sunday. Neither one would permit the other to be even five minutes late in returning the boys from a visitation. Cheryl complained to confidants that Brad brought the boys back in faded old clothes, although they left her house in new garments. Phillip's new carseat disappeared and was replaced by an old one.

The most basic chores of everyday living had become a struggle. Cheryl had a brief respite when she took the boys on vacation with her. Her fear dissipated with every mile away from Portland. She spent Labor Day with her half sisters Debi Bowen and Kim Roberts – Floyd Keeton's daughters by his second wife, Gabriella – and their families in Vacaville, California. But she had to leave early to get back; she had to be sure that Jess had a good start at his new school.

September 2 was Jess's first day at Bridlemile School. Eric had arranged to pick up Cheryl very early in the morning so they could drop Michael at his preschool, and also avoid Brad if he came to the house. Cheryl and Eric had just arrived at Bridlemile School with Jess when Brad suddenly appeared, carrying Phillip. Moments later, they were engaged in a clash of wills that appalled the principal, Peter Hamilton. Never before and never again would he see parents so out of control. 'These people *hated* each other,' he would recall.

The cause of their argument was not that unusual. Hamilton had seen any number of divorced parents who disagreed over where their children would go to school. It was the ferocious intensity of the fight between Cheryl and Brad that alarmed Hamilton. While scores of parents, first graders, and kindergartners stared, stunned, Brad was calling his wife a 'slut' and a 'cunt' and he looked at her with venom and naked hatred in his eyes. Here in a sunny hallway that smelled of wax and crayons and fresh first-day-of-school clothes, Cheryl and Brad seemed about to come to blows. Hurriedly, Hamilton ushered them into his office where they could talk without everyone in the building hearing them.

Brad was enraged because he wanted Jess to go to Chapman School in downtown Portland, where *he* lived. Further, he was furious that his name did not even appear on the application for enrollment to Bridlemile. Cheryl had left the square marked 'Father' blank. For twenty minutes, Brad and Cheryl railed at each other. Even with Hamilton's attempts at mediation, nothing was settled – except they all agreed that Brad's name should be added to the Bridlemile registration card. There was no agreement on where Jess would go to school.

The excited little boy's first day of school had been ruined. And Hamilton was so shaken by the confrontation that he jotted down what had happened on a five-by-seven card. He really didn't have to; he could never forget the hatred that had suffused his office with an almost palpable cloud. He wondered how those two parents could ever have gotten close enough to each other to conceive the poor little boy who shrank against the wall as they fought over him.

Brad told Sara about the scene at Bridlemile. He reported that Cheryl had yelled and screamed at him, that she had hit him, and that, in general, she had behaved like a trampy fishwife. 'My impression from Brad was that Cheryl had caused the scene,' Sara recalled. 'Brad said he was holding little Phillip in his arms and Cheryl screamed and caused a really big commotion. He said she almost hit Phillip while he was in Brad's arms. He was very angry and upset.'

After all the screaming and fighting, Jess was finally allowed to attend first grade at Bridlemile. He went to Bridlemile from September 2, 1986, until Friday, September 19. He had seventeen days of an almost normal childhood. After that, everything would change.

Seeing her son in tears because his first day at school had been ruined, something in Cheryl had rebelled. She would give her little boys a normal childhood, no matter what it took. She would no longer allow Brad to play his terrible games with their lives. Yes, she had agreed to shared custody, but she no longer believed that either she or the boys would survive emotionally if that continued. She now wanted full custody; she wanted Brad out of her life, and out of their lives. She had been gathering evidence for months, and she was finally ready to face the thing she feared most.

And that was Bradly Morris Cunningham.

29

Cheryl continued taking notes of everything her estranged husband said to her – both at home and when he called her at her office. She often read her notes aloud to Jim, or handed over the tablet for him to read. Eric Lindenauer was also aware that Cheryl was documenting all of her contacts or calls with Brad. Ostensibly she was getting ready for her day in divorce court. But literally, and almost unbelievably, she was preparing for another eventuality. If she should not be around to face Brad in court, she wanted a written record to exist of all that had taken place in the final months of her marriage.

Jim didn't want to talk with Cheryl about the dread

possibilities she sometimes envisioned, but he listened as she spoke softly to him. 'She let me know that she had changed her will so that Brad would have no control over her estate,' Jim said. Cheryl was no longer fearful only of losing her sons. She was afraid that they would lose *her*, that something might happen to her, something so subtle that it would seem tragic – but not criminal.

One night Cheryl looked hard at her brother and said, 'Jim, I fear for my life. Short of my collapsing and dying in front of you, I want you to assume that any accident involved *wasn't* an accident. Pursue it. *Pursue it.*'

Three times, Cheryl told Jim the same thing.

Three times, he told her not to be frightened.

The terrible scene at Bridlemile School had given Cheryl a glimpse into the searing rage Brad was capable of. Certainly, she had seen him angry before, although he had usually shown his public face, the smooth, charming facade of a man who had his life and his emotions under perfect control. But Brad had lost it at Bridlemile, just as he had once lost it at the boys' Montessori School. No, not just; this time Cheryl sensed that he had been ready to kill her for having the temerity to register *his* son in the school she had chosen.

She knew it was going to get worse. She hadn't even brought out her big guns yet, her list of witnesses from Brad's past. And when she did, she could envision what Brad's reaction would be. It terrified her. She was fully prepared to do whatever was necessary to keep Jess, Michael, and Phillip with her. Cheryl never wanted them to be the object of the kind of wrath that Brad was capable of. But she also knew full well that she might die trying to save them from that.

After Cheryl had made up her mind to divorce Brad in February, she had returned to Portland with an iron resolve. She had also been seized with the premonition that she might have less time than she expected. She had called her friend and coworker Kerry Radcliffe. They had attended law school together, and they both were employed by Garvey, Schubert – Kerry on the business side and Cheryl in litigation. Kerry still worked in the Seattle branch of the firm.

'She called me from Portland,' Kerry later said, 'in the third week of February, on a Wednesday or a Thursday. Cheryl was agitated. She said, "I'm going to ask you a huge favor. This might sound unreasonable – and demanding – but I need to have this done." She said she had gathered her strength and filed for divorce. She wanted to have her will changed that day, and have me Federal Express it down to her so that it would be effective right away. She was not her normal self. She was very much upset.'

Kerry had drawn up both Cheryl's and Brad's wills five or six years earlier. At that time Cheryl had expressly stipulated that all of her estate was to go to her spouse, Bradly Morris Cunningham. Now she wanted to invalidate that will immediately. She told Kerry that she feared Brad's reaction. But she wanted to be sure that, in case of her death, nothing she owned went to Brad. Jess, Michael, and Phillip should inherit whatever she had. She also told Kerry that she didn't want Brad to be named guardian of the boys.

'I told her that until the divorce was final, this will might not have the full legal effect,' Kerry said. 'But Cheryl said, "I want this down. I want it in my will." I told her that if Brad were still alive, the court would probably make him guardian, and she said, "I know that, but I want my intent in my will. I don't want him to be guardian."'

Cheryl's first will had been pretty much a 'boiler plate' will in Washington, a community property state. All property acquired after marriage becomes community property of the two spouses in equal shares. What each partner brings into the marriage is separate property, and that includes later bequests or inheritances. Cheryl was adamant that her new will override the community property statutes. She was filing for divorce in Oregon, which is not a community property state.

Kerry did exactly as Cheryl asked. And she did it so hurriedly that she actually FedExed it with a few typographical errors.

Cheryl's new will was blunt. It said she was married to Bradly Morris Cunningham, but was separated from him and in the process of dissolving the marriage. It stated her intention to leave all of her property to her three sons, and 'to make no provision for Bradly Morris Cunningham.'

The will Kerry Radcliffe prepared was a long document. On page nine, it read, 'If it becomes necessary that a guardian be appointed for any of my children, I name my mother Betty Marie Vandever. If she is unable to act in this capacity, I nominate my former stepfather, Robert McNannay. . . .'

Cheryl had considered a number of people who would take good care of her children if she were no longer around to do it. She asked Sharon McCulloch if she and her husband would take them, and Sharon said, 'We considered it, and we would have if she'd put us in her will – but our children were so much older than Cheryl's boys.' Susan McNannay and her boyfriend, Dave Keegan, were also willing to raise Jess, Michael, and Phillip, even though Susan wasn't twenty yet. They agreed between them to reassure Cheryl of their commitment to her children.

Cheryl had also tried to provide for the eventuality that Brad *would* become the guardian of their children. If she could not prevent that, she would stop him from spending the money she left them. She directed that any funds from her estate were to go directly to pay for their education, their medical care, et al., and that nothing should ever pass through Brad's hands first.

Kerry did not know, at that point, how completely Cheryl's marriage had crumbled – or why. 'Cheryl told me that she felt very strongly that the children should not stay with Brad. She talked about his having guns and firearms around. She said something about a place in eastern Washington that he'd filled up with canned goods . . . as if he had a survivalist type of mentality.'

Legally, the job of a 'guardian' is basically to act as a substitute parent and provide a home and love to a minor child. A 'trustee' is the guardian of a minor's money. Often, of course, one person serves both functions. However, it is not unusual for a guardian and a trustee to be two separate people. A loving parental substitute may have little knowledge about money matters. Cheryl named her longtime friend John Burke as the executor of her will. He would become the personal representative of her estate and have her will probated. She also named John Burke and Bob McNannay as alternate trustees of her sons' inheritance.

Cheryl knew what she was doing when she picked her old friend to look after her boys' money if she should die. 'She told me that of all the lawyers she knew,' Kerry said, 'she trusted John Burke to be very strong in that position. He was somebody who could stand up to Brad. She knew that a lot of pressure would be put on this person. She said, "Brad is very manipulative and he can wear people down."'

Above all, Cheryl didn't want Brad dipping into what belonged to the boys. She hadn't been able to put much aside, not with the expenses she had carried for so many years. But she had a retirement fund with Garvey, Schubert. And she had life insurance. If she were dead, her estate would be worth a few hundred thousand dollars.

Cheryl's secretary, Florence Murrell, witnessed the will that had been drawn up so rapidly. She had been Cheryl's friend as well as her legal secretary, and she had watched the steady erosion of her confidence and peace of mind about what might happen in the months ahead. Kerry Radcliffe had too. It seemed impossible that *anyone* could get her down the way Brad did. 'Cheryl was incredibly intelligent, very organized; she was a very strong presence,' Kerry would say later, fighting back tears. 'She just took control when she came into a room. She was a wonderful attorney and a wonderful person.'

Cheryl continued to perform well for Garvey, Schubert, but by the late summer of 1986 almost everyone in her Portland offices and many of her coworkers in Seattle knew that she was living in a state of siege. She was embarrassed by that, ashamed that her nerves were so close to the surface and that she jumped whenever a door slammed or a phone rang. She had also been losing weight steadily until she weighed less than a hundred pounds. That wasn't nearly enough for a woman almost five feet six inches tall. And she was engaged in the litigation of her life. Never had she had an opponent as dogged, or as malicious.

Florence Murrell tried to be a wall between Cheryl and Brad. She saw how often Cheryl was upset and distraught. She was chain-smoking, but she wasn't eating. 'Brad called constantly,' Florence remembered. 'At Cheryl's request, I screened all his calls. I spoke to him *many* times. I hardly ever put him through to her. She was so upset and trying to work. She kept notes of all his phone calls.'

Florence saw that Cheryl was especially uptight after depositions and her visits to psychologists in the continuing struggle over the three little boys. 'I was separated myself,' Florence remembered. 'And we talked about our mutual problems. By that time, I was definitely stronger than she was. I'd buy her flowers and give her cards. . . .'

Florence had an unsettling experience in the late summer of 1986. She came into work early one morning, sometime between 7:00 and 7:30. 'The sun was shining through the east windows. I saw Brad coming out of one of our offices. No one else was there at the time. I was startled – very startled. We passed and I said, "Hi, Brad."'

Brad had had the area to himself. He smiled thinly at her, and walked through the glass doors, disappearing into one of the elevators.

Florence didn't see the unaddressed, unsealed envelope

that lay on the receptionist's desk. Later, a receptionist idly opened it to try to figure out who it belonged to. Inside she found photographs and negatives. They were nude pictures of Cheryl, pictures she had posed for in the early days of her marriage. They weren't provocative; they were actually lovely, artistic studies of a young woman with an exquisite body. But Cheryl was mortified. She knew that Brad had intended to cause her embarrassment. Worse than that, he had apparently had free rein to wander through the offices of Garvey, Schubert before they were officially open for business.

'When I told Cheryl, she was very upset,' Florence recalled. 'She said, "Those doors – they stay locked – until someone's at that front desk!"'

Sharon Stewart Armstrong was a Superior Court judge in King County, Washington, in 1986; she had worked with Cheryl at Garvey, Schubert beginning in 1979. Sharon took over Cheryl's caseload when she was on maternity leave and during the time she was in Houston. Like everyone who worked with Cheryl, Sharon admired her tremendously. 'Cheryl was an exceptionally fine lawyer, and we were very good friends,' she said. 'She was very, very bright. She had a fine strategic sense; she was excellent in the courtroom. She was also a mature person, able to cope with stress and strain. She was very warm and very funny. I adored her. She was a wonderful person.'

When Sharon Armstrong became a Superior Court judge in August 1985, her schedule was packed and she and Cheryl didn't see each other or even talk on the phone the way they often had. In 1986 Sharon knew 'a little bit' about Cheryl's divorce, but it was August before she heard from mutual friends about the depth of her friend's ordeal. She called Cheryl immediately and was distressed to hear that the information was true. Cheryl needed friends and Sharon offered to come and visit in Portland on the weekend of September 19–21. She would bring along another of their old friends. Cheryl was so happy to hear that, and was looking forward to the September reunion.

Tragedy seemed to hover over Cheryl and her friends that summer. On August 23 Sharon Armstrong and her husband and daughter were in a terrible automobile accident. Sharon almost lost her husband and child, and they remained hospitalized for a long time. She herself was injured, although not as critically as the rest of her family. 'I couldn't go to see Cheryl,' Sharon remembered. 'I was still too weak and in too much pain to go to Portland. I *did* talk to her on Wednesday or Thursday before the weekend we planned to get together. She told me that Brad was "being a beast" about the divorce.' Cheryl also confided that the psychologist had just recommended that Cheryl have custody of the boys and that 'Brad flipped out.' He was going into court to ask for a second report.

'After this,' Sharon said, 'she told me she thought he would kill her. I thought this was startling. I asked her, "Why on earth do you think that?" She said, "I think he will do anything to keep me from having the kids." She said his mother and sister were very afraid of him, that they wouldn't let him know where they lived because he had assaulted them. . . . I became concerned. We talked about how she needed to be careful. That was the last time I heard from Cheryl.'

Kerry Radcliffe talked to Cheryl often in August and early September. And when Kerry learned about Sharon's accident, she relayed the awful news to Cheryl. 'With the Armstrongs' accident, we talked about how fragile life was. She was really looking forward to the weekend of the twentieth.' Now, of course, Sharon wouldn't be coming after all. But Cheryl was grateful that Sharon and her family were still alive. After that, Kerry called often to update Cheryl about Sharon's progress – until Sharon herself was strong enough to call.

Kerry talked to Cheryl again early in September, two weeks before the weekend of September 19–21. Cheryl told her about the scene at Bridlemile when she had tried to enroll Jess. She said that Brad had screamed and yelled at her, and had yanked on Jess's arm, trying to pull him away from her. Jess was embarrassed. She was embarrassed.

'How are *you* doing?' Kerry asked.

'You don't want to know,' Cheryl answered, sounding so tired. 'I get up each morning, gather my strength together, and I get through the day.'

There was little that Kerry could say. Suddenly Cheryl blurted, 'Kerry, if I die, Brad did it.' She asked Kerry if she could come down on the weekend of the nineteenth, since Sharon couldn't come.

'I didn't go. I couldn't that weekend,' Kerry remembered sadly.

There would never be another weekend.

30

On September 16, 1986, Cheryl and Brad met at the offices of Kell, Alterman and Runstein in the Bank of California Tower in Portland. Reporter Michael R. King would record their depositions. Cheryl would have much preferred to give her deposition without Brad in the room, but she had no choice.

Brad was deposed first. Betsy Welch was representing Cheryl, and as she attempted to get some idea of Brad's financial status, she understood what Cheryl had said about his talent for being evasive about money. He wasn't sure how long he had worked for U.S. Bank or how many hours he worked. He was beyond that. 'I probably don't work – when you say "work," I mean I think about my job *after* work. I think about my job at night sometimes. But, you know, my physical presence is not something I keep track of – I'm an exempt employee.' That was true. Nobody at U.S. Bank checked on Brad; he came and went as he pleased.

Brad had no idea how much money he had made in the early 1980s. 'How much did you earn?' Welch asked.

'I don't remember. I would have to look at our tax returns.'

'. . . Mr Cunningham, you haven't filed a tax return since 1981, have you?'

'No – I think '82.'

'I hand you your '82 return. . . . I would like you to take a look at whatever you need to look at there and tell me what your income was for 1982.'

'It says here it was five thousand two hundred eight dollars.'

'I think . . . if you look . . . in the back, Mr Cunningham, that that's Cheryl's income for the year.'

'*Oh?*' Brad replied. 'Well, it's a joint return.' He had no idea what his income had been. He said his accountant did his tax work. Welch pointed out that his Schedule C Profit and Loss Statement showed that he had had no income at all in 1982 but had claimed $159,000 of expenses. His 1981 form showed income of $1,800 in his 'consulting and appraisal' business and claimed a $142,000 loss.

Brad said his Chapter 11 bankruptcy had been filed in 1984 and mentioned his ongoing lawsuit. 'The major assets of the estate, which is this lawsuit against the contractor and his bonding company and the parent corporation, needs to be tried.' His case had been filed in Texas in the 295th District in October of 1982, but he had no idea when it was going to trial.

'When was the last time you had a trial date?'

'Gosh,' Brad said, looking bemused. 'I don't know. In Texas, they do things different than we do here. They don't have trial dates, you understand?'

'I don't understand.'

Welch knew that Brad was intelligent, but he was acting

ingenuous, as if he had no idea what was happening in his multimillion-dollar suit in Houston. He had no legal costs, he said, but Vinson and Elkins might take up to 40 percent of any judgment.

'What's it about?' Welch asked.

'Messed up the construction – incredible. Violated Uniform Building Code, Uniform Electrical Code, Plumbing Code, improper construction of the concrete. I got a videotape on this stuff. It's incredible. . . .'

'. . . What's the prayer in that case? What are you asking for in money?'

'I don't know. My attorneys prepared it. It's quite a bit of money.'

'How much?'

'I don't know; twelve million . . . maybe it's fourteen million.'

Brad, the financial wizard, the entrepreneur, suddenly didn't know what was going on. He had had no income – at least according to his IRS forms – for years, but he thought he might be suing for as much as fourteen million dollars. He agreed that he hadn't filed tax returns for 1983, 1984, or 1985, but that was not his fault. It was because his tax picture was 'one of the most complex things I have ever seen in my whole life. I don't understand it.' He was planning to get rid of his accounting firm in Seattle, which, he said, didn't seem to understand it either. And he certainly had no money to pay Cheryl.

Cheryl gave her deposition next. Ted Runstein was now representing Brad, and she was frightened, jumpy as a rabbit, when he questioned her. She estimated that their basic living expenses, prior to Brad's moving out, were $10,000 a month. Early in their marriage, Brad had prepared their financial statements, and she had signed them. In 1982, Brad's figures showed total assets of $4,074,000 with outstanding liabilities of $1,200,000. This was during the time that the Houston project looked as if it was going to be a go. 'I relied on what Brad said the values of these figures were,' Cheryl said. 'I had no reason, at that point, to believe that they were untrue.'

'Okay,' Runstein said. 'Let's go to 1984 now. Mr Cunningham – in early 1984 – commenced sharing a residence with you again?'

Yes, Cheryl said, he had been more or less back with them in 1984, and they had moved to Portland because Brad wanted to. 'He felt he could not get employment in Seattle because of the bankruptcy and so many creditor banks in Seattle – so many *enemies*, as he put it.'

Cheryl had had to pass the Oregon bar and took a bar review course. They hired Marnie O'Connor as a baby-sitter. 'She did not live in until about two weeks before she was fired,' Cheryl testified.

'When was she fired?' Runstein asked.

'. . . late August or early September.'

'. . . Was this the young lady that Mr Cunningham told you he was intimate with?'

'. . . yes.'

Runstein went on to ask if she and Brad had discussed open marriage.

'Brad had raised the subject numerous times, yes.'

'Brad had? You had not?'

'. . . no.'

Cheryl lost her composure. Brad was making faces and comments. She said she could not continue. Runstein admonished Brad to make no comments.

'My question,' Runstein continued, 'is just prior to finding out about this young baby-sitter, had you told him that you had had intercourse with someone during the marriage?'

'Absolutely not. And I had not,' Cheryl said firmly. She had never, ever gone along with Brad's enthusiasm for open marriage.

Cheryl answered questions about the terrible scene on the first day Jess went to Bridlemile School. It was still bitterly fresh in her mind; it had happened less than two weeks earlier. She trembled as she recalled that morning.

Cheryl admitted that she had balled her hand into a fist and held it out 'real hard to stop [Brad] from pushing me backwards.'

'. . . You were not angry at this time?'

'I had been upset ever since he called me the night before. I was *extremely* angry at this man for causing this scene [in front of] my little boy. You bet I was.' For a moment, Cheryl showed her old fire.

It was a long and tedious deposition, and Cheryl was strung so tightly she almost vibrated. Runstein asked her questions which seemed designed to trip her up, but Cheryl remained steady. She described the weekend when Brad moved back into the Gresham house as 'absolutely frightening.'

'Does the guest room have a lock?'

'Not to my knowledge. If it did, he put it in when he and Marnie screwed in it. . . . I did notice one there as I was cleaning the room when I moved out. And I believe Brad put that on himself, as I said, probably for privacy with his baby-sitter.'

Runstein's questions now touched on a volatile area. He asked if Cheryl felt Brad should see the children out of her presence. She tried to avoid a direct answer. She could feel the heat of Brad's rage. But Runstein kept needling her until she blurted, 'No, I don't think he should see them at all.'

'*Ever?*' Runstein breathed.

'Considering what he's done lately, I don't think he shows himself to be mature enough to be a father figure for them.' She cited the Bridlemile School spectacle. 'I think that speaks for itself.'

'Okay. When was the first occasion when he struck the children, leaving welts and bruises?' Runstein was fishing; Cheryl had not mentioned her concern about that, but now she had to speak. 'You see,' she began, knowing she was on treacherous ground, '. . . I have a feeling I didn't know about that a lot of the times. The children got a lot of bumps and bruises that you think occur falling down. The one time we're talking about here occurred shortly after we moved from Seattle in 1985 . . . when Michael was three years old. . . .'

'What did you do,' Runstein asked, 'when he had beaten the children so severely that they had welts and bruises?'

'I confronted him with it. I told him that if he ever did that again, I would report him to the police . . . and he basically told me it was none of my business and that if I wanted to have a few welts myself, he could give them to me.'

Brad could not contain himself, and Cheryl turned to look at him, alarmed. 'I'm not going to sit here and be intimidated by him. He scares me.'

Cheryl was almost beyond fear now, but she plunged on. She described welts and bruises on Michael's thigh.

'And did it ever happen again?' Runstein asked.

'He struck them a lot of times after that, but generally so as not to leave welts and bruises,' Cheryl replied. She said Brad had hit the boys on their bottoms and that 'he generally confined his striking of the children to times when I wasn't around.' But the boys had told her.

Brad was seething. Runstein showed Cheryl an affidavit she had signed six months earlier saying that Brad could see the children as often as he wanted.

'I would agree to *anything* to get him out of the house, Mr Runstein – anything to get him physically out of my house. I figured the Court would take care of him if he abused the children.'

'Okay.'

Cheryl drew up every inch of her frail body and fixed her eye on Ted Runstein. 'If you are trying to imply I don't care about the well-being of my children, you are off base.'

'You are not angry, are you?'

'Yeah, I'm real angry. You are upsetting me a great deal. It's been a long day.'

Runstein suggested that they break for the day. The deposition adjourned at 4:04 P.M. The court reporter, Michael King, rode down in the elevator with Cheryl and saw that she was barely holding back tears. She had every reason to be upset. She had just broken all of Brad's rules. She had defied him, she had humiliated him in public, and most dangerous of all, she had officially accused him of child abuse. Brad viewed himself, above all else, as the perfect father. But Cheryl had held nothing back as she described him as an abusive father, a terrible father, a damaging father who was not fit to be with his sons. Never before had she made those accusations to his face and now she had not only said it, she had said it for the record. Cheryl had covered for Brad for all the years of their sons' lives, sticking colored pins on maps, telling the little boys that their daddy loved them and would be home with them if he weren't working so hard, letting them believe that their daddy was perfect.

Now she had spoken what she felt to be the truth. As a father, Brad was a monster.

When Brad returned to his Madison Tower apartment that evening, Sara Gordon saw 'the most anger I'd ever seen him exhibit.' He was furious, pacing back and forth, repeating to Sara over and over again that Cheryl had lied about everything. He was consumed with his rage over her deposition, the veins standing out on his forehead. He would talk of nothing else. Finally, he strode to his bedroom to call Cheryl. Sara sat on the bed and listened. 'He was so angry that his speech was pressured,' she recalled. 'Brad was actually having trouble getting his words out.'

'You lied at the deposition today,' he growled at Cheryl through a throat tight with fury. 'I'm going to get even – or you're going to pay. . . .'

Sara sat, frozen, on Brad's bed, her mind recording this previously hidden facet of her lover's personality. She had never seen him out of control. She had never known him to make such a call before and she was shocked at his venom. And yet, she was amazed to see how rapidly Brad's fury dissipated once he hung up the phone. It was as if he had blown out a pressure valve and everything was back to normal. He stopped pacing. He stopped repeating his epithets about Cheryl. Internally, something had changed. Perhaps he had made some decision. He had told Cheryl that he would have his revenge, and that seemed to make him feel better.

31

From the nineteenth to the twenty-first of September, Sara Gordon spent what was, at least for her, a fairly normal weekend. She had always worked harder and longer hours than any of her friends. That was a characteristic she shared with Cheryl; both of these brilliant women had fought for an education, fought for a career usually enjoyed by men, and once they attained their toeholds, they had worked twice as hard as any man to succeed.

During the summer of 1986, Sara was totally in love with Brad and she would have preferred to spend far more time with him than her practice allowed. But, in a way, she was working for both of them, for their future. She continued her usual fifty to sixty hours a week on call at Providence. It seemed even more important now that she and Brad had begun to talk about marriage. He had reluctantly told her that Cheryl was a profligate spender, and that he had had to file for bankruptcy. Although he had high expectations for the eventual windfall that would come from the suit Vinson and Elkins had filed on his behalf in Houston, the bottom was still falling out of the Houston economy and he had been temporarily brought to his financial knees.

How difficult it must have been, Sara thought, for this proud man to tell her the details of his bankruptcy filing so he could save what little he had left. She admired him for his honesty and she had no doubt that Brad would regain his financial footing soon. The man was a genius, and he had vision. He saw what the American public was going to need, and he set out to provide it way, way ahead of the pack.

Brad hadn't lost everything, of course. He had his new job as an upper-echelon executive with U.S. Bank. And he told Sara that he had formed his own corporation, also called Spectrum, and that it was a going concern, untouched by the bankruptcy. Although things were in the hush-hush stage, he said confidentially, his biotechnical division scientists had come up with a drug that would alleviate almost all the pain and symptoms of herpes. It was called Symptovir and he said there was great excitement in the medical community about early test results.

Sara was impressed. As a physician, she knew that the drugs in current use were often ineffective; they were little more than placebos. With studies projecting that a third of the population of the United States would contract genital herpes sooner or later, any company with a better drug to treat the disease would make not millions but billions. Sara's talent wasn't business acumen, but she knew what Symptovir could mean. Brad would be back on the top of the heap. And she was working double shifts to help him get enough money together to rebuild his financial empire.

Brad wanted her to mention Symptovir to her ex-husband Dr Geoff Morrow, but she was understandably hesitant to do that. He didn't really need her to pave the way for him, anyway. But she was fully prepared to back Brad in his business, and to help him take care of his children. From those confidences he had told her so haltingly and with such embarrassment, she realized that he had never had a woman who really loved him. Sara cared deeply for him, and it seemed sad that a man with so much love to give had been so unlucky with the women in his life. Even his own mother had apparently been cold and selfish, although Brad spoke about her only vaguely, and Sara didn't know whether she was alive or dead.

But Brad had loved his father, and he had been desolate in July when Sanford Cunningham succumbed to his third heart attack, suffered while on a fishing trip. Sara knew that Brad was still hurting from the loss. Sanford's pickup was parked in the basement of the Madison Tower, virtually unused now.

On Friday, September 19, 1986, Sara rode along with Brad in his Chevy Suburban van when he drove to Cheryl's house to pick up Jess, Michael, and Phillip. It was his weekend to have the boys. Sara waited in the car as always; she had yet to meet Cheryl, although she was extremely curious about the woman who was putting Brad through such an emotional wringer. And like any woman, she was curious to learn what she could about all the women who had come before her.

A wild and gusty storm hit the Portland area that Friday night and Sara could barely see through the Suburban's windows as sheets of water shut out the world beyond the glass. She could see that Cheryl's brother Jim's car was still parked there. He was usually around when Brad picked up his sons. Squinting, Sara watched Brad dash into the house to get the kids. Even without sound and at that distance, she could sense that Cheryl seemed 'frazzled' as she moved quickly past the windows, getting the boys' coats, helping them push their arms into the sleeves, running back to get someone's 'special blankey.'

Brad's mouth moved constantly. Sara wondered what he was saying to Cheryl. She felt like the outsider as she watched the two of them interact with each other in the warm light of Cheryl's home. They must have been in love once; they had three children together. Sara felt a little shiver of jealousy, but she told herself not to be dumb. Brad cared only about his sons. He had said often enough how he detested Cheryl. If Sara just thought rationally, she knew she had nothing at all to be jealous about. Cheryl looked attractive, but she also appeared to be a nervous wreck. Her movements were stilted and awkward. If everything Brad said about her was true, she had good reason to be nervous.

Sara could see now that Brad was carrying Phillip as he herded Jess and Michael ahead of him through the rain. Cheryl stood silhouetted in the doorway, looking after them as if she were straining to catch a last glimpse of the boys, almost as if they were going away from her for more than a weekend. That was odd, Sara thought, since Brad said that the kids drove Cheryl nuts and she could hardly wait to be rid of them so she could go out and have fun.

'What were you talking about in there?' she asked Brad as they buckled the boys into carseats and seat belts.

'Remember how I told you I'd never eat anything at home when we lived in Gresham?' Brad said.

She nodded. Sara had heard this before. Brad had told her that just before he moved out of the house he shared with Cheryl, things were so bad that he was actually afraid to eat anything she cooked. He had to have the boys taste it first because he suspected that Cheryl was trying to poison him. He told Sara now that he had reminded Cheryl that he was fully aware that she and her mother, Betty, had been trying to destroy him.

'I was telling her about how I listened in on those phone calls she had with her mother when I had to go over there to be sure the boys were okay,' Brad said, 'the calls where they talked about poisoning me to get rid of me. How they said that nobody would ever prosecute a case where a husband died like that.'

Sara said nothing. It always struck her as bizarre that Brad could be so matter-of-fact about his estranged wife and her mother talking about poisoning his food. And she had to admit – at least to herself – that it was odd that he would risk the boys' safety by having *them* taste food he thought was poisoned. Maybe it was like Solomon and the two women who each claimed to be the mother of a baby. The *real* mother cried out as the sword descended to cut the baby in two. Cheryl, however lacking she was as a mother, would never have let her sons taste poisoned food. And Brad would know that.

Sara listened as Brad ranted on about Cheryl. She worried because he never censored his conversation in front of his sons. He always blurted out whatever was on his mind. The little boys were listening now, and Sara didn't want Brad to get into the details again about some weird poison plot. Cheryl was, after all, their mother, and Brad could get a little histrionic. The boys appeared to love their mother a lot, no matter what. Sara wasn't a mother, but she knew enough about psychology to know it wasn't good for kids to have to choose up sides between parents, or to hear such accusations.

'What'd you guys have for dinner?' Sara asked, changing the subject as she turned to face toward the second seat of the Suburban.

'Orange juice,' Jess answered.

Brad rolled his eyes. He said he was sure that Cheryl did that on purpose – filled the boys up with liquid so they would wet their beds in his apartment. Anything she could do to make life difficult for him, she would do.

Back at the Madison Tower, Sara and Brad tucked the boys into bed in the room that Brad kept just for them – Jess and Michael in their bunk beds, and Phillip in his crib. The storm eased and everything was serene again.

Sara was on duty at Providence the next morning. She tiptoed out of the apartment and left them all sleeping; she had to be at the hospital by 6:30 A.M. The mass of Portland is divided in two by the Willamette River, and the Madison Tower is in the western part, while Providence Hospital is in the eastern section. Even so, Sara had only about seven miles to drive, crossing the river via the Morrison Bridge. She drove her Toyota Cressida; it was white and she had treated herself to the deluxe leather interior. Her commute was a quick trip along the rain-scrubbed, empty streets of an early weekend-morning Portland.

Sara knew Brad planned to take the boys to Jess's first soccer game that day. All of them, with the possible exception of Phillip who was too young to understand, were excited about it. Jess was going to play for the Bridlemile Buddies. Then Brad was going to take the boys to Dunkin' Donuts after the game. Sara hoped they all had a fun day.

As it turned out, it wasn't a fun day – at least not for Brad. When Sara got home Saturday evening, she found him fuming. He told her that Cheryl had broken the custody rules again. This was supposed to be his weekend, and Cheryl knew that, but she had shown up brazenly at Jess's soccer game, deliberately horning in on his time with the boys. It had ruined the game for Brad. He had to look at Cheryl sitting there in the bleachers as if she had every right to be there. One of Cheryl's Gamma Phi Beta sorority sisters from the University of Washington, Nancy Davis, had a son on the Bridlemile Buddies too, and her husband was the boys' coach, so Cheryl had sat there with Nancy. Brad told Sara that he had picked up Phillip and Michael and walked to the other side of the field to avoid her.

It had gotten to the point where Brad and Cheryl seemed to be fighting over even the most minute details of custody, and, to Sara at least, it seemed such a waste of emotion – but then she had never had a child and she didn't like to judge Brad's reactions.

They tucked the boys in, then Brad and Sara went to bed, but her beeper sounded at 2:30 on Sunday morning and she was called back to Providence Hospital to administer anesthesia for emergency surgery. After the patient was stable and out from under the anesthesia, she went back to Brad's apartment and caught a few hours' sleep. Exhausted, she still forced herself to get up so she could have breakfast with Brad and the boys. She was supposed to meet a girlfriend for brunch, but she was too tired; she called and canceled.

Brad could see how tired Sara was, so he thoughtfully took the boys out to play in the park after breakfast. Grateful, she crawled back into bed until one, and was back on duty at the hospital at 3 P.M. She had scarcely seen Jess, Michael, and Phillip all weekend, so she suggested that they all have supper with her that Sunday evening. The American Dream Pizza Company was kitty-corner from one wing of Providence, and the boys loved pizza. At 5 P.M. Sara left the medicinal-smelling hospital corridors and walked to the restaurant, enjoying the sunny September afternoon.

Brad was always on time. That was just one of the many things Sara liked about him. If he said he would be someplace, she could count on him. She thought he looked handsome as he strode toward her with his sons, but then Brad always looked handsome to Sara. Later, she remembered he was wearing a burgundy golf shirt, casual slacks, and a brown leather jacket. She couldn't recall if he was wearing boots or tennis shoes. At the time, it didn't matter.

They had a leisurely meal, enjoying each other's company and the beautiful Sunday evening. Grinning devilishly, Brad urged the boys to drink more and more Pepsi. Cheryl had delivered them to him with their bladders full of orange juice; now he would return the 'favor' and take them home full of soda pop.

Toward the end of their meal, Brad told Sara that something was wrong with his Suburban: it was missing and stalling, and he suspected he had probably gotten a tank of dirty gas that was plugging his gas line. He asked the boys to demonstrate the sound his van made and they all laughed when Jess and Michael obliged by snorting and hiccuping.

'Could I borrow your car to take the kids back to Cheryl?' Brad asked.

Sara nodded. She wouldn't be needing her Toyota

Cressida that evening, anyway. She would be either in the doctors' lounge, in the on-call room, or in surgery.

Brad drove his Suburban over from the pizza place and parked it next to Sara's car in the doctors' lot. Sara walked back with the boys, reluctant to leave the clean air and dappled sunlight of that lovely evening. Brad was pouring some kind of gas additive into the tank of his van when they caught up with him. 'It needs to sit in the tank for a while,' he said. 'It'll work better that way.'

Sara knew absolutely nothing about the inner workings of a car. She didn't know that a gas additive doesn't even start to work until the vehicle is actually driven and the additive circulates through the adulterated gas lines. She gave Brad her key ring. He took off her car key and handed back her other keys and the keys to his Suburban, although neither one of them expected she would need them. If Brad was nervous about driving the Suburban because the engine was missing, *she* certainly wasn't about to venture out in it. Anyway, Brad promised he would be back to visit with her in the doctors' lounge within the hour.

It was about ten minutes to seven when Brad and the boys were ready to go. As usual, things were a little hectic. Brad suddenly remembered that he had left Jess's 'special blankey' back at his apartment. 'Maybe I'll call Cheryl and have *her* pick up the boys for a change,' he said. 'I can hand her the blanket then.'

As far as Sara knew, Cheryl had never before picked up her sons at the Madison Tower, nor had she delivered them there. She wondered if Cheryl would even agree to that. She seemed to give Brad such a hard time about everything. One thing Sara *did* know. There was no way that Brad was going to get to Cheryl's house in the West Slope area by seven – not from Providence Hospital. He still had to go through downtown Portland and then swing west onto Route 26, the Sunset Highway.

Brad gave Sara a quick peck on the cheek and again promised he would be back to spend the evening with her until about nine. Brent had been gone all weekend on a scuba diving trip to Hood Canal and was due home after that. Brad wanted to be there when he got back.

When Brad and the boys drove off, Sara waved goodbye and headed back to the doctors' lounge. Her schedule demanded that she remain on trauma call all night. The hospital provided a suite, not unlike a nice hotel suite, for physicians who were on call overnight. She would begin her regular operation schedule first thing Monday morning. It was possible that she would be working almost around the clock. If she was lucky, she would get a good night's sleep. At about 7:30 she was watching television in the lounge when the hospital operator paged her and she picked up the phone. It was Brad.

'I called Cheryl,' he said. 'She's going to pick up the boys. I still should be over there before eight.'

Sara was relieved. They chatted for about five minutes, and then she turned her attention back to the television. She expected to look up at any moment and see Brad coming through the door of the lounge. He had been there often enough to know exactly where to find her.

But Brad didn't appear. If she was expecting anyone else, Sara wouldn't have been concerned, but Brad was such a punctual man. She called his apartment shortly before eight and was surprised to hear the phone ring five, six, ten times. His answering machine *always* came on by the fourth ring, but this time the phone just rang endlessly. At 8:30 she dialed Brad's number again. And again the phone rang emptily. Until that night, Sara had never known Brad to leave his apartment without making sure the answering machine was on. With his business interests, with his concern about the boys, with his graciousness in always being available to *her*, he just automatically left it on.

Sara was disappointed, and a little irritated. If Brent was due home at nine, Brad wouldn't be able to come and spend any time at all with her. Their times alone together were precious because they were so infrequent, and now they had lost another evening.

Sara kept glancing at the clock. It was getting dark outside. And now she was not only annoyed, she was getting worried. There was such enmity between Brad and Cheryl; Sara had seen Brad enraged, frustrated almost to the point of tears only five days ago. She felt a presentiment of doom. Maybe she was superstitious. Just when everything was as close to perfect in her own personal life as she had ever imagined it might be, she didn't want to lose the man she loved. 'I remembered what Brad had said about Cheryl trying to poison him,' Sara would recall. 'I didn't take it seriously, but . . .'

Maybe Brad had had an accident. He had been in such a tearing hurry when he left. And those darling little boys wouldn't be as safe in her sedan as in the big Suburban. Every time she heard a siren approach the hospital, Sara flinched. She didn't just love Brad; she loved Jess, Michael, and Phillip too.

It was so out of character for Cheryl to go to Brad's apartment to pick up the boys. Why would she agree to do that tonight? Sara wondered. And if she had agreed, why wouldn't Brad be there? The night no longer looked lovely; it looked dark and empty outside the hospital window. Her work in the trauma unit reminded her every day that people someone loved often never went home again. And most of them had parted saying, 'I'll see you—'

Just before nine, Sara tried Brad's number again. This time, to her great relief, he answered.

'Where have you *been?*' she asked angrily.

Brad sounded out of breath and a little excited when he spoke. 'We've been down waiting for Cheryl—' he said.

'For an hour and a half?'

'Yes,' he said, and then elaborated. He told Sara that he had called Cheryl at 7:30 and asked her as nicely as he could if she would come and pick up the boys. But it had been clear to him, he said, that she had not been alone. 'I heard someone in the background – she probably just went out partying.'

Sara slammed down the phone. She wasn't sure if she was mad at Brad or at Cheryl, but she felt guilty and foolish almost immediately. From everything Brad had told her about Cheryl, she might very well have left him waiting that long. Contrite, she called Brad back.

'I'm sorry,' she said. 'I'm calmed down now. I was just worried that you were either out killing Cheryl or that she was killing you! This is the first time since I've known you that you weren't where you told me you would be—'

Brad sounded upset, too, as he accepted her apology.

'What were you telling me about hearing somebody at Cheryl's house?' Sara asked.

'I just heard some guy. The second time I called, she wasn't home. She probably just decided to go out and party.'

'Well, where have *you* been, Brad?'

'Like I said, waiting for Cheryl downstairs. She never showed.'

They agreed it was too late for Brad to drive over to the hospital. Besides, Brent wasn't home yet, and there wasn't anybody for Brad to leave the boys with. Sara told him she was going to go to bed, and he said he would tuck the boys in at his apartment. Sara was disappointed, but she was no longer angry at Brad. It was hard for her to stay mad at him for very long. She loved him too much.

32

Cheryl's last weekend was bittersweet. She had gone to Jess's soccer game even though Brad had told her that on *his* Saturdays she was not allowed to go to the games or to speak to the boys or even to act as if she knew her own sons. She had called her mother either on Friday night after Brad picked the boys up or on Saturday morning. 'Cheryl wanted to go to Jess's game,' Betty would recall, 'but she didn't want to make it bad for them.'

Betty and Marv Troseth were all too aware of the terrible strain Cheryl had been under for most of that year. They lived in Longview, and so did her sisters Julia and Susan, and her former stepfather, Bob McNannay. They all loved her but none of them could do much to help – except listen. Betty and Cheryl had grown extremely close and they talked constantly by phone.

'The main issue, of course,' Betty would say later, 'was the custody of the children. At first she was afraid she wouldn't get them. I told her that was ridiculous. Cheryl said, "He will lie in court. He will *kill* me to get them." I tried to talk her out of shared custody. I really preached. He wasn't fit to have them.'

Betty remembered that Cheryl had looked at her once and said with complete resignation, 'I'll have to put up with him. For the rest of my life, I'll have to deal with Brad.'

Cheryl had felt cautiously confident after Dr Sardo decided that she was the primary parent. Right up to the last week, she believed she would have custody, although she knew it wasn't going to be easy. She told her mother that she and Brad had both given depositions on September 16.

After the soccer game on Saturday morning, Cheryl got in her Toyota van and headed north across the bridge that separates Oregon from Washington. She was going home to Longview. She was afraid. Her mother saw it. Betty had seen Cheryl afraid for a long time, but this weekend was different. There was a kind of tragic acceptance about Cheryl, as if she had done everything she could for her children, for herself, for the slightest chance that she and her three boys might have a happy future – or *any* future together.

Cheryl was strangely low-key on Saturday. She had always been a woman of tremendous energy, and the contrast with the way she had once looked and acted was shocking. 'She just looked terrible,' her sister Susan remembered. 'She was exhausted, and she was so thin that you could see her rib cage. Her cheeks were caved in.'

On Saturday night, when Betty got up from the table to wash the supper dishes, Cheryl didn't move to join her. 'She let me do the dishes alone,' Betty said. 'Cheryl *always* jumped up to help me.' But she seemed, at last, to have run out of strength. She didn't talk about the custody battle, but she did speak of her worries about Phillip, her baby. 'She said he was starting to stutter, and she was going to take him to a doctor.'

Betty's role over the previous year had been to calm Cheryl down. But she wasn't agitated that evening; she seemed beaten down. 'My highs are not quite as high as they could be,' she said. 'And my lows are lower.' Then she said quite softly, 'I know you don't think he's going to kill me, Mom, but he *is* going to kill me.'

Betty stopped what she was doing and stared hard at Cheryl. It wasn't that this was the first time Cheryl had said she feared Brad would kill her; Betty had heard her say it almost a dozen times since November of 1985. She responded as she usually did. 'He's too selfish to risk his butt.' But then Betty felt a chill. This time she believed Cheryl and she warned, 'Don't be alone with him, Cheryl.

Don't try to talk to him the way you would with other people. Watch your car.'

Cheryl sighed. 'I have to live my life, Mom. There are things I have to do.'

Cheryl spent that Saturday night at her mother's home. They watched a movie, *Queen of the Starlight Ballroom*, a sentimental story about romance between lonely people in their sixties, with Maureen Stapleton and Charles Durning.

On Sunday Cheryl told her mother that she wanted to visit her sisters. That was rather unusual; Susan and Cheryl had always been very close, but Cheryl hadn't seen Julia for six years. When Julia graduated from high school, she had left Longview immediately and headed for Seattle. She had been back in her hometown for only a short time. 'Julia lived a few blocks from Mom's place,' Susan said. 'Cheryl and Mom walked over to see Julia. Then they drove over to my house.'

Susan still lived with her father, Bob McNannay, in the house that had been Cheryl's home too when she was in high school. The kitchen had just been retiled in shades of cobalt blue, and this was the first time Cheryl had seen the remodeling completed. They all sat around and talked. Michael's birthday was coming up in about five days, and Susan suggested that they all come down for a birthday party. Cheryl tried to be enthusiastic.

'Cheryl was calm, even docile,' Susan would remember. 'She was usually moving a million miles an hour, but she was very peaceful. She wasn't depressed: she was passive. She was like someone I didn't know very well. She was *subdued*. That was *not* typical.'

Another thing Susan noticed was that Cheryl didn't talk about her divorce or the custody battle. That seemed strange because they had all talked about those topics for months. Susan had just baked rye bread and they all had some. Cheryl praised her sister's baking, and then Susan played the piano for them.

In a way, it was just like their usual visits. But Susan kept

BRAD CUNNINGHAM
Soph. Class Pres., Wolverine Guard, Honor Society, Modern Language Club, Football, Lettermen's Club Vice-Pres.

Brad's picture in his high school yearbook in 1967. He was handsome, strong, and headed for success—with both academic and athletic scholarships to the University of Washington. He was the kid who had it all.

Sanford Cunningham holds his first-born children: Bradly Morris and Ethel. He would always consider Bradly, his son, to be absolutely perfect.

Sanford and his wife, Rosemary, who was Colville Indian. No matter how bad things were at home, the Cunninghams always seemed to get along on their camping trips.

Below, Brad and Rosemary posing affectionately. In fact, he was hostile to his temperamental mother, and eventually came to deny her very existence.

Loni Ann Ericksen at sixteen, Brad's high school sweetheart who became his first wife. She adored him and bore him a daughter, Kait, and son, Brent. Their marriage was not what she had expected.

Cheryl Keeton as a freshman at the University of Washington. Beautiful and brilliant, she would go on to get her law degree from the same university.

Cheryl pledged Gamma Phi Beta at the University of Washington *(middle row, fourth from left)*. Her sorority sister and best friend, Lauren Swanson, would become Brad's third wife after he had married and divorced a wealthy older woman.

Cheryl and Lauren *(facing camera)* meet for dinner with friends. Cheryl and her first husband often socialized with Lauren and Brad, but their friendship would end abruptly in bitterness, when Lauren was pregnant with Brad's second daughter, Amy.

Cheryl was deliriously happy to be married to Brad. She thought he was wonderful.

Cheryl played part-time mom to her much younger half sister, Susan McNannay. Susan would always stick by Cheryl, too.

Brad and Susan aboard his sailboat in the San Juan Islands. Angry that he found no mooring slip, he dropped anchor in the dangerous shipping lane, terrifying Susan and Cheryl.

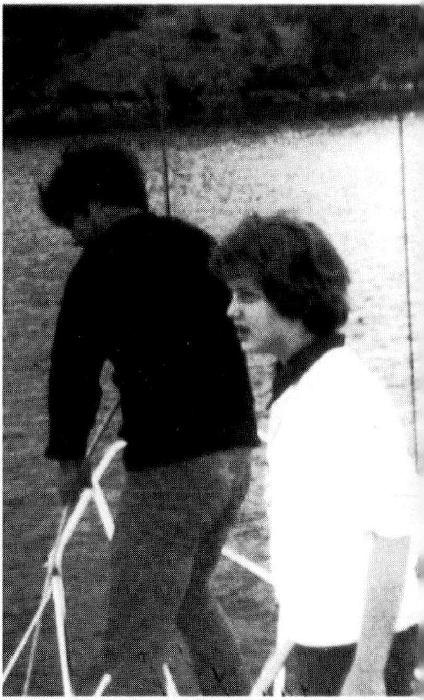

Brad and Cheryl began their married life in this house in the Laurelhurst tion of Seattle. He was a rising star in real estate and construction. She practicing law and on her way to becoming a top litigator. Brad would s estimate their net worth in the millions. They were a stunning couple and t future seemed limitless.

In 1981, Brad and Cheryl moved to Houston where Brad was having this lu rious house built for them. He expected to make a fortune constructing a h business complex. When the bottom fell out of the Texas economy, his fir cial empire collapsed.

Brad poses proudly with Jess, his firstborn son.

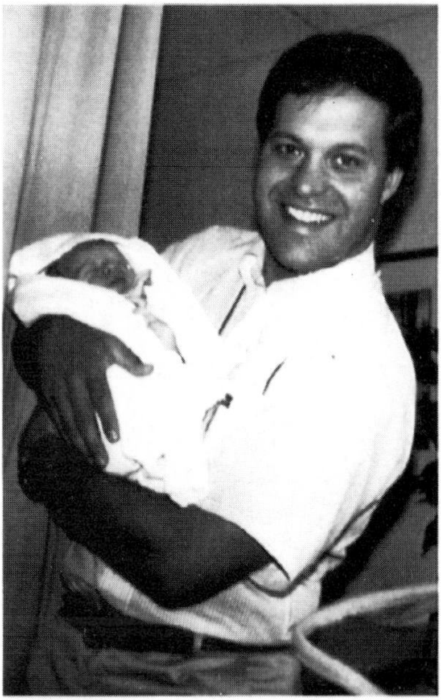

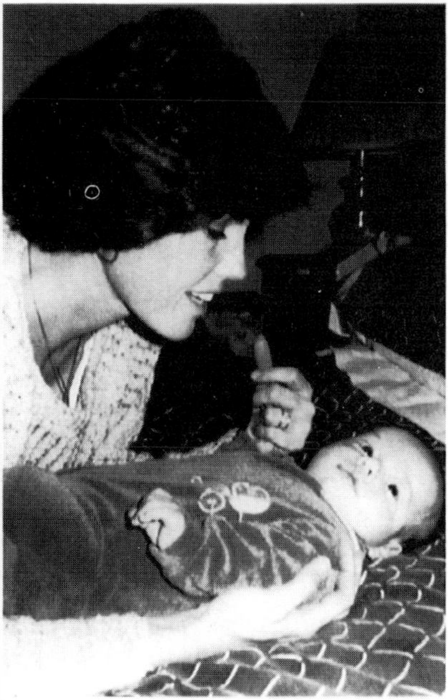

Cheryl bore Brad three sons in six years, even while she practiced law to help him regain his business. Here she plays happily with Jess.

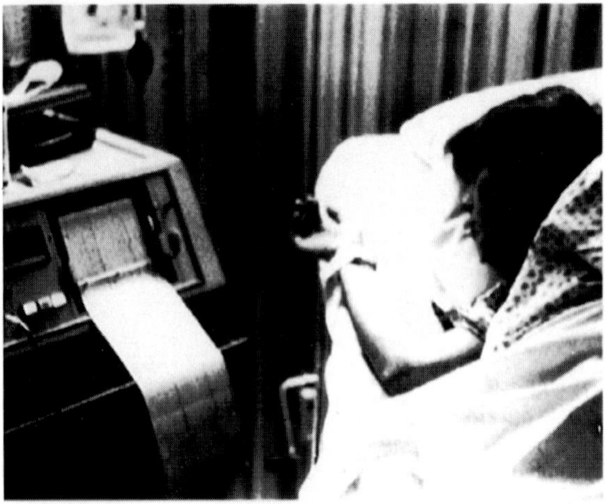

Cheryl was not happy when Brad took photographs of her in labor.

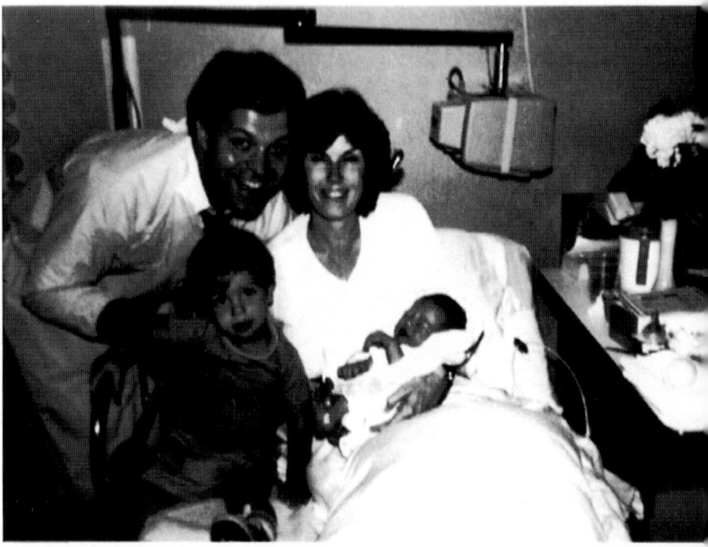

Brad, Cheryl, and Jess with newborn Michael, another son for Brad.

Outwardly, Brad seemed to be the ideal father. But he often shunted aside Brent and Kait, his oldest children, even though Cheryl and her family always welcomed them.

Left, Brad poses with Amy, his daughter by Lauren, with Jess on his back.

Michael, Jess, and Phillip Cunningham, Brad's three perfect sons.

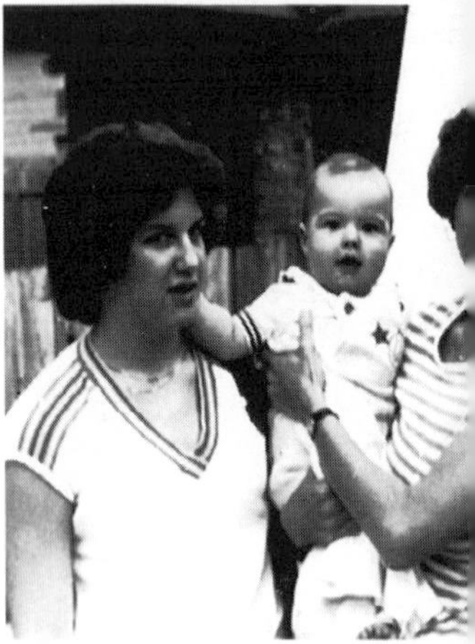

Cheryl with the three members of her family who tried desperately to protect her from the thing she would come to fear most: Jim Karr, her half brother *(above)*; her half sister Susan *(right)*; and her mother, Betty *(below)*, who was the last person to speak to Cheryl on September 21, 1986.

rad's father, Sanford, the only person he always ared about, with his second wife, Mary, on the rry to Bainbridge Island to see Brad and Cheryl's ew home.

All the Cunningham boys were bright. Here Jess, three, plays chess with his aunt Susan. His intelligence and memory would be put to a severe test when he was only six.

Cheryl with Jess, Phillip, and Michael. Her marriage to Brad had come apart, and nothing in the world was more important to her than her sons.

Sara Gordon, a beautiful and successful doctor, fell deeply in love with Brad and sympathized with his efforts to keep his sons from their "unfit" mother. They hoped to marry when he divorced Cheryl.

Randy Blighton was driving on the Sunset Highway on September 21, 1986, and risked his life to move a stalled van from the fast lane. He discovered horror inside.

The scene at 79th and the Sunset Highway on September 21. Cheryl' blue Toyota van was only slightly damaged but she had suffered massive head wounds.

Oregon State Police Detective Jerry Finch was among the first investigators to arrive at the scene, and would remain deeply involved in the investigation of Cheryl's death.

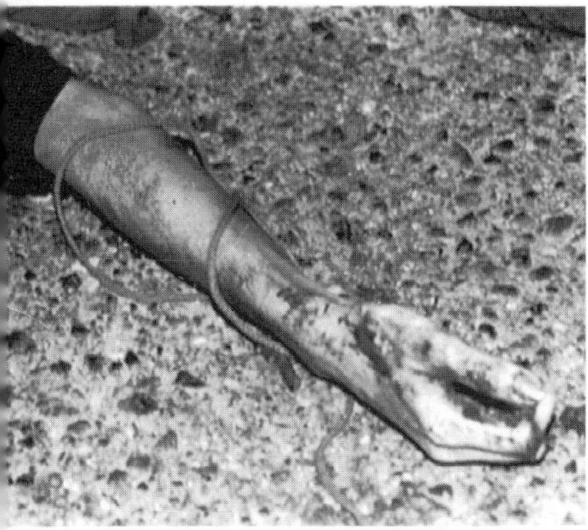

Oddly, a key on a blue shoelace was entwined around Cheryl's bloody arm. The explanation was heartbreaking.

Suspected of Cheryl's murder and determined that her family would not gain custody of his sons, Brad fled with them to this tiny house in Tampico, Washington. But no evidence surfaced to link him to the crime.

Brad was the epitome of the successful businessman during his marriage to Sara Gordon. He drove Mercedes-Benzes and pursued grandiose financial schemes. But it was Sara who paid all the bills, and their divorce was eerily reminiscent of Brad's divorce proceedings from Cheryl.

Dana Malloy in her high school graduation picture *(right)*, and as a beauty pageant contestant *(below)*. Hired as a "nanny" for the Cunningham boys, she soon fell under Brad's spell. And when he convinced her topless dancing was an art, she was the next woman to pay for his extravagant lifestyle.

Brad gave Dana this picture, taken in 1975. It was the way he liked to see himself—a man on top of the world.

Dana *(below)* posing with her sister and Brad's three sons. She was their third "mother" in three years and loved the boys. But like all Brad's women, she was soon living in terror.

Greg Dallaire, managing partner of Garvey, Schubert and Barer *(above)* joined John Burke *(right)* in seeking justice for Cheryl Keeton.

Mike Shinn and his assistant, Diane Bakker, took on the difficult task proving that Cheryl's murder was a case of "wrongful death." In a tr Brad never deigned to attend, the jury awarded an astoundingly lar sum to Cheryl's estate in May 1991.

Incredibly, Brad acted as his own defense attorney during his crimi trial for murder in 1994.

Charming and quick-witted, Brad was confident he could convince the jury he had had nothing to do with the brutal assault on his estranged wife.

Greg Ebersole

Greg Ebersole

Greg Ebersole

The Oregon State Police investigators who were dogged in their determination to bring Cheryl's killer to justice: Detective Mike McKernan *(left)*, Detective Jim Ayers *(fourth from left)*, and Sergeant Greg Baxter *(fifth from left)*.

Washington County District Attorney Scott Upham *(left)* led the criminal prosecution against Brad. Oregon State Police Detective Mike McKernan *(center)* and D.A.'s Investigator Jim Carr *(right)* were important members of his team.

Judge Timothy Alexander presided over the trial with remarkable skill and patience, even instructing Brad about the rules of criminal defense.

Cheryl's family and friends try to look cheerful as they anxiously await the jury's verdict on the afternoon of December 22, 1994. *Front row from left:* Kim Roberts, Katannah King, Debi Bowen, Jack Kincaid, the author, Marv Troseth, and Dave Keegan; *back row from left:* Bob McNannay, Billy Bowen, Donna Anders, Betty Troseth, Mike Shinn, and Susan Keegan.

Cheryl chasing her oldest son, Jess, as he heads for deep water. Her love and devotion as a mother, her capacity for caring, and her fierce determination to fight the evil that finally overwhelmed her—all remain in the memories of her family, her friends, her colleagues, and everyone who investigated and prosecuted her killer.

glancing at her sister and she was appalled. Cheryl looked as if she was starving; she was pale and she was so terribly quiet. 'I hugged Cheryl when she left, and she felt almost nonexistent,' Susan said. 'She was so thin. Our last hug was much longer than usual.'

After they left Susan's, Betty and Cheryl went to Sears and Cheryl bought some underwear and socks for the boys, paying with her Sears credit card. When they got back to Betty and Marv's house, they talked with him out in the driveway. Marv had been changing the oil in his car and he noticed that Cheryl's Toyota van was dirty. He offered to wash it for her, and she thought about it for a moment. 'No,' she finally said. 'I have to get back for the boys. There might be an accident on the freeway or something and I might be late. Thanks, Marv – maybe next time.'

Late that afternoon Cheryl headed south on the I-5 freeway. The drive to Portland ordinarily takes an hour, and even though she had to stop briefly at her office at Garvey, Schubert to pick up some papers, she would be at the house on the West Slope in plenty of time to welcome her three boys home from their weekend visit with their father.

Jim Karr had also been in Longview for most of the weekend. He headed down to Gresham on Sunday to visit a friend and watch the Seahawks game. He planned to be back at the West Slope house in time to help Cheryl put the boys to bed.

In Longview, Marv Troseth returned from the grocery store a few minutes after seven. Betty told him that Cheryl had called, very upset. The boys weren't home yet. Brad had called her and said that he was having trouble with his gas line. Betty was worried. She thought maybe Cheryl should call the police and ask them to look for Brad and the boys. 'I told her that you couldn't call the police just because someone was fifteen or twenty minutes late,' Marv said.

That made sense and Betty tried to be calm. But she

had caught Cheryl's fear the way you catch a virus, and her dread grew with every passing minute. She called Susan between 7:10 and 7:15. 'Mom said Cheryl was very upset because the boys weren't back,' Susan remembered. 'Mom was on edge because Cheryl was unreasonably concerned.'

It was unusual for Betty to call Susan and be so agitated. It was actually the first time Susan had heard her this way. 'Mom wanted to go to Cheryl's house, and I told her to relax.'

Betty and Marv's phone rang just before 8 P.M. It was Cheryl. 'Brad called and he wants me to meet him at that Mobil station down by the IGA store – but I know that station's closed. . . .'

'No!' Betty said. 'Don't go down there.'

'I have to get my kids.'

Betty begged Cheryl to wait until she and Marv could drive down to Portland and go with her to pick up the boys, but Cheryl argued that would take an hour at least. She was going to go. She had to go.

Betty couldn't change her daughter's mind. 'You call me the second you get back to the house. Don't wait for anything. I want to know you're safely home.'

Cheryl promised she would.

When Betty called Susan again that evening, she was on the edge of hysteria. She was terrified that Cheryl was going to meet Brad and told Susan that she thought she and Marv should head for Portland immediately.

'Go to Portland, if you want to go, Mom,' Susan said. Now Susan was catching the fear too.

'Something's not right,' Betty said. 'I don't know what's happening.'

Susan put down the phone and told her father about Betty's two frantic phone calls. 'I got very nervous too. I had a lump in my throat all evening,' Bob McNannay said.

Betty waited anxiously for Cheryl's call. Trying to ease her mind, Marv placed calls to both Cheryl's number and

Brad's. There was no answer at either, and no answering machine pickup. At Betty's urging, Marv kept calling but no one answered.

The next call that Betty received from the West Slope house was from her son Jim. She grabbed the phone before the first ring was over and when she heard Jim's voice, she cried, 'She's dead, isn't she? Cheryl's dead!'

Jim said that wasn't true. He didn't know where Cheryl was, but he had found a note from her and he was going to go look for her.

Betty was inconsolable. She *knew* her daughter was dead.

And, of course, she was right.

Brad had hired three separate attorneys to represent him in his divorce from Cheryl, dismissing them one after the other even though they were the best in the business. He had consulted almost a dozen others. He need not have bothered. How ironic that he didn't need a divorce now. Nor would there be any more custody battles.

Cheryl was dead.

And Jess, Michael, and Phillip were his alone.

Part IV

Sara

33

Brad Cunningham had emerged as the prime suspect in the death of his estranged wife, but the time frame of Cheryl's murder was vitally important in establishing the possibility of his guilt. Brad could account for his movements on that Sunday night almost to the minute. If Danielle Daniels, one of the residents living along 79th where it entered the Sunset Highway, *had* heard the sounds of someone beating Cheryl to death, the time of the murder would have been between 8:20 and 8:25. In order for Oregon State Police detectives to be satisfied that Brad had nothing to do with the crime, they would have to talk to witnesses who could back up his alibi for that Sunday night.

Brad didn't have to prove anything. In America, suspects and defendants are innocent until proven guilty. The legal burden of proof rested heavily on the detectives' shoulders and on the Washington County District Attorney's office. If they could not gather evidence and/or witnesses that they believed would prove Brad guilty beyond a reasonable doubt, he would go free.

There were numerous ways of checking on Brad, and the investigation was still fresh. Investigators could check phone records. Perhaps they could find outside witnesses who had had no interest in his activities that night but who would remember seeing him. The problem was to locate everything and everyone who might be able to either validate Brad's story or discredit it.

Brad's own six-year-old son had told the grand jury that

his father had left the apartment on Sunday night while he was watching a video and television. Children have little sense of the passage of time, but detectives did check the running time of *The Sword in the Stone* and of *Rambo*, the two movies Jess had been watching. If the boy's recollection was correct, Brad would have been away from the apartment for more than an hour.

Officer Craig Ward of the Portland Police Bureau had a far better time sense than a six-year-old boy, and so did Lilya Saarnen, Brad's former lover. Ward didn't see Cunningham that Sunday night, although he was in the Madison Tower parking garage, but Lilya did. And so did another tenant in the building.

Officer Ward arrived at the Madison Tower between 8:21 and 8:27 Sunday evening in response to a 'car prowl' complaint from Terry Houghton, a men's clothing salesman whose company van was parked in the garage on the B-2 level. Ward took an elevator from the ground floor to the B-1 level and then walked to B-2. His notes reflected that he had spent ten to fifteen minutes at the van. Houghton had lost more than a hundred sample suits and other items. After Ward had taken down that information, he and Houghton walked to the security gate and inspected it. 'I was aware that two or three vehicles drove past,' Ward recalled, 'but I never saw any foot traffic at all.'

Rachel Houghton, however, *did* see a man and a child in the garage. She and her husband lived on the seventh floor of the Madison Tower and they had two parking spaces in the garage. 'We returned from a weekend trip to find our van had been broken into,' she said, 'and we called the police. While we were talking to the police, I saw someone come down the driveway into the parking structure – running. It was a man and a child, entering the garage in a slow run or a fast walk. I had just been telling the officer how people got into the garage. The man had on shorts and a T-shirt; he was barefoot and he had wet hair.'

Later, Rachel Houghton would identify that man as Brad Cunningham. She sensed that he was startled to see a policeman in the garage. 'He stopped abruptly, and walked to a car, and put something away, and then he headed toward the Tower.'

The child and the running man in the shorts with wet hair hadn't meant anything to Rachel Houghton – not until she read about Cheryl Keeton's murder in the papers. She hadn't mentioned it to her husband, who was busy showing Craig Ward how the security gate operated. Later, she called police and told them what she had seen. She estimated that it was sometime around 9 P.M. when she saw the man and the little boy. Officer Ward cleared the Madison Tower at 'roughly nine P.M.'

Lilya Saarnen, who lived on the first floor of the Madison Tower in G-42, had been late for a shower given by a friend's mother that night. It was just past 7:30 P.M. when she stepped out of her door and encountered Brad and his small son Michael. Brad was carrying keys in his hand.

Early the next morning – Monday – Brad had called Lilya before she was even out of bed, asking her if she remembered seeing him in the hall the evening before. When she said she did, he said, 'At eight P.M., right?'

'No, Brad,' she corrected. 'I saw you at seven-thirty.'

Brad abruptly hung up the phone.

Lilya told her surgeon boyfriend that something about Brad's manner worried her. Later that morning at work, a friend called and asked, 'Have you read the paper?'

Lilya said she hadn't had time.

'Cheryl Keeton got murdered last night,' her friend said.

'That's funny,' Lilya said. 'I just talked to Brad, and he didn't say anything about it. . . .'

Lilya told Detective Jerry Finch about seeing Brad on Sunday evening. 'My front door was one of four on the ground-floor level. The elevator is on one side and the garden gate on the other. I was moving toward the garden gate at seven-thirty and Brad and Michael were leaving the elevator. . . .'

'How was he dressed?' Finch asked.

'Casually . . .'

'How casually?'

'Khaki pants, I think – and a jacket.'

'When Mr Cunningham and his son left the elevator, where were they headed?'

'Toward the garage.'

On October 10, Oregon State Police investigators served a search warrant on Brad Cunningham's apartment. Richard McKeirnan, Greg Baxter, Les Frank, and Jerry Finch conducted a search and found nothing that seemed truly helpful in their probe – either in the apartment or in Brad's storage locker at the Madison Tower. They did see a reflectorized vest with orange or yellow stripes which they seized and marked into evidence. It might have been the vest that Jess said his father was wearing when he came back from 'jogging' on the night of the murder. Or it might not have been. Brad would claim later it was a seldom used hunting vest.

Tests revealed no evidence of blood on the vest.

If the detectives had hoped to find a heavy blunt instrument with many surfaces that might match the wounds Dr Karen Gunson noted on Cheryl Keeton's autopsy report – and they had – they were disappointed. They found no weapon, no bloody clothes, and no running shoes with traces of red still etched in their bas-relief bottoms.

To solve a murder, investigators need to show means, motive, opportunity, and physical evidence. The detectives assigned to the Keeton case were convinced they had a motive. Brad had hated his estranged wife, particularly after the deposition she gave five days before her murder. Brad also had the means. He was a strong man and had access to all manner of weapons. And he could have had the opportunity – *if* he had been able to fit a murder into an extremely tight timetable.

Some of those who could verify where Brad had been that night or establish time sequences – Dr Sara Gordon, Officer Craig Ward, the Houghtons, Lilya Saarnen – would make impeccable witnesses *if* they chose to cooperate with the State. Then there were his own little boys, although Jess, the oldest, was probably the only one whose recall might be accurate. But Sara Gordon loved Brad Cunningham and they had plans for the future. Lilya Saarnen had once been intimate with him, and she was still his friend – as well as Sara Gordon's. And his own sons idolized their daddy. Detectives hoped that more witnesses would either come forward on their own or surface during the investigation.

Just as a medical examiner may find that the last time the deceased was seen alive is the best way to establish time of death, the activities of a murder suspect are best charted by the last time he was seen before the murder by competent witnesses, and the first time he was seen after the crime. Lilya Saarnen had seen Brad and Michael emerge from the elevator at the Madison Tower at 7:30–7:35 P.M. that Sunday. Cheryl was murdered between 8:20 and 8:30 P.M. And at around 9:00 P.M. Rachel Houghton saw Brad and a small boy in the garage of the Madison Tower. For an hour and a half, Brad's whereabouts were unaccounted for.

Had he been taking care of Jess, Michael, and Phillip during that time, waiting impatiently for his heedless, drunken, estranged wife to come for them? Had he left the apartment on the eighteenth floor only briefly – to peer down over the rail to watch for Cheryl, to put boots into Sara's Cressida, to pick up the mail? That would fill up the vital time period.

Or had he planned every minute of that Sunday evening, and planned it with vile intention? Had he left Jess and Phillip alone in his apartment and taken Michael with him as he set out to murder their mother? That would fill up the vital time period too.

Detectives would drive the route from Providence Hospital to the Madison Tower to the West Slope and back to the Madison Tower with stopwatches in hand to prove that Brad could have done that on the night of the murder. It was certainly possible. Still there was absolutely no physical evidence linking him to the crime.

34

In the days immediately following Cheryl's murder, Brad told confidants that his biggest fear was that her mother would take his children away from him. He had been trying to spirit Jess, Michael, and Phillip away from Portland, but the best he could do was keep moving them from one house to the next over the ensuing three or four weeks. The first week, along with Sara, they were mostly at his sister Margie's or Gini Burton's, and that weekend they stayed with another of Sara's sisters, Shirley, who lived in McMinnville, Sara's hometown. Michael had his fifth birthday on September 26, and he wanted to celebrate at Chuck E Cheese's. While the flowers were still fresh on his mother's grave, Brad and Sara tried to give Michael a wonderful birthday.

Then suddenly, after Brad's three sons had become such an integral part of Sara's life, they disappeared. It was just one more component in a world that was growing steadily sadder and more frightening. 'I didn't see the boys after that,' Sara would recall. 'Not for weeks. I asked Brad where they were, and he told me that he had had them taken out of state. I didn't know where they were.'

Brad had been unsuccessful in preventing his oldest son from appearing before the Washington County grand jury, of course. Still, when no arrest followed his testimony, he must have felt vindicated. The damn police had come and pawed through his apartment and his storage locker, but if they were looking for evidence that he had killed his wife, they didn't find it. How could they? He said he hadn't murdered Cheryl, and he didn't know who had.

Brad's career with U.S. Bank faltered after her murder. His superiors were understanding when he didn't come in to work the first week. His estranged wife's death was a shock to everyone. But Brad never really went back to work. He showed up only sporadically. He had been considered a valuable employee for the almost five months he was with U.S. Bank. He was a man with an eye for property with potential. But now he had made unsavory headlines in Portland, and that was not the image that U.S. Bank – or any bank, for that matter – would choose to project. Even so, Brad was given the benefit of the doubt.

However, his poor attendance at work was brought to the attention of his boss, Larry Rosenkrantz. Given Brad's apparent disinterest in his job, it was only a matter of time before U.S. Bank had to demand some response from him. Did he intend to come back to work? Brad met with Rosenkrantz and poured out a story of a life that left little time for his career. 'He indicated to me that he was being harassed by the police, and that he was being hounded by his mother-in-law,' Rosenkrantz recalled.

That might explain why Brad had checked out two bank cars from the car pool in the ten days after Cheryl's murder. One had to be retrieved from an airport lot in Seattle. Brad had apparently used them so that no one could follow him. He had had Sara's car, his truck, his Suburban, his Cabriolet, and the pool cars so that he could vary his transportation often. He wasn't fired from the U.S. Bank job, but a mutually agreed arrangement was made. His contract was bought out, and he received twenty-three thousand dollars.

Everywhere Brad looked that fall, he found another facet

of his life shattering. His sons had no mother. He had no job. His suit was jammed up in the Texas courts, and he told Sara he lived in terror that he would lose his sons. He knew that Cheryl's law firm was helping Betty and Marv Troseth, Bob McNannay, and John Burke in their efforts to gain custody of his children. Everyone but Sara seemed to be against him.

Finally, Brad came to the decision that the only way he could keep his sons was to hide them. He could not even tell Sara where they were. He had possession of his sons, and he intended to keep them. The problem was that he needed help. He wasn't so naive that he didn't know the police were still following him, aware of most of his movements. He couldn't simply drive his sons away himself, he believed, without someone knowing where they were.

His father would have helped him – he always had – but Sanford Cunningham had died two months before Cheryl. Brad detested his mother, and he had nothing good to say about his sisters Susan and Ethel. He refused to go to them for help with his sons. (Later, his sisters said that they would have gladly sheltered the little boys.) Brad was still close to his uncle Jimmy, but he lived in Burien, Washington – Brad's old hometown – and anyone looking for his boys would check there first.

Brad had other relatives in Washington State. Although he hadn't seen his aunt Trudy Dreesen for decades, he thought of her now. Trudy was one of his grandfather Paul Cunningham's daughters by his second wife, a half sister to Sanford and Jimmy, but a decade younger. She was married to Dr Herman Dreesen, a chiropractor in Lynnwood, Washington.

Trudy Dreesen, the onetime Seattle SeaFair Queen, was still a beautiful woman in her fifties. She was also tender-hearted, and when she received Brad's call for help, she rushed to do what she could. She was appalled at the tragedy that had struck him and his children. And when he explained that it wouldn't even be safe for *her* to keep his sons with her in her Lynnwood home, she perceived the depth of his anxiety. She could see that Brad was shaken by what had happened and was terrified that he would lose his boys too.

'I have friends who will help,' she said quickly.

Trudy Dreesen talked with Florence Chamberlain, who lived in Port Angeles. Although Trudy had met Florence only twice, her son was dating the Chamberlains' daughter, and Trudy knew that the Chamberlains were good people who lived in a three-story, six-bedroom home. After Trudy explained that Brad was a widower who needed someplace for his little boys – but only for a few weeks until he could find a permanent spot for them – Florence agreed to take Jess and Phillip in. Brad had told his aunt that his six-year-old and his two-year-old should be together, but he wanted Michael, just five, to be in another safe house. He didn't tell her why and she didn't ask.

Trudy and Herm Dreesen brought Jess and Phillip to the Chamberlains' home. Florence showed them through the house and gave them their choice of the empty bedrooms. Jess selected the room with only one bed. It was clear that he and his little brother needed to be together. Florence saw that Trudy was very upset, truly fearful that someone was trying to snatch or somehow harm Brad's sons.

Trudy asked her friend Jean Count, who lived in Bothell, if she would take Michael. Jean agreed readily, touched by the pathetic story Trudy told and how upset she was. Brad and Trudy brought Michael to her home. During the two or three weeks that Michael stayed with Jean Count, Brad came only once when he picked Michael up to take him to visit with Jess and Phillip.

In Port Angeles, Florence Chamberlain never met or spoke to Brad in person. When he brought Michael to see his two brothers, it was Trudy who took them outside to meet Brad and Michael. The three little Cunninghams romped on the lawn for about half an hour. Brad never called Florence to check on Jess and Phillip.

Florence Chamberlain and Jean Count were women in their middle years. They were very kind to the little boys in their care, even if they were slightly puzzled about why they had to be separated from their father. The children had arrived without even a change of underwear or socks, but Trudy gave her friends more than enough money to ensure that they had whatever they needed.

'I spent twenty-five dollars on underwear for them,' Florence Chamberlain would recall. 'That was all.'

Their mother had been dead for such a short time, and Jess, Michael, and Phillip had already been dragged from pillar to post, moving almost every day. They had stayed with Sara's friends and family, protected by a father who feared the police, unnamed assassins, *and* his ex-mother-in-law – three entities he sometimes spoke of as equally dangerous. Now for most of October the boys were completely separated from their father, from Sara, from anything they could remember of their former life. It had to have been worst for Michael; he didn't even have a brother to talk to when the lights were turned off at night.

Almost instantly, Trudy Dreesen had become one of Brad's staunchest supporters. Even though she had not seen him for longer than she could remember, she was there for him now. That was the kind of woman she was, and her husband Herm backed her up.

The Dreesens and Brad's other loyal supporters understood that he was hiding his boys to protect them. But there were others – Cheryl's family and friends – who felt he was determined to hide them from the police for fear that one or all of his sons might have some memories of the night of September 21, memories that he hoped time would erase completely.

Brad's eighteenth-floor apartment in the Madison Tower stood empty. When his rent came due on October 3, Sara paid the twelve hundred dollars. On the seventh, she made his car payment. He had enough problems without having to face eviction or repossession of his Suburban. U.S. Bank owned his Cabriolet now.

On October 3, 1986, Sara testified before the Washington County grand jury, which was still looking into Cheryl Keeton's murder. The ordeal she herself was undergoing was obvious. Twelve days after Cheryl's death, she didn't know where Brad or the boys were. She didn't know if they were alive or dead. Sara was a small woman to begin with – one hundred pounds was a good weight for her – but she hadn't weighed that much for months; now she was down to about eighty-five pounds, and there were dark circles under her eyes.

She answered the grand jurors' questions about her contacts with Brad on the night of September 21, and she told of her calls to him after he left her at Providence Hospital, calls that went unanswered. She did not tell them about the purple bruise she had seen beneath Brad's arm when they showered together on September 24. He had explained that to her satisfaction.

'I answered everything they asked,' she said later. 'I didn't volunteer information.'

Sometime later that month, Brad got in contact with Sara. 'He told me that he had taken the boys on a "journey." Later, he said that he took them to Salt Lake City and he was looking for an "underground system" so that Cheryl's family could never have them. He told me he knew he would be taking a chance because even *he* might never be able to find them.'

After a few weeks, Brad had picked Michael up from Jean Count and met the other boys at the Bainbridge Island ferry dock where Florence Chamberlain brought them. Apparently he had decided against sending his boys into long-term hiding, or maybe he never found the 'underground system' he was looking for. He brought them back from the 'journey' and made new plans. One thing was certain; he refused to stay in the Portland area, or even in the State of Oregon.

Brad and Cheryl had purchased property east of the Cascade Mountains in Tampico, Washington, in the early 1980s. The little crossroads town west of Yakima was located between the Cowiche Mountains and the Lost Horse Plateau. Sanford Cunningham had lived there until his death, and Brad had been drawn to the area. He had taken most of his wives to Yakima County to hunt or to camp. After he lost the real estate project in Houston, he and Sanford had started their abortive businesses together there – the gas station, laundromat, and car wash.

He and Cheryl owned two large parcels of land in Tampico, on which Brad had grown hay and built a barn and sheds. He fancied it had potential as a working ranch. There was a small house on the property, a rental, and the larger shell of what Brad would always call 'the family home.' It was presently nothing more than exterior walls and a roof. This Tampico property was the refuge that Brad ran to around Halloween 1986.

Even though the previous tenants had trashed the place, he and the boys moved into the rental house. Brad, Brent, Jess, Michael, and Phillip were now living in a tiny house with cheap vinyl floors, urine-soaked carpets, and scarred walls. The place needed new wallpaper and cabinets too. It was a radical departure from the lifestyle that Brad had become accustomed to – the huge homes and sumptuous apartments.

Brad was down but far from out. He had the twenty-three-thousand-dollar severance pay from U.S. Bank, Sara had paid all his legal bills and his monthly obligations for September and October, and he was not unskilled as a carpenter. He bought supplies and quickly refurbished the rental house. It was anything but elegant, but it was warm, clean, and comfortable. Jess, Michael, and Phillip were glad to be with their father, to sleep consecutive nights in the same beds in the same house, and to begin to trust that they would not have to move on soon again. The Cunningham boys were living in their own house, literally in their own house. Since they too qualified as tribal members, Brad had borrowed money from the Colville tribe in his younger sons' names to buy this property.

To her relief, Sara was once again part of Brad's life, and of the boys' lives. Perhaps they had a future after all. When Sanford died the previous July, Sara had worried about how his widow, Mary, would manage, and she had bought the Prowler trailer that belonged to Brad's father, deliberately paying Mary way over book value. Now, Sara parked the Prowler in Tampico, next to Brad's little house.

The boys still believed that their mother had died in a car accident, and Brad felt they were much too young to know the truth. They were his children, and Sara didn't try to interfere with his decision about what to tell them and when.

Every chance she got, Sara spent time in Washington with Brad and the boys. She either drove east on Highway 84 alongside the Columbia River, crossing the river to head north on Route 97 into eastern Washington, or she caught one of the little commuter airlines into Yakima. 'When I visited,' Sara remembered, 'Brad and I slept in my trailer, and Brent and the little boys slept in the two bedrooms in the house.'

Brad told his youngsters that their mother was gone but now he had found them a 'new mom.' 'He wanted them to call me Mom,' Sara recalled. 'And he always referred to Cheryl by her first name, so they began to call her Cheryl too. He told me that he didn't think the kids would miss Cheryl at all.'

It was true that Sara had never seen the boys cry for their lost mother. She was concerned that they seemed never to have gone through a grieving process. It was almost as if Brad had them under some kind of mental control. There was no question that they admired him and she never saw him punish them physically. But she wondered at the 'excessively long time-outs' Brad enforced. Often one son or another was ordered to stand in the corner, arms at his side, with his nose an inch or two from the wall, and instructed not to waver. Even Phillip, who was not yet three years old, did his time at the wall. 'If they moved, Brad extended the time,' Sara said. 'It might start at ten minutes' time-out and end up being an hour.'

Sara wasn't present at the supper table in Tampico one night when one of the boys suddenly asked where their mother was. Had she heard Brad's reply, she would have been horrified. Brent was at the table and stopped eating when he heard his father's reply. 'Your mother's turning to dust. Now eat your supper.'

A month or two after Cheryl died, Sara accompanied Brad and the little boys to Bunker Hill Cemetery outside Longview. They were still confused about where Cheryl had gone. It was a raw day and it wasn't easy to find Cheryl's grave. It did not yet have a marker or a tombstone on it. Finally they located it far up at the top of the hill, near the section that had been there for a hundred years. Brad pointed to the grave and told the boys their mother was buried there in the earth. Michael looked at the spot and Sara heard the five-year-old boy ask, 'But how can she breathe?'

It was arduous for Sara to make the trips to Brad's house in Tampico. She had to arrange her on-call schedule very carefully and she couldn't cut down on her work. She had been meeting not only her own financial obligations but Brad's too, plus his legal expenses. Still, she had fun when she was with Brad and the boys. It snowed early in Yakima County that year, and they made popcorn and hot chocolate after they played in the snow.

Brad was resolute that he would never move back to Oregon. He told Sara he could never get work in Portland – there was too much media interest in him there. He was making a life for himself in the Yakima area. He was taking care of his boys and building a shed for one of his tractors, and he had joined the local volunteer fire department. If and when he moved, it would not be back to Portland. 'He wanted me to move my practice to Seattle,' Sara said. 'He wanted me to leave my family, my friends, my patients – my *security* – in Portland and start all over again in Seattle. I made some inquiries about openings for anesthesiologists in Seattle – but I didn't want to go.'

Despite her love for Brad and his sons, living with the aftermath of Cheryl's murder wore on Sara. Although she believed absolutely that Brad had had nothing to do with her death, she had never really gotten over the memory of those first few weeks of terror, of their moving from place to place to escape the unseen forces that Brad insisted were stalking them. Brad had come into her life at Easter and made it wonderful, but by Thanksgiving it was hard for her even to remember those happy, carefree days. When Cheryl died, much of Sara's joy had died too.

Sara was having second thoughts. 'It wasn't just that he wanted me to move my practice to Seattle,' she said. 'He did things that upset me. He showed up at Providence Hospital one night looking like a street person. He was dirty, scroungy – he needed a shave. I was embarrassed.'

Never once did Sara complain about how much money she had spent on Brad. Money in and of itself had never mattered to her. People did. It was the complete upheaval of her life, her belief system, that made her rethink her decision to marry Brad.

Brad seemed unaware that she was backing away. He and the boys went to McMinnville for Thanksgiving dinner at Sara's sister's house and they had a pleasant time. Later they spent the night at Sara's apartment in the Madison Tower. Brad had long since given up his own apartment. Regretfully, Sara had made up her mind that she couldn't continue with Brad. After the boys were tucked into bed, she told him gently that she wanted to break up with him. 'Brad pleaded with me not to leave him,' she recalled. 'He told me that he would have a very hard time finding another "partner" at that stage in his life.'

Sara would not be dissuaded. She had agonized over her decision for a long time before she told him. She had fallen in love with a handsome, charming, self-confident, successful bank executive. She barely recognized that man in Brad anymore. She was shocked to learn he was nearly broke. He had spent the twenty-three thousand dollars U.S. Bank had given him to buy out his contract in September, spent it in two months! He seemed to have no discipline and no brakes on his behavior. It was true that he had bought building supplies to fix up the house in Tampico, but even so, he should have had half of that money left.

They went to bed, finally, with Brad still refusing to let Sara go. He loved her. He needed her. Some time later, Brad shook her awake. 'Sara,' he said, 'if something happens to me, will you take care of my kids?'

'Yes,' she answered sleepily. 'Of course.'

The next time Sara woke up, Brad was gone. She looked around the apartment and couldn't find him. Alarmed, she got dressed and went down to the garage. His Suburban was gone. Where would he go in the predawn hours?

Sara paced the floor of her apartment as Brad's sons slept, unaware. Brad was gone for three or four hours. And when he came back, he looked terrible. He looked like a broken man. 'I was going to jump off the fourteenth floor,' he told her hoarsely. 'I didn't have the nerve. I went out on the freeway and was going to drive into a pole or something—'

'Why?' Sara asked.

'I couldn't live without you. I can't get a job. I'm being harassed by the Oregon State Police. What do I have to live for?'

Sara stared at him, wondering if he meant what he was saying. But, finally, she believed him. There was no way she could walk away and leave a man in such desperate straits. Brad needed her. The boys needed her. 'All right,' she said. 'I'll stay with you for one year. But I'm not going to leave Portland. If you don't get your life together by then, I'll leave you.'

Brad smiled at last and folded her into his muscular arms.

35

Sara realized that if they were all going to be together, they would need larger living quarters. Her apartment and Brad's tiny house 190 miles away would do only as stopgap measures. Counting Brent, there would be six of them when they merged their families. Sara started looking for a house big enough for herself, Brad, and his four sons. Eventually they settled on a beautiful estate in Dunthorpe, an upscale area in Lake Oswego. There was a huge gray house, a guest house, and a sweeping lawn where the boys could play. It would need some remodeling, but it was well worth the quarter-million-dollar asking price.

Brad and his sons moved back to the Portland area in February 1987. He pointed out numerous things that he didn't like about the Dunthorpe house. The kitchen needed modernizing, and he felt a sweeping circular driveway would suit their estate better. Brad did some of the work himself, grading the driveway before a contractor paved it. He was quite adept at operating heavy equipment.

'He took the cabinets out in the kitchen,' Sara said, 'and tore down the kitchen wall.' Mostly, however, she hired carpenters, electricians, and plumbers to do the work. In the end, it cost her one hundred thousand dollars to remodel the Dunthorpe estate to Brad's specifications. She also agreed to finance a 1988 Whitewater Jet boat that Brad felt would be fun for all of them.

Brad had apparently been correct in his assumption that he couldn't get a job in Portland. 'He tried for banking jobs,'

Sara said. 'He had a good interview at Rainier Bank but he said U.S. Bank quashed that.' So they soon settled into a pattern. Sara was the breadwinner and Brad was the househusband. She left for work early each morning, and Brad gave the boys breakfast and took care of them until the sitter arrived. Brent went to Lincoln High and Jess was in first grade, but Michael and Phillip were still too young.

Sara changed her bank account at First Interstate so that Brad's name was on the checks and he could sign them. Now she was not only paying for child care, dental and medical care, and all the other expenses for Brent, Jess, Michael, and Phillip, she was also paying Brad's support payments for Kait to Loni Ann. Indeed, she was paying for everything, even $210 a month on the baby grand piano that had impressed her so much when Brad first took her to his eighteenth-floor apartment in the Madison Tower. Michael was taking piano lessons. That alone made the piano worthwhile for Sara.

Brad's contribution was to write the checks and sign them with his flamboyant signature.

A year passed and although Brad had not really 'gotten his life together,' he and Sara were married on November 27, 1987. She was his fifth wife; he was her fourth husband. She was determined to make this marriage work. She truly loved Brad and she cared for his sons as if they were her own.

Brad still couldn't seem to find a job, nothing in keeping with his education and talents. He had overseen a six-hundred-million-dollar project in Houston, and he had been a top bank executive in Portland. He couldn't very well lower himself to taking an ordinary job. He and Sara decided that he should go back to college. He registered at Portland State University in 1987 and 1988, and Sara paid his tuition and expenses. Brad had no income at all. The Houston lawsuit continued to wend its weary – and expensive – way through the courts in Texas. Vinson and

Elkins had taken the case on a contingency basis. If and when there was a judgment in Brad's favor, the law firm would take a large chunk of that.

Beyond Sara's support, Brad had another money source to tap: Cheryl's estate. He submitted a budget for the cost of raising Jess, Michael, and Phillip – which included money to pay *him* for child care. He told Bob McNannay, one of the trustees of Cheryl's estate, that he needed just under four thousand dollars a month for the boys' expenses. He said he had to pay for their medical and dental bills, clothes, food, shelter, and for child care. He didn't mention, of course, that Sara was already paying for all of that. When McNannay resisted and John Burke backed him up, Brad sued Cheryl's estate. In essence, the estate that she had set up for her sons then had to pay legal expenses to protect itself, but at least Brad wasn't able to penetrate the trust.

He had another ingenious financial scheme. There was no question that he had suffered crushing business losses for years, and he said he had talked to a C.P.A. who told him that Sara could take advantage of those losses. She would have the benefit of 'two million dollars in tax loss carry-forward,' Brad said, and would pay considerably lower taxes than if she hadn't married him. There would even come a time when Brad would claim that Sara married him only *because* she wanted his tax write-offs.

Nineteen eighty-seven was the first year they filed their income tax jointly. However, Brad told Sara that he learned on the very last day of the year that his tax loss could only be used against *his* income. He told Sara that a C.P.A. suggested that she pay Brad a salary of fifty-five thousand dollars on December 31, 1987. The sum was supposed to be returned into her account. Sara did what she was told to do. 'I signed a lot of signatures I shouldn't have signed,' she would say years later. 'That was certainly one of them. . . .'

Shortly after their marriage, Brad suggested to Sara that she adopt his youngest sons. He said that she was their mother now, and there was no reason why she shouldn't cement her emotional bond with them legally. She agreed readily. Sara loved Jess, Michael, and Phillip as much as she could love any child she gave birth to. In March 1988 she legally adopted the three little boys.

New birth certificates were issued. Now Sara's name appeared on the line for 'Mother.' There was no longer any mention at all of Cheryl Keeton, the mother who had given birth to the boys and loved them so deeply. It wasn't Brad's idea, and it certainly wasn't Sara's. She never wanted to replace Cheryl as the boys' mother; it was simply the way Oregon adoption law is written. But it was a little sad to see Cheryl's name erased from her sons' lives, Sara thought, as if she had never existed at all.

If Cheryl herself had set out to find a mother who would love her little boys, she could not have found a better one than Sara. But if she was sometimes disappointed that her relationship with Brad was not as idyllic as she had hoped it would be, Sara was never disappointed with Jess, Michael, and Phillip. She loved them devotedly. Without realizing it, she had given hostages to fortune.

Brad remained the consummate entrepreneur. He was constantly thinking of ways to get back into the world of business. While he was attending classes at Portland State, he saw that there was a real need for a coffee shop close to the college; not everyone wanted to eat at the college-run cafeteria. He visualized a bakery with fresh muffins, rolls, and bread, sandwiches and coffee. He could even add a call-in/take-out lunch run. If it was managed correctly, he figured that students and anyone with business near the campus would flock to patronize his small restaurant – good smells and a warm place to get out of the rain.

Brad checked out buildings around the college and found one that seemed perfect. They could gut it, remodel the interior, and use the lower level for the bakery/coffee shop. Later, when they got a liquor license, he envisioned a gourmet 'bistro' upstairs. It was hard for Sara to imagine that the deserted building could ever be turned into a desirable restaurant. 'The kids said it best, I guess,' she remembered. 'The first time they saw it, they said, "This is a piece of junk."'

Brad assured them all that the building was not junk; it was a tremendous opportunity. He had not lost one whit of his sales ability. When he believed in something, it was difficult not to catch his fervor, and Sara was soon involved in his plans. 'I agreed to finance the bakery,' she later said. Brad would call it the Broadway Bakery. And the money drain began when Brad wrote a check on their joint account on April 11, 1988, to the City of Portland for a building permit: $115.63. Sara would pour some $200,000 into the remodeling of the old building, transforming it into a bright, inviting restaurant.

Brad was totally in charge of selecting the bakery equipment, and hiring contractors and employees. Sara paid the bills. The bakery opened in 1988, and the Bistro – the upstairs restaurant – in July of 1989. The bakery barely kept its head above water, even though there was an enthusiastic response from customers. The Bistro was a financial flop.

Sara had hoped that the Broadway Bakery and the Bistro would provide some center and purpose for Brad. He had been through so many bad years. He no longer had a profession, or at least he could not find work in real estate or banking in Portland. He was only thirty-nine and she couldn't picture him sitting around the Dunthorpe estate as some kind of glorified baby-sitter.

Brad reassured Sara that Symptovir, his formula for the alleviation of herpes symptoms, was still viable. She had never been enthusiastic about that product, however, whose base ingredient was olive oil. But Symptovir was no longer Brad's main interest. It wasn't going anywhere, although Sara had paid those bills too, buying cases of olive oil and chemicals, getting business cards printed.

Brad chose Spectrum, the name of the division of U.S. Bank for which he had recently been an executive, for his corporate name. Actually, he had several small corporations. Every time he opened up another section of the bakery building, he became another corporation. Sara could not understand why he did that, but she had never claimed to have a head for business.

A number of puzzling things happened to Sara in the summer of 1989. She didn't understand all the ramifications, but an old friend of Cheryl's – an attorney named John Burke – was apparently trying to sue Brad over Cheryl's death. Brad didn't take it seriously, although he was incensed at almost anything Burke did. Burke and Bob McNannay administered the boys' trust fund and Sara knew that Brad felt that they were deliberately keeping him from getting money that the boys needed.

Sara was surprised when she learned the name of John Burke's attorney, Mike Shinn. She had gone to college with Mike and, worried about Brad and her sons, she wrote and chided him for causing new grief in her family's lives. They had all been through so much already. Shinn delayed a reply until he was more familiar with the case.

In the autumn of 1989, Sara and Brad were having dinner at Jake's, a popular downtown Portland restaurant. She recognized Mike Shinn sitting at another table and pointed him out to Brad. Later, Brad left their table briefly and she saw him bend down to say something to Shinn. Brad brushed her questions aside when he came back.

At about the same time, Brad hired a young woman named Lynn Minero* to work as assistant manager of the bakery. He was telling Sara about his new employee when he suddenly volunteered, 'You don't have to worry about her, Sara – she's happily married and has two daughters.'

Sara laughed at first. '*You're* happily married and you have two daughters and four sons.'

Sara had never been concerned that Brad might be unfaithful to her. They had had their differences, but this was simply not a problem that had ever crossed her mind. Now she looked up at him sharply. Why would Brad tell her not to worry about a new bakery employee just because she was a woman? He had been extolling Lynn's virtues and telling Sara how attractive she was, but that hadn't worried Sara.

For the first time, she wondered. Was Brad protesting too much? They spent most of their days apart now; both Sara and Brad had to leave the Dunthorpe house so early in the morning – she to go to surgery, he to head for the bakery – sometimes as early as 4 A.M. Their baby-sitter Shannon Farrell lived in the guest house on the property, and they knew the boys were well taken care of.

If Sara had a flaw, it was that she could be too trusting, too accepting, too generous. But she was an extremely smart woman and, once the first atonal *ding* of doubt sounded, she didn't have to be told twice. In retrospect, she realized that Brad had been much too complimentary of his new manager's appearance and much too enthusiastic about her as an employee. But he made his fatal error when he tried to allay suspicions his wife hadn't yet felt.

Now she *was* suspicious.

They spent Thanksgiving of 1989 on Sara's brother's huge ranch in eastern Oregon. Brad was not the same. Sara's feminine instincts told her that something was going on. And hell hath no better private detective than a suspicious wife. Sara began to keep a journal, just as Cheryl had written notes before her. She began writing down her thoughts on Saturday, January 17, 1990. Her marriage was slightly more than two years old, she had adopted Brad's three youngest sons, she had invested almost a million dollars in his enterprises and in their Dunthorpe home, and now she had the sickening apprehension that he was cheating on her at the very workplace she had funded to give him one more chance for financial success.

'Jan 27: Brad went in to bakery at 4 a.m. At 8:30, I called and he *wasn't at bakery*. . . . He called at 9. Said he had put his new tire on and had gone to a cycle shop to fix something he had broken.

'Feb 1: Brad met me at Fulton's Pub. . . . He said he had given Lynn a ride, . . . said she couldn't get hold of Gary* [Lynn's husband] so she called him and asked him to give her a ride home. . . . Brad left bakery at 4:20. I called on portable phone at 4:50, 5:10, 5:25 with no answer.

'Feb 2: Brad met me . . . to sign loan papers. He left at 3:05–3:10. I know he went right back to the bakery and picked Lynn up. . . . I called his phone. . . . He said he found the phone had been turned off accidentally.

Sara's journal noted numerous instances almost every day when Brad had not been where he said he was. She also wrote that Brad was 'very resentful about my asking about her [Lynn] being around.'

In February 1986 Cheryl Keeton had changed her will and the beneficiaries of her life insurance policy. In February 1990 Sara Gordon changed the beneficiaries of *her* life insurance policy, and also the terms of the loan she had just signed with Brad at First Interstate Bank. She did not tell Brad what she had done.

Although Brad always had a plausible explanation for why he never seemed to be where he was supposed to be and why he didn't answer his mobile phone, Sara's careful charting of his movements proved to her that Lynn Minero was often with him. Brad's behavior was now diametrically opposed to that of the man she had first known. Then, she could count on him to be exactly where he said he would be. He had always arrived for their dates on time. The only time he had faltered was the night Cheryl was murdered.

Brad came down with stomach flu, he said, and he slept on the couch so that he wouldn't bother Sara. She had another explanation for his behavior.

'February 6: Brad stayed down on the couch all night. . . . Seemed angry with me – Said he felt that Burke et al were persecuting him for something he had not done. Then said how he felt I was like them and persecuting him for something he had not done – ie. affair with Lynn. . . . Called me at work at 8:00 A.M. . . . said his SeaFirst Visa account had not been paid for two months and was I intentionally not paying his bills? Seemed rather upset.'

Sara now knew in her heart that her marriage to Brad was not working out, but a faithless husband is far easier to say goodbye to than three little boys. She loved Jess and Michael and Phillip so much that she wondered if she could bear to give them up. 'I knew that Brad would never let me have the boys,' she would recall wistfully. And she had to remember the vicious struggle that went on between Cheryl and Brad over their three sons.

It would not be exaggerating to say that Sara was going through emotional agony. If she stayed with Brad, she knew there would be countless early mornings and nights when she didn't know where he was or with whom. If she left him, she would lose the children who considered her their mother. And they would lose her.

36

Four years had passed but police files had never been closed on Cheryl Keeton's death; the investigators from the Oregon State Police and the Washington County District Attorney's office simply ran out of leads. They had been unable to link Brad to Cheryl's murder with physical evidence. They had found no weapon, no bloody clothing, and no telltale trail of blood. They had talked to scores of people and found many who knew nothing that would help and a number who were reluctant to become involved. Those who knew Brad did not want to go into detail about their relationships with him.

On television and in the movies, circumstantial cases move along smoothly and charges are filed, witnesses burst out with new information or outright confessions, and the last five or ten minutes of fictional mysteries always seem to bring satisfactory answers to complicated puzzles. There are usually even wonderfully convoluted 'double-reverse twists' to make the denouement more suspenseful. The death of Cheryl Keeton was, however, a tragically authentic event. Real life. Real death, as it were. After an exhaustive investigation, it began to look as if the person who had caused her death was going to walk away and any footprints left behind were going to grow fainter and fainter until there was no trail at all.

The detectives who had worked their way back through Cheryl's life – and through Brad's life – found themselves against a brick wall. Cheryl's murder went unsolved. At least, it went unprosecuted, because all of their evidence was, thus far, circumstantial. On Sunday, September 21,

1986, Brad had had ample time to drive from the Madison Tower to the West Slope area to meet Cheryl, to strike her on the head and face two dozen times, to send her van containing her body onto the Sunset Highway, and to drive back to his apartment. No one had seen him between 7:35 and 8:50. But a man cannot be arrested because he hated his wife and because no one had either seen or talked to him for an hour and fifteen minutes, not even if his wife had died a brutal death during those seventy-five minutes.

If Brad had killed Cheryl, he had found a place to wash himself clean of blood afterward (although blood spatter experts would one day testify that 'cast-off' blood from a bludgeoning weapon doesn't necessarily land on the killer who holds that weapon). When Lilya Saarnen saw Brad at 7:35, he had been wearing casual slacks – just as Sara recalled. Sara never again saw the wine-colored shirt that Brad had worn to the American Dream Pizza Company earlier that evening, although that was something else she had not volunteered to the police during their initial investigation. If Brad washed up, no one knew where he had done it. When Rachel Houghton saw him entering the garage around nine, he was wearing shorts and a T-shirt; he was barefoot and his hair was wet. That was forty minutes after Cheryl's estimated time of death. Had he come through the pool area of the apartment tower? Had he stopped in a gas station restroom somewhere along the way home? Had he made it back to his apartment without being seen at all and washed up in his own kitchen or bathroom?

These questions had never been answered.

Cheryl Keeton's coworkers at Garvey, Schubert and Barer had felt a certain sense of serenity after the memorial service they held for her in Seattle's Public Market the week after her death. 'We *did* have closure,' managing partner Greg Dallaire said, 'but we expected the police to do something. . . .'

Civil attorneys are not usually trained in criminal law, nor are they any more aware of police procedure than someone in an entirely unrelated profession. It is necessary to be caught in the middle of a criminal case – in one manner or another – to really understand how very difficult it is to bring criminal charges against a murder suspect and then to actually *convict* that defendant.

But Oregon State Police detectives Jerry Finch and Jim Ayers hadn't forgotten Cheryl. Washington County Prosecuting Attorney Scott Upham and Assistant D.A. Bob Heard hadn't forgotten her. Nor had OSP Sergeant Jim Hinkley and his wife, OSP criminalist Julia Hinkley. Every officer and every paramedic called to the side of the Sunset Highway on the evening of September 21, 1986, remembered Cheryl Keeton. But they didn't have enough to arrest someone. Brad remained their only suspect, but they couldn't bolt under pressure and arrest him too soon.

Brad also remained the prime suspect in the minds of Cheryl's family, friends, and colleagues. Greg Dallaire and other partners at Garvey, Schubert knew that Cheryl had been convinced for months before her murder that Brad was going to kill her. They knew that she had begged her friends to see that her boys did not go to their father if she should die. They knew that, fearing she would die, she had done everything humanly possible to prevent Brad from gleaning one penny from her estate.

Cheryl had insurance and her estate had money coming from her Garvey, Schubert retirement account. 'The firm also gives five thousand dollars in the case of death,' Dallaire said. 'We didn't want to give it to Brad. And we were concerned about the kids. We did hire a Portland attorney to help get custody from him so that the boys could go to Betty and Marv Troseth. But Brad was taking care of them – and we couldn't prove otherwise. That petered out.'

Sharon Armstrong, Kerry Radcliffe, Eric Lindenauer, and Dallaire were 'extraordinarily frustrated' as they saw everything that Cheryl had feared become reality. Both Sharon and Kerry had tried to be emotionally supportive of Cheryl, as only women can be with one another. Neither of them could be with her on the last weekend of her life and they may well have wondered if things would have been different had they been there – if somehow, some way, they might have protected her. It would be only natural.

Eric Lindenauer had been there for Cheryl as often as he could be. He had made the trip to Bridlemile School with her to try to protect her – and the boys – from Brad's rage. But he couldn't be with her all the time. No one could, and in the end, all Eric had been able to do was call the Oregon State Police the day after her death and tell them about the horror she had been living through in the months before her murder.

Greg Dallaire had never been as close to Cheryl – he had seen her around the office, of course, and had lunch with her once or twice – but she had almost always seemed happy and vibrant. Dallaire was a gentle man, a man who used his legal knowledge to help others. In 1970 he set up the first battered women's program in America through his work with the Evergreen Legal Services in Seattle. He had never realized how emotionally battered Cheryl was. When he did, it had been far too late to help her, and he agonized over that.

Three months had passed since Cheryl's death without an arrest. It was early 1987. Somewhere, her little boys had their first Christmas without their mother – but none of Cheryl's former coworkers knew where. Brad and the boys had completely disappeared. As much as they wanted to fulfill the promises that Cheryl had extracted from them – the promises that they wouldn't let Brad have her little boys – they had no legal avenue to stop him. He was their father. Their mother was dead. And if Brad had killed Cheryl, no one had yet found a way to prove it.

Yet it didn't seem possible that someone as alive as Cheryl could die so horribly and that no one would be punished. 'We went to Hillsboro,' Dallaire recalled. 'Eric Lindenauer and myself. We talked to Bob Heard and Jim Ayers. They said that they were attempting to put a case together, but they told us it was a circumstantial case. They said, "We *know* he did it, but . . ."'

The civil attorneys were learning more about the criminal side of law than they had wanted to know. Some months later, they returned to the Washington County Courthouse and talked once more with Bob Heard. 'All he could tell us was that it was still under investigation,' Dallaire said.

Eighteen months after Cheryl died, Lindenauer and Dallaire traveled again to Hillsboro. They could sense at once that their meeting with Bob Heard, Jim Ayers, and Jerry Finch would not be a fruitful one. None of the three men seemed to want to meet their eyes. They made small talk and glanced at the thick files in front of Heard. Finally Heard took a deep breath and spoke the words that he didn't want to say and none of them wanted to hear, 'We're declining to prosecute.'

The room was silent as the words began to sink in. Dallaire and Lindenauer were stunned and disappointed. More than disappointed, they were outraged that Brad seemed to have beaten the men and women who had been on his trail for eighteen months. 'The cops were unhappy,' Dallaire remembered. 'You could tell they didn't like this decision.'

The five men in the room all wanted the same thing, although they were coming at it from different angles. There had to be some way to construct a case against Brad Cunningham that would hold up in court. Cautiously, they explored the possibility that a civil case might be brought against him, a case that – if successful – might put enough pressure on Brad to force his hand. 'If – if—' Dallaire began, 'if we brought a case that would establish civilly that he killed her, would that be helpful?'

The room was silent and then Heard, Ayers, and Finch said, 'Yes!' almost in the same breath. 'Yes, that would help.'

It was a backdoor way to convict a suspected killer who

had apparently escaped every criminal investigation ploy, but it *was* a way to begin. The Washington County D.A.'s office provided Dallaire and Lindenauer with a copy of the police files on Cheryl's murder, and Ayers and Finch offered whatever help they could give.

Dallaire returned to Seattle carrying a heavy box of files. Alone, he began to read the official follow-ups that described Cheryl's death and the aftermath. 'I was devastated,' he said later. He read the autopsy report in horror, fully aware for the first time of how brutal Cheryl's murder had been. He tried to visualize the sunny, bubbly, brilliant young woman he had known and, for the moment, could not. He decided he couldn't share the awful details of her murder with most of his staff.

And then Dallaire came to a copy of the note Cheryl had left behind as she went to meet her killer. He held it in his hand, unbelieving. 'I have gone to pick up the boys from Brad at the Mobil station next to the IGA. If I'm not back, please come and find me . . . COME RIGHT AWAY!'

It was almost as if Cheryl was in the room, talking directly to him. 'I was flabbergasted when I came across the note. And I got really angry,' Dallaire said. 'I thought, *Why didn't they* DO *something?*'

Maybe there hadn't been enough for the prosecutor's office to go with a criminal charge against Brad, but Dallaire knew that the note he held in his hand was enough evidence to bring a wrongful death suit in civil court. At the next executive committee meeting of the law firm, he went in and said, 'DO something!'

He got no argument. Everyone at Garvey, Schubert who had known Cheryl was anxious to do whatever they could to bring her some modicum of justice. 'We figured we had two ways to go,' Dallaire recalled. 'We had some money that was in her estate – Cheryl's profit sharing and the five thousand dollars. We thought, Let's wave the money in front of Brad like a red flag and he'll sue us. We can get him into court and we can prove wrongful death.'

The second plan for hoisting Brad on his own petard was more complicated. There had been a murder in Washington State on July 26, 1974, that had eerie similarities to Cheryl Keeton's. Ironically the killer, Anthony Fernandez, had come from Longview just as Cheryl had, although it was unlikely she had ever known him. Fernandez had been in prison on fraud convictions by the time Cheryl was in high school.

'Tony' Fernandez was forty-eight and a paroled con man when he met a pretty forty-two-year-old widow named Ruth Logg in Auburn, Washington. He didn't mention his criminal background, of course, to Ruth. He appeared at her door to look at the house she was offering for sale. He told her he was *Dr* Anthony Fernandez and was in the process of setting up a counseling practice in Tacoma. He even showed her an article from a local paper announcing the opening of his practice. Ruth was a wealthy woman, as Fernandez noted when she showed him around her sumptuous home. As it turned out, he didn't have to buy the house; he simply moved in.

Despite her family's reservations, Ruth Logg fell in love with 'Dr' Anthony Fernandez and married him six months later. With his counsel on financial affairs, she changed her will so that he would inherit everything she had, uncharacteristically disinheriting her two young daughters. Two years later, Ruth suffered what appeared to be a tragic accident. The Winnebago motor home she and Tony had rented plunged off a dirt road on Snoqualmie Pass in Washington's Cascade Mountains. Ruth was found dead halfway down a steep embankment; the Winnebago was 150 feet further down the slope. She had succumbed to a fractured skull and a blow to the stomach, but she had no wounds that pathologists would expect to find in someone who had gone over a cliff in a vehicle.

Tony Fernandez survived. He hadn't even been in the Winnebago. He told authorities that Ruth had driven away from their campsite and he had followed twenty minutes later in another vehicle. Washington State Patrol investigators and detectives from the King County Police were suspicious of him, but they were working with a highly circumstantial case. There was no arrest.

Eighteen months after Ruth Logg Fernandez died on a lonely mountainside, her daughters brought civil action against the man who had by then spent most of the assets of their dead mother's estate. Judge George Revelle found that Anthony Fernandez 'participated as a principal in the willful and unlawful killing of Ruth Fernandez.'

The aspect of the landmark Fernandez case that appealed to the Garvey, Schubert partners was the fact that Fernandez was then charged *criminally* with the murder of his wife – more than three years after her death – and he was subsequently convicted and was serving life in prison.

'We decided on our second option,' Dallaire remembered. 'We would go for the civil trial. The committee at Garvey, Schubert told us, "Go forward!" We wanted to shop this case out to a lawyer to see if there might be something there. Eric Lindenauer started looking around because he knew Portland attorneys. John Burke backed us up.'

At that point, no criminal charges had been filed against Brad. Not in 1986. Nor in 1987 or in 1988. The world went on for everyone, except for Cheryl. But nothing was over in the pursuit of her killer. Everything was only suspended in time.

It wasn't as easy to find an attorney to go up against Brad Cunningham as the Garvey, Schubert partners had originally thought. As it turned out, there were few attorneys in Portland who were not already familiar with Brad. He was a most litigious man, and it was his policy to consult several attorneys on each of his legal actions before he chose one. After three or four turndowns, Dallaire and Burke and Lindenauer realized that finding an attorney willing to joust with Brad would be a challenge. Lawyers with families said they didn't want to chance it. One said, 'I have a daughter who walks to school alone. I won't risk taking him on. Try

Shinn.' He said that Mike Shinn, while he certainly enjoyed the company of women, had no wife – and he was notorious for loving a good scrap.

That's what the attorneys from Garvey, Schubert needed. They knew it would be far safer for a prosecutor to go up against Brad in a criminal case. If he were convicted criminally, he would go to prison and would not be a threat to anyone for years. But if a civil attorney should prevail, Brad would still be free. It would be a moral victory, and it might well be the springboard for a criminal charge. But even with a win, Brad would be as free – for a period of months – as he was at the moment. And if, as the lawyers who were about to set a net for him believed, he was a devious and dangerous – and vengeful – man, the civil attorney who brought him down would have to watch his back. Nobody but an attorney with a rebel streak, a maverick, would touch this dicey case.

Mike Shinn was indeed a maverick, descended from a long line of mavericks. His great-grandfather was William Jasper Kerr, onetime president of Utah State University, Brigham Young University, and Oregon State University. Shinn's mother Miriam's ancestors had come from Pennsylvania by wagon train, members of a religious commune with a charismatic – but eccentric – leader. They made it to Oregon and founded the community of Aurora. His great-uncle William Kerr was the U.S. prosecutor for the Japanese war crimes trials, the Asian equivalent of the Nuremberg trials. And Shinn's father, Bill, was an underwater demolition expert in World War II, a fearless swimmer whose assignment would compare to Navy Seals today. Tragically, Bill Shinn died of cancer at forty-two when his only son was in high school.

Mike Shinn was a natural athlete and particularly gifted at football. He was one of the fastest and most nimble quarterbacks the Willamette University Bearcats ever had. He wasn't very big, but he was smart and he was tough. Like his father before him, he excelled at risk taking. In 1968 the Bearcats were ranked number three in their division in the nation. They were led by Mike Shinn who threw for 1,508 yards and eighteen touchdowns. The whole 1968 team was inducted into the Willamette University Athletics Hall of Fame in 1993.

In his forties Shinn was still a risk taker and a dogged opponent. In his forties, he played world-class rugby and checked the weatherman's wind forecast before he glanced at his schedule for each day. If the wind was going to blow, Shinn was going to be out on the Columbia River windsurfing. He was a 'board-head' and, like all windsurfers, hopelessly addicted to gliding across the water as fast as he could, wrestling with his sail to stay upright.

Actually, Shinn's major in college was English. 'What I really wanted to do was go to film school and make movies, or go into publishing,' he said. 'I never thought I was smart enough to go into law because I could never figure out who did it in the Perry Mason shows.' Shinn turned out to be a lot smarter than he thought he was, of course. 'I ended up in law school at Willamette,' he said. After Willamette, Shinn clerked for a federal judge and then did some criminal work. 'The last criminal case I defended, I got a guy acquitted of five bank robberies,' he recalled, 'and I figured it was a good time to quit criminal law – while I was ahead.'

It was late summer of 1989 when Mike Shinn listened as Greg Dallaire and Eric Lindenauer took him through the tragic details of Cheryl Keeton's death. John Burke was on the phone, a participant in this hard sell. Ideally, they were hoping to convince Shinn to undertake the civil action against Brad on a contingency basis.

Shinn was intrigued by the case; he remembered reading about Cheryl Keeton's death on the Sunset Highway, though he hadn't heard anything more for three years. Still, as he listened to the twists and turns the investigation had taken since 1986, he realized that this would be a colossally complicated case to prosecute civilly, criminally, or any way.

'There were three reservations I had about taking the case,' he said later. 'One of them was the very concept of filing a civil suit against a man for murder when he'd never been indicted . . . you don't have the constitutional protection that you do in a criminal case. . . . My second reservation was that I might get killed. I knew two other lawyers who had looked at the case and said, "I don't want to expose myself to this kind of risk."'

When Shinn was told that Brad was now married to Sara Gordon, that further complicated his decision. 'The third concern was Sara,' he said. 'I remembered her as a real perky, bright-eyed, intelligent, energetic, charismatic, neat lady. But it wasn't just Sara. It was the idea of the kind of grief that would be brought to bear on the whole family. I didn't know the kids, but it was inevitable. We never asked for it, but this was the kind of story that was going to lead to big-headline coverage.'

Shinn realized how much time it would take, how many contacts would have to be made, how many hours would be billed by private investigators – and suggested that he be paid by the hour. He couldn't afford to take the case on a contingency basis. Brad had allegedly gone through millions of dollars and no one knew if he had anything left. Even if Shinn won a civil suit against him, his cupboard might very well be bare.

'It was going to be such an undertaking for me,' Shinn said. 'It would mean doing little else. I told Dallaire and Lindenauer that I was willing to do it – but I'd go bankrupt if I did it on a contingency basis.' He estimated that the civil case would cost about fifty thousand dollars. But he couldn't be sure. 'If Cunningham *has* any money left,' he told Dallaire and Lindenauer, 'he'll probably hire someone like F. Lee Bailey, and, unlike other cases, there's no bottom to this until the guy gets convicted of murder.'

Dallaire never blinked at the fifty-thousand-dollar figure

– or at the possibility that it might be more. He took the information back to the executive committee and they signed off.

'We entered into an agreement with Mike Shinn in 1989, but we had to be cautious,' Dallaire remembered. 'We were afraid that Brad would find out what we were doing by somehow seeing certain bills. *We* were the client hiring Shinn, but we didn't want Brad to know that. On paper, then, the client was John Burke for Cheryl's estate – but Garvey, Schubert was paying Mike Shinn. If Brad hired a lawyer to face off John Burke, we were concerned that he would find out the firm was paying and we'd have to grant discovery.'

And too, if Brad should find out how many people from his past Shinn's private investigators were prepared to interview, he might try to intimidate them so that they wouldn't talk. He was, demonstrably, a past master at intimidation.

Going into what was inherently a criminal case for the first time in many years, Shinn was a little apprehensive, but he moved ahead. He filed the civil suit, and it did indeed make headlines in the *Oregonian*.

'One of the first things I remember is getting a letter from Sara,' Shinn recalled. 'It said, in essence, "Gee, I haven't seen you in ten years. I thought you were a nice guy. And now you've done this horrible thing to my family—"' She also wrote that all the employees of the Broadway Bakery that she and Brad owned had walked off the job, and that her sons' friends wouldn't play with them or return their phone calls. Shinn felt rotten. But he had anticipated that Sara would be angry, and he would just have to live with it.

'The next letter I got,' he said with a grimace, 'was from Brad's first lawyer. He said there wasn't a scrap of evidence against Brad. Brad had told him that probably John Burke killed Cheryl. . . . Then Brad's lawyer threatens me with disbarment and a lawsuit. I'd met Greg and Eric, but I didn't know John Burke beyond his voice on the phone. I wasn't sure *who* the bad guy was. Sometimes I even wondered if it *was* Burke – if somehow I was being set up. . . .'

Not sure what was going to develop – but now totally committed to the case – Shinn went ahead with traditional discovery work and the filing of motions. Brad was scheduled to file his first deposition in early 1990. 'The night before, I get a phone call,' Shinn said. It was from one of Portland's top attorneys, Forrest Rieke. He had Brad Cunningham in his office, along with Wes Urqhart, a bigger-than-life Texas lawyer from Vinson and Elkins in Houston. It was Brad's opinion that Shinn's suit had been filed to keep Brad from prevailing in his Houston lawsuits.

'It became like guerrilla warfare,' Shinn remembered.

The first shots from both sides had been fired in the case, but Shinn had yet to learn how tenacious Brad could be, and how calculating. If he had known that he was stepping into a runaway stagecoach whose horses were about to stampede, would he have said 'no' to Greg Dallaire and Eric Lindenauer?

Probably not. Mike Shinn always loved a good fight.

37

There is a rule of thumb in homicide investigations. The chance of finding and convicting the guilty person or persons diminishes in inverse proportion to the time that passes after the crime is committed. Given a choice, detectives want to catch the killer in twenty-four hours. They feel fairly comfortable with forty-eight hours. After that, they wonder if they will *ever* solve the case.

Mike Shinn was reopening a murder case that was almost

three years old. He wasn't a criminal attorney, and he wasn't even a crime buff. All he really had to bring to this project was a new point of view, a brilliant legal mind which he hid beneath a somewhat sardonic wit, and an inborn refusal to give up long after anyone with common sense would have thrown in the towel.

He had his own 'negatives.' Not only had too much time passed since Cheryl's death, but he knew the Washington County District Attorney's office was not particularly happy to have a civil attorney take on a case in which they had exhausted all possibilities. It was akin to an internist striding into an operating room, seizing the scalpel from the surgeon already in the middle of an operation, and saying, 'Let me do it – I think I see where you're going wrong.' Human nature being what it is, D.A. Scott Upham and Mike Shinn were probably not fated to be best buddies.

Criminal prosecution works under different guidelines than civil trials. To prove a case criminally, the judge or jury must be convinced beyond a reasonable doubt that a defendant is guilty. That is, a reasonable man, after hearing the evidence and the testimony of witnesses, could come to no other conclusion. A civil case is proved by a preponderance of evidence. A judge or jury weighs the evidence presented by each side and decides which has the most compelling argument. Thus, it follows naturally that a civil case is easier to prove.

In the end, after all the investigation by the Oregon State Police and Upham's own office, they had concluded that they did not have enough evidence to charge Brad with Cheryl's murder. That did not necessarily mean that Upham and his staff or Jim Ayers and the other detectives who had followed Cunningham's movements with keen interest for the past three years believed he was innocent. They felt in their gut that he was guilty. But they doubted that they had enough firepower to prove guilt beyond a reasonable doubt. If they arrested him and tried him, and he was acquitted, they could never try him again. Double jeopardy would attach.

All detectives and prosecutors can cite cases where they know full well that a man, or woman, is guilty but is still walking around free – and probably always will be unless he or she commits another crime. It is not one of their favorite topics. Brad was still walking around free and Shinn hoped to uncover something that everyone else had missed, but he didn't really think he would. Only Perry Mason did that, and Shinn had never been able to second-guess Mason.

Shinn started with nothing but a three-ring black binder – the summary of the police investigation of Cheryl's murder in 1986 and 1987. If he was lucky, somewhere in that list of witnesses and law enforcement personnel he might find someone whose perception and recall would help him in his civil case. 'I didn't really expect to find new witnesses,' he said. 'I hoped to *expand* on the witnesses who were around. Maybe my style was different, I could analyze differently, and my philosophy was different. I had the advantage of coming into this case fresh.'

To reinterview people who had not been very receptive to interviews in the first place was going to take some innovative and empathetic private investigators. As he always did, Shinn went to experts for advice on how to find the best. 'Steve Houze is one of a handful of the best criminal defense lawyers in Oregon, and I asked him who he would recommend as an investigator,' he said. 'I told him about the case, and that, although this was a civil case, it was going to be almost like prosecuting a homicide. I need an investigator who's used to doing criminal work.'

Houze pondered Shinn's question and then said, 'Well, the very best investigator in the state is Chick Preston – but you can't have him because he's working for me.'

'Later,' Shinn said, 'I found out I'd played football against Chick when he went to Whitman University.'

'Second,' Houze said, 'would be Connie Capato, but she's working on the Dayton Leroy Rogers case right now.'

Shinn grimaced. Rogers was a suspect in the serial murders of Portland prostitutes whose bodies, their feet neatly severed, had been found in a lonely Oregon forest. Fortunately, Connie finished her work on that case in time to help Mike Shinn.

Connie Capato had come to the field of private investigation by a circuitous route. At one time she had considered becoming a nun but found that the religious calling was not for her. She liked people, she was good with people, and for her the 'calling' of the P.I. was a better way to connect with them. Along with Connie, Shinn hired another female P.I., Leslie Haigh, who worked in Connie's business, CLC Investigations.

When it came time to file the complaint and serve Brad with the official notice, Shinn didn't know where he was living. 'Somebody had heard he was working for a doughnut shop or something. Eric Lindenauer thought that was hysterical because he'd known Brad as this hotshot bank executive. I was sitting in the "Y" in the sauna room one day, going through the *Downtowner*, and there's a picture of Brad. It says, 'New Guy on the Block,' and there's Brad with this new Broadway Bakery. So that's how we found him,' Shinn said with a laugh. 'With *great* detective work. So I called Connie's office and said we needed someone to serve the complaint. She said she'd send Leslie Haigh over, and I said, "Maybe you'd better send a guy. . . ."'

When slender little Leslie showed up, Shinn had his doubts. 'This case has some elements of danger – that's why I asked for a guy,' he told her. 'This guy you're serving a complaint on is suspected of murdering his wife.' Her eyes sparkled, and she said, 'Oh, really? That's interesting.'

'Yeah, it's interesting, but it might be dangerous. Are you sure?'

Leslie was sure. Shinn arranged to have a male P.I. follow Brad when he left the Broadway Bakery after Leslie had served the complaint. And Leslie promised to return to Shinn's office and report on how Brad had reacted to the news that he was being sued in civil court for responsibility in his former wife's death.

She was back in a short time. 'I went in the bakery,' Leslie reported. 'It's a really nice little place. And there was this long, cafeteria kind of line you stand in, and Brad Cunningham was at the end of the line—'

'Yeah?' Shinn asked expectantly.

'So I got to Brad, and he said, "Can I help you?" and I told him I had some papers for him. I handed them to him—'

'Yeah?'

'He read them.'

'Did he say anything?'

'Yes, he did. He said, "Thank you," and then he looked at me and said, "Would you like a muffin?"'

For weeks after that, Brad Cunningham was referred to in Mike Shinn's office as 'the muffin man.'

A civil suit accusing a man of murder was not the kind of story that a newspaper would ignore – and the *Oregonian* and the wire services did not. The headlines hit in July 1989.

LAWSUIT BLAMES HUSBAND FOR SPOUSE'S DEATH

Portland, Ore. (AP) Family and friends of a slain lawyer have filed a $15 million wrongful death lawsuit in Multnomah County Circuit Court against her estranged husband.

Court documents say that for months before she was bludgeoned to death on September 21, 1986, Cheryl Keeton had feared she would be killed by her estranged husband, Bradly M. Cunningham, a developer, entrepreneur and banker.

But neither Cunningham nor anyone else has ever been charged in Keeton's death. Despite an investigation that a prosecutor called exhaustive, the homicide case remains open.

Portland lawyer Michael Shinn filed affidavits and court documents to support the lawsuit Monday. . . .

The wire services quoted an outraged Brad Cunningham who said that the lawsuit was clearly an abuse of the legal system, the result of a 'vendetta' against him by John Burke, the personal representative of his wife's estate. He said that his three sons – nine, seven, and five, who lived with him and his new wife – believed that their mother had died in a car wreck. 'It's very upsetting to me that the system will let someone go and file something like this,' Brad told reporters. 'It was bad enough to live through the death of my wife, and now we have to live through this . . . just when we thought life was normal again.'

When Shinn's legal assistant read the paper, she was appalled. She had no idea what he had undertaken, and she didn't like it when she found out. 'I'll never forget,' Shinn said. 'She read the article in the paper and she walked into my office with her hands on her hips. She just looked at me and said, "*What* have you *done?*"' And within a few days, she resigned.

Shinn didn't really blame her. It was going to be heavier and more dangerous work than any legal assistant in her right mind would choose to take on. But he was now involved in what would be the biggest case of his life, and he didn't have a legal assistant. He had never needed a good right arm more than he did at this moment, and he realized a little ruefully that he was going to have to find a woman who was something of a daredevil – as he was.

Shinn went to several attorney friends and asked if they knew of anyone who might meet his rather unusual specifications. He was looking for someone who would work overtime and have an uncanny ability to talk to people and get them to trust her enough to share secrets they had kept for years. She would have to have the soul of a detective, and she would have to be utterly fearless.

One of Shinn's former partners, Mark Bocci, heard him out and then said, 'You should have asked me before. I know who you need. I know the one who's the best in the State of Oregon, and she was looking for a job too –

but she just got hired. She's working for a company that defends civil cases.'

'See if she's really happy there,' Shinn urged. 'See if she'll leave and come with me.'

The best legal assistant in the state turned out to be Diane Bakker, a slender and striking blond in her thirties. Fortunately for Shinn, she was already bored with her new job, and she was intrigued with the Cunningham case, listening avidly as Shinn gave her an overview of what lay ahead. 'There's a negative to this,' he said finally. 'If you come in on this, there's likely to be some danger.' He looked up apprehensively, expecting that he was about to lose any chance he had with Diane. Instead, she was grinning.

'She lit up like a Christmas tree,' Shinn recalled. 'It turns out she's fascinated with true crime books. Diane is into the "Serial Killer of the Week" and all that stuff that I knew nothing about. I didn't read those kinds of books. Diane did. Nothing scared her; it only whetted her appetite for the job. I was fortunate that she came on this project. I never could have done it without her.'

Brad Cunningham, who had accepted his complaint papers with such seeming equanimity, was not the sanguine 'muffin man' at all, of course; he had the capability of being a sinister and dangerous presence. And he resented some guy named Mike Shinn interfering with his life.

'It must have been the fall of 1989, a few months later,' Shinn remembered. 'We were at Jake's, and I was having dinner with Dave Jensen, who was president of the Oregon Trial Lawyers' Association two years after I was. We were still on the board together. We were standing in the bar waiting for a table, and Dave asked me if I had anything interesting going on. I said, "Funny you should ask." So I was telling him about this Cunningham case. Then we moved to the tables near the bar to eat, and we were sitting there, still talking about the case. I'd noticed out of the corner of my eye that some guy seemed to be looking at me. All of a sudden, he looms up over me and he's got this funny grin on his face.

'He leans over and he's kind of peering at me and he says, "Are you Mike Shinn?" I was trying to figure out who he was, and I thought maybe he was an old fraternity brother. I was trying to buy time to remember who he was, and I said, "Yeah, I'm Mike Shinn. How ya doin'?'

'He says, "I just wanted to see what you looked like." Then he turned on his heel and walked away. Dave says, "Who in the hell was that?" and suddenly I knew who it was. I said, "That was *him*." I just made the connection, and then I looked closer at the woman he was with – and it was Sara.'

Shinn's encounter with Brad was brief. He would remember only that the guy was big and dark. He didn't expect to see Cunningham again until they met in court – if he showed up in court. He sure wasn't showing up to give depositions.

38

Brad had more problems than the legal action against him. His fifth marriage was turning sour. Marital fidelity or even discretion had never been part of his makeup, and his falls from grace were becoming more transparent.

By February 6, 1990, Sara could no longer talk herself into believing that her marriage was working. Half the time she had no idea where Brad was; most of the rest of the time she knew he was with Lynn Minero. She knew because she had hired a private investigator to follow him. That day she told Brad she was thinking about divorce, and he barely reacted.

Despite his flat reaction, Sara was worried because he had been very ill the night before. She tried to find Brad when she had a little time away from the OR, or when she could get to a phone. She called him and got no answer or got the answering machine. Brad always had a reason why he couldn't answer her calls. 'I was on hold on another call' or 'The machine was turned off accidentally' or 'The phone stopped ringing just as I reached for it.'

Brad was running both the Broadway Bakery and the Bistro now, as well as delivering lunch orders. But he had a cell phone and there was no legitimate reason why Sara could never reach him. Half angry and half worried because of his history of heart problems, she kept trying to locate him.

Sara jotted notes in her journal for February 6:

'11:50 – Called Bistro – Lynn answered. Said Brad had been back. She gave him message – He left again to deliver sandwiches. I asked her if he was okay. "Yes," Lynn answered. "He seemed okay the little bit that I've seen him." I said, "You picked him up this morning, didn't you?" She said yes.'

Sara finally got a call back from Brad an hour later. She had agreed to pay a twelve-thousand-dollar retainer to a divorce attorney. Brad had no money. He called to say things had gone fine with the attorney. 'I said I was concerned about him – He sort of grunted. Then said he didn't believe me. I said he was scaring me. He said he was sorry – didn't mean to. I asked him if he loved me. He said, "Sara, we have to talk, but I can't talk now." . . .

'13:40 – I called Brad. Asked him if he was able to talk now. He said he was too busy. He said he didn't think he'd feel like talking today. Said he felt like going out and having a few drinks tonight. I said, "With me?" He said, "No, maybe just by myself." He said he felt like I wasn't being honest with him. Would not be more specific. Just in general I was not being honest with him.'

Brad was a master at projection; he could turn criticism

away from himself as if it were a boomerang that he could direct back the way it came. He told Sara that afternoon that he felt she didn't love him, that she was dishonest, that he would not answer her questions anymore. 'He feels I grill him, and that he might want *me* to move out. I'm not the person he thought I was.'

Brad told Sara he was 'upset' about everything – the civil lawsuit that Mike Shinn had filed against him, the fact that she had been talking to a divorce attorney too, the knowledge that he had been followed for the past four or five days. It was true. She had grilled him and she had had him followed, and his answers never matched the truth.

At that point, if Brad had made any effort toward reconciliation or any admission of his culpability, Sara might have stayed in the marriage – for the sake of Jess and Michael and Phillip. She might even have still loved Brad on some level, though she didn't trust him. Perhaps she *wanted* to trust him.

The next day Brad packed his pickup and left for a trip to Seattle. Sara was certain that Lynn had gone with him, but she was surprised later to see Lynn and her husband Gary together. Sara and Gary had talked; they were both worried that their marriages were crumbling because of an affair between Brad and Lynn. Sara got more response to her concerns from Gary than she did from Brad. In fact, she already considered her marriage over, and she had made plans to move out of the big gray house in Dunthorpe and find an apartment in the new Portland complex at Riverplace. Brad didn't seem to care one way or the other if she left. And Sara didn't tell Gary that she was leaving Brad.

Brad didn't get back from Seattle until Saturday afternoon, February 10, and he left the next day for Houston. After she drove him to the airport, Sara took Jess, Michael, and Phillip to look at the Riverplace Athletic Club. The boys hoped to join, and it would be a way for her to see them often.

Brad called Sara the next day from Houston, but it wasn't a pleasant conversation. He was furious with her because she had talked to Gary Minero. 'Lynn's going to quit the bakery now because you're trying to ruin her marriage. If she quits, I'll quit too,' he fumed.

Enough. How much more was Sara expected to take from Brad? She had gone to the bakery once late at night and found Brad alone – but Lynn's purse was sitting out in plain sight; she had found Lynn in the restroom, and Lynn looked anything but innocent. It had happened again, or close to it. When Sara drove up to the bakery one night, she recognized Lynn's car parked in front. She discovered that someone had taken the bakery key from her key ring, and by the time Brad let her in, minutes had gone by. There was no trace of Lynn, but when Sara left, she saw that Lynn's car was gone.

All this had taken an emotional – and physical – toll. Sara's resting heart rate was way over one hundred, she was afraid even to take her blood pressure, and her weight was under ninety pounds.

Sara rented a studio apartment at Riverplace. She had bought the big house for the boys and she wanted them to be able to live there and go to school where they had friends. Above all, she didn't want them to be uprooted one more time. She would move and would continue to pay the mortgage on the big house so they would still have their home. 'I was prepared to make the payments on the Dunthorpe house until the boys were grown,' Sara would say later. 'I wanted them to be able to stay there – to have some stability, even if my marriage to Brad was over.'

Sara and the boys picked Brad up at the airport when he returned from Houston. They went out to eat and Brad started to tell his sons that he and Sara were splitting up. She begged him not to do this in public, but he had said too much already. Michael and Phillip started to cry, and Jess bit his lip.

'The boys drew wonderful pictures for us to stay together,'

Sara wrote sadly in her journal. 'Brad and I talked for several hours. He was surprised that the boys were upset.'

That astounded Sara. How could Brad *not* know that his little boys would be hurt by yet another loss in their lives? Their mother had been dead for only three and a half years. They had bonded with Sara and now she was their mother – both legally and in terms of love and caring. She didn't know how she could bear to leave them. She had been going to counseling just to find the strength to do it. If Brad would let her have the boys, she would be overjoyed – but she knew him better than that. She had had a ringside seat to his terrible battle with Cheryl over the boys. The most Sara could hope for was that Brad would let her see them, and that they would still know how much she loved them. She agreed to sign a lease on a Volvo station wagon so that Brad would have transportation for the boys. He couldn't get a lease in his own name because of his bankruptcy.

'I always think of February sixteenth as a kind of anniversary,' Sara said later, not without a trace of bitterness. 'Brad and I met early to go over property settlements before meeting with Al Menashe [Brad's attorney].' Brad had already met with another attorney who had told him that Sara should pay him between eight thousand and ten thousand dollars a month child support. Sara was surprised and explained that she was currently spending eighty-five hundred dollars on the bakery/ bistro and three thousand dollars on malpractice insurance. She said if she gave Brad what he felt he should have, 'that left very little for me.' She remembered his reaction vividly. 'Brad said he knew how much I liked to work and now I'd have more time to work.'

Sara stared at this wonderful man she had once loved so much. He was a stranger.

But something happened that day that completely changed Brad's treatment of Sara. From the Bistro, he spoke on the phone with one of his criminal attorneys about this pesky civil case that some lawyer named Mike Shinn had filed against him. And for the first time, he seemed to grasp how dangerous it could be for him. The lawyer told Brad if he was found civilly responsible for Cheryl's death, he might very well face criminal charges. Brad finally perceived that he stood a very good chance of actually going to jail. He had laughed off Shinn's suit as ridiculous; now one of the best attorneys in Portland was telling him that it wasn't funny. Brad later told Sara that his lawyer also advised him to keep his marriage intact. Having a woman like Sara beside him, a woman with a fine reputation in the Portland community, would make his acquittal in the civil trial far more likely. It would not look good for him if he was going through yet another divorce while he was being sued civilly over the death of his fourth wife.

It was at precisely that moment that Sara walked into the Bistro. Brad was a pale shade of gray and there were beads of sweat on his forehead. This was not the same man who had sneered, 'I know how much you like to work, and now you'll have more time to work.' He was frightened. 'Brad had a revelation on that February sixteenth,' Sara would remember wryly. The man who hung up the phone clung to her like a lost child.

'Brad became almost nonfunctional with the realization of the gravity of the civil suit,' Sara said. His attitude toward her changed from bitter sarcasm to tender affection all in the space of a few hours. 'He was on the phone with his attorney when I walked into the Bistro. He begged me to stay around the Bistro with him. He felt better just having me around. His behavior toward me changed totally. He *loved* me and needed me. He needed his family to be together. He couldn't handle the boys being sad about my not being there, etcetera etcetera. His whole demeanor toward me changed to how it used to be. I told him I was in no hurry to leave, and could stay until his lawsuit was finished.'

But Sara was not deluded. She knew that Brad needed her only as window dressing during the civil trial. She didn't try to get out of her lease at the Riverplace apartment. She kept it as her escape spot. Brad helped her move a bed, a table, a sofa, and some chairs to the studio apartment. She knew that she would be leaving the marriage soon, but she relished the reprieve she had been given to be with her little boys.

On February 21, 1990, Sara lived through one of the most bizarre nights of her life. She met Brad for drinks at the exclusive Alexis Hotel in Portland and they talked. He said that he was thinking of moving to Seattle or to Colorado Springs when 'this is all over.' She didn't know if he meant their marriage or the civil trial. She didn't care which, but she started to cry because if Brad moved so far away, Jess, Michael, and Phillip would be far away too.

Later, Sara wrote down the events of that night in her journal. 'Brad became depressed when I told him I would not stay with him after the lawsuit – too much pain for too many months, all of his lying to me, etc. I left for home [the Dunthorpe house] so Rhonda [their baby-sitter] could leave and Brad went for a walk. He called me a little later from the Morrison Bridge, and made it sound like he was considering jumping. I called the cellular phone a couple of times but he didn't answer.'

Brad's threats to commit suicide had worked once before when Sara had said she was leaving him. She had capitulated and promised to stay with him. But this time, she was weary of his games. Brad simply used these threats to bring people into line. Besides, the Morrison Bridge was so close to the water. Even if he jumped, he would only make a small splash and get wet. There were higher bridges in Portland – much higher – if Brad was serious about killing himself.

'Later, he called me from the East Bank Saloon,' Sara wrote. 'Said he would like to have some hope that we might stay together, wished that I would just "lie" to him so that he could have that hope. Brad eventually got home about 10:15 p.m. I was in bed sleeping. He wanted to talk and I told him I needed to sleep. He got out of bed, said he should just end his life, and started reaching for the gun in his closet.

'I got up, pulled him away from the closet. He went downstairs and I followed. He started crying, "I want my Daddy." I tried to talk him into going to the hospital for help but he wouldn't.'

Sara watched in horror as Brad got a box with a gun in it from a cupboard in the laundry. She was pretty sure he wouldn't shoot himself, but she wondered if he might just shoot *her*. 'I was scared beyond belief but stayed calm. I told him I wanted to leave and he said to go ahead. I had to go upstairs to get my purse and keys, and grab a coat. I only had my Mickey Mouse night shirt on and Jess's slippers. I was very frightened that he would get the gun while I was upstairs.'

Brad allowed Sara to leave the house. She drove away with tremendous relief and went to Providence Hospital. She called the house a couple of times but Brad didn't answer. She knew he was trying to make her think that he had, indeed, killed himself.

Sara realized too late that she was dealing with a manipulator, a master puppeteer. She had no idea yet to what lengths Brad would go to get what he wanted. She had begun, however, to wonder what had really happened to Cheryl.

39

Mike Shinn's private investigators, Connie Capato and Leslie Haigh, had set out to walk through Brad's past, to find the women he had married and divorced, the mother and the sisters whose existence he barely acknowledged. Somewhere in that past – some of it decades old – they might find enough to help Shinn in his civil suit against Brad.

Connie Capato found Loni Ann Cunningham in Brooklyn, New York, on August 24, 1989. Although she had not lived with Brad for seventeen years, Loni Ann was still afraid of him. Theirs was the only one of Brad's divorces where money was not an issue. 'Neither of us had money,' Loni Ann said. 'It was Brad's power and dominance over me. He punished me by getting at me through my children.'

With Capato's promise that her whereabouts would never be revealed to Brad, Loni Ann began to open up. Her marriage had been hellish, she said, full of emotional and physical abuse. She had dreaded Brad's moods. Sometimes he hit her when he didn't even seem to be angry. She might be watching television and he would hit her and say, 'Take that for a lesson,' and then sit down and watch with her as if nothing had happened.

Loni Ann detailed the disintegration of her life with Brad from the time she was a happy young bride until the last terrifying days when she actually feared for her life. 'In the beginning he would argue, and then he would throw things and then hit me. At the end, he would walk in the door after having a bad day and start beating on me.'

Loni Ann confided that Brad had a history of fighting going back to high school. 'If there was a fight going on, Brad would do anything to get involved – even if he wasn't part of the fight in the first place.' She said Brad had told her that he and his friends had a 'good time' going downtown in Seattle and beating up 'winos' and 'queers.' 'One time he beat up one guy so badly that he didn't know if he had killed him – but he didn't stick around to find out.'

Loni Ann said the most frightening time of her marriage was when Brad had worked at Gals Galore. Whether it was true or not, he had always talked as if he was heavily involved with organized crime figures.

She described his reaction once when he was picked up

for parking violations. She told Capato that Brad was livid that his fingerprints were on file.

Loni Ann also told Capato that she thought he had a lot of money '—although you could never prove it by his paperwork.' Every time she had tried to file for support to help raise her children, Brad managed to look like a pauper on paper. Whenever Kait and Brent visited their father, they came home and told Loni Ann about 'the hundreds and hundreds of dollars in cash' and all the material things their father had. 'He would talk about how he was giving his "current" three sons three-wheelers and very expensive toys, and Kait and Brent basically got nothing. It was as if he was throwing it in their faces – that if they came to live with him, he would give them things, but since they didn't, he wouldn't give them anything.'

She told Capato about the time Brad had taken Kait to Houston, but when she asked Loni Ann if Kait would testify about that, she shook her head. Kait wanted only to be as far away from her father as she could be.

Loni Ann had had a difficult time surviving when she was alone with Kait and Brent. 'One of the things that Brad would do was write support checks – and then stop payment on them,' she said. 'He knew that if the welfare department believed I was receiving support from him they wouldn't give me any money. I couldn't cash his checks, but the welfare people wouldn't give me money either. . . .'

Hesitatingly, Loni Ann told Capato about the terrible night when Brad had left her, drunk and disoriented, standing on the cliff above the river. And as for Cheryl's murder, she had thoughts about that. She felt that if Brad had paid someone to kill Cheryl, he would have made sure that many, many respectable people saw him in the vital time period. Since no such witnesses had come forward, she said that Brad himself had probably beaten Cheryl to death. Loni Ann had been frightened that he would murder *her* during their divorce and custody battles.

Loni Ann told Connie Capato that she had never known

anybody who was so vindictive and had such a strong need for revenge and control as Brad. That was the major reason that she had fled the Northwest and found work as a kinestheology therapist as far away from him as she could get and still be in America. Asked if she would testify against Brad in the civil trial, she turned white and stammered 'N-n-no!' She wasn't even sure about a deposition. There was no guarantee that Brad wouldn't come after her. Even if he was found responsible for Cheryl's death, she knew he wouldn't be locked up.

Connie could see how afraid Brad's first wife still was of him – even though he had had four other wives since she divorced him. She asked if Loni Ann would think about giving a videotaped deposition that Mike Shinn could present in the civil trial.

Loni Ann said she would think about it.

Leslie Haigh located Brad's older sister Ethel. Ethel – who went by 'Edie' – was living in the Northwest, although she, like most of the women in Brad's past, didn't want her address revealed to him. Unlike Loni Ann, Ethel wasn't hesitant to relate her memories of her brother. She remembered him as being violent since his high-school days. He had beaten her and he had beaten their mother.

Ethel regretted that she had persuaded Brad to marry Loni Ann when she became pregnant at seventeen. She hadn't realized the abuse that Loni Ann had suffered in her marriage. 'She was just beginning to establish a relationship with my husband and me and she finally opened up to us. . . .' Ethel looked at Leslie Haigh and confided, 'I have no doubt in my mind that Brad murdered Cheryl. What is so sad is that all the women who have been involved with Brad truly believed that he wouldn't hurt them. They believed that he loved them.'

Ethel had never really known Cheryl – not until near the end of her life. They had talked in the spring of 1986 after Cheryl and Brad had separated. Ethel had offered to help

Cheryl in her divorce and custody proceedings, and she had invited Cheryl to her daughter's wedding.

Ethel said that Cheryl had told her about one time when Brad disappeared for two weeks. Cheryl had asked him where he'd been and why he had left. 'Brad's response to Cheryl,' Ethel said, 'was "If I ever hit you, I'll kill you."'

Cheryl had called her the Friday before she died and told her about the deposition she had given a few days before. 'She told me, "I'm going to nail him – I'm not going to let this happen." I begged her, "Don't be alone this weekend. He'll try to get you to come to him. Under no circumstances should you go to him." Cheryl said, "I'll be careful. I'll tell somebody if something looks like it will happen."'

Ethel made a strange comment to Haigh about Brad's perception of children. 'Children are nonentities,' she said. If Brad were to strike his wife and the children were present, it would be as if they were not really there – not in Brad's mind. 'It is quite conceivable that the child [Michael] *was* with Brad on the night of Cheryl's death,' Ethel said, 'and he might actually have *seen* what he did. It is quite conceivable that he took no precautions to make sure that the child did not see anything because no child was "there" to see anything.'

It was a chilling thought – almost as if Brad equated children with dogs or cats. Crimes could be committed in front of animals with impunity. Who would ever know?

As far as Michael Cunningham's memory went, the police files weren't very encouraging. Mike Shinn saw that Michael had refused to talk with Jerry Finch and Susan Svetkey in the days immediately following his mother's murder. He had been four then; now he was almost eight. The chance that he remembered *more* after three and a half years was almost nil. But like Jim Ayers, Shinn hoped in his heart that Michael hadn't seen the terrible violence done to his mother.

* * *

In September 1989 Connie Capato found Brent Cunningham, who was still living in Portland – but not with his father, who had thrown him out a year earlier. Brent agreed to talk to Capato. His memories of his childhood were not particularly pleasant. His father had left his mother when he was only a year old, and during the next ten years he saw him only during summer vacations and sporadic visits. When Capato asked Brent to describe his father, he said he was more a 'competitive parent' than a 'loving father.' Brad had always flashed money in front of him and Kait and told them that when they were old enough they could decide which parent they wanted to live with.

Brent said that he had had minimal contact with his father's second and third wives. He recalled being in a van with Brad and Cynthia Marrasco and watching them fight. 'My dad slapped her.' As for Lauren Swanson, Brad's third wife, Brent had never seen any abusive language or physical violence. But, of course, Brad had been married to Lauren less than a year.

Brent's first prolonged contact with his father in years was on the Tampico property. He was eleven then and he was given so many chores that he felt like a 'slave.' And just as Brad had once had Jess, Michael, and Phillip collect 'souvenirs' of dead things on their trips to Yakima, he had made up for lost time with his eldest son. He decided that Brent needed to learn how to kill and he forced the eleven-year-old to watch as he killed a young steer. But Brad didn't know how to carry out a clean kill. In the end, he took a hatchet and finally a chain saw to the animal, and the barn stall was a bloody abattoir. It was an image burned forever into Brent's mind.

Brent had hay fever and farm chores aggravated it. His father hadn't believed him and told him he was 'faking it' and 'lazy.' 'He grabbed me by the back of the neck and said, "You're your mother's product and I don't want you around if you are going to be like that."' Then he threw Brent onto the ground. In a rage he ordered Brent to stay in the barn all day, and promised to deal with him later. Frightened, Brent ran away to his maternal uncle's house.

'My dad called and said I could come back and take my punishment or go back to my mother and forget that I ever had a father. I decided to go back to my mom's.' But first, Brad insisted that Brent return all the clothes he had bought for him over the summer. Brent collected them and returned them to the Tampico ranch, but Brad noticed that he was still wearing clothing he had purchased for him. 'I had to take them off and leave them,' Brent remembered. 'I left with half my clothes gone and barefooted. That was the last time I heard from my dad for about four years.'

The passage of time since his days on the Tampico ranch had faded his bad memories of his father, and Brent visited Brad in Oregon in the late spring of 1986. Brad had just left Cheryl. 'Everything went really well, and I stayed in Portland,' Brent said.

And so he became witness to the bitter divorce between his father and his third stepmother. He remembered well the night that Cheryl was murdered and the fear they had all lived through in the days that followed. Brent said he had gotten home from his scuba diving trip about 10:30 that Sunday night. 'When I asked my dad why the message machine wasn't on when I tried to call, he told me he'd just gone down to check the mail. After this . . . we all went to bed. Sometime later the police were beating on the door but no one could hear them . . . the apartment was near the freeway. . . . I went in and woke my father up and we were scared because we didn't know who was pounding at the door in the middle of the night. My father got two pistols out and gave one to me.'

Brad went to the door and opened it cautiously to find the police there. 'The police said, "You don't want your son to hear this," so my father told me to go back to my room . . . but I listened from the door and I could hear the police say, "Your wife's been killed."' After a long time, Brad came to Brent's room with tears in his eyes.

He told him that Cheryl had been murdered and that he was a suspect.

Brent told Connie Capato that when his father had his heart attack in Phil Margolin's office two days later, all of his four sons had ridden to the hospital with him. But it was Brent that Brad wanted to talk to privately. 'He pulled the curtains and got real close and we talked secretly about trying to get the boys out of town. He gave me a lot of business cards and names of people who could help get the boys hidden so that Cheryl's mother wouldn't take them. My dad told me to drive them out of town myself if I had to.'

Brent wasn't yet sixteen at the time and it was an awesome responsibility. He looked at the names in his hand and saw that his father had listed his attorney Phil Margolin, Jerry Elshire, a private investigator, his sister Susan in Seattle, his uncle Jimmy Cunningham, and Herman and Trudy Dreesen. As it turned out, of course, Brad's heart attack did not prove fatal and the burden was off Brent. But he had been caught up in the paranoia that followed Cheryl's murder and he fled with Brad and the boys to the ranch in Tampico, back to the scene of his black summer of 1981.

Once the pressure over Cheryl's murder was somewhat off Brad, he started in on Brent again. He didn't like his personality, he was too quiet, and he was boring. He told Brent that he thought he would probably turn out to be a serial murderer or someone like John Hinkley because he was too quiet. Brent was smart enough to feel that his father was projecting his own personality onto him.

Asked about Brad's treatment of his three younger sons, Brent told Capato he thought the three little boys were 'scared to death' of their father because of his rigid schedules and routines. When Phillip was being toilet trained, for instance, Brad had sometimes punished him for mishaps by forcing him to sit on the toilet for as long as six and a half hours, 'half the time crying, and in the dark.'

Sara had tried to intervene when she was there and asked Brad to let up on the boys. She had also gone to Brent's defense when Brad tried to kick him out over some transgression. 'He threw a suitcase on the floor, threw all the dresser drawers on the floor, and began throwing things at the suitcase,' Brent said. 'Sara came in crying and it was later resolved and everything was back to "normal" as if nothing had happened.'

Gradually, Mike Shinn and his investigators were going through the list of possible witnesses against Brad Cunningham: Lilya Saarnen, Betty and Marv Troseth, Jim Karr, all of whom had informative and often startling viewpoints on the man Shinn was about to meet in court. Jim Ayers was a tremendous help in re-creating the night of Cheryl Keeton's murder and the investigation that followed. Greg Dallaire, Eric Lindenauer, and dozens of Cheryl's coworkers at Garvey, Schubert and Barer were prepared to testify to the terror Cheryl had felt during the last year of her life.

Shinn, Diane Bakker, Connie Capato, and Leslie Haigh were peeling the layers of Brad's life away, and the further they peeled, the darker and more filled with poison he seemed to become. Here was a man who had had everything in life – good looks, money, success, power, beautiful women, perfect children – and yet nothing had been enough. Again and again, he had turned on the people who loved him – on his wives, on his children, on his mother and sisters. He was a cruel man and he appeared to be completely devoid of conscience. The more they learned about Brad, the more convinced they became that he had, indeed, been the person who bludgeoned his wife and the mother of his three little boys to death.

But could they prove it?

40

Sara was back in her shaky marriage, if only temporarily. February 1990 was obviously a time of revelation for her, and she was coming to terms with some brutal truths. She was a strong woman; she had to be to have come so far in her career and to survive this strange and treacherous union with Brad. She no longer felt threatened by Brad, at least most of the time, and thought she could handle his temper tantrums and his hysterics. She recognized the 'games' and the histrionics for what they were, and she still planned to stay only until the civil suit in Cheryl's death was over.

Since she had listened to his pleas to stand beside him through his trial, Sara certainly didn't expect Brad to continue to cheat on her with Lynn Minero. A bargain was a bargain.

But then, Brad was Brad. Sara was still wary, and still writing in her journal. '2–22–90, Thursday: Sometime during this week Brad repeated part of a conversation I had had *only* with my sister Rosemary from our bedroom phone when he was in Houston [Feb. 11]. It involved my losing a checkbook from U.S. Bank and wondering if he had taken it. I figured out that he must have recorded somehow in our bedroom. I had had numerous conversations from the kitchen phone and the office phone without his knowledge.'

Now, Sara remembered that Brad had known other things he should have had no way of knowing. He knew that she had hired a private investigator, and he knew that she had asked her banker to change the credit line at her bank so Brad could not withdraw any more cash. Those were also things she had told her sister on the bedroom phone.

Something was getting to Brad. He was 'frantic' when he found out that Sara had spoken to Bill Schulte, a divorce attorney. 'I told him no plans were made to file for a divorce – I simply wanted information and to secure an attorney for myself, since Brad had seen so many attorneys in the past.'

On February 27, Sara wrote: 'I walked over to the Hilton to wait for an 8:30 a.m. meeting with Brad and Wes [Urqhart, Brad's Houston lawyer]. . . . Wes's concern was about my guaranteeing the legal fees for Brad's civil lawsuit. I told him I would do that. I also told him I had not filed for divorce and was unsure when and if I would. . . . Wes met with 'Joe' Rieke and Jerry Elshire. Rieke also wanted me to guarantee Brad's legal fees which I verbally agreed to do.'

Sara did not delude herself that Brad wanted to keep her as his wife because he loved her. He needed financial cover, and she would do that. But she wasn't doing it for Brad, she was doing it for the boys. She still believed they needed a father who was not in prison.

Later that same day, Sara met again with Lynn Minero's husband, Gary. She must have felt she was being pulled in a dozen different directions. Gary needed money too; Lynn was no longer working at the bakery and that put him in a bind. He said he needed $3,500, but only for sixty days; he would pay her back $5,000. Although the guilt was not her own, Sara knew it was Brad's deviousness that had destroyed Gary's marriage; he had small children, and his wife was clearly besotted with Brad. Sighing, she wrote a check for Gary's living expenses.

'We talked nonstop for an hour and I guess my overall reaction was one of relief because he confirmed almost everything that my instincts had been telling me about Brad and Lynn's relationship. . . . Anyway, he asked Lynn if she was involved with Brad and . . . she broke down and told him everything. Things had started out with messing around in the office. She said they started having intercourse in the middle of December. . . . They usually went to the Red Lion Motel.'

There were many more encounters, all the times when Brad had been away 'on business.' According to Gary, Lynn blamed the affair on Sara. Brad had told her what 'tight control' Sara kept over him. Sara and Brad had always talked two or three times a day 'but he had come to resent the checking up on him. Brad had told Lynn he didn't love me, he couldn't stand to be around me, and he wanted her to leave Gary for him. Gary was concerned for my safety because Brad had told Lynn, "Don't worry about Sara. I'll take care of her," with no mention of working through a divorce with me.'

'2–27–90: . . . Brad came home around 8:00 and did very little talking. Brad and the boys went to bed. . . . They were all in our bedroom and Brad locked the door. . . . I went to the apartment to sleep. . . . The next day, I decided to go ahead and file for divorce. I didn't sleep very well at all at the apartment and decided to just stay at the hospital every night after that.'

On February 28, Sara called her attorney Bill Schulte and told him about the past two days. She mentioned that she had given Brad's attorney a check for fifteen thousand dollars and had promised to guarantee Brad's legal fees in the civil suit. Schulte was appalled. For the first time in a long time, Sara had a champion – someone on *her* side. 'Schulte went over to Rieke's office and said I wouldn't guarantee the fees. . . . Schulte was told that I had been having an affair with 'this doctor in Baker' and that we [Brad and I] had always had a very open sexual arrangement.'

Sara called Betty Troseth to tell her that she was leaving Brad. She wanted Cheryl's mother to know that if anything ever happened to Brad she would look after Jess, Michael, and Phillip. Betty felt a familiar chill. She told Sara about the pervasive fear Cheryl had lived with in the last months of her life, of her belief that Brad would kill her. In the end, it had done Cheryl no good to be on guard. Betty said she was frightened for Sara, and for the boys too. She warned Sara to be very, very careful.

Sara wrote, perhaps naively, 'I look forward to the time when this whole mess is over with, and I can find out from Betty what Cheryl was really like. Of course, Brad has not painted a very flattering picture of her to me – just like he painted a bad picture of me to Lynn. Betty said the first time she met me, she thought, "Oh no, there's another Cheryl." It will be so good for the boys, especially Jess and Michael, to know what Cheryl was really like.'

When Brad found out that Sara would no longer guarantee his legal fees, he began another fervent campaign to win back her love. He used pleas, and he issued threats and warnings. 'Friday, 3–2–90: My case in surgery was cancelled. Thank Goodness! Had one conversation with Brad. He called me and said Burke and Shinn have won. He loves me and wants to talk with me. . . . He said Schulte doesn't like him and might affect my feelings toward him. . . . Brad called again, says he's lost 32 pounds, pleading with me not to get a divorce. There's no good reason that our marriage should end. He can't take another battle, another hassle in his life right now.'

Brad warned Sara that 'adversarial divorces' could have attorneys' fees running over one hundred thousand dollars. 'He says Rieke will not defend him if I don't guarantee the legal fees. . . . He always loved me, but with "the knowledge of what I was doing," he sought comfort from Lynn. . . . It was due to the stress he was under from Shinn. . . . He said he never had anything [sexually] to do with Lynn. . . . He said we can gain trust in each other again.'

Sara listened to Brad's glib and persuasive words without expression. She recognized his lies too well now.

Later that day, she took the three little boys to McMinnville to spend the night at her sister's. Her cell phone rang twice but she didn't answer it. She finally shut it off. She had other anesthesiologists covering for her at the hospital; no one needed her – except for Jess, Michael, and Phillip – and she didn't want to hear any more of Brad's pleas for reconciliation. He didn't miss her, he missed her checkbook. He was about to find out that she had made her first and last payment on the Volvo station wagon Brad wanted to lease. That would make him absolutely furious, but she had decided to stop paying his way.

The next morning, Sara called the boys' baby-sitter and learned that Brad had been taken to Good Samaritan Hospital, suffering from chest pains. Once she had run to the ER, stricken with fear that she would lose Brad to a fatal heart attack. Not now. She had heard his cry of 'Wolf' too many times. She took Michael and Phillip back to their sitter, and later, as she drove Jess to his basketball game, her car phone rang. It was Brad's psychologist. 'She said Brad was having an anxiety reaction. She wanted to talk with me to see how much of an emotional support I could be for Brad.'

Emotional support, indeed. Sara did not rush to the hospital. She watched Jess play basketball. But her pager beeped. It was a nurse from Good Samaritan who told her that Brad asked that Sara stop by her apartment at Riverplace to pick up a letter he had left there for her.

After the basketball game, Sara took Jess home and then went by her apartment. She felt an icy apprehension when she saw that somehow Brad had circumvented the tight security there and managed to slide a letter under her door.

'I visited Brad in the ICU [intensive care unit] and he looked very pitiful and pathetic,' Sara wrote in her diary. 'He had some IV's in, was getting a Lidocaine infusion (No PVC's on his EKG for a change) Nasal O/2 [oxygen] and was trying to sound very weak. He had me read the letter and then continued to tell me how much he loved me and wanted us to be together.'

Brad told Sara how easily he had gotten into her apartment complex. 'I told some women who were going in that my wife wasn't answering the phone and I thought her phone wires were disconnected. They let me right in.'

Sara knew she could never stay in her apartment again. Brad had such a guileless, charming way; he would always be able to get into any apartment she had – even the most security-conscious complexes. He was like smoke, able to creep beneath doors, through locked windows. There was no safety for her anymore.

Looking at the 'sick' man in the hospital bed, Sara felt nothing at all, except relief that he was in the hospital; it meant she could have one more night with the boys. 'We went to dinner at Wan Fu's and then stayed overnight in the trauma call room. It was a nice evening with them.'

Sara kept the letter Brad had slipped under her door. Later that evening, something made her reread it. Brad had printed it in sprawling letters.

> My dearest wife,
> . . . I love you very much. . . . It may be too late . . . [but] our family is the most important part of my life.

Brad wrote fervently that their problems should in no way be considered cause for divorce. He could not bear to let Sara go.

> We are humans. . . . I want to . . . rebuild our trust. I have made some mistakes – I sought refuge in Lynn when I thought there was no friendship or trust from you. . . .

Brad explains, with his odd talent for reversing blame, that their marriage is in trouble mostly because of Sara's omissions. If she had only given him an ultimatum sooner, everything could have been worked out. In essence, he was saying that it was *her* fault that he had continued his affair with Lynn for so many months.

Moreover, he blamed his stress over the Houston lawsuit for whatever poor judgment he might have shown. Somehow, those worries had affected the way he felt about Sara.

But he felt he was 'o.k. now,' thanks to the fatherly concern shown by his attorneys, Wes Urquart and Joe Reike.

Brad again reminded Sara that she had been less than direct with him. She should have been firmer when she accused him of having an affair with Lynn, and she should have told him he was working too many hours. 'I know you think you were – but to me it takes a big message – in neon. . . .

'I need you honey,' Brad pleaded,

> I need your love and affection – your mind, and your body. I can defeat those beasts in Houston with you. . . .
>
> I will renew our vows, pledge my support and understanding to you and work like you have never seen to strengthen our marriage and relationship. . . .
>
> I love you Honey,
> I need you.
> Your Husband

Sara folded the letter and tucked it, without emotion, into her journal.

The next day, Brad tried another tack. He told Sara he thought John Burke killed Cheryl. 'Sunday, March 4: The motive was unrequited love. He then warned me to watch out – he may try to kill me too. Brad said to make sure I was always around people when I was on vacation.'

Sara got the message. Brad had just told her that the person who killed Cheryl might try to kill her too.

Apparently unaware of how seriously Sara took his not-quite-subliminal warning, Brad tried every device he could think of to keep her from filing for divorce. Since money was of paramount importance to him, he assumed everyone felt the same way and he kept reminding Sara of how much a complicated divorce would cost, upping the figure with every call.

Next, Brad tried total honesty. 'He said he'd like to tell me every detail about him and Lynn,' Sara wrote. 'I told him I didn't want to hear it.'

* * *

Only six months earlier, Sara had been shocked to learn that Mike Shinn was attempting to file a civil suit against her husband, and she had chastised him for bringing more pain to her family. Now, she reached out tentatively to Shinn. She was not ready to admit to herself – and certainly not to anyone else – that she suspected that Brad had killed Cheryl. And yet she needed to know more. She needed to make some contact with the man who had been her friend years ago at Willamette University.

Brad himself gave Sara an excuse to call Mike Shinn. He had been working out at the 'Y' and he'd told Sara that he had seen Shinn there, watching him. 'Brad felt intimidated by Mike Shinn,' she recalled. 'He thought Mike was dangerous.'

Sara knew that was patently ridiculous, but she called Shinn at home on March 4, 1990, and left a message asking him to call her at the hospital. He did a short time later, and she asked him if he belonged to the 'Y' and worked out there.

'Yeah, I do,' he told her.

'Brad thinks you're there to watch him.'

Shinn laughed. 'Sara, I wouldn't recognize Brad if I bumped into him. He may have seen me working out, but I never noticed him. I only saw him once – at Jake's – and that was for about half a minute.'

An hour later, Sara talked with Brad. There was no way he could have bugged her phone at Providence Hospital, but it was almost as if he knew she had called Mike Shinn and that they had had a friendly conversation after she had asked him about the 'Y.' Earlier in the day, Brad had begged her to stay with him because he loved her so, because 'the family' needed to be together; now he was cold.

'It was obvious already that I was now his enemy and the war had been waged. I couldn't believe how fast he changed his whole demeanor toward me. He said we would each spend fifty thousand dollars in legal fees. He also said something about my using a fraudulent financial statement when getting the increase in credit at First Interstate Bank . . . *this* is a financial statement *Brad* prepared in January. . . .'

Sara at least realized that even a pretense of marriage was impossible. Brad was now ready to talk about dividing up their furniture.

41

In the spring of 1990 the same rhododendrons bloomed in Portland, the same azaleas, the same sweet daphne – everything in nature was the same as it had been in the spring of 1986. And yet everything had changed and Sara's world had reversed itself from a place filled with wondrous love to a dark abyss where loss and fear walked with her constantly.

She had decided to move out of the house in Dunthorpe on March 5, and her journal entries showed that once Brad had accepted that, he set himself on what was, for him, a familiar path. 'March 5, 1990: Brad moved all my clothes over to Rhonda's [the baby-sitter's] guest house in the morning. All my hanging clothes were on the couch. The clothes from my dresser and shelves were placed in brown paper bags and boxes.'

Sara had arranged for a restraining order to keep Brad from being present when she went to the house in Dunthorpe to collect her belongings. She had paid for this house and she was willing to let Brad and the boys live there while she continued to pay for it, but she found that he had stationed a private investigator at the house to be sure she didn't remove items that Brad considered his.

'March 6, 1990: . . . I was totally stunned. . . . Brad had removed an incredible amount of my stuff from the house. . . . All my cancelled checks and registers from 1985 on were gone . . . files, a basket of paid bills and papers that needed to be filed. . . . He must have been up all night going through things and packing them into [his] pickup or car.'

Brad had also demonstrated an uncanny instinct for taking things that had sentimental or special meaning to Sara: 'He had removed *all* the placemats, my Waterford goblets, most of the wine glasses, all of the bottles of wine (including presents to me . . .) and all of the cookbooks. The kitchen, though, was the most cleaned out. Both drawers of utensils were gone.' It was odd. She had asked Brad for an oak cabinet and said the boys could have whichever TV and VCR they wanted. Brad had left those but taken the cabinet.

The next day, a very shaken Sara had an appointment with her psychologist. 'Dr T. Thought that Brad's statements about John Burke trying to kill me and not ever being alone were a direct warning to *me*,' she wrote in her journal. '[He told] me not to let Brad find me in those situations where he might be tempted [to kill me.] I was scared when Brad had said that to me, but became even more fearful for my safety after discussing it with Dr T.'

Brad gave two weeks' notice to Rhonda, their baby-sitter. He told her he planned to stay home with the boys and he needed to rent the guest house to make money. He changed all the locks on the Dunthorpe house. And Rhonda told Sara that she had overhead Phillip and Michael talking. 'Rhonda said . . . Phillip was telling Michael that Mom doesn't like Dad anymore and Mom hired people to kill him,' she noted in her diary. When Rhonda tried to tell the little boys that wasn't true, Michael took Phillip to their room and shut the door.

Sara realized that Brad had begun to wipe her from

the boys' minds in a most terrible way, just as he had systematically erased Cheryl from their memories. Now, it was Sara who was not 'Mom' any longer; she was an evil person who was trying to kill Dad.

'March 9, 1990: . . . First Interstate Bank called me, saying that Brad . . . wants a copy of my financial statement. . . . Brad went to AAI and asked for my deposits. They told him they were not at liberty to give them to him. . . . At U.S. Bank, the Broadway Bakery Account is $2758 overdrawn.'

Sara soon learned it was worse than that. A bakery employee with loyalty to Sara told her that many bills had gone unpaid for at least three months, even though she had provided money to Brad to pay them. The total of these bills – combined with unpaid salaries – was over twenty thousand dollars. Furthermore, Brad was negotiating to lease the Broadway Bakery premises – even though it was Sara who owned the property.

In an affidavit Sara drew up, she would list Brad's machinations that began when he realized she was truly going to divorce him. 'Upon the Respondent learning that I was filing this proceeding, he failed to deposit the receipts from the bakery or from the delicatessen. . . . I do not have any idea what happened to the money or how much money he took. He also immediately took large amounts of money from my credit cards on cash advance. . . . I have now learned the Respondent has taken equipment that is encumbered with debt . . . it can [not] be sold or used to reduce the debts I am personally responsible for. I know he has a fax machine, a copier, an espresso machine and a coffee grinder (a large commercial model). . . . Respondent has left a van at the bakery in a parking lot that is in danger of being towed. . . . I have paid $27,000 in recent months over his being accused of killing his former wife. . . .'

Sara realized that she would probably have to sell the Dunthorpe house. It was the only way out of the morass of debts Brad had piled up. But the money drain was not her biggest concern; she was worried sick about Jess, Michael, and Phillip. Rhonda was still there and she told Sara that the boys were wearing old clothes she had never seen, that no laundry had been done, and they had no toys to play with because they came to the guest house after school, instead of the big house, and Brad had locked all their toys up. Michael wasn't practicing the piano and botched his piece at his recital. Sometimes Brad didn't come home until late and the boys had to sleep on Rhonda's couch.

From Rhonda and the boys' piano teacher, Sara learned that Brad was telling people that she had left him for a doctor, that she didn't care anything about the boys, and that she was happily vacationing with a new lover. It wasn't true. She was working double, triple shifts to forestall financial disaster. An affair with another man was the last thing on her mind.

Brad's attorneys were going after Sara for huge monthly support for him and the boys. He claimed the only income he would have was $350 from the rental of the guest house, while his monthly expenses were $11,422 – including $450 a month for the Volvo lease, $590 a month for payments on a new truck (with camper), $439 for his boat payment, and $5,000 for his legal fees. Married to Sara, Brad had become accustomed to an even higher standard of living than he had enjoyed with Cheryl.

And he had no intention of lowering it. Brad felt it would be 'demeaning' for him to have to submit bills to Sara's attorney. He requested through his attorney that Sara simply keep his checking account solvent so that he could continue to write checks. She thought not.

Sara willingly continued to make the twenty-five-hundred-dollar house payment, all insurance payments – including medical insurance for Brad and the boys – all taxes, the bakery payment, and all other monthly obligations. She also paid Rhonda eleven hundred dollars a month for as long as she stayed. At least Sara knew that Rhonda cared about them. She asked only for a temporary restraining order to keep Brad away from her Riverplace neighborhood and from Providence Hospital.

On March 12, 1990, Sara signed her newly drawn will, four years and one month after Cheryl Keeton had signed her hastily prepared will. The language in Sara's will bore a somber resemblance to that in Cheryl's.

'I declare that I am married to Bradly M. Cunningham. A proceeding is pending in the Multnomah County Circuit Court to dissolve our marriage. I have intentionally made no provision for my husband in this will.

'It is my intention that my husband Bradly M. Cunningham not receive any assets by virtue of my death. I have three children, Jess K. Cunningham, Michael K. Cunningham, and Phillip K. Cunningham. . . .'

Sara set up a 'Sara Gordon Trust Fund' that would be administered by members of her family and was to benefit her three adopted sons.

Brad let her see the boys only once; Sara was ecstatic. When they were together, it seemed as if they had never been apart and that somehow, someway she was still their mom.

On March 30, 1990, Rhonda called Sara to tell her that the boys weren't in school. 'They aren't here and I called the school. Brad told them he was taking the kids to Seattle for a few days and they might be back to school by Wednesday.'

Three days later, when Brad and Sara were to appear at a support hearing, he didn't show up and Sara learned that Brad had called Michael's school and said he wouldn't be back. Period. Sara wasn't sure where Brad and the boys were. On April 11, someone called her at the hospital – at 7 A.M. – and said he was her attorney, Bill Schulte, calling collect. Hospital operators had permission to put Schulte's calls through. But when Sara was paged and picked up the phone, she heard only a dial tone. She called Schulte and he assured her he had not called her – collect or any other way.

The Dunthorpe house was empty. On April 21, Sara had the front door rekeyed so that she could get in and clean the house before she listed it with a realtor. She had to fax a copy of a court order to a Dunthorpe security officer in order to get into her own house. The agreement was that he would let a realtor with a prospective buyer in to see the house – but when he tried to get in, he found all the locks had been jammed.

Brad called Jack Lang,* the security man, from Houston, threatened to sue him for trespassing if he let realtors in, and said that he was going to change the alarm code. Lang called his attorney, who advised him not to let anyone into the house since ownership was in contention.

In the last week of April 1990 Sara got a phone call at Providence Hospital. It was Jess, and her heart convulsed when she detected that he was crying. His first words to her were, 'Mom, why do you have to sell the boat and the house?'

'Jess,' Sara said urgently. 'Where are you?'

'Texas.'

'When are you coming back?'

'I think when school is out . . .'

'I love you and I miss you very much,' Sara said. 'I thought you were coming back sooner.'

'*Why*, Mom?' Jess repeated, obviously coached. 'Why are you selling our house and our boat?'

'Your dad can tell you why, Jess.'

'Why can't *you?*' he asked.

'We have to sell them, honey, because we need the money.'

Sara thought she heard ten-year-old Jess mutter something like 'bullshit' and he hung up on her.

That wasn't like Jess. Sara's hand rested on the phone and she frowned. The phone rang again a few minutes later. It was eight-year-old Michael.

'Where are you living, Michael?' Sara asked.

'Texas.'

'Do you live in a house, Michael?'

'No, we don't have enough money.'

'Are you in a hotel?'

'No, in an apartment.'

Sara rushed to tell him that she loved him and missed him and his brothers. But Michael asked about the house too. How could she sell their house? She repeated what she had told Jess – they needed the money. Now, she was sure he was being coached. She could hear Brad's voice whispering to Michael.

And then Michael said, 'You make thirty thousand dollars a month!' and hung up on her.

Both the boys sounded so angry; they were almost yelling at her.

Things got worse. The leading realtor in Lake Oswego told Sara there was a 'big problem' with showing the Dunthorpe house. Apparently, Brad was back in Oregon. He had confronted a real estate saleswoman at the house and said he planned to move back in, and she was not to do anything about listing it or selling it. All the women in her agency had had a meeting and they agreed that they didn't feel safe handling Sara's property.

Brad was making it virtually impossible for Sara to sell her own house and attempt to recoup some of her losses. He was also keeping everything of any value. The computer that she had paid for had been removed on Brad's orders, 'to be cleared of Brad's information.' Bill Schulte was supposed to pick it up from the dealer but somehow it was never ready. Eventually, Sara learned that the sixteen-thousand-dollar system had 'been sent to Houston.'

The Volvo station wagon was in Houston too. She had stopped paying for the car Brad was driving, but she was still legally responsible for the debt. Sara felt if she could just get it back and turn it in to the bank, she might be able to cut her losses some. Brad finally dumped it in Houston. Sara eventually had it brought back to Oregon; it was less than a year old but it was dented and run-down, far more than it should have been for such a new vehicle. To unload it, Sara had to pay the dealership the five-thousand-dollar difference between its book value and its actual worth.

On May 21 Sara received a message from the sales manager at the Volvo dealership. 'Brad Cunningham called me . . . because he said he is restrained from talking to his wife. He said she caused their Volvo to be repossessed and there were some items of personal property in the car: children's clothing, children's toys, and baseball cards. . . . He'd like her to try to get them back.'

None of the boys' possessions had been left in the Volvo; Brad's call was simple, almost childish harassment. He was never averse to using his sons to manipulate Sara. Two days later, she received a Federal Express overnight letter from Vinson and Elkins. Inside there was a single lined sheet, printed laboriously in what seemed to be a child's hand.

> Dear Mom,
>
> We get out of school this Thursday. We have no way of getting back home. We have no money. Could you send some money and airplane tickets so we can get home?
>
> Singed [*sic*] by,
> Jess
> Phillip

Sara didn't respond. She knew that Brad had either dictated this sad little letter or written it himself, imitating a child's handwriting.

That bleak spring, something made Sara walk to the park blocks near her former home, the Madison Tower. She remembered the huge purple bruise under Brad's upper arm – the bruise she had seen when she took a shower with him four days after Cheryl's murder. Brad had explained it easily enough. 'Oh – that. I was playing on the jungle gym in the park blocks with the kids on Sunday while you were sleeping. I slipped at the top, and I caught myself on the bars on that arm.'

Now, in the spring of 1990, Sara saw that there *was* no jungle gym in the park blocks. There never had been.

42

In her affidavit to obtain a restraining order against Brad, Sara had stated what she had come to believe with growing horror. 'I have been married to the respondent for slightly more than two years. Prior to our marriage, my husband was the subject of an investigation concerning the murder of his fourth wife, Cheryl Keeton, in September, 1986. The Grand Jury did not indict him. He has now been sued in the Multnomah County Circuit Court for causing Cheryl Keeton's death. . . . Because in the past I had a belief that he did not cause Cheryl Keeton's death, I married him. My belief now is not so certain, and I am in great fear of my husband. . . .'

Sara had her attorney, Bill Schulte, on her side, and she had begun to trust Mike Shinn again, although she had asked in vain to have Brad excluded from the room when she gave Shinn a deposition. 'I remember what happened to Cheryl within days of the deposition *she* gave when Brad was in the room,' she said. Brad was present, but Sara never looked at him.

Mike Shinn had consulted with a Portland psychiatrist, Dr Ron Turco. Turco was an associate clinical professor of psychiatry at Oregon Health Sciences University and he was particularly qualified as a consultant to Shinn. Not only was Turco a psychiatrist, he was also a commissioned police officer. He had testified on the psychopathology of a number of defendants, and he willingly agreed to look over the material Shinn had gathered thus far on Brad Cunningham. After he read carefully through the huge file, red-flagging scores of pages, Turco warned Shinn that men like Brad were extremely dangerous.

'How do I find him – or at least more about him?' Shinn asked, brushing aside Turco's warnings.

'Go to his women. Get them to talk to you,' Turco said. 'I think you'll find most of his secrets there.'

Shinn was doing exactly that in preparation for his court action against Brad. And he would have no paucity of witnesses. Quite apart from his five wives, Brad's past was teeming with women.

On March 21, even as Sara was acknowledging that she didn't really know the man she had married, and that she not only no longer loved him but feared him – feared him so much that she didn't want to give a deposition in his presence – Loni Ann Cunningham was about to give her own deposition. It was, perhaps, the most terrifying thing she could imagine – short of actually confronting Brad in a court of law. Mike Shinn, Diane Bakker, and Brad's attorney, Forrest 'Joe' Rieke, traveled out of state to depose Loni Ann. She was much too frightened of Brad to come to Oregon. She had finally agreed to a videotaped deposition on neutral ground.

The camera caught Loni Ann as she waited for the questions to begin. She was a pretty woman, slender, with thick brown hair. She wore a purple sweater, which only added to the pallor of her face. She looked for all the world like a mouse that had been backed into a corner by a cat just before a kill. Almost two decades had not diminished her fear of Brad one iota.

Joe Rieke, a big-boned man with a deep gravelly voice, began the tape with his objections. His client Brad Cunningham objected to Loni Ann giving testimony on his alleged 'prior bad acts'; such remote information should have no legal import in the civil action against him in Cheryl Keeton's murder and should not be used to find some propensity for violence on Brad's part in recent years.

'Secondly,' Rieke said, 'my client asserts all marital privileges that exist with respect to statements made by him to this woman during the course of their marriage.' Rieke promised that each statement Loni Ann made would be judged on whether it had been privileged communication during her marriage to Brad.

In response to Shinn's questions, Loni Ann forced herself to go back over her life with Brad ever since she had first met him in 1967 at Evergreen High School. Her marriage to him had lasted four years and two months.

'When you married Mr Cunningham, were you in love with him?' Shinn asked.

There was a long pause. It was clear that Loni Ann had to search far back in her mind to remember if she *had* once loved Brad. Finally she said, 'Yeah . . .'

'Did that change during the course of the marriage?'

'Yes.'

Loni Ann said that her divorce had been obtained after she filed on grounds of 'cruel and unusual treatment.' Asked to explain, she said, 'He was physically abusive, he was violent . . . he was emotionally abusive . . . he was sexually abusive.'

Loni Ann described her shock, her fear, her shame over the abuse that Brad had heaped upon her eight months after their wedding. As she related incident after incident, a haunted look washed over her face. 'He said I was really stupid – he couldn't understand how he could have married someone as stupid as I was. . . .' Her voice was laced with unshed tears and old terror when she told of the night Brad had left her on the edge of an embankment over a river – left her, she was sure, to step forward and drown.

'Did you ever seek professional counseling or help for the psychological or emotional effects Mr Cunningham's abusive conduct during your marriage had on you?' Shinn asked.

'Only just recently. . . . I was told that everything would probably be all right in time, to give it time, but it's been seventeen years and it's not okay.'

'What's not okay about it?' Shinn asked.

'It just still stays with me . . . I have problems because of it.'

Loni Ann said she had allowed Brent to live with his father in the spring of 1986 because he hated living in Brooklyn, where she was working.'

'When and why did he stop living with his father?'

'In July of 1987. His father threw him out – he didn't want him anymore.'

Loni Ann said that her daughter Kait did not want to talk to Mike Shinn 'or to be involved in any of this.' Both her children had suffered pain during the long separations from their father, and 'when they did see him, they were never happy when they came home.'

'Did you ever witness any abuse to Brent when he was a baby?'

'When we were married . . . his father would throw water at him for crying or throw water at him for not wanting to eat. He didn't beat him too much . . . he was only two. I didn't see any reason for disciplining a two-year-old . . .'

'*Did* he?'

'Yes.'

'How?'

'He would slap him. . . . After we were divorced, and Brad returned the children from visitations, I noticed that my son had bruises on him on his backside, almost from his waist to his knees, and he said his father had spanked him . . . for wetting the bed.'

Asked about weapons Brad owned, Loni Ann had seen a rifle and a small machine gun. 'He said he knew people who – for the right price – would do anything he wanted them to do. . . . 'You know I can do whatever I want . . .

I always win. I never lose.' . . . He told me I should know better than to mess with him.'

Reluctantly, Loni Ann answered Mike Shinn's questions about an incident that had occurred *after* her divorce. Brad had come very early in the morning to pick up the children when she was still asleep and he told her he would wake them up and get them dressed. 'I went to take a shower. He unlocked the bathroom door with a screwdriver and he came in and he just took me into the bedroom. He told me not to make any noise or it would wake up the kids, and he didn't care if the kids saw it . . . and afterward, he said he didn't know anyone could hold their breath that long.'

'Did you report this to the police?'

'No . . . I didn't think anybody would believe me.'

'And after you discovered that he had left you on the cliff, did you report it to the police?' Shinn asked.

'No.'

'Why?'

'It wouldn't have made any difference. They couldn't do anything about it, and if he found out, things would only be worse. . . . I just knew I had to get away from him . . . somehow.'

Mike Shinn finished his questions; his part of the deposition had taken an hour and a half, and Loni Ann looked devastated. When Rieke began to question her in more detail about the night that Brad left her beside the river, she suddenly began to sob and ran from the room.

Diane Bakker went with Loni Ann to the ladies' room and held her. 'Her whole body shook with racking sobs,' Bakker said later. 'She started talking to me. I guess I didn't ever know that someone could be so afraid of somebody. She told me how Brad terrified her – even to this day – and to remember that incident, and how close she came to dying, was something that she could hardly deal with. Not only that, it brought back all the memories of her marriage to him. She proceeded to tell me many things that didn't come out in the deposition that were unbelievable.'

Loni Ann told Diane what she could not bring herself to describe in detail in the deposition. Brad's idea of sex had been, as she testified, 'that I would do anything that he wanted, *when* he wanted it.' But it was more than that. She said having sex with Brad was like being raped.

Loni Ann was finally able to retake the witness chair and face Joe Rieke. Rieke reasserted his client's express desire to bar all privileged marital communication. Any attorney working for Brad Cunningham would have sought to strike the devastating deposition Loni Ann had just given, citing Brad's marital privilege. But this was not a task that any defense attorney, much less Joe Rieke, would relish. The woman was so frightened.

Rieke asked Loni Ann about the incident at the party, apparently in an effort to imply that she had been responsible for Brad's behavior. He also attempted to establish that she and Brad had had consensual sex after their divorce. If possible, Loni Ann shrank even further into the witness chair. It was obvious that the thought revulsed her and when he asked her why she had not fought back when Brad opened the bathroom door with a screwdriver and raped her, she looked at him with a hopeless expression. She had never been able to fight back. 'Brad always outweighed me by at least a hundred pounds – except when I was pregnant. . . .'

The deposition had begun at one that afternoon of the first day of spring in 1990. It was over at 3:38 P.M. Loni Ann had smiled only once in two hours and forty minutes – and that was when Mike Shinn stumbled over pronouncing 'kinesiology.' But it was all on videotape, and Shinn would be able to use it in the civil trial.

Sara didn't know that Shinn had taken Loni Ann's deposition. She didn't know Loni Ann. She had known none of Brad's former wives; Cheryl was the only one she had ever seen and they had not spoken. She had yet to realize how much they all had in common. Her own deposition was scheduled for August 20 – five months away.

On April 25, someone from Sara's past returned, someone who sparked mostly happy memories for her. She had not seen Jack Kincaid for a long time, not since they had stopped dating in the spring of 1986. And there was an irony in his coming back into her life at that particular moment. If he had not taken another woman to Easter brunch in March of 1986, Jack and Sara probably wouldn't have broken up. She would not have been inclined to accept a second date with Brad Cunningham. Kincaid had often regretted losing Sara, but when he heard she was involved with Cunningham – and then *married* to him – there was nothing he could do.

'It was funny,' Kincaid would recall. 'Clay Watson and I had been in the service together, and after he was a surgeon at Providence, it was Clay who introduced me to Sara in the first place – back in 1986. And he told me I'd blown my chance and I was a fool to let her go. He called me in April of 1990 and said, 'Well, it looks like you've got another chance – Sara's filed for divorce.'

'Clay told me a little bit of what Sara was going through. I didn't waste time. I sent flowers to Sara at the hospital, and then I called her. It was April twenty-fifth when we met for drinks at the Harborside near her Riverplace apartment. She told me she couldn't live in her apartment – she was afraid.'

Jack and Sara went for dinner at Nick's Coney Island, and they talked about the decisions they had made over the last four years. He could see that she was thinner than she had ever been and more worried. The circles beneath her eyes seemed permanently etched there. If ever Sara needed a strong, solid man to lean on, it was now. And Jack Kincaid was that kind of man.

As far as anyone knew, Brad and the boys were living in an apartment in Houston. He had been served with a court order to have Jess, Michael, and Phillip appear for a hearing in Portland on April 16, 1990. On April 13, his attorney reported that Brad's Houston case had been postponed yet again, and that he expected to move back to Portland in the next few weeks. His attorney told Bill Schulte that Brad had no money to move, no money to have a phone at home, and that he had to sell his luggage to have 'money for food.' That would explain the 'children's letter' to Sara Gordon, begging for a ticket home.

And then suddenly on May 27, Brad was back in Portland and in the Dunthorpe house. So far he had won every flurry. He wanted the house and he told Sara that he would stop at nothing to keep it. Along with the wives he had left behind, he had walked away from some wonderful houses – but none as grand as this one. He liked the huge gray house, the sweeping circular driveway, the guest house. He and his sons were living in one of the best neighborhoods in the most desirable suburb of Portland. He informed Sara that he was in no hurry to leave.

Sara had wanted the Dunthorpe house to be there for Jess, Michael, and Phillip. But that was before she found out she had co-signed too many times for Brad and was now responsible for bills all over the Portland area. As hard as she tried, she didn't see how she was going to be able to pay the bills and keep the house too.

Brad was unemployed. Since U.S. Bank bought out his contract in the fall of 1986, he considered his suit against the Houston contractors his real profession, a kind of 'legal career.' The Broadway Bakery – even the Bistro – had never been his true style. He had only been marking time, and now he was bored with the bakery. In any event, he had run it into the ground financially.

There were so many papers to be filed in Brad's marathon legal suit, so many details to keep abreast of. Vinson and Elkins – the second largest law firm in the state of Texas, with five hundred attorneys in its employ – still believed in his case. There was still the chance that Brad would be awarded several million dollars. If he won, they won. Several of the firm's top litigators, including the dynamic and colorful Wes Urqhart, had been working on it for years now. And Brad's input was so vital that Vinson and Elkins always made a private office available to him whenever he was in Houston.

For the moment, however, Brad was comfortably ensconced in the Dunthorpe house, living there with Jess, Michael, and Phillip, who were now ten, eight, and six. Sara missed the boys terribly. She was their legal mother, and she had been their mother in every sense but biological since Cheryl's murder – but Brad made it very difficult for her to see them. Nevertheless, he was prepared to sue her for child support. They were her Achilles heel, and Brad knew it. Sara had seen the boys only once – for two and a half hours – since she filed for divorce in March. But then, surprisingly, Brad allowed her to take them out for a visit on June 10. They had a good day together and Sara bought them clothes. Whatever might happen in the civil suit against Brad and their divorce proceedings, she hoped that this might be the start of regular visitation.

Part V

Dana

43

Brad had long since dismissed Rhonda, but he did need someone to take care of his sons while he was involved with his business endeavors. He advertised for a nanny who could live in. He placed ads in the *Oregonian* for months and interviewed scores of women. The applicant he finally chose would have to be just right, the perfect woman for his sons and, quite possibly, for him too. He was, after all, alone now.

Brad's ads for a nanny were enticing. The successful applicant would earn a thousand dollars a month and would be provided with all living expenses. She could choose whether she wanted to live in 'the mansion' or in her own guest house on the property. There would be travel, some entertaining, and flexible hours. There were many applicants and Brad eliminated most of them because they were too old, too dowdy, too stodgy, had no social graces, or they did not live up to the picture he had in his mind. He wanted class, he wanted physical beauty, and he wanted a malleable female who would fit into the lifestyle he envisioned for himself.

Brad had told applicants that he would need someone who could start in May of 1990. Some of them he put on hold; he told the patently unsuitable ones that the job had been unexpectedly filled. When he had winnowed the profusion of applicants down to a handful, he called his first choice back.

Dana Malloy* was twenty-three years old, although she

could have easily passed for eighteen. She was tall and slender, with a spectacular figure and luxuriant ash-blond hair that surrounded her face like a halo and fell to the middle of her back. She had smoky green-blue eyes and the small, even features that Brad always seemed to seek in each new woman whose path crossed his, each woman who became his wife – and his victim.

Until she was twenty-two, Dana Malloy's life had been as normal and wholesome and happy as any small-town girl's in America. 'I grew up in a little town in southern Oregon,' she remembered. 'There were four of us kids, and we were raised strict Catholic. I was Brownie and a Girl Scout. I was a cheerleader from the fifth grade until I graduated from high school. My folks sent me away for my last two years of school so I could graduate from a Catholic school.'

Dana and her sister Allie* were in 4-H, and Dana grew up crazy about horses. She could ride bareback; she could ride facing forward, backward, or crosswise. She was such a complete country girl that it was hard to picture her any other way. 'My mom saw that we had tap dancing lessons, and ballet, and baton twirling. She didn't push us; she just wanted us to have the best chance to succeed. I was in every beauty pageant I heard about. But it was *fun*. It was just the "girly thing" to do. If I didn't win, nobody cared. It wasn't as though my folks were pushing me. It was just fun.'

Dana kept a scrapbook with a blue gingham cover, and in the pictures of one of the early pageants she was in, pretty, slender teenage girls were wearing modest formals in pastel colors as they walked along a runway covered with red velvet and edged in white fake fur. The audience beaming in the background was full of parents, sisters, brothers, and townspeople. Dana's lovely eyes were slightly tilted and her smile was wide and confident even though, inside, she was scared and her knees trembled. She usually placed in the top two or three contestants.

The Malloys were strict parents, but loving. Their values

were a little old-fashioned, shaped by their own parents and the church. When Dana went to the prom, she wore a modest high-necked dress with long sleeves, daisies in her hair, and a corsage of white carnations. Her cheerleader's costume was a long-sleeved red sweater, a swingy red and white miniskirt, red and white saddle shoes, and huge matching pom-poms.

Dana had been in love with Mark Rutledge,* a tall, dark-haired basketball star, for as long as she could remember. Everyone who knew them assumed they would get married within a few years of graduation. In the meantime, they dated and Dana sold cosmetics and cut hair.

After high school she still entered beauty pageants, but where she had been merely pretty, Dana had become startlingly beautiful. Her hair was a few shades blonder and her gowns were sewn with glittering sequins. She strutted along the runways with more confidence now, even during the bathing suit competition of the 'Miss Oregon, U.S.' pageant. The audience was more sophisticated, but she was still having fun. Dana had no particular aspirations beyond marriage and babies.

'I really loved Mark and my parents thought that "living in sin" was wrong. I was twenty when we got married. It was July 26, 1986 – how could I ever forget that date?' It was a beautiful wedding. Mark wore white tails, and Dana's dress had a flouncy lace train. She carried a white lace fan decorated with pink flowers as her father walked her down the aisle. Her mother and her bridesmaids wore gowns of pale dusty rose.

It should have been a happy ending, but it wasn't. 'Mark was a workaholic. I mean, he worked *eighty hours a week,*' Dana said. 'We bought a nice home with land in a little town twenty miles north of Portland. But I was alone there all the time. Mark worked on projects in Las Vegas or in California, and he couldn't even come home on weekends. He told me there was no point; he'd just get home Saturday and have to fly back on Sunday. He came home about once a month.'

Dana knew that Mark worked all the time before she married him, but as so many woman before her have believed, she thought marriage would change him. 'He didn't change,' she said. 'I couldn't go out because I was married, and besides, I didn't want to. I wanted children. I wasn't a women's libber. I believed a woman should stay home. But I couldn't have babies with Mark – I would have had to raise them alone. I felt he was hurting me.'

The marriage was probably doomed from the beginning. It just kind of wore itself out by September 1988. Dana moved to Portland and got a job selling high-end cosmetics in a department store. Sometimes she cut hair to supplement her income. 'I sold Estée Lauder – I went to the brands and the stores where I could make money.' Dana was divorced from Mark in 1989. It was not an acrimonious divorce. Not at all. 'We're still great friends today,' she said. 'We just couldn't be married.'

Deep down, Dana knew she was pretty, but she wondered if she had anything else to offer. Her own husband hadn't cared enough about her to come home more than once a month, even during the honeymoon phase of their brief marriage. Her confidence was shaken, and she was particularly vulnerable to men who responded positively to her. She dated some; men came on to her everywhere she turned. There was one man, Nick Ronzini,* who sold men's clothes in the department store where she worked. Dana liked Nick a lot and he was very handsome, but when he drank, his personality changed.

Dana was at a crossroads in 1990. If nothing came along to change her life, she might stay with Nick. Or she might go home to southern Oregon and stay with her family. As it turned out, something – *someone* – did come along: Brad Cunningham. 'He called me and told me that he remembered me,' Dana said, 'even though there had been people "standing in line" for the nanny job.' She had almost forgotten that she had applied for the job.

When she went to the Dunthorpe house for her second

interview, Brad told her that he was separated from his wife, Dr Sara Gordon. 'We aren't getting along,' he said. 'I live here with my sons.'

Dana assumed that the huge home with its sprawling grounds and two-story guest house belonged to Brad. She found him 'very distinguished.'

Brad was forty-one in the spring of 1990, but he didn't look it. He was running ten miles a day and was in peak condition. He dressed in expensive dark suits and drove a new (rented) Mercedes. 'He was so charming,' Dana said, 'but he was humble, too, and quiet.'

When Brad told her that she had won the nanny job over all the other applicants, Dana was thrilled, but she looked upon it only as a job. She would care for his three little boys during the week and live in the guest house, but she planned to continue her job selling cosmetics on the weekends.

Sara had to sell the Dunthorpe house. The cash drain of the bakery and then the bistro was bad enough, but the payments on the big house, not to mention the taxes, were more than she could handle – even if she worked twenty-four hours a day. But Brad blocked her every attempt to sell the house. It was outrageous, and it was ridiculous, but Sara understood. She knew Brad's charisma, and she had learned how frightening and relentless he could be to get what he wanted. If she had not had Jack Kincaid to back her up, she might have buckled under the pressure.

Sara's money had paid for the Dunthorpe house *and* the Riverplace apartment, but she no longer lived in either. In truth, she really didn't live anywhere; she was a woman in hiding. The few items she had managed to take out of the Dunthorpe house were in the Riverplace apartment – but she wasn't. Instead she slept at Providence Hospital, feeling some slight sense of protection with her coworkers surrounding her. She never slept in the suite she had shared so many times with Brad and the little boys. Brad knew where that was, and there was always the chance he might encounter some new employee who didn't know about him and talk his way into the suite. Sara knew what a glib talker he was. So she slept behind doors that were behind doors that were behind doors, deep in the bowels of the hospital. If anyone called for her, *anyone*, the ground rules now demanded that the caller never be told where she was. All of her calls were transferred to trusted friends inside Providence. Only then would the call be passed on to her.

Once again Sara's work was her life, just as it had been when she first met Brad in 1986. However, by 1990 she no longer took her life for granted. The memories of being able to concentrate on her work, to walk without fear into the parking lot, to live without fear in her own home, were only that – memories. Somehow Brad always seemed to be aware of where she was.

Sara never knew what she might find. Sometimes she found black spray paint along the sides of both her cars – an Audi and a Volvo – sometimes splashes of paint across their hoods, the edges drying into segmented clots, the way blood dries. The cars were white and she saw the damage immediately. It didn't matter where she parked. Once, when she had spent the night at a girlfriend's house, she found that twelve nails had been pounded into her tires. For some reason the tires hadn't gone flat and she was able to drive to a tire dealer and have them repaired. But worst – because of what they symbolized – were the flower petals. Some unseen hand had sprinkled rose petals all over her car, as if casting flowers on a grave.

Even when she went to bed in one of the on-call suites deep in the inner sanctum of the hospital, Sara didn't sleep well. It was hard not to think of all she had lost. Most of all, she missed her sons. 'If I hadn't been afraid of Brad, I would have sought custody of the boys – but I didn't dare.'

Sara harbored the hope that she might have Jess, Michael, and Phillip for three weeks in June. Seeing the boys meant seeing Brad, but she wasn't afraid of him in the daylight. It was the unexpected that frightened her. Brad would never let her have the children for long periods, but he allowed short visits. Meanwhile, their divorce proceedings inched along. An uncontested divorce in Oregon took only three months, but Brad claimed federal law guidelines and said his pending bankruptcy gave him an automatic stay. And, as usual, he changed attorneys. It would be fall at least before Sara could hope to have her divorce finalized.

On June 10, Sara met Dana Malloy when she returned the boys to the Dunthorpe house after they had visited her. The two women liked each other, and Sara went away somewhat relieved at Brad's choice of a caregiver for the boys. She noticed one thing that shouldn't have surprised her. Dana looked a lot like herself, same coloring, same general facial features. Dana was taller, of course, and about ten years younger than she was, but their resemblance was remarkable. Sara was glad she liked Dana. But if she hadn't, it wouldn't have mattered to Brad. He no longer listened to anything she said.

Dana had settled happily into her job at the Dunthorpe house. If she couldn't have babies of her own, Brad's sons were great little kids and she soon became very attached to them. She looked after Jess, Michael, and Phillip, saw that they got to school, cooked, washed dishes, and made the beds. The work wasn't hard, and Dana enjoyed being with this little motherless family. She did not know, of course, that there had been two mothers whom Brad had ruthlessly cut out of their lives.

Before a month had passed, Dana was surprised but a little pleased, too, when it became obvious that Brad was attracted to her. 'When I went to work for him, I had my own life,' she said. 'I had my weekend job. He didn't even *know* me but, within a month, he didn't want me working weekends. He got obsessed with me – I guess that's how you'd describe it. He put me on a pedestal. He wouldn't let me make beds or wash the dishes. After I was with him thirty days, he hired "Molly

Maid" to come in. But cleaning was supposed to be *part* of my job.'

Dana believed that Brad was a wealthy businessman. She had no idea that the house they lived in belonged to Sara and that Brad had no income at all – beyond $1,608 a month he collected in Social Security survivors' benefits for Cheryl Keeton's boys, and the sporadic payments that he got from the Colville tribe.

Brad began to court Dana avidly and she was dazzled. 'He ordered these exotic flowers flown in from Hawaii – flowers I'd never seen before. I didn't even know you could buy flowers that way.' The five of them – Brad, Dana, Jess, Michael, and Phillip – went out to dinner often as a family. It was pleasant and fun, and Dana found herself falling in love with Brad. It wasn't much more than a month after she began working for him that they became intimate. 'He was a wonderful lover – a passionate lover. When he kissed you, you believed you were the only woman in the world for him.'

Dana had been ignored by her husband, but now she had become the center of Brad's universe, completely unaware of the bitter divorce and the terrible struggle he and Sara were having over the house. Dana never knew about things like that; Brad took care of his own business affairs. He dictated what they would do, where they would go, how she would dress, whom she would see. She was so happy to be with him that she didn't notice how short her leash was becoming.

Life with Brad was sheer joy, but it wasn't perfect. Dana's awe of him lasted for a relatively brief time, and some things really bothered her. She didn't like the way Brad disciplined his sons, even though he seemed to love them. She watched him administer the precise number of 'swats' that he had toted up during the boys' lapses when they were away from home. Once they knew that punishment was awaiting them, most of the fun of their outings vanished. And Dana was as horrified as Sara had been to see another form of control. For some minor misdeed, Brad would order the miscreant to stand inches from a wall, warning him that he must not allow his nose to touch the wall itself. 'Sometimes, they'd have to stand that way for an hour,' Dana said, 'even Phillip.' Brad was their father, Dana knew, and she never interfered – but it bothered her to see a little boy like Phillip doing his time against the wall like a Marine recruit.

Sometime in the summer of 1990, Brad announced that they were all moving to Seattle. Dana assumed that he must have sold the Dunthorpe house, and agreed to go with him. The move caught Sara completely by surprise and added to her torment. 'The last time I saw the boys was July 8, 1990,' she remembered. 'After that, it would be such a long, long time before I saw them. I didn't have any idea where they were. . . .'

On that Sunday, July 8, Sara brought the boys back to Dunthorpe and saw a large U-Haul truck parked down the street. A little alarm sounded in her brain. Later, she learned that Brad had pulled it into the driveway and packed it full. Before he, Dana, and the boys pulled out, he told the security force at Dunthorpe that he was 'putting a few things in storage' and taking his sons to Canada for a vacation. He said there would be no way to contact him, and he didn't know when he would return.

When Sara called the Dunthorpe house two days later, she found the phone had been disconnected. She went to the house with two realtors and discovered that once again all the locks had been changed to high-security locks which were almost impossible to disable. In order to get in, she had to break a window in the laundry room. The house was a mess. But she didn't know if Brad was gone for good; he had left a house-sitter in the place.

Sure enough, he returned on July 14 and hooked up the phone. When Sara called him to once again discuss listing the house, he was curt.

'Am I going to see the boys for dinner?' she asked.

'Not unless you want to go to Bellingham.' Bellingham was three hundred miles north of Portland.

'Brad, you're disobeying court orders by taking them away,' Sara countered.

He hung up on her.

Neighbors called Sara to tell her that Brad had had movers at the house and had hauled away a tremendous load of stuff. He had told his 'renter' in the guest house that he was moving to Seattle for 'six to ten months to sell a drug product.' Sara asked the security patrol to check the house. They reported that the key she had given them still fit in the lock in the back door, but Brad had apparently done something to the door so that it wouldn't open. All the windows on the ground floor had also been nailed shut.

When Sara finally gained entry to the house, she was stunned. The place had been gutted. 'Besides removing all of his furniture and personal belongings,' she wrote shakily in her journal, 'Brad removed the washer, dryer, and refrigerator, . . . a $3,000 armoire, $1800 china cabinet and $600 coffee table that I purchased prior to our marriage. Most surprising, he cut wires and totally removed two Genie garage door opening systems, . . . all the closet components (shelves et al) installed by Closets to Go . . .'

Brad had pried out the fireplace insert, taken down light fixtures, and generally dismantled and removed everything that could possibly be carried away. Lightbulbs, fireplace screens, towel racks, Sara could not imagine what use he had for them; no, Brad was simply leaving his signature.

On July 18, Sara went to get the Ford truck she had bought Brad from the World Trade Center parking lot where he said he had left it. She felt fortunate that he had obeyed a court order to return the dark blue one-ton pickup truck that she was paying for. It was there, still with Brad's vanity plate that said BBIIGG. 'The pickup would not start and was towed to Coliseum Ford,' Sara noted in her diary. 'They found that both gas tanks contained at least 50% water.' It would cost at least five hundred dollars to get the truck running again.

None of it mattered to Sara as much as the fact that her three little boys had once again vanished. And she had no idea how long it would be until she saw them again.

44

As they moved through 1990, Mike Shinn, Diane Bakker, and Shinn's private detectives quite possibly learned more about Brad Cunningham than anyone ever had. Perhaps confident that the police had long since lost interest in him as a suspect in Cheryl's murder, Brad for a time had not been as careful of his movements as he had once been. But now that the civil action had been filed against him, Shinn was always right behind him and Brad was once again moving frequently. Shinn had yet to wrest so much as one deposition from him. Forrest Rieke's law firm no longer represented Brad – not since Sara's attorney, Bill Schulte, informed them that she would not be paying his legal bills. And he and the boys had abruptly moved to Washington State.

In May of 1990 Shinn believed he had finally succeeded in getting Brad to give a deposition. It meant that Shinn had to travel to Seattle to obtain it, but it was worth the two-hundred-mile trip. He arrived at the appointed place and time, and at the last minute Brad did appear, carrying some kind of legal document. 'There!' he exclaimed and threw the document on the table. 'There will be no deposition. I have an automatic stay of all legal action.'

The document was a Chapter 7 bankruptcy filing. By switching from his Chapter 11 bankruptcy action to the

Chapter 7, Brad had indeed removed himself from the requirement of giving a deposition in the civil action against him concerning Cheryl's murder. Without Sara's support, Brad argued – correctly – he had no funds. And he would not have funds until his pending Houston suit came to fruition. As a virtual indigent, without legal counsel and protected by Chapter 7, he was temporarily untouchable. To the best of Shinn's knowledge, he had seen Brad only twice – once when he came over to his restaurant table in Portland and once when he slapped his Chapter 7 papers down on the conference table in Seattle.

Shinn began to wonder if it was humanly possible to get Cunningham into a courtroom. The guy wasn't an attorney, but he had been involved in so much litigation over the years that he was savvy about how to delay and distract. Shinn became a regular in bankruptcy court in Seattle, appearing several times over the next six months to file motions to lift the stay. Finally, in December of 1990, Judge Samuel J. Steiner did accede to Shinn's motions. Brad named a date when his Houston trial would take place, and then ignored one deposition request after another. For Shinn, it was like jousting with a shadow.

That fall, Mike Shinn had learned to his disgust that the date Brad had given for his civil suit against the Parkwood Place contractor and the bonding company in Texas was false. There was no trial date set in Houston. But Shinn moved steadily ahead on the civil case in Oregon. Depositions or not, Brad was going to have to answer questions he had avoided for four years.

Shinn wanted to re-create, if he could, the events of September 21, 1986. He had to prove that it was possible for Brad to have left his sons – or at least Jess and Phillip – in his apartment in the Madison Tower and driven to the Mobil station on the West Slope to confront Cheryl Keeton. He had to allow time for the killer to strike the victim more than twenty times, send her van onto the freeway, run back to the Mobil station, and then drive home and answer Sara Gordon's phone call at 8:50 P.M. If that wasn't possible, Shinn wouldn't have a case. Lilya had seen Brad at 7:30. The window of opportunity was, almost certainly, little more than an hour and fifteen minutes.

It was now the third week of September 1990. No moment in time is ever *exactly* like any other, no sunset or sunrise, no ebb and flow of tide. But Shinn chose the night of September 21, 1990, to run his test. Conditions were as close as he could get to the night Cheryl was murdered. The weather was almost the same, warm and pleasant. Only it was four years later, and September 21 was a Friday, not a Sunday. Traffic would be a little heavier.

At 7 P.M. the test car pulled up to the exit of the parking garage at the Madison Tower. The man who was playing the 'killer' was driving; Shinn was in the backseat. It was still full daylight and there were two reasons why Shinn figured that Brad would not have left the Madison Tower until an hour later. He would have waited for darkness to carry out a murder; and Betty Troseth had talked to Cheryl just before eight on the night she was murdered. The last thing Cheryl had said to her mother was, 'I'm going to meet Brad at the Mobil station.'

Diane Bakker was playing the 'victim' in the test. Shortly after 8 P.M., the time when Cheryl had ended her conversation with her mother, she left the West Slope house that Cheryl had rented. Driving a Toyota van, Diane clocked the distance to the Mobil station at seven-tenths of a mile. 'It took just a couple of minutes to get down there,' she remembered. She parked the van and waited.

8:07:00: It is dusk when Shinn and the 'killer' pull out of the Madison Tower parking area and head for the Sunset Highway. They will be careful to travel at legal speeds. A camcorder in their car automatically registers the passing of seconds and minutes.

8:09:44: The arrow to 26 West appears; the car moves left onto the approach toward the westbound tunnel.

8:13:28: The car emerges from the tunnel and onto the Sunset Highway. The speed is fifty-five miles an hour.

8:16:32: They reach the location of the Mobil station.

8:17:00: They pull in and park in the shadows there. The 'killer' slips on gloves. He walks slowly around from the back of the station to the 'victim's' van parked out front. He pounds on the 'victim's' window, forcing his way in. ('I was trying to think as Cheryl would have that night,' Bakker remembered. 'I sat in the van waiting, looking all around for "Brad." But even though I was waiting for someone to attack me, I didn't see him. He was just *there* suddenly. . . .')

8:18:20: He is inside the van. (This period could never be absolutely reconstructed. Had Brad pulled up close to Cheryl's van so that she could see that Michael was in the car? Or had he left Michael – with orders to 'take a nap' – in Sara's car behind the station. Or conceivably, could he have left all three boys in his apartment? Furthermore, no one could really know where the savage beating of Cheryl Keeton had taken place. More than likely, it was a continuous attack in the van, although she might well have tried desperately to leap from the passenger door, only to be yanked back by the belt of her jeans. Her injuries had been inflicted by a heavy object. Shinn was inclined to believe it was a 'police-type' flashlight, although he could never locate it.)

8:22:10: The 'victim's' van, with the 'killer' at the wheel and the 'victim' dead or unconscious in the passenger seat, is stopped on 79th Street a minute or two away from the Mobil station. The eastbound lanes of the Sunset Highway are just ahead.

8:22:48: The 'killer' sends the van toward the freeway. He then jogs back toward the Mobil station. He is wearing shorts and a T-shirt now, and carrying a bundle of clothes under his arm like a football.

8:30:50: The 'killer' arrives back at the Mobil station where his car is parked.

8:32:28: The 'killer' gets in his car, checks traffic carefully, pulls out of the Mobil station, and heads toward the Sunset Highway going east. He is slightly out of breath from his jog.

8:37:40: The 'killer' is back on the Sunset Highway, headed east toward the Madison Tower.

8:38:13: He is in the tunnel going east.

8:42:07: He pulls into the Madison Tower parking garage.

8:42:34: He exits his parked car.

The reenactment of Cheryl's murder was only a drama. It wasn't real – but it seemed real. 'I relived it,' Shinn recalled. 'I was sweating, *my* heart was pounding like crazy, even though we knew it was just a reenactment. It was almost as if it was really happening.'

Brad could have easily been back in the Madison Tower garage at 8:42 P.M. In two more minutes, he would have been able to ride the elevator to the eighteenth floor and enter his apartment in time to take a phone call. With ten minutes to spare.

'If Brad had not answered the phone when Sara called just before nine,' Shinn commented. 'He would not have locked himself into such a tight time frame. . . .'

But it was loose enough. The test run had proved that it was, indeed, possible to drive from the Madison Tower to the West Slope and back in thirty-five minutes – even allowing for almost five minutes in which to strike a helpless victim almost two dozen times. But if Brad was Cheryl's killer, he may not have had ten minutes to spare. Later, experts estimated that it would take almost fifteen minutes to bludgeon someone two dozen times.

In late 1990, Mike Shinn's office was in the Bishop's House, in a remodeled parish house that was once a part of a church complex. Because it had been built in a time when crime in

Portland was not a major concern, the Bishop's House had had to be beefed up with security devices. Iron grilles were placed over windows on the ground and second floors – not just in Shinn's offices but for all the offices located in the building.

Brad Cunningham was a man who resented anyone snooping into his business and his life. Judging by the huge stack of reports from Connie Capato and Leslie Haigh, there was ample evidence that Shinn had done both. And the civil trial was fast approaching. It seemed a wise thing that his office was secure.

Diane Bakker began to receive obscene phone calls at Shinn's office. The male voice was Asian, or at least disguised to sound Asian. 'I know who you are,' he breathed. 'And I'm going to come up there and rape you.' He added some ugly details about what he planned to do.

By the third call, Bakker was ready for him. She kept saying, 'I can't understand you – could you repeat that, only *slowly?*' and every time the obscene caller tried again, she pretended she couldn't understand the string of obscenities he uttered because of his accent. 'I don't think it was Brad,' she recalled. 'But maybe it was someone Brad hired. The guy finally got so exasperated with me because I couldn't "understand" him that he hung up. That was the end of the phone calls.'

But not the end of the pretrial incidents. Diane Bakker went to work early one morning and found Mike Shinn's office a mess. Someone had come in during the night, someone with a very explicit mission. It was easy enough to find the point of entry. Powerful arms had twisted the iron bars away from the bathroom window of the second-floor office complex. 'Someone broke the window to the bathroom and took powdered cream and sugar from next to the coffee machine in the hall and scattered it all over the hall and Mike's office,' Bakker said. 'They didn't touch the other two attorneys' offices.'

What was odd – and disturbing – was that nothing of

value was missing. There were computers, typewriters, all manner of office machines, and Shinn had any number of paintings and sculptures in his offices that were worth thousands of dollars. The intruder had taken nothing, nor had he damaged anything in Shinn's offices. He seemed, rather, to have broken in just to leave a message.

'The only thing that was disturbed,' Shinn said, 'was the Brad Cunningham case file. Whoever broke in had taken that from where I kept it and scattered it all over the hall. That was what was under all that spilled sugar and cream. Whoever came in during the night may have read the file, but he didn't take it away with him. He just left it in sheets scattered all over my office – like a calling card.'

Shinn figured he must be getting to somebody, forcing him to look over his shoulder and annoying the hell out of him. But he was not about to quit. He was hot on the trail.

Someone was hot on his trail, too. His car was broken into – not at his office but where it was parked near his houseboat. The message was clear: *I know where you work, and I know where you live . . .*

Mike Shinn wasn't the only target. Some of Dr Russell Sardo's records of his sessions with Brad and Cheryl during their custody battle disappeared. And Sara Gordon received a scribbled letter that might have been meant to be reassuring, but it was unsigned, and anonymous messages frightened her.

> Dr Gorden [*sic*],
>
> We heard about your testimony today. Our police friend tells us based on what you've said they can almost arrest him and by the end of your sworn statement we expect he'll be in jail by end of month. Hang in there – you have our support.
>
> Your friends in
> Washington

What friends in Washington? What testimony? Although

Sara was prepared to testify in the civil trial, only a few people knew about it.

Superstitious people, those who believe in omens and in the power of evil, might have felt a pall over the years-long quest for justice in Cheryl's murder. Oregon State Police Detective Jerry Finch, who had been the lead detective in the criminal investigation of Cheryl's death, had succumbed to lung cancer in 1988, almost exactly two years after Cheryl herself died. He had been in his early forties. Connie Capato, the private investigator who had been most active in Shinn's civil investigation of Cheryl's death, was barely thirty when she also developed cancer, a deadly fast-moving malignancy of the brain. She was dead within a few months and did not live to see the civil trial she had worked so hard on come to fruition. Nor did Bob Burnett, another P.I. who had worked on the case.

Mike Shinn and Diane Bakker were not afraid, but they had long since become cautious. Nothing about this case was going to be easy.

45

'We always had very nice houses. Brad insisted on a very glamorous lifestyle,' Dana would recall, speaking of their sudden move in the summer of 1990. 'The Seattle house was brand new, and I'm not even sure where it was – except I remember it was close to the Sand Point Naval Air Station. It was a beautiful house, over three thousand square feet.'

Dana had gone willingly with Brad and his sons to Seattle in July, but within weeks she had some reservations. Being chained to a pedestal was beginning to cloy. She yearned for some small bit of freedom. She had no job, she didn't know anyone in Seattle, and her life had suddenly become only Brad. He was there everywhere she turned – not hovering, but *enclosing* her. He was not nearly as humble or distinguished as he had seemed to be at first. And he had a one-track mind. 'Brad talked about sex all the time,' Dana said. 'Sex was his thing. I asked him not to talk the way he did, but he didn't stop.'

Brad tried to persuade Dana to go to topless dancing bars around Seattle and she was appalled. Watching other women dance nude – or next to nude – was not something she wanted to do. Even though Brad was insistent that it would be fun, she refused.

There were other things about Brad that puzzled her. She often found rubber gloves in his pockets and she could not for the life of her figure out why he needed them. When she asked him what they were for, he was evasive. Since his estranged wife was a doctor, she supposed it was possible that Brad had access to such things. But it was something that she tried to shut away in her mind. 'Brad was crude, too,' Dana recalled. 'I don't like to repeat the words he used or the way he referred to . . . *things*. He'd use initials, but he'd tell me what they meant and it was the same as if he said it all out loud.'

After Dana had been with Brad and the boys for four months, she began to feel so smothered that she could barely breathe. She was twenty-three and Brad was forty-one. Traits that had once seemed sweet and romantic now seemed like little fences going up around her. Brad clearly considered her far more than a nanny, far more even than a mistress. He talked of a future where they would always be together, and Dana wasn't ready for such a commitment. She didn't know if she ever would be.

Brad had plans to move to Houston and he assumed that she would go along. Instead, Dana left him, went back to Portland, and moved in with Nick Ronzini. It was perhaps the first time any woman had left Brad without discussion or wavering. Dana was just gone. And she was naive enough to believe she was free and clear.

'Brad moved to Houston. A couple of weeks later, he called and said he was in Portland,' Dana said. 'He asked me to have dinner with him – just so we could end our being together on a friendly note. I didn't see why I shouldn't do that – so I said yes.'

That evening with Brad was one of the weirdest Dana ever experienced. It started out well enough. She was all dressed up as Brad had suggested, and when she met him, he seemed to be his old wonderfully charming self, not even upset that she had left him. He took her to a very expensive restaurant. 'It was one of those restaurants where they served course after course after course,' Dana said. 'You know – salad and soup and appetizers and then sherbet, and then something else. It was very expensive and very impressive. They had special wine that went with each course. I don't drink very much, but Brad kept urging me to. . . .'

At some point during that autumn evening in Portland, Dana lost track of time and place. Everything took on a dreamy quality. And she would still sound puzzled when she remembered what happened next. 'When I woke up the next morning, we were in Houston. I had no idea how I got there. I didn't remember getting on a plane or leaving the restaurant. Brad just kept telling me, "I'm so in love with you. I can't live without you." And so I stayed with him in Houston.'

Dana had, at the very least, ambivalent feelings about Brad. She hadn't even said goodbye to Nick. One minute she was having a wonderful meal in Portland, and the next thing she knew she was breathing in the humid, muggy air of Houston. Even if Brad loved her, he had tricked her.

Nick Ronzini soon figured out where Dana was and followed her to Houston. When he tracked her to the apartment where she was living, he encountered Brad and the two men had a fist fight. Neither won, really, but it was Nick who left. 'I would have gone back to Oregon with Nick,' Dana said. 'But Nick had problems and I knew that wasn't the way out. Besides, I was so insecure that I felt I was trapped with Brad.'

Dana had begun her 'tour of duty' with Brad. Sometimes things were good. When Brad was happy with a woman, no man could be more charming or more fun. 'I don't want to say that it was all terrible,' Dana said. 'Thinking back, we had a wonderful time in Houston. We did most things as a family. Brad took us to Galveston. We had parties. We had fun. We always lived in big "executive" homes. Brad always had new cars. When we were first in Houston, Brad had a new van. We needed a van because of the three boys. . . .'

Back in Portland, Sara hoped against hope that she was free of Brad. Her divorce was finally granted on October 21, 1990. Circuit Court Judge Kathleen Nachtigal looked over the documents showing how many of Brad's debts Sara had to pay and listened to recountings of his vandalism of their property. She awarded the house, the Broadway Bakery and Bistro, its stock, the cars, the Whitewater Jet boat, and all bonds, personal property, and pension assets to Sara. Brad received his formula for Symptovir and one lot in Tampico, Washington. In addition, Judge Nachtigal denied Brad's petition for child support and ordered that he pay Sara the sum of fifty thousand dollars immediately. If he did not, interest at 9 percent would accrue. He didn't pay.

Sara had paid $220,000 for the Dunthorpe house. And she estimated that she had poured more than $100,000 into it to remodel it to Brad's specifications. After they separated, she had made mortgage payments faithfully on a home occupied by her estranged husband and his nanny/ mistress. Real estate was booming in Lake Oswego in the late eighties and early nineties, but when Sara finally managed in May of 1991 to sell the honeymoon house that had become a horror to her, she barely broke even. It had been an investment only in terror. And she still had the financial burden of the bakery and the bistro.

Sara's relief at having Brad gone was offset by her pain at losing her sons. From the time she had adopted them in March of 1988, she had considered them as much hers as if she had carried them in her womb. Now, she had no idea where they were. Every day there was something that reminded her of Jess, Michael, and Phillip and her heart hurt, thinking of them, wondering if they were safe, if they were happy. She didn't even know if they were alive. Sara tried to believe that Brad loved the boys – it was a funny, skewed kind of love, but he had fought so hard to get them away from Cheryl that he *must* love them.

And she took some faint comfort in the thought that Dana Malloy seemed fond of the boys. But Dana was young and would be so easily intimidated by Brad. Sara knew that if push came to shove – as it so often did with Brad – he would tromp right over Dana. Maybe Dana wasn't even with them any longer; Brad went through women so quickly.

As it happened, Dana *was* still with Brad. He wanted her to marry him. Brad had rarely been an unmarried man since he wed Loni Ann in 1969. When his marriage to Sara officially ended in October, Brad just naturally assumed that Dana would be anxious to marry him.

She wasn't. 'Brad always called me his "wife,"' Dana said, 'but I just giggled when he kept proposing to me. I didn't want to marry him.'

Brad had carried out a carefully choreographed plan to bend Dana to his will. She didn't have the education that his other women had, she was younger than most of them, and she had never been an assertive person. Dana was adamant, however, on one point. Some instinct kept her from accepting Brad's marriage proposals.

It wasn't easy. As he had with all his women, Brad quickly isolated Dana's weak points. In his most loving tone, he would call her over to show her a diagram he had drawn.

With his arm around her waist, he would tap his pencil on a line near the bottom of the page. 'See, angel,' he would say. 'You're at this level here – and *I'm* way up here. You're a beautiful woman, but you're uneducated; you're gorgeous but you're not very smart. You *need* me – you'll never find someone as smart as I am.'

She believed him. But she still wouldn't marry him.

Brad talked to Dana about all his other wives. He hadn't married any of them for love, he said, and he wanted her only because he loved her. He went through the familiar litany: Loni Ann had been pregnant and they were both very young when they married. Cynthia had been much older than he was and, he told Dana, 'my second marriage was purely business.' He confided that he might have stayed with Lauren, 'but Cheryl wouldn't let me alone. She was completely obsessed with me, and I simply couldn't get away from her.' As for Sara, he said she 'wanted to marry me to save money on her taxes.'

Remembering Brad's explanations for his many failed marriages, Dana said, 'At the time, that made sense to me. That made total sense to me. Especially when Brad cried and told me over and over, "But I've never loved anyone the way I love *you*."'

They moved often in Houston. Each house was lovely, so Dana didn't really mind. Brad told her about the civil suit that was looming back in Oregon – something to do with his fourth wife's death. 'You know, angel,' he said, 'the police and the D.A. up there totally botched their investigation into Cheryl's murder. They're trying to get me for it because they have to have *someone*. The D.A. will lose his job if he doesn't get somebody.'

Dana would remember 1990 and 1991 as 'scary.' Part of her felt sorry for Brad when she heard him sob aloud about how much he loved her, how much he needed her. And yet part of her wanted to break free of him. 'He hovered over me,' she said. 'He was working for that law firm – Vinson and Elkins – that was handling his lawsuit. He brought me to his office every day so he could watch me, so he knew where I was.'

She wasn't bored exactly. 'No, not really,' she said. 'I'd sit in the corner and read magazines while he'd work a little bit in the morning, and then we'd go out to lunch. There were hearings or trials on his lawsuit and he took me to court with him. We went to the park or to the underground section or shopping. We had fun. It wasn't so bad. But he always watched me.'

It seemed to Dana that Brad was omniscient. He knew everything she did, everyone she talked to on the phone, and even what they had talked about. It was almost as if he could read her mind. 'I'd call my mom or she'd call me, and I'd tell her that I just didn't know what to do. That night, Brad would ask me if I was "confused" about anything, and when I said, "No," he'd grin and say, "Oh, *really* – that's not what I heard. I heard you didn't know what to do about your life."'

Finally Dana realized that Brad had hooked up a tape recorder to the phones in the house. He was checking on all her calls, listening to every conversation she had while he was away from home. 'He was becoming more obsessive – more possessive,' Dana said.

Brad had been insistent that he didn't want his 'angel' to take a job in Houston. He wanted her available to him, with him all day, and on his arm looking like a million dollars when he dined out with partners of Vinson and Elkins. Dana was very impressed when they went out to dinner with his high-powered attorneys. 'There I was – nobody, really – sitting there with those wealthy lawyers. I really enjoyed going out to dinner with them, and I was happy that Brad wanted me along.' It was Brad, of course, who had brainwashed Dana into believing that she was essentially 'nobody,' a woman blessed with great physical beauty but with limited intelligence.

Dana had grown used to dining in fine restaurants. She was seduced by Brad's grand lifestyle. She loved that part, but he still urged her to go to strip joints with him in Houston – just as he had tried to get her to go to girlie spots in Seattle – and she still refused. One night in 1991 Brad took her to a sumptuously decorated restaurant called the Men's Club. Dana had never been to a club that was so impressive; she believed it to be a place where Houston's high society went. 'I thought it was a "five-star" restaurant,' she remembered. 'Everyone was eating filet mignon and lobster. All the women wore sequined gowns.'

Dana was eating her meal when she had a shocking revelation. Suddenly, beautiful young women, scantily clad, emerged from behind curtains and strutted down a stage in the center of the room. The Men's Club was not an exclusive restaurant at all; Brad had finally succeeded in getting her into a topless dancing club. It was much nicer than any of the Seattle area clubs, but Dana saw well-dressed men slipping bills into the garter belts and G-strings the girls wore. She turned and looked at Brad accusingly.

He gave her a big smile. 'You're more beautiful than any of those girls up there,' he said.

It took a while before Dana realized that Brad must be working on another of his plans. He bought her sequined G-strings and spike heels and filmy little costumes. He had always liked to see her dressed that way. Now he suggested that she could be a star at the Men's Club. All she had to do was wear the things he bought her to wear in the privacy of their bedroom.

Dana was shocked. If Brad loved her so much, how could he ask her to get up on stage and dance for other men?

'You're a hundred-thousand-dollar-a-year girl, angel,' he murmured. 'You make everyone else look plain. You could do it, baby.'

'But, Brad—' she protested.

'You know what your problem is, angel? You're suffering from "Malloyism." Your parents raised you up in a repressed, small-town way. They have little, closed-down minds, they do everything the same way their parents and their grandparents did. They never opened up their eyes to possibilities. And you're just like them. You're not living in reality, angel.'

Besides, Brad patiently explained, he needed her to work, to take a job that would help them get by until his lawsuit was settled.

'But you always said you didn't want me to work,' she argued.

'Not just any job,' he said. 'You have it all, Dana. You have class. Your body is your fortune.'

She couldn't do what he asked – not at first. Although she admired the statuesque beauties who danced at Houston's most popular club for males, Dana couldn't picture herself out there wearing only a G-string. Parading in front of strangers nearly nude was not the way she had been raised. She knew Brad would scoff at her for her 'Malloyism' mentality, but she couldn't do what he wanted. 'If we need the money that bad, Brad,' she finally said, 'I'll be a cocktail waitress. Those girls get really good tips too.'

Brad grinned. 'Get dressed, angel. We're going out.'

Dana began as a cocktail waitress at the Men's Club, but it wasn't long before Brad convinced her she was wasting her most valuable assets. When he opened the packages he brought home and produced beautiful – if tiny – costumes, when he told her that the Men's Club wasn't some sleazy honky-tonk place but rather a showcase for the greatest beauties in Houston, Dana began to believe him. Finally she agreed to dance, and just as he predicted, she was a real moneymaker. 'It was different in Houston,' Dana would remember. 'When you were one of the popular dancers at the club, you were almost a celebrity. People would come up to me in the mall and ask for my autograph. It didn't seem cheap.'

Dana was 'Angel' now – and she was much in demand. With her natural beauty, her professional knowledge as a makeup expert, and her exquisite long-legged, full-breasted figure, she was as lovely as any movie star and more graceful. All of her years of tap, ballet, and beauty pageants made her a natural on the polished stage of the Men's Club.

Brad had promised his 'Angel' she would have his full support, his protection. And every night, after the boys were tucked in, they went to the Men's Club. Dana didn't like leaving the boys alone, but Jess was ten and extremely capable, and Brad assured her he could handle any emergency that might come up. He had the number of the club and Brad's beeper number. But it was ironic, Dana thought. She had been hired as a nanny – someone to look after Jess, Michael, and Phillip. Now they were home alone almost all night while she danced at the Men's Club and Brad watched, gloating that the woman up there desired by every man in the room was *his* woman.

'Each private dance was for four minutes, and we got twenty dollars for that,' Dana said. 'If a man wanted you to come to his table, he would slip a five-dollar bill into your G-string . . .' She usually danced for eight hours every night and was making three hundred dollars an hour or more, but Brad didn't allow her to keep any of the money for herself. 'He was waiting to take my money right after work. He told me I was selfish when I wanted to keep some.' She never had time to count the money she made dancing for rich men. She might have been surprised if she had. She wasn't a lawyer like Cheryl or a doctor like Sara, but Dana was bringing in almost twenty-five thousand dollars a month.

And as the dawn turned rosy over Houston, Brad and Dana drove home to one or another of the fine homes he had rented for them and his sons.

Brad told Dana very little about the civil suit against him in Portland, nothing more than that the charges were trumped up, and that he was the fall guy because no one really knew who had murdered Cheryl. According to what he said about Cheryl's promiscuity, it sounded as if anyone could have killed her. He warned Dana not to give out information about him to anyone. If he was on one of his trips, she wasn't to tell where he was. If he was in Houston, that went double.

46

With the the civil trial set to begin in the first week of May 1991, and no indication at all from Brad Cunningham that he would be present for that trial, Mike Shinn tried every channel possible to notify him. The last thing Shinn wanted was for Cunningham to be able to say he had not even known there *was* a trial.

First of all, Shinn sent subpoenas to every attorney that Brad had ever employed – at least those Shinn knew about – and that list alone was formidable. 'I must have contacted more than a dozen of Brad's former attorneys,' he said. It appeared that he had spent most of his adult life involved in litigation. 'They all said they were no longer in touch with him, they had no idea where he was, and they had no way of contacting him.' Or if they did, they weren't saying.

Since Shinn knew that Brad spent a great deal of his time in Houston, he decided to look there. In early April he hired a private investigator in the Houston area, Charles Pollard of Greenwood, Texas. Shinn gave Pollard Brad's date of birth (October 14, 1948) and his Social Security number (537–48–7732) and told him that Brad supposedly was living with his three small boys who were attending St Ann's Catholic School in Houston. He should have been fairly easy to find. But Brad had become a master at hiding in plain sight.

Pollard first tried the usual routes to trace an individual. He did computer checks of voter registration, assumed names, marriage license records, criminal records, and deed records in Harris County. He came up with a driver's license for Bradly Morris Cunningham, but Brad had moved from the address listed. Pollard searched through all Texas vehicle registrations and found nothing. He finally got a hit. Houston Lighting and Power had Bradly Cunningham in their records as a customer at 4824 Bel Air Boulevard. And Pollard discovered why Brad was so hard to trace. He had routinely changed one digit in his Social Security or driver's license numbers, a subtle adjustment in the age of computers that was enough to prevent someone from being found.

On April 18 Pollard went to the Bel Air Boulevard address. The neighborhood was definitely upmarket, and the home where Cunningham was supposed to be living was opulent. Pollard spoke with the woman who lived next door and she said that a dark-haired man was living there with three boys.

Pollard reported this to Shinn, who sent him documents to be served on Brad about the upcoming civil trial. On April 24 Pollard returned to the Bel Air Boulevard house at 4:30 in the afternoon. He noted a blue Volkswagen van parked in the garage with the Washington license plate 567-CZD. It was the vehicle that Sara learned Brad had bought in Washington after he dumped the pickup truck with the BBIIGG license.

Pollard assumed that he would find his quarry inside the house. But it wasn't going to be as easy as it seemed at first. He rang the bell and after a time the door was answered by a dark-haired boy with freckles who looked to be about eight or nine.

'Is this where Bradly Cunningham lives?' Pollard asked.

The dark-haired boy nodded. 'But he's asleep.'

Before Pollard could say anything, the boy disappeared and an extremely pretty young woman with long blond hair came to the door. When he asked her name, she shook her head, refusing to identify herself. Pollard wondered if she might be Dana Malloy, the woman Shinn believed to be living with Brad. But he wasn't going to find out from her. She seemed nervous.

'I'm the baby-sitter,' she told him with little inflection in her voice. She said Mr Cunningham was in Portland, Oregon. 'The only way I have to reach him is through some relatives of his. A Dr Dreesen and his wife in Lynnwood.'

Grudgingly, the 'baby-sitter' gave Pollard a telephone number to the Dreesen home.

Pollard doubted that Cunningham really was in Portland; he suspected he was hiding in one of the bedrooms of the huge house. It was obvious that Cunningham didn't want to talk to him or to accept any papers from a lawyer in Oregon.

Pollard was stubborn, however. He figured the next best place to confront Cunningham was at St Ann's School. He arrived there the next morning at 7:30 and parked where he could watch parents dropping children off. The blue Volkswagen van didn't appear, nor did the Cunningham children. Pollard then returned to the Bel Air address. This time he saw a white Chevrolet Beretta parked in the driveway. It bore Texas plates that identified it as a rental car. He knocked on the door again, and again the same young boy answered. 'My father's out of town,' he said immediately.

'Where's Dana?'

'She's asleep. She worked late last night.'

Pollard asked the boy to waken Dana, and when she came to the door, he handed her the summons informing Bradly Cunningham of his impending trial. There was also a letter from Judge Ancer Haggerty, dated in February, advising the defendant of his May 6 trial date and requesting that he appear to give his deposition on May 4.

Later that day Pollard searched deed records for the legal owners of the house on Bel Air Boulevard. As he suspected, Cunningham was renting it. The couple who owned the house said that it was indeed rented by a man named Bradly Cunningham, although it was also currently for sale. With no job and no money, and even in hiding, Brad was living well. The landlords said he was paying rent of $1,900 a month and was prompt with his payments, but they understood he was moving soon to somewhere in the Northwest – either Washington or Oregon, or perhaps even Alaska.

On May 1, 1991, Pollard delivered copies of the legal documents to the secretary at St Ann's School. 'I probably won't see Mr Cunningham,' she said. 'He took his children out of school about a month ago. Someone in their family is very ill, and he said he was taking the boys to Portland, Oregon.' Pollard didn't tell her that the Cunningham boys weren't in Portland at all – that they were spending their days behind the closed drapes of the house on Bel Air Boulevard, only blocks from the school.

There was little question in Mike Shinn's mind that Brad knew about the May 6 trial date. Beyond all Shinn's notifications, he had proof from Brad himself that he knew about the civil trial. Brad had written a letter to the editor of the *Oregonian* complaining of the odious plot against him. And in that letter, he referred to the upcoming trial.

He knew. In the end, however, Brad could not be bothered with such a penny-ante legal event as this civil trial. But it would proceed even if the defendant's chair was empty. Defendants in a legal action have the right to face their accusers and to defend themselves in a court of law; it is not illegal for civil defendants to absent themselves from their own trials. It is, however, highly unusual.

Mike Shinn had gathered scores of witnesses for the trial to be held in Judge Ancer Haggerty's courtroom. Many of them had new information – or information that they had been hesitant to reveal before. Many of them were very frightened. Sharon McCulloch, who had been Jess Cunningham's first caregiver and who had become Cheryl's close friend, wanted to testify but vacillated. 'I was afraid to testify in the civil trial,' she remembered. 'I knew Brad. I knew the things he could do and how he just broke a strong woman like Cheryl. One day I would decide I would do it – and the next day, I'd lose my nerve.'

Chick Preston had come on board to work the Cunningham case with Shinn after Connie Capato's death. He was a remarkably good private investigator, and just before the May trial he went to Shinn bearing good news. 'Doc Turco always told me to "follow Brad's women," and Chick had talked to yet another one,' Shinn said. 'I remember Chick telling me a week before the trial, "I've found somebody! I have found you a dynamite witness! Wait until you hear what she has to say."'

Preston had talked to Karen Aaborg and asked her if she would come in to see Mike Shinn. She had had a brief affair with Brad in the months before Cheryl's murder and had seen him again in the days that followed. 'Karen came in with her fiancée,' Shinn said, 'and she told me, "I'm not sure why I'm here. I have nothing that will help you." And I just said, "Let's wait and see." She actually didn't *know* how much she knew. I knew that Karen Aaborg was going to prove to be one of the missing links we'd been searching for so long.'

Given Brad's history of violence and intimidation, Dr Ron Turco had warned Shinn to cover his back. He wasn't just imagining things; there was every chance that Shinn was in danger. Nobody knew for sure where Brad was. Dana had said he was in Portland and perhaps he was. And he might be quietly watching Shinn, waiting for a chance to take on the attorney who was causing such trouble in his life.

Shinn decided to listen to the advice of the experts in psychopathology he had consulted, Ron Turco among them. They suggested this was no time to be a sitting duck – or, in his case, a *floating* duck in his houseboat on the Multnomah Channel. He abandoned the houseboat and at least became a moving target. 'I ended up living in hotels for that entire trial,' Shinn recalled. 'I'd stay in one for a while and then move on. I didn't want Cunningham to ever get a fix on where I was.'

Brad might not be planning to go to his own trial, but he had been seen in Portland recently and nobody knew exactly why.

Part VI

A Civil Matter

47

Multnomah County Circuit Court Judge Ancer Haggerty was something of a legend. Like almost every other male connected to the Cunningham case, Haggerty was an athlete. He had grown up in North Portland and played guard for the University of Oregon, where he had been All Pac-10. He had served as a Marine captain in Vietnam. In fact, Haggerty and Multnomah County District Attorney Mike Shrunk had gone through officers' training together. Haggerty, wounded in battle, was highly decorated for valor.

Haggerty was a massive presence in a courtroom, standing over six feet two inches tall, weighing in somewhere around 260. He had a wry sense of humor and a quick wit, but he had never looked favorably on defendants who simply ignored the justice system – as Brad Cunningham apparently intended to do. The trial was going ahead whether he was present at the defense table or not.

By May 6, 1991, a jury had been selected. Charlene Fort, a science teacher, was elected foreman of the twelve-member panel, which was equally divided between males and females. Before testimony began, the jurors were taken for a 'jury view' of the intersection of 79th and the Sunset Highway so they could visualize the physical dimensions of all they would hear in the weeks ahead. They knew, of course, that something of great importance to this case had happened there. They did not yet know what.

Mike Shinn did, and he had a prickly feeling at the back of

his neck and along his spine as he stood looking at the spot where Cheryl's body had been discovered. 'I hate to admit it,' he said, 'but I couldn't help but wonder if someone was back in those trees taking a bead on me. . . .'

The trial began the next day. Judge Haggerty's courtroom looked like all courtrooms. He sat behind the bench in black robes beneath the state seal of Oregon, the American flag on his right, the flag of Oregon on his left. Shinn was at the table of the complaining party – John Burke, representing the estate of Cheryl Keeton – who was not present. Diane Bakker sat beside Shinn, her long blond hair caught back and falling to her waist.

Cheryl's relatives and friends sat in the back of the courtroom. But somehow the usual air of excitement was missing. There was no one at the defense table. No defendant. No defense attorneys. As Shinn would comment later, 'It was like playing tennis by yourself; there was no one to return my serves.'

Before the jury filed in to hear testimony, Shinn detailed for Judge Haggerty the arduous steps he had taken to locate Bradly Cunningham, listing the names of all Brad's previous attorneys whom he had notified of the trial date. He also said he had taken a deposition from Trudy Dreesen, Brad's aunt in Lynnwood, Washington. Mrs Dreesen acknowledged to Shinn that she talked to Brad at least once a week. 'She begged me not to depose her,' Shinn told the judge, 'but I had to.' Trudy Dreesen, who was now terribly ill, admitted that she had talked to Brad the morning of her deposition and informed him that his trial was due to start in Portland within two weeks.

Shinn told of hiring Charles Pollard, 'who is one of the best investigators in Texas and claims he can find anyone in twenty-four hours.' Pollard *had* found Dana Malloy, and Jess, Michael, and Phillip Cunningham; he had not found Brad Cunningham. He had hand-delivered Judge Haggerty's order to trial to Dana Malloy one week before the trial. Whether Pollard ever saw Cunningham wasn't really the point. Brad had clearly gotten the message. Within two days, Brad, Dana, and the three little boys had vacated their lavish fortress of a home in Houston. 'No one knows where Brad Cunningham is now,' Shinn said flatly.

The jury then filed in to hear the story of Cheryl Keeton's tragically short life and to listen to the witnesses Shinn had gathered to help him tell it. He held up a large picture of Cheryl. She was wearing a tan trench coat and she was smiling through raindrops at the cameraman. Ironically, the photographer had been the man Shinn alleged had killed her: Brad Cunningham.

'In 1986 Cheryl Keeton was thirty-four – or so,' Shinn began softly. 'As you can see, she was a beautiful woman. She had a brilliant future ahead of her, [she was] a woman who played many difficult roles at the same time. First of all, she was the mother of these three little boys. . . .' He held up another picture. It was a heartbreaker – Cheryl with Jess, Michael, and Phillip. 'In 1986 the oldest, Jess, was six; Michael was four, and the youngest, Phillip, was two years old.'

The jury next looked at a photograph of a laughing woman clinging to a darkly handsome, smiling man as they stepped through a doorway toward their future together. 'She was the wife of this man – Bradly Morris Cunningham,' Shinn said. 'This was taken on their wedding day. She thought at the time she was his second wife. She later found out she was his fourth.'

It hadn't been difficult to pick a jury who knew nothing of the case – there had been little coverage of Cheryl's death, and she had been dead for almost five years. 'Who were these people?' Shinn asked. 'Mr Cunningham . . . was one of the most intriguing personalities you are ever likely to encounter. . . . He had a charm about him, a charisma. . . .'

Could Shinn do it? Could he paint a true picture of a man the jury was likely never to see? Could he bring Cheryl back to life and make her real enough for the jury to understand how devastating her murder had been to so many people? Could he explain why there was 'something fundamentally disastrous' about their relationship? Would the preponderance of the evidence he presented to the jury prove that Brad had murdered his wife?

Shinn began almost at the end of Cheryl's life, setting up an enlargement of Cheryl's last will and testament on the easel in front of the jury. He described the tearing hurry Cheryl had been in to have a new will drawn up – a will barring her husband from inheriting her estate or even having any control over it. 'She told her friend Kerry Radcliffe, "I think he's going to kill me,"' Shinn said.

He held up another picture of Cheryl, the last picture taken of her, a shockingly graphic photograph that showed how she looked on the night of September 21, 1986. 'She was beaten over twenty times,' Shinn said. No one would have recognized this battered corpse as the smiling woman in the first picture.

The first witness was Randy Blighton, the young truck salesman who had seen Cheryl's van bumping against the median barrier and had bravely dashed across the Sunset Highway to get it out of harm's way – and to save approaching motorists from disaster. He told of his shock when he saw the dead woman lying across the front seat.

Karen Aaborg was next. Brad had had so many women throughout his life that it wasn't surprising his brief affair with Karen Aaborg had managed to escape the notice of the original investigating team in 1986. Karen had been in her early twenties when she worked for Brad at Citizens' Savings and Loan, a young attorney fresh out of law school. Lilya Saarnen's affair with Brad had virtually overlapped his affair with Karen. Add to that the fact that he was simultaneously sleeping with his sons' baby-sitter, and it was easy to see why just keeping up with his sexual conquests was a challenge for police investigators. Karen Aaborg had simply slipped through the cracks.

Karen had had some misgivings about Brad's activities in late September 1986, the time of his wife's murder, but she hadn't wanted to hold up her hand and say, 'I was involved with Brad too!' In fact, she had been relieved when no one questioned her about him. She hadn't really known anything that would help the police anyway. But then Mike Shinn's private investigator Chick Preston had discovered her relationship with Brad and seemed fascinated with her recollections. He urged her to talk to Shinn – whose eyes lit up when she told him about events of the week after Cheryl died.

Karen walked to the witness chair, a slender, almost girlish-looking woman, her golden hair swept back from her face and caught in a black ribbon. If she wore makeup at all, it was so lightly applied that it was invisible. Shinn had noted that Karen was what seemed to be Brad's type – the same small features, the same symmetry and delicacy. And she was nervous. All of the women in Brad's life were nervous when they spoke of him, and most of all when they did so for the public record.

Karen told the jury that she had been interviewed for the first time only about ten days before this civil trial – when Chick Preston approached her. She had worked for Brad for a little less than a year at Citizens' Savings and Loan in Lake Oswego, beginning in June or July 1985. An attorney, she was a loan closer, while Lilya Saarnen was a loan officer.

She said she started going out with Brad in May or June 1986.

'How long did you date him?' Shinn asked.

'Two or three months.'

'Were you in love with him?'

'No.' There was no emotion in Karen Aaborg's voice.

'Did you have an amicable parting?'

She nodded. She and Brad, who was fifteen years older than she was, had remained friends and had been in contact.

'Do you remember when Cheryl Keeton was killed?'

'Yes. . . . It was a Monday around lunchtime [when I heard]. . . . One of our temps from Citizens' called me and said a person named Cheryl Keeton had been killed – or found killed – and wasn't that Brad's wife?'

Karen didn't know Cheryl; she had met her once very briefly. She had immediately called Brad. 'I said, "Hi. How are things going?" He said, "Okay," and I said, "Brad, what's going on, really – I heard that Cheryl was dead," and he said that, yes, that was what had happened.' He had told her that he was just leaving to go talk to an attorney.

'This is the Monday following Cheryl's death?'

'Yes.'

Karen testified that Brad had come to her apartment the next day, Tuesday, and talked to her about his movements on Sunday night. He showed up unexpectedly and spent an hour or so, telling her what he had done on Sunday night in much detail. She repeated to the jury what Brad had told her.

His story began very like the version he had told police – about eating with Sara and the boys in the pizza place. Then he had had trouble with 'bad gas' or 'water in his gas tank' with his Suburban. Brad told Karen that after he got back to the Madison Tower, he was supposed to return the boys to Cheryl. He said he called Cheryl to tell her he was having car trouble but it was his impression that she was busy, that she had someone there and wasn't interested in talking with him. '[He said] she sounded mad at him – just leave her alone – she'd been drinking, she didn't care about getting the kids back. Then he decided the kids would stay with him that night.'

But from that point, the version Brad had told Karen became a little different.

He told her he had gone down to the parking garage to get the boys' backpacks and especially Phillip's blanket, and took Phillip – not Michael – with him, leaving the two older boys in the apartment. He said he ran into Lilya Saarnen in the garage and he also mentioned seeing a police officer in the garage.

'Was this all in the same trip?' Shinn asked.

'Yes, I think so. . . . [He said] he got whatever he needed to get out of the car. He went back upstairs – the kids watched a movie, they fell asleep, and the next thing he knew there was a police officer knocking on his door about midnight or one o'clock.'

'Did he tell you that he had more than one conversation with Cheryl that night?'

'. . . Yes, at least two – maybe three . . . I think what I remember is that Cheryl called him and suddenly wanted those kids – changed her tune – and wanted him to return those kids *right now*. I think he argued with her . . . because it sounded like she was with somebody and had been drinking.'

Karen had just cut a large hole in Brad's alibi for the night Cheryl was killed. He had told everyone else that he had been *waiting* for Cheryl to come and get their sons. He had never said that he refused to let the boys go home to her because she was 'drunk' and had a man with her. He had made a big point of saying that he had gone out on the balcony to watch for Cheryl, but that she had never shown up.

Karen further testified that she had seen Brad several times that first week after the murder. She even took care of his boys while he was at his attorney's office. She kept them at different times for an hour or so.

'Did he express to you his attitude about the police investigation that was going on?' Shinn asked.

'Yeah, he said the D.A. in Washington County was really out to get him – that this guy had almost a vendetta against him—'

'A *vendetta?*'

'Yeah, he said that he was convinced that Brad had done it, and that he was going to get him. Brad felt he was going to be arrested at any time.'

'Did he express his attitude about Cheryl's mother?'

'Well, yeah. He was concerned that Cheryl's mother . . . would get the kids.'

'Did he ask you to do anything about that?'

'Yeah, he asked me to take the boys and get out of the state, and just kind of keep them, get them out of town, when things were very traumatic and he could get arrested at any time.'

'Where were you supposed to take them?'

'Out of the state – not out of the country. He didn't want to know where they were.'

'Why?'

'Because if he was arrested, he didn't want to know where they were. If he was asked [by authorities] he didn't want to know.'

Karen said that Brad had given her three thousand dollars he took out of an account at First Interstate Bank. She went with him to get the money. She had kept the money for a day or two, because she had tentatively agreed to help Brad hide his children. But then she changed her mind and returned the three thousand dollars.

Karen Aaborg was finally excused. What would the jury think of a man who was willing to have his children spirited away so far that even he couldn't find them? They had just lost their mother, yet he had planned to hide them completely, delivering them to strangers somewhere. He had wanted to take them away from their mother, but he apparently had been willing to abandon them so that their grandmother could not have them – or so that they would not be vulnerable to other enemies of Brad.

As the trial progressed, still without Brad in attendance, Shinn varied his witnesses – some from the past, some from the present, some from Cheryl's career world, some from her family and her social world, and some detectives and criminalists from the investigation of her murder. And gradually the jury began to see the image of Brad's life psychopathology emerge.

Another friend from work, Janet Blair, told of witnessing Cheryl's new will not long before her murder. 'As we were witnessing the will, Cheryl said, "I want this all taken care of so that if something happens on this trip, Brad will not get anything and the children will get everything." And the other thing she said – and I will never forget this – is, "If I'm ever found dead, Brad did it."'

Sharon McCulloch testified, and Cheryl's cousin, Katannah King, and any number of women who had worked for Garvey, Schubert and Barer. They described a woman who had once had guts and strength and brilliance, but who had become so subdued that she lived in fear that her estranged husband was going to keep her children from her – even if he had to kill her to do it. All the women spoke in voices tremulous with tears. None of them had been able to save Cheryl; all of them had tried.

Katannah King testified in a voice so soft that the jurors had to strain to hear her. Cheryl had told her that Brad was at least three years behind in filing his income tax. A few weeks before Cheryl was killed, Katannah said she had been alarmed when she listened to Cheryl speak on the phone to Brad. He was asking her to come and help him with his income taxes. And it made her angry. 'Cheryl said to him, "No way. I'm not going to help you. We're [meaning Brad's sister Ethel] working against you, and I'm going to hang you for it." Brad said to her, "Well, I'm not going to worry about it anyway – because you're not going to be around to do anything."'

'When was the last time you saw Cheryl?' Shinn asked.

'The last time,' Katannah said softly, '. . . was on Saturday night at Cheryl's mother's house. She was very quiet, *very* quiet. She was very calm. . . . We talked and she took me home, and she said, "You take care of yourself, Katannah," and I said, "No, *you* take care of *yourself,*" and that was the last I ever saw her.'

Chief Criminal Deputy D.A. Bob Herman was the next witness. He testified that after Cheryl's body was discovered in the van, he had accompanied OSP Detective Jerry Finch to her house on 81st Street. There they met her brother, Jim Karr, and the three of them went into the house. When they walked into the kitchen, Herman said, 'Jerry found a note on the drainboard—'

'Let me show you my client's Exhibit Two,' Shinn said, holding a blowup of what Finch had found in Cheryl's kitchen.

Herman read it aloud. 'I have gone to pick up the boys from Brad at the Mobil station next to the IGA. If I'm not back, please come and find me . . . COME RIGHT AWAY!'

Jim Karr had told Finch and Herman about the bitterness of his sister's divorce, and her habit of taking notes on her conversations with Brad.

'Do you remember any evidence of alcoholic drinking?' Shinn asked Herman. 'Beverage glasses? Wineglasses?'

Herman shook his head. 'The house was neat as a pin.'

'Thank you. You may step down.'

Sara Gordon took the witness stand to testify against her former husband. Almost five years earlier, she had been adamant that he was an innocent man hounded by the police. She had never lied – she was not a woman who could lie – but she had answered only those questions asked of her. Now, Sara knew through bitter experience what kind of man lurked behind the charming facade she had fallen in love with. And she was prepared to tell the jurors about the *real* Brad Cunningham.

Sara was remarkably pretty, and almost fragile in appearance. For her day on the witness stand, she wore a dark wine suit with a white blouse. And it was obvious that she was nervous – perhaps even frightened. It was also obvious that she was resolute.

As the jurors listened, enthralled, Sara relived her first meeting with Brad and all that had transpired between them since the spring of 1986. She had to open up her private life, reveal things that no woman would want to tell. It was terribly difficult for a woman of exceptional intelligence to have to admit that love had temporarily obliterated her common sense.

She described how rapidly her affair with Brad had progressed. 'He made me feel very, very special. He spent a lot of time with me, and involved me in the activities with his children. . . . He seemed like a very successful business person to me. He was a lot of fun to be with.' Brad had been Everywoman's ideal man at first, but he had soon revealed himself to be an opportunist, adulterer, thief, and stalking predator. He was also a liar and had convinced Sara of a number of things that were not true – that Cheryl was a loose woman, that *he* had been designated the better parent by psychologists, that Cheryl and her mother had been plotting to poison him. 'He told me that he stopped eating at home unless he took one of the kids' plates or ate something that they hadn't finished,' Sara testified. 'He didn't eat until they had eaten it first.'

Mike Shinn led Sara through the events of September 21, 1986, when she had lent Brad her Toyota Cressida, the vehicle that Shinn submitted was the car he had used when he ambushed Cheryl at the Mobil station. That whole week had been strange – Brad's rage after Cheryl's deposition on September 16, his phone threats to Cheryl that night, and the fight they had on the stormy night of September 19 when he and Sara picked up the boys. Sara said she was surprised at his rage, and surprised how quickly it dissipated after he told Cheryl that he would make her 'pay.'

Shinn asked Sara when she had last seen Brad without clothing during the weekend of September 19–21.

'. . . Friday night.'

'Did he have any bruises on his upper body?'

'No.'

'*After* Sunday night, when was the first time you saw Mr Cunningham without clothes on – on his upper body?' Shinn asked.

'. . . Wednesday or Thursday morning – we were taking a shower together.'

'Did you see anything on his body that you had not seen prior to Sunday night?'

'Yes. I saw a very large bruise under his arm – like huge . . . I can't remember if it was the right or left arm. It seems like the left – just the back of the upper arm. . . . I remember being very shocked when I saw it – and gasping. It was very large – like this size—' She held her hands apart and demonstrated a circle the size of a cantaloupe.

Sara gave the jurors a precise time schedule for the night of Sunday, September 21. She had said goodbye to Brad and the boys shortly before seven, she began.

'When is the next time you actually heard from Mr Cunningham?' Shinn asked.

'He called me at the hospital right at seven-thirty. . . . He said that Cheryl was coming to the apartment to pick up the children. . . .'

'When is the next time that you actually *talked* to Mr Cunningham?'

'That was at ten minutes to nine.'

'That was an hour and twenty minutes later?'

'Yes.'

'What did you think he had been doing? . . . At eight-fifty, when you finally got him on the phone – tell us what was said?'

'I asked him where he had been,' Sara said. 'He said he had been waiting for Cheryl to pick the boys up. He sounded very escalated – very excited.'

'Did he say anything about ever leaving the apartment?'

'. . . I recall in my first conversation, I thought they were in the apartment. He said they were actually down in the lobby. . . . The next day, he started saying no, Michael was with him. They were doing errands, getting the mail, taking shoes down to my car.'

Shinn asked Sara how long such errands would have

taken, the elevator ride and then the walk to the garage or the mailboxes.

'Five minutes.'

Sara was no longer on Brad's side. She now had come to realize what kind of man he really was, and she was testifying to everything she remembered from the night of Cheryl's murder, knowing full well that the details she recalled did not mesh with Brad's explanations to the police or to Karen Aaborg. She could understand now what Cheryl had lived through in the last months of her life.

Sara went on to describe how they had kept on the move the first week after Cheryl's murder, and how Jess, Michael, and Phillip were taken out of state.

Shinn asked how long it was before she saw Brad and the three little boys again.

'They eventually came back and I think they stayed with his aunt and uncle in Seattle – Herman and Trudy Dreesen.'

'Were you in love with Mr Cunningham by then?'

'Yes.'

'When?'

'I was very committed to him and his children by that summer.'

'You married him?'

'Yes . . . in November of 1987.'

'You adopted his children . . . ?'

'Yes.'

The testimony moved into the rapid deterioration of their marriage, the huge amounts of money Sara had given Brad to finance his various ventures and expensive lifestyle, and the tremendous debts she had been saddled with when they separated and divorced. Nothing she had to say helped Brad's case. She no longer cared. She had been frightened when her testimony began, but as the hours passed, she seemed to experience a catharsis. She could almost see the humor in Brad's constant manipulation. She had been much more frightened during her marriage.

And she had had to tell this same story in her deposition before the civil trial while Brad was sitting at the same table. Only his attorney Joe Rieke was between them then. Even though she faced away from Brad, she had been frightened. Today he wasn't in the courtroom; no one knew where he was. Telling her story to Mike Shinn and the jury was so much easier than what she had already been through, and she seemed to relax as her testimony drew to a close.

'When did you file for divorce?' Shinn asked.

'March seventh, 1990.' And then Sara recounted the terror she had lived through during their divorce: the threats and harassments, the sudden appearances and disappearances, the demands for money, the destruction of the Dunthorpe house, the stalkings. Now all that was in the past. Brad had cost her a million dollars. But even that didn't matter. What mattered was that she had not seen the three boys she had legally adopted and had loved as her own for so long. Her sons were growing up without her. She didn't even know if they were safe, living with a father who was capable of violent rages and physical abuse.

'One final question,' Michael Shinn asked. 'During that second phone call to Brad on September twenty-first, when you found him at home, what did you say to him?'

'I was angry. My first response was, "When I can't get hold of you, I don't know if you're out killing Cheryl or Cheryl's killing you."'

'You were kidding, weren't you?'

'. . . no, I was serious. I was really concerned. I didn't know where he was. It was *so* unlike him not to be in touch with me. . . .'

'That relationship had reached such a peak . . . where you were actually partway serious . . . ?'

'Yes.'

'What was his response?'

'He didn't respond.'

48

Dr Karen Gunson, who had performed the autopsy on Cheryl, used photos during her testimony that showed the terrible damage done to the victim. Dr William Brady, a legend in forensic pathology who had been Oregon State's medical examiner for more than twenty years, testified next. Tall, slim, and dapper with a neatly trimmed snowy-white mustache and Vandyke beard, he had studied the Cheryl Keeton case at Shinn's request.

'Of all these autopsies and homicide investigations you've been involved in,' Shinn asked, 'how would you rate the level of violence in the Cheryl Keeton case?'

'The amount of violence . . . would certainly have to be at the top of my particular scale. . . . Actual physical assaults or beatings are uncommon. . . . Of those I have had experience with, they fall into two categories, . . . a few blows . . . and the other narrow category of repetitive, extreme violence, of what we call "overkill." Of that now exceedingly small group, . . . this one certainly with the number of injuries, the distribution, character type of the injuries . . . would rank this . . . right up at the top of anyone's scale.'

Dr Brady went over each injury and told the jury that there were minutes – 'quite some minutes' – before Cheryl actually died. Her death had not been instantaneous. 'She may well have been alive for a good time *after* eight o'clock. . . .'

'As much as twenty minutes or thirty minutes?' Shinn asked.

'That's not unreasonable. Probably less, but it may have been that long.'

'So we have fifteen to thirty minutes of beating?'

'I certainly wouldn't want to suggest that the beating occurred all that time, because we have motion – a change of location of the automobile—'

'For some reason,' Shinn said, 'there's a lull, and there's more beatings?'

'What we can say medically is that there is a period of survival during which time this lady had been beaten, lived, and died. . . . We're not talking about a single beating and then death – no.'

'It's not a merciful killing, was it?'

'That's an understatement.' Based on his experience, Dr Brady said that this particular type of overkill was 'a crime of passion.'

Dr Russell Sardo, who had attempted to find some equitable way for Brad and Cheryl to share their custody of their three little boys, testified to his finding that – in the end – he had chosen Cheryl as the primary parent. Dr Sardo was on the stand for a long time, and he did an excellent job of explaining the dynamics he had seen between Cheryl and Brad – his aggression and her willingness to bend as far as she could to reach some kind of a solution. He commented that often divorcing parents view children as 'possessions,' something to be 'won' from the other party like a house or a car or a boat. Although that was not true in Cheryl's case, it was in Brad's.

Lieutenant Rod Englert of the Multnomah County Sheriff's Office was a much sought-after expert in a somewhat arcane area of expertise – blood spatter evidence. He could read all manner of things from blood spatter, splatter, spray, drops, and stains. He could actually reconstruct crime scenes, showing direction of force, and he could decipher whether blood spatter was of low, medium, or high velocity. He was also an expert on crime scene psychology.

Englert had viewed the evidence from the Keeton homicide. In his psychological reconstruction of Cheryl's murder, Englert first considered what type of person might carry out the 'overkill' of two dozen violent blows. Then he tried to connect a sequence of events that had taken place inside the Toyota van. Englert began, 'We have four different motives to consider: Was it a fear thing? . . . Was it revenge? Was it sex? Or was it theft? Most homicides fall into one of those categories.

'In crimes of violence, blood is often shed. And through that bloodshed, you can make interpretations.' Englert showed the jury that round drops are usually low-velocity spatter – 'cast-off blood.' If a person's hand is bleeding or if the weapon in the hand of a killer has blood on it, and he throws it back, the blood will be cast off onto a surface in an elongated shape with a 'tail.' The tail always points toward the direction of travel.

Medium-velocity impact spatter is blood shed by blunt trauma. 'If I hit Mr Shinn with a baseball bat,' Englert said, 'there will be no blood from the first blow. There will be a laceration.' He moved his arm to demonstrate and Shinn never flinched. The jury watched, fascinated. 'The second blow – or even the third – will produce medium-velocity spatter. . . . As a result of my striking Mr Shinn with this "baseball bat," we start creating a spatter pattern – and I can hit him ten or fifteen times, and you'll see a horribly bloody scene, but you can look at me and you could swear I didn't do it because there will be very little blood on the prepetrator. There may be some on my shoes, there may be some right here under my cuffs. There may be some on the back of my hand, but very, very little. The force is *away* from the person doing the striking.'

In Cheryl's murder, there would have been massive amounts of blood around where her head had been – but virtually no blood on the person who struck those blows. Englert had selected eleven photographs of the Toyota van to show the jury what had happened to her.

'In my opinion, the first time she was hit was in the driver's seat. You say, "There's no blood in the driver's seat," but that's why. The blood was directed *away* from the driver's seat. . . . Most of the blows are to the left side of her body and to the back of her head. . . . The first blow would not have shed any blood, but the next blow—'

Englert pointed to the child's carseat behind the driver's seat. The tails of blood were there – pointing to the rear of the van, away from the direction of blows. 'She was in the driver's seat, her head leaning toward the passenger seat. There were defensive bruises on her arm where she tried to ward off the blows. That's position number one.'

Position number two was on the console between the seats. 'She's down. She's bloody, . . . she's moving her hands and transferring blood, cloth on cloth [Cheryl's shirt moving against the upholstery], and struggling. Her only route of escape is toward the [passenger] door.'

Cheryl was hit so many times that she was weakening. This was chilling testimony. The courtroom was absolutely still, save for Englert's voice. Position number three, he demonstrated, was where most of the damage was done to the back of Cheryl's head. She was down, disoriented. She was stretching for the door but her head was at the headrest. The medium-velocity spatter showed on the passenger window. At this point, Englert felt that Cheryl was rendered unconscious. 'She was struggling – but slowly – to get out the door before this. See the low-velocity blood where she rested? The tails are pointed downward on the back of the seat – as they would as if from a nosebleed. She also tried to open the door to escape. There is medium-velocity spatter on the inside of this doorjamb and it couldn't have gotten there unless the door was open.'

There was only one more position. Position number four. 'Her buttocks were on the console, her head is down and stationary, and she's bleeding, saturating blood into the carpet on the passenger floor.' Englert held a photograph of the plastic bag found on the floor of the passenger side.

There were transfer bloodstains there from Cheryl's hair – but there was no movement at all. Englert agreed with Dr Brady that it had taken many minutes for the attack to take place. Cheryl had bled for a long time.

'If I understand you correctly,' Shinn said, 'the blood spatter trail that you can read for us is more reliable than if we'd had an eyewitness in this case.'

'It's scientific,' Englert said. 'It's reliable – as opposed to witnesses sometimes, who are not as reliable – including myself.'

'What kind of weapon was used?'

'It's a linear object.' Englert picked up a long police flashlight – a Kell light that Shinn had procured. The murder weapon, he said, would have been something similar, with many different-shaped surfaces. The blood on the ceiling of the van was cast-off blood, flung from the blunt object used to bludgeon Cheryl to death, as her killer hit her again and again.

Shinn asked Englert what he felt was the motive for this murder. Englert wrote four words on the easel, and crossed them out one by one. 'Sex? No. Theft? No. Because this is what I would term "overkill." This is one of the very few that you'll see with that much overkill.' Englert said if he had been there on the night of the murder, he would have ruled out everything but 'Fear' and 'Revenge.' The fact that the van had been rolled out onto the freeway, combined with the overkill, made him believe the motive was revenge.

'You can just see the hatred in this case,' Lieutenant Englert commented, 'because of the four different positions I described to you. You see a male who has a very strong personality, a very domineering personality – he wouldn't be afraid.'

Both Oregon State Police Sergeant Greg Baxter and Detective Jim Ayers had always believed that Brad had taken his four-year-old son Michael along with him when he went to confront Cheryl at the Mobil station.

'You mean her own son was used as bait to lure her to her death?' Mike Shinn asked Baxter when he took the stand.

'That's exactly correct.'

Ayers testified next. He had worked closely with Shinn in reconstructing this case. When he took the stand, he was as anxious as the people who had known Cheryl Keeton in life to see that her killer was brought to justice.

Nobody ever knew what Ayers was going to look like; he worked undercover as much as he did routine detective work. He sometimes looked like an accountant, but just as frequently he would resemble a truck driver or a bearded biker. Even those who knew him well could often stand right next to him and fail to recognize him. He was extremely proficient on any detail – be it drug enforcement, sex crimes, or homicide – and he was a natural chameleon. On the day of his testimony, his hair was cut short and he wore horn-rimmed glasses. He was dressed in a striped shirt, dark suit, and tie. He was, for the moment, in his 'accountant' garb.

Ayers told the jurors that when he and Detective Jerry Finch went to Brad's Madison Tower apartment a few hours after his wife had been found dead, they were there only to inform him of her death. There had been no reason to read Brad his rights under Miranda. He was not a suspect; he wasn't in custody.

'When you first got to Mr Cunningham's apartment,' Shinn began, 'you didn't know anything about him – or about her, did you?'

'No, other than that she was dead,' Ayers said.

Ayers recalled the one-hour-and-fifty-minute conversation he had had that night with Brad. It was to be the last time Brad would ever talk to him about anything. After that, he had made himself unavailable to the investigators.

'I asked him about the last time that he had seen Cheryl,' Ayers said. 'And he stated he had seen her Friday evening when he had picked the kids up.'

Ayers testified that Brad told him Cheryl had agreed to

come to his apartment and pick up the boys. When Ayers said he had information that Brad had planned to meet Cheryl at the abandoned Mobil station on the West Slope, he denied it.

'What was the next conversation?'

'I asked him if he'd killed Cheryl.'

'What'd he say?'

'He said, "No."'

'How'd he say it?'

'He had a very brief display of emotion – and I mean brief . . . a fifteen-to-twenty-second display of emotion. My interpretation of what that was wasn't emotion over Cheryl having been killed, but he was frightened by the fact that I had asked him that question.'

Ayers repeated Brad's oft-told stories about Cheryl's affairs with a number of men and her fondness for country-and-western music. He said that she hung out at a truck stop and often went to the nude beach on the Columbia River. At that point in the investigation, Ayers said, he had no reason to doubt Brad's description. Later, he said he had discovered that Brad had been lying and he saw it as an attempt to suggest that any number of people might have had a motive to murder Cheryl.

'Did he say he ever left the apartment?' Shinn asked.

'Yes, he did,' Ayers testified. 'He said he left one time just long enough to take some things down to the garage, because he had an inspection to do the next day.'

'Did he tell you that he and the three little boys were sitting in the lobby for a long time waiting for Cheryl to show up?'

'No.'

'Did he tell you that he took Michael with him for a while, wearing his jogging costume and his hunting jacket?'

'No. . . . I asked Cunningham if he was athletic,' Ayers said. 'He stated, "No."'

'He denied he was athletic?'

'Yes.'

Shinn reminded Ayers and the jury of Brad's background as a star football player. And whoever had killed Cheryl had probably been someone of considerable strength and almost certainly jogged from the crime scene to the Mobil station to get his car. Beyond Jim Karr's suspicions, Ayers had no reason to believe that Brad was lying. In retrospect, however, it seemed that he was denying anything that might have linked him to Cheryl's murder. And he would not have done that unless he already knew how the crime had been committed.

Ayers testified that at one point Finch had asked if he could talk to the boys. 'Cunningham just said, "NO! – not until I talk to an attorney about it."'

'Why did you want to talk to the boys?'

'My strong suspicion,' Ayers said, 'and greatest fear, was that all or at least one of those children were with Brad Cunningham—'

Suddenly, Ayers' voice faltered and he closed his eyes against tears, swallowing hard. He could not speak. Judge Haggerty realized that, for the moment, Ayers could not go on. He called for a noon recess. And when court reconvened that afternoon, the jury listened to other witnesses before Ayers returned to the stand. He had regained his composure and was able to continue his testimony in his usual professional voice. 'I had substantial concern – that was shared by all the investigators in this case – that Brad had taken at least one or all the boys with him. That one or more of those boys might have been a witness to their mother's death.'

'He never let you talk to those boys?' Shinn asked.

'No, not willingly.'

'Eventually, you had to subpoena them,' Shinn said, 'and they had a lawyer by then. . . . Is it common for little children to have a lawyer when their father is a murder suspect?'

'I've never encountered it.'

In fact, six-year-old Jess had offered testimony to a grand jury that implied his father had been absent from the Madison Tower apartment at the time of his mother's murder. But that had not been enough to indict Brad for the crime. And no one investigating the case had been able to speak to the boys again.

When Jim Ayers stepped down from the witness chair, he hoped his testimony would help to nail Brad Cunningham. For years, he had wanted to face Cunningham in a court of law. Brad was not there now. But it didn't matter; the jury could still render its verdict. If it ruled against him, Cunningham could eventually face a criminal trial, and Ayers would willingly take the witness stand again.

49

Ordinarily, the family of the defendant testifies for the defense. In this trial, there was no defense – only an empty table. But had there been a defense, the female relatives from Brad's past would not have testified for him. They came to Judge Haggerty's courtroom to testify for Cheryl's estate.

Ethel Cunningham Bakke, Brad's elder sister, wore a white pantsuit and a dark aqua blouse. She was blond with dark brown eyes and bore a resemblance to her brother. 'Brad was so suave and so sweet-talking with the girls,' she testified. 'He made money. He knew how to turn a dollar—'

'Did you know his wives?' Shinn asked.

'Yes, I met Loni Ann because she was my baby-sitter when he was in high school. I met Cynthia because I went to court to help Loni Ann keep her children. . . . I ran into my brother in a restaurant and I met Lauren, who was about to have her baby. . . . They separated within a month after that, and Cheryl came into his life. . . . My daughter got married on June twenty-eighth, 1986, and my father said, "Have you called Cheryl?" and I said, "I don't know Brad's address or phone number."'

Sanford Cunningham had told Ethel that Cheryl and Brad were having problems and that she could 'be nice and invite Cheryl to the wedding.'

'Did you call Cheryl?' Shinn asked.

'I did. . . . This was in April. . . . I invited her to the wedding . . . and she said, "I would like to know more about you and your mother—" I said, "My mom's alive," and she said, "You're kidding!" and I said she would be at the wedding.'

Cheryl told Ethel that she was very afraid of Brad and that he had threatened her. 'You're not the first,' Ethel answered. And so a friendship had developed, and Cheryl, her brother, and her three boys all came to Ethel's daughter's wedding. Sanford, who had less than a month to live, came to the wedding too. 'That was the first time I had seen my dad in all this time,' Ethel said. 'My dad then died on July twenty-sixth. . . . Cheryl called me after the funeral and told me she felt partly responsible for my dad's heart attack . . . and that Brad had told her not to come to the funeral. . . . I told her Brad had shown up with Sara and tried to pass her off as Cheryl . . . I nipped that in the bud.'

Shinn asked Ethel about her relationship with Cheryl later that summer. 'Did she talk with you about "witnesses"?'

'Yes.'

'Did she talk to you about who they were?'

'Yes.'

'In the conversation Cheryl had with you about taxes and bankruptcy – what did she tell you in connection with the evidence she intended to present in the divorce and custody proceedings?'

'She was going to break Brad. Break the bankruptcy

statements. She was going to prove that he was getting money . . . he was avoiding taxes with the IRS. . . . I gave her any information she needed. . . . She told me she had prepared a list; she was keeping it secret—'

'Did you have conversations with her,' Shinn asked, 'where she was afraid of the consequences?'

'Not only was she afraid of the consequences to her but to those of us who were going to testify. . . . She made a list but it was a "protective" kind of list. She told me that on the Friday before her death.' It was clear from Ethel's testimony that she believed her brother was capable of violence, of revenge, of murder. She said he had beaten her too.

Shinn elicited testimony from Ethel about her final conversation with Cheryl. It had been on Friday, September 19, 1986, after Brad picked up the children. Cheryl said they had argued as usual, and she had insisted he have the boys home on time on Sunday because they had school the next morning. 'They'd started to argue and fight,' Ethel said, 'and he was raising his arms and everything, and all of a sudden he stopped and said, "What's the matter with me? Sunday! You're not going to be here after Sunday. I don't have to worry about you." I sat right up and said, "Cheryl, *Cheryl*. He's not just making threats anymore. He means to do it *this* weekend. He's got a plan. I know Bradly . . . He doesn't have to argue with you because it's settled in his mind. . . . He's going to do it." I even tried to warn her. I said, "Cheryl, listen to me. . . . He's not going to attack you in your house. Has he ever threatened you with the children being harmed if you don't do what he tells you to?" and she said, "Yes, I'd lay down my life for my kids, you know that."'

Sobbing on the stand, Ethel recalled that she had warned Cheryl that Brad was going to do something to call her out of her home, alone, tell her that something was wrong so she would have to go out to get the kids, that he would draw her away from security.

'How did you know this?' Shinn asked.

'He plans and he creates and he figures out how he's

going to go after somebody,' Ethel said. 'He was this way in junior high.'

Rosemary Kinney, Brad's mother, took the stand next. She looked nothing like snapshots of the lovely young girl Sanford had married, or the attractive middle-aged woman standing next to him on a camping trip. The years had been unkind to her. Her hair was still raven black, but it was pulled into a knot on top of her head, and her face was deeply lined, her eyes almost hidden by pouches of flesh. Shinn asked her what the nature of her relationship with Brad had been over the previous decade.

'I haven't seen my son,' Rosemary said, the pain of many losses bringing tears to her eyes. 'I saw him at his father's funeral in July. [Before that] it had to be at Loni Ann's [custody] hearing.'

'You testified against your son?'

'Yes, I did – of his treatment of the children. He came to the cabin with the children and I had fixed dinner. He dished their plates up – they were small – and he walked into the kitchen and said, "Eat that food!" Kait said she couldn't eat any more. He started force-feeding them. Kait finally vomited her food into her plate. . . .'

'Did you know Mr Cunningham's second wife?'

'Only time I seen her was in court. She was quite a bit older than Brad.'

'. . . his third wife, Lauren Swanson?'

'No, I didn't know her. I got a glimpse of her one time. Loni Ann was going to let me have the children one weekend, because Brad would never let me see them. I went to Loni Ann's mother's house, and I put my car behind the house so Brad wouldn't see it. They drove up, and I got a glimpse.'

'Were you invited to their wedding?'

Rosemary looked astonished. 'To *Brad's* wedding? No.'

Rosemary told of the first time she ever met Cheryl Keeton. Kait had given her Cheryl's address, and she wrote a letter to 'explain who I was, and my nationality – I'm a registered member of the Colville Confederated Tribe, and I'm French, Indian, English, Hawaiian. I knew Cheryl probably didn't know anything about me, and I wanted her to realize that Brad did have a mother, and I did care about the children. When she got my letter, she called me. It was really wonderful to get to talk to her.'

Rosemary had finally met Cheryl at Ethel's daughter's wedding in June 1986. 'I was standing in the church, and this pretty lady came up in front of me with these three beautiful boys, and she said, "This is your grandmother," and these little boys gave me a hug—'

Rosemary put her head in her hand and sobbed. She had never even hoped that she would meet Cheryl or her youngest grandsons. She got a chance to visit with Cheryl at the reception and to have her picture taken with her and the boys. 'I told Cheryl, "I'll tell you one thing – don't ever trust Brad—"'.

'Why do you say that?' Shinn asked.

'Well, after my first husband left me, I got a job as a teacher's aide in eastern Washington, and it was a break from school and I came home because I still had the house. I'd changed the locks so no one could get in. I drove up and there was lights on and I went in and my son was there. There was this woman – Brad's second wife. He said he was there to get his things. We had words. He hit me and knocked me on the floor. I tried to get up, and every time I tried, he hit me again. . . .

'Finally, he went out the door, and every time I tried to go out, he hit me with the screen door. He finally hit me so hard in the chest with his arm and fist, I landed out in front of the house on my neck and shoulders. I went to the neighbors and called the sheriff.'

When the deputy arrived, Rosemary said, Brad came charging in and said, 'I'm the one that called you.' But the deputy didn't believe him. He waited until Brad had removed some things he had in his mother's garage and left the house.

'The following Monday, I went to Roxbury Court and filed charges against my son,' Rosemary said, beginning to cry again. 'I figured that if I filed charges against him, he would never do anything like this to anybody else. I knew he had been cruel with Loni Ann – so I filed the charges. The day he was supposed to go to court, I was there – but Brad had an attorney. The judge said Brad wouldn't be there. I had to leave to go back to work. Nothing ever happened about that.' Rosemary went on to tell the jury that she had been afraid of Brad, her own son, ever since he was in high school.

Shinn handed her a letter that Brad had once sent to her. It was remarkably similar to the letter he would send to Sara, and to any number of women who had angered him. He warned her that, if she didn't change her ways, she might end up killing someone.

Like her daughter Ethel, Rosemary testified that she would have done 'anything in the world' to help Cheryl keep her children. In the end, of course, there was nothing they could do. The 'protective witness list' that Cheryl had drawn up, the battle plan that she believed would bring Brad down and protect her little boys, had been as fragile as a cobweb held up against a bazooka.

Loni Ann Cunningham testified through her videotaped deposition. Her taut, pale little face filled the screen and the jurors listened as she recalled the horrors of her marriage to Brad. Kait Cunningham testified by phone. In a flat voice, she told about the spring she had spent in Houston when she was twelve or thirteen and had been humiliated and held captive by her father. One overwhelming fact was becoming obvious. The women in Brad Cunningham's life had been disposable, dispensable, the objects of derision and hatred – and ultimately expendable.

Even his wives.

Even his daughter.

Even his sisters.
Even his mother.

The civil trail went on. There were no objections; there was no one there to object. A long line of Cheryl's friends and former law partners walked to the witness stand and spoke briefly of their memories of her. In that courtroom Cheryl came to life, and the jurors began to sense the enormity of her loss.

Stu Hennessey, Cheryl's friend from her early days at Garvey, Schubert and Barer, attempted to sum up what a superb lawyer she had been. 'Cheryl was clearly the best. As the pressure grew, she just got better and better.'

He also recalled Brad's possessions. 'Brad *really* liked Mercedes-Benzes,' he said. 'He almost always had two or three at a time.' Hennessey described the Unimag as a 'huge moon buggy' with tires six to seven feet high, a vehicle used by the Israeli Army to move troops. 'Brad told me he had the only Unimag in the United States . . . it had absolutely no purpose as a car.'

'What about a yacht?' Shinn asked.

Hennessey remembered that Brad had acquired a yacht early in his marriage to Cheryl in trade for some project. As he recalled, Brad was renting it out for charters.

'Did he have a police car?' Shinn asked.

'Yes,' Hennessey said. 'That was a source of great frustration to Cheryl. Brad got in his mind that he wanted a police car – like the State Patrol's in Washington – the big white highway cruisers? They don't sell those to regular people, but Brad *wanted* one. He bugged some dealer until finally – it took months – they ordered him one. Poor Cheryl would have to drive this thing . . . it's like you don't have any springs . . . it's really a horrible car – there's nothing inside it. You know, it was kind of scary. It was white. Except that it didn't have a light on the top, it was just like a police car.'

'You know what he used it for?'

'I haven't a clue.'

'How would you describe Mr Cunningham physically?'

'He wasn't a huge guy but he was powerfully built,' Hennessey said. 'He told me he had to have all his shirts custom made because his neck was so big.'

Cheryl's family – Betty and Marv Troseth, Susan Keegan, and Bob McNannay – had told their last memories of Cheryl to the initial investigators. They testified now in the civil trial, old griefs coming back sharply. And they were prepared to testify again and again and again, if need be. There were no surprises in their testimony, nothing the Oregon State Police detectives and the Washington County D.A.'s office hadn't heard back in 1986.

Jim Karr, Cheryl's half brother, identified Exhibit 6 – the 'protective witness list' that Cheryl had prepared, the list meant to fight Brad but which had probably been Cheryl's death warrant. Mike Shinn read it aloud while Karr nodded. It included Brad's mother and elder sister, two of his former wives, baby-sitters, and Cheryl's family, friends, and colleagues – all people who would have been able to demonstrate Brad's pattern of abusive behavior.

Sara Gordon's sister Margie Johnson was the 'Megabucks' spokesperson for the Oregon Lottery and her face was well known to Oregon television viewers. She was as vivacious on the witness stand as she was on the small screen, a pretty, bubbly woman. She said that when U.S. Bank bought out Brad's contract shortly after Cheryl's murder, they asked for the return of all the pool cars he had borrowed. One was in Seattle, and she said that she had driven Brad to Sea-Tac Airport so he could drive it back. She had found Brad a nice person, but she barely knew him. Her sister Sara had only been dating him for a few months. 'He was very upset,' she testified. 'Even though he hadn't done it, [the murder] would put a cloud over the bank.'

Margie had also heard yet another version of Brad's movements on September 21, 1986. 'He said that they waited in the lobby. . . . I was under the assumption that

Cheryl was supposed to pick up the kids about seven o'clock and he had the kids in the lobby—'

'Did you know she had been unwilling for months to come there to pick up those kids?' Shinn cut in.

'No. . . . [He said] when she didn't show up, they went back upstairs. . . . Jess and Phillip were watching a movie, and he was with Michael, and they went to check the mail.'

According to the testimony of various witnesses, Brad had given many different versions of what he had done between 7:30 and 8:50 on the night Cheryl was murdered. He told Jim Ayers he had left his apartment just once – to put shoes and work clothes in Sara's Cressida. He first told Sara that he and the boys had been in the lobby waiting for Cheryl to come for them. A day after the murder, he told her he had been doing errands – picking up mail, leaving his boots in her car. Brad told Karen Aaborg that he had refused to let Cheryl have the boys at all that night because she was drunk and with a man, and that he had gone to the car with Phillip to get the boys' blankets and backpacks. Lilya Saarnen saw Brad and Michael at 7:30, but Brad called her the next morning and tried to get her to say she had seen him at 8:00. Margie Johnson, Sara's sister, had heard the 'waiting in the lobby' story and that Brad and Michael were doing errands around the Madison Tower. Jess Cunningham remembered that his father said he had been 'jogging' around Sara's hospital, and that he had been gone for a long time. Rachel Houghton saw Brad and a little boy in the garage around nine, and Brad had been wearing shorts and his hair was wet.

Where *was* Brad during that hour and twenty minutes? Was he in his apartment, waiting in the lobby, watching for Cheryl from the rail around the walkway, doing errands all around the building, jogging, settling the boys down for the night? Or was he following a carefully thought-out plan to lure Cheryl to the deserted Mobil station and her brutal death? Were his car problems a pretense? Had he selected the weapon he would use? Had he provided himself with a change of clothing? If this was a crime of 'revenge,' as Lieutenant Englert had testified, was it also a crime of deliberate premeditation? It was certainly beginning to look that way.

50

Mike Shinn called Dr Ron Turco. A compactly muscled man with a thick head of hair, Turco looked younger than his age and nothing at all like a psychiatrist.

'What is your profession?' Shinn asked.

'I'm a physician and I specialize in the practice of psychiatry,' Turco replied. 'The medical model of psychiatry [which] views early development and early training as being very important in later behavior.'

Dr Turco said he had dealt with criminal behavior often in his studies, particularly in constructing psychological profiles. When Shinn asked him to explain to the jury what that meant, Turco said, 'A psychological profile is a product of the technique that utilizes known psychological theory as well as very specific information to formulate an idea of what a person is like. This goes back a very long time. Freud himself did a profile on Leonardo da Vinci and Michelangelo by studying the work they did – and their family background and information available.'

Turco went on to say that Freud had also done a psychological profile on Woodrow Wilson. Profiling was not a new technique at all. During World War II a profile was done of Adolf Hitler. President Kennedy had received a psychological profile of Nikita Khrushchev.

Constructing a psychological profile of a criminal was

slightly different. 'You don't know the person,' Turco said. 'If someone has committed a crime, you take information and put it together and try to then make predictions about a person you don't know. This is what happens with a serial murderer – several people are murdered – we take information from the crime scene. We look at the way the body has been handled, we look at the blood splatter, the kind of weapon used, the specific nature of the assault, put together, and we hypothesize. . . . We also try to take crime scene pictures and autopsy reports and study those. . . . Even when no body had been discovered,' Turco added, 'we take whatever information we have and we try to formulate a profile.'

Each type of murder has particular patterns, whether domestic, serial, stranger-to-stranger, or person-to-person. Turco and his fellow psychiatrists and criminologists had come to a place where they could predict with no little accuracy which types of human beings commit which crimes. Turco told the jurors that he himself considered four or five things when he did a profile: current behavior, development, physical health, and the psychodynamics of the crime. 'If possible, I use the crime scene information.' He stressed, however, that profiling was not a technique to *convict*; it was a technique to predict human behavior, used to aid investigators and all those concerned with the psychopathology of the criminal mind.

Shinn pointed out that, unlike some witnesses, Dr Turco was not 'living in an ivory tower. Tell the jury a little about yourself.'

'I have at least ten years' experience as a homicide detective,' Turco remarked. 'I'm a commissioned police officer in the State of Oregon. I've investigated many homicides. Detective Rod Englert and I worked on a serial murder case together.'

In fact, Turco had worked with the FBI, and with police agencies all over America. At Shinn's request, he had reviewed a stack of documents on the Cheryl Keeton murder and read the long chronology of both Brad's and Cheryl's lives. 'Almost too much – including a letter that Mr Cunningham sent his mother,' Turco said.

'Mr Cunningham,' Mike Shinn began, getting down to the case at hand, 'is a man who, from outward appearances, seems to have the characteristics and background that were totally inconsistent with the kind of brutal murder that killed Cheryl Keeton. . . . I want to understand what went on here between him and Cheryl Keeton.' He asked Turco what he might have found significant in the materials he had studied on this particular murder case.

'Outward appearances are not very helpful,' Turco said. 'At least, in the everyday behavior observed by strangers. This is what we call a "false self." The individual projects an image of what he is really not. It's only in the intimate situation that you find what he is really about. That's the so-called true self that is hidden.' Turco cited Dr Jeffrey McDonald, the Green Beret doctor convicted of killing his wife and small daughters, as an example of an individual who projected the false self. 'His *public* image was exemplary,' he said.

Shinn reminded Turco and the jury of Brad Cunningham's many achievements – his athletic stardom, his intelligence, his business career where literally millions of dollars were under his control, his love relationships with any number of beautiful, successful women. 'It's totally contradictory that he could do something like this,' he remarked.

'Not at all,' Turco said. 'The "I-5 Killer" fits the profile you just gave of Mr Cunningham. He was a football player, well liked, had lots of girlfriends, very smooth, very social.'

'That's [Randy] Woodfield?'

'Yes. Ted Bundy is another person who would fit that category. . . . We did the profile of Mr Woodfield in 1980–81. . . . It's not unusual. That's a typical pattern. It's one of the reasons why these people surreptitiously murder. Why not just get a divorce? Why not just leave town? But these people maintain a facade – an image.

In order to do so, these people have to destroy someone who can show that they don't meet that image. They're destroying the "evidence," so to speak. That's one of the reasons they always profess to be innocent. In a sense, they even believe . . . that they had the right to do what they did. . . . It's a narcissistic presentation . . . *malignant narcissism.'*

Turco explained that people like Woodfield, McDonald, Bundy, and Cunningham had character disorders; they were unable to relate in any meaningful way to anyone. They had no consciences. 'It's the way they live,' he said bluntly. 'Narcissists cannot love in a genuine way. It's an incapacity.' It was indeed, he testified, a kind of blindness, an inability even to see that one is doing something harmful.

'In the materials about Mr Cunningham . . . I see projection. Particularly in the letter he wrote to his mother,' Turco said. 'In projection, there's a tendency to take one's own feelings – usually negative feelings – and to project them onto the environment, and anticipate that they will be coming back at you. He accuses many people in his life of doing things to harm him – a representation of his underlying rage – I think it's intimately tied up with the parental relationships.'

Turco went on to note a number of deliberately cruel patterns of behavior that Brad had exhibited, behavior he had seen again and again in depositions and testimony from both his former wives and his family. He commented particularly about the fact that his first wife Loni Ann had been totally dependent on Brad's child support checks, and yet he had invalidated them after he gave them to her – so that she would be destitute.

Speaking of this kind of cruelty carried to the point of murder, Turco said, 'We call it sadism – egosyntonic sadism – which means there are people in this world who are just basically very comfortable with cruelty. It's almost a way of life for them to be cruel to others – in small ways and in big ways. Reading through these records, that pattern becomes apparent.'

'Could you give us an example?' Shinn asked.

'. . . behavior toward his former wives – to the women in his life. That's pretty well documented,' Turco responded. 'I think there's really a very serious indication of loss of impulse control. This person is not just cruel on a level of canceling checks or cheating. It has an aggressive component that's really quite substantial.'

Shinn held up the letter that Brad had written to his mother on January 28, 1974, when he was twenty-five years old. 'What does that reflect about his feelings about his mother?' he asked Turco.

'Briefly stated,' Turco said, 'this letter reflects his perception of his mother as being very cruel, and being a very inhumane person who is out to destroy his life and the life of his father. . . . Actually there are two elements to this letter. We would have to assume that his allegations are false. . . .'

The letter that Brad had sent to his mother was three pages of single-spaced typing. It was packed with vituperative accusations, beginning by castigating her for her 'thinly veiled offensive . . . to cover your own tracks because you had opened and destroyed my first-class mail,' and moving on: '. . . You liken me and my father to conspirators in your divorce. . . . You clearly . . . know that your bizarre and unexplainable actions . . . caused the man to seek out peace of mind away from you. His most serious heart attack [was] caused by one of your relentless ranting and raving sessions. . . . Your threats to kill people . . .

'I have made a concerted effort to divorce myself from your sphere of influence,' Brad continued in his hate letter to his mother. 'You have ignored my right to quiet enjoyment, harassed my person . . . ostracized and impugned my character and reputation . . . attempted to alienate my children's affection. . . . You have physically attacked the woman with whom I associate, calling her a slut and a whore, and threatening to kill us both. . . . You have pawed through my personal belongings like an animal. . . . I can subpoena witnesses to state . . . they heard you threaten to kill various people. . . . You also said you should blow off my father's head with a gun. . . . I speculate and believe that you will need the professional help of a psychiatrist. Without this assitance, I fear you may commit an irretrievable act in carrying out one of your earlier . . . threats.' Brad had ended his letter to his mother, 'Consider yourself informed as to my feelings on these matters via this letter. Any continuance of further actions on your part to harass, intimidate, or malign me or my family or friends will be met with appropriate and swift legal restraints.

'Yours, Brad M. Cunningham.'

Analyzing this letter for the jurors, Turco said, 'You basically see an individual projecting . . . his own rage, hostility, paranoia, etcetera, to another person. In this case, onto his mother. The second element . . . what is or isn't true, whether his mother is a terrible person or an angel – is irrelevant. It is that he *views her as such* and that is extremely, extremely bad . . . the relationship with a mother is very important, and this [letter] is a projection of his own hostility.

'Take this a step further. Individuals who *believe* that their mothers are that bad almost instinctively reenact the same rage toward other women in their lives . . . they lack the ability to *not* be aggressive. . . . They have the inability to relate in any fashion. . . . This man doesn't have empathy. . . . He's *using* people – only to get something out of them.'

'Do you notice that – not just in his dealings with his wives, but with his children?' Shinn asked.

'Yes,' Turco agreed. 'I noticed that quite specifically. He's basically relating to them with respect to wanting complete control.'

Brad Cunningham's whole life with other people then had been one of wanting to dominate and to control.

'Would the words "Jekyll and Hyde" be used here?' Shinn asked. Privately, he often referred to Brad as 'either Prince Charming or Darth Vader.'

Dr Turco said that this was just another way of saying 'true self' and 'false self.' He explained that the more a person's private self matched his public self, the more likely he was to be a 'pretty well integrated' person. Brad Cunningham had been two widely disparate 'selves' for more than three decades. His wives had been drawn to a man who was a kind, tender lover – and had awakened to find they were tied to a man who detested all that was female.

Was it possible that Brad had been in the grip of his own psychosis the night of the murder, that he was insane? Turco said he had studied the murder of Cheryl Keeton and discerned the M.O. of a person who had carefully and meticulously planned each detail. Because this was a civil trial, but mostly because Brad had chosen not to present a defense at all, the jurors were able to hear an extremely comprehensive overview of the psychopathology of a narcissist, an antisocial personality – a man certainly capable of murder. No defense attorney jumped to his feet to object.

Shinn asked Turco how a personality like the one they were discussing would relate to his children.

'The children to him are objects, so to speak,' Turco replied. 'In other words, he *owns* them. . . . This is an important issue to consider again. . . . The father in this case wants to say, "My children love me, I have them, I have control," even though they may not [love him]. The other part of it is – he's going to hurt the other person by taking control of the children, a valuable possession, from this mother.'

Turco agreed that the fight over custody of the children, coupled with Cheryl's threat to expose Brad's tax irregularities, was more than enough to provide a murder motive for a man who fit Brad's profile. 'It's the utilitarian use of people for one's own gain . . . malignant narcissism,' Turco said. And this was a character and/or personality disorder that was totally untreatable. Brad Cunningham was not crazy, not insane. In Turco's words, he was 'totally in touch with reality.' He was smart and charismatic and selfish and terribly dangerous – and still a completely free man.

51

It was nearing the middle of May and Brad still had not appeared at his trial. His living ex-wives, however, were not all represented. Sara had testified in person, but Brad's first and third wives were too afraid to do that. Loni Ann's videotaped deposition had been convincing. Cynthia Marrasco had talked only off the record. And only a month before the trial, Shinn had traveled to where Lauren Stoneham lived to ask her questions about her memories of Brad while a court reporter recorded their words. Although Lauren hadn't realized it, she had important information. Brad had called her on October 5, 1986, to tell her that Cheryl had been killed two weeks earlier. At that point, only the time the van had been found – 8:45 P.M. – had been released to the media. 'Brad said that the estimated time of her death was eight-fifteen P.M.,' Lauren told Shinn. 'He said that he had been downstairs in the garage at his apartment house at that time.'

At 11:05 on Thursday morning, May 16, 1991, Mike Shinn began his final arguments. He had to convince twelve jurors that the preponderance of evidence proved that Bradly Morris Cunningham was responsible for causing the death of Cheryl Keeton almost five years earlier. The jurors had listened to more than five dozen witnesses, visited the site of the 'accident,' and looked at scores of photographs. Shinn did not, however, have physical evidence to offer them. His case was purely circumstantial.

Shinn's opening remarks had painted a picture of the kind of woman Cheryl Keeton was, 'one of the most brilliant legal minds in the United States.' All the lawyers who had praised Cheryl, he submitted, were effective witnesses. And yet it was the secretaries, the paralegals, the women she had worked with, who had really given the picture of who Cheryl had been as a mother, a friend, and a human being.

'Once I got involved in the case,' Shinn said, 'we conducted an exhaustive investigation, including interviews with hundreds of people, and not one person in this entire world was found with a bad word to say about her – except perhaps Lauren Swanson . . . who thought Cheryl had stolen her husband, and later we found that wasn't what had happened at all. There was nobody who had any rational reason to murder this woman.'

Shinn then moved through the facts of the case, stressing that not only had Cheryl's killer struck her two dozen times, he had been quite willing to murder other people who were driving on the Sunset Highway the evening of September 21, 1986, and who would have died in a multiple pileup of flaming cars.

Shinn admitted that one of the facets of his investigation was that he kept getting back such 'bizarre' information that he himself doubted it – at first. 'Children's coffins – letters that Mr Cunningham wrote to his mother, to Cheryl, to other people . . . I was afraid to present them to the jury. *If people see this stuff, they're going to think it's just too impossible to believe*. There was no mystery about *who* had killed Cheryl. The questions, Shinn submitted, were 'why?' and 'how?'

He then began a litany of Brad Cunningham's sins, and he used as a framework the letter that Brad had written to his own mother – that diatribe filled with accusations and show-off vocabulary. It was an answer to a letter his mother had never written. Brad had done the same thing to Cheryl – written her answers to questions she had never asked. It was a familiar dodge for him; if answers to letters existed, then those letters must also exist. But all the searching in the world could not turn up the ugly letters Brad loved to cite. They had never been written. His letter to his mother was particularly chilling in that it was a prime example of projection. All the things that Brad accused his mother of were not her flaws, they were his own.

Shinn quoted the experts who had testified about the nature of Brad's behavior. He quoted those who had suffered because of it. 'The horror is unimaginable,' he commented after giving many examples, '– *except* that it's come from so many sources.' But Cheryl had been prepared to stand up to Brad and he could not allow her to live to bring her witnesses into the courtroom. He could not allow her to talk to the IRS. He could not allow her to have sole custody of her sons.

'You know what a Beefeater is?' Shinn asked the jurors. 'I never did until I went to the Tower of London on a rugby tour. I found out a week before this trial from Dr Sardo that Brad asked him to keep a secret. "What is the secret?" I asked Dr Sardo, and he said, "Brad believed that Cheryl and her mother were going to poison him." When I asked Sara if Brad was really serious about the poison plot, she answered, "Yes, he was so serious that he had his own sons sample his food first to make sure Cheryl wasn't poisoning him."

'He was making them Beefeaters,' Shinn said. 'Kings had Beefeaters who would taste their food, and they would watch them for an hour to see if they died of poisoning before they would eat the food. That's how much Mr Cunningham thought of his sons. . . .'

Mike Shinn had spoken for fifty-two minutes when Judge Haggerty broke for the day and those in the courtroom walked, blinking, into the warm May afternoon, their minds filled with the horror of malignant narcissism at work.

Shinn began the next morning with a description of Brad's character, calling him a tyrant and a coward. He commented on Brad's collection of guns, his arsenal, bullet-proof vests, his hideout in the woods, and his police car. 'Where's his military record?' he asked the jury. 'When this country needed men who were really men – that had to use guns – where was Mr Cunningham? He's my age. I haven't heard about any disabilities. Why didn't he go to Vietnam or to the desert? Mr Cunningham was trying to get rich. He was collecting automobiles. MercedesBenzes. Stables of them. . . .'

Shinn pointed out a pattern in Brad's behavior that was so clearly predictable. 'Mr Cunningham uses vehicles against women. . . . Stealing cars. Hiding keys from his wives. . . . When Lauren Cunningham was delivering her baby in the hospital, he calls her up, "I've just repossessed your car."' It was true. Brad collected exotic cars as symbols of his masculinity. He also used them to get even with the women in his life. He had *killed* Cheryl in her car.

Step by step, Shinn reminded the jury of the many 'bizarre' actions that witnesses who knew Brad had testified to. Using charts, photos, maps, and the videotape of the reenactment of the crime, he once more called up the last moments of Cheryl's life. He sounded angry. He *was* angry. It would have been impossible to spend so much time immersed in her life and tragic death without coming away with a compelling need for justice.

Brad Cunningham was not there in that courtroom on Friday, May 16, 1991. But his image was flayed, pinned to the wall, and laid out for the jurors to study. He was a coward, a con man, a sadist, a monstrous father, a faithless husband, a killer.

The jury retired to deliberate. Mike Shinn had not suggested to them a specific amount of damages. He asked only for a verdict that would serve as a memorial to Cheryl 'so that her life didn't end in total vain. You're the only people who may ever have the power and the authority to bring some kind of deliverance to the victims – her little boys. With her death, half of them died too – maybe more. Bring back a verdict that reflects the conscience of you people . . . a verdict that will follow Mr Cunningham around the rest of his life, one that will reflect his ego and that he will take notice of.'

The jury would decide whether to award money for Cheryl's wrongful death, the pain and suffering of her children, and their loss of their mother, as well as punitive and exemplary damages.

Deliberations took a little more than five hours, and even Shinn was shocked at their decision. They had agreed with all of his arguments. They believed that Brad Cunningham had indeed beaten Cheryl Keeton to death. But they went further than he could have imagined. Shinn had privately been hoping that they might return with a judgment of $15 million. He wasn't naive enough to think that the money would ever actually be paid. It would likely be a Pyrrhic victory. Brad would undoubtedly claim poverty.

The jury had added in losses that even Shinn hadn't thought of. There should be money for Jess, Michael, and Phillip to go to college. There should be money for counseling. They announced that they had awarded Cheryl Keeton's estate $81.7 million. It was one of the largest civil judgments – if not *the* largest – in Oregon history.

Interestingly for a man so hard to find, television camera crews had no difficulty locating Brad in Houston. Sitting on a couch in his tastefully appointed apartment with his sons and Dana standing nearby, he said that no one knew the pain he had suffered over Cheryl's death. 'I miss her – terribly. I had nothing to do with her death, and yet my whole life has been ripped apart as if I did,' he said with a slight catch in his voice. He refused to discuss any evidence or suspicions that linked him to Cheryl's murder, but he said, 'Yeah, I would like to know what happened to her. . . .

'This has been a very tough time for my family. And it's very difficult on *me*. I'm not the same person I was a year ago, or two years ago. Just a lot of unnecessary pressures and stresses on the children and I – reading what's been printed in the newspaper, the people not hearing any other side of the story, and us being unable to give that other side of the story. . . .

'I have no money to fight this. The boys and I live on Social Security. We have very little money. We haven't had hot water in our house for some time. We haven't paid our rent – we're not being evicted, but we're leaving.' How could he be expected to pay Cheryl's estate $82 million?

Jess faced the cameras. 'It makes me kind of sad because he had to go through that,' he said. 'He's my dad. I love him. He couldn't have done what they said he did.' And then the cameras followed Brad, Dana, and the boys as they stepped into a taxi. Dana looked like a movie star in her clinging blue dress and dark glasses, and Brad smiled benevolently at his sons.

52

When the trial was over, several jurors said that they were going to write letters to Governor Barbara Roberts and Attorney General Dave Frohnmayer to urge them to seek a criminal indictment against Brad Cunningham. 'I think everyone on the jury felt he was responsible,' said juror William Tyrrel. Charlene Fort, the foreman, said, 'I think he should be tried in a criminal hearing.'

Brad's aunt Trudy Dreesen denounced the trial and

questioned the motives of everyone who had testified against her nephew. 'All this that's being said about him is a landslide of lies and network of half-truths and twisted things,' she said. She would die believing that Brad was a sad young widower who longed only to care for his little boys.

Washington County District Attorney Scott Upham declined comment on the verdict. 'The Keeton case is open and it has always been open,' he said. 'It is being actively investigated by the Oregon State Police.' Pressed, he explained the concept of double jeopardy and the conflict his office had faced since 1986. The civil verdict put the D.A.'s office in an uncomfortably hot spotlight. It had been between a rock and a hard place for almost five years now, agonizing over which way to go to see that permanent justice was done in this case. But it had yet to seek a criminal prosecution against Brad. Mike Shinn had done a masterful job of proving Brad civilly responsible for Cheryl's death. He had given the jurors the 'clear and convincing' evidence required for a wrongful death suit. Still, most people watching television and reading newspapers didn't have the faintest notion of the difference between winning a civil case and winning a criminal conviction.

Shinn now had tossed a gauntlet in Scott Upham's direction. And it wasn't a subtle gauntlet. In his final arguments, he had said in plain language that the justice system in Washington County 'has been either too impotent or too cowardly to deal with it. The legal system has utterly failed with this individual.'

In this case, justice delayed was not justice denied. It was, however, justice delayed once more. Upham had never given up on his quest to gather enough evidence to convict Brad of murder in a criminal court. In a sense, Mike Shinn's civil victory heartened him. But in another sense, it was as if someone had just lit a red-hot fire underneath him.

Shinn had had three distinct advantages in the civil trial: (1) He was unopposed; (2) He had had only to win with the preponderance of evidence, while Upham would have to prove that Brad was guilty beyound a reasonable doubt; and (3) Many witnesses called in the civil trial would be considered 'hearsay' witnesses or witnesses to 'prior bad acts' of the defendant, and never would be allowed on the witness stand in a criminal trial. As Upham explained to *Oregonian* reporter Joan Laatz, 'Those rules are put in place to demand that prosecutors seek justice. Suspicion, feeling, innuendo, and motive do not amount to evidence.' And a man cannot be convicted of murder simply because he is a mean S.O.B. Sometimes 'similar transactions' – similar crimes from a defendant's past – *can* be admitted into a criminal trial, but their admission has often opened the door to appeals.

Upham and his chief investigator, Jim Carr (not Cheryl's brother whose name is spelled 'Karr'), and Oregon State Police Detective Mike McKernan finally decided to pursue a criminal indictment against Brad. If they failed, they failed. If they got a criminal indictment and Brad was acquitted, he would go free. It was a risk Upham was prepared to take.

For Mike Shinn, it was over – or as close to over as it could be for anyone who had ever jousted with Brad Cunningham. Gratefully, he vacated his latest hotel and returned to his houseboat. He was sick of hotel food, sick of city noise, and he wanted to be back in his floating home in the wild preserve. He had no reason to feel any safer; in fact, he had reason to feel less safe. Brad was still free. But the civil trial was finished; two years of intense investigation had paid off. It was time to move on.

Scott Upham was an Oregon native who had attended Portland State University and got his law degree from the University of Oregon. With his thick, rapidly graying hair and a luxuriant mustache, glasses, and tweed jackets, he looked like a college professor. He was serving his fifth term as D.A. of Washington County. Hillsboro is basically a small town, and Upham was so approachable to his constituency that his name was listed in the phone book. It was not unusual for his evenings to be interrupted by someone who had a quarrel with the judicial system of Washington County. 'They have the right to complain,' Upham said. 'It doesn't happen very often, and it helps me keep in touch.'

In his mid-forties, Upham jogged, worked out, and played golf, soccer, and softball. He liked a beer after work and, most of all, a good cigar. He was a familiar and popular figure around Washington County. He was also an excellent courtroom strategist. He knew his cases inside out, and he was rarely surprised by anything the defense might throw at him. He was a man with a wicked, deadpan sense of humor. But by mid-1991, he had lost all sense of humor about Brad Cunningham. Gathering enough evidence to return to a grand jury and secure a murder indictment, and then trying the case in court, would prove to be the toughest challenge of Upham's career. If any man knew the ins and outs of the legal system, it was Brad.

There is a special kind of stress inherent in preparing for a criminal trial – *any* criminal trial – and when it is a homicide case, the stress grows exponentially. Upham and his wife Mary Ann had three children – two daughters and a son. They were planning to build a new house. But with the Cunningham case, Scott and Mary Ann Upham would find that they scarcely saw each other often enough to draw up plans for a chicken coop, much less a house. Before Upham was finished with the probe into Brad's past – both criminal and personal – his office and adjoining rooms would spill over with thirty thick three-ring binders and twenty-four cardboard boxes full of detailed information.

Had Cheryl's body been found a few hundred feet to the east, her murder would have occurred in Multnomah County, the most populated county in Oregon – with, naturally, a much bigger D.A.'s staff. Indeed, the Toyota van was discovered so close to the Washington/Multnomah county line that Upham could still have chosen to decline the case and turn it over to Multnomah County. He just couldn't do that. As she did everyone else, Cheryl Keeton haunted him.

Brad simply ignored the $81.7 million judgment against him in the wrongful death suit in Portland. It was as if it had never happened. He was concerned only with his multimillion-dollar lawsuit against the Houston contractors. He and Dana and his sons were living in Houston again, and living well. He had lost, but in Brad's mind he had won.

Sara had not seen her sons for more than a year, and she was thrilled – if cautious – when she received a letter from Phillip on September 6, 1991. She recognized Brad's distinctive printing on the green-and-white envelope and saw it was from Vinson and Elkins in Houston. Sara immediately wrote to Phillip, enclosing a hundred-dollar check for his birthday, and sent it by certified mail. 'I was so happy to get your letter. I love you, Phillip. How are Jess and Michael? Tell them I miss them too and I love you all very much. . . .'

Sara knew Brad could not resist cashing her check. He would have to show identification, and she hoped she might get the address where the boys were living. She had seen them all on the television news when Brad proclaimed his innocence and pleaded poverty. She had watched, horrified, as Jess faced the cameras and mouthed the words she knew Brad had programmed into his brain – just as he dictated their letters to her.

When her plan to find out his address worked and Sara tried to learn more about the boys, Brad was furious. Jack Kincaid was trying to help her see the boys, and Brad vented his rage on him, too. Kincaid's opinion of Brad was, if anything, lower than Brad's of him. Kincaid never called Brad by name. He referred to him simply as 'Killer.'

To intimidate Sara, Brad resorted to a familiar tactic. He sent a fax to Providence Hospital full of venom and ugly aspersions on her, hoping it would circulate around the hospital.

> Sara . . .
>
> Sara, you suffer from both physical and emotional afflictions . . . demonstrated by your cruel toying with the children's minds and emotions. . . . You also have symptoms of the Burke Syndrome, . . . wherein the sufferer wrongly punishes the minor children of an individual they do not like.
>
> I know so well of the hatred you harbor for me. God knows how you have inaptly [*sic*] demonstrated it in your failed collaboration with Michael Shinn. . . . How you can fabricate and lie under oath amazes me. . . . Your outwardly attractive appearance and seemingly sweet facade hides the conniving control freak that you really are. . . .

In the fax, Brad described Sara as a manipulator and a career wrecker who enjoyed having her friends and associates feel sorry for her and who deliberately contrived stressful situations. He also named names of physicians at Providence and said that Sara had started rumors about them. His loathing and disdain for Sara oozed from every line. He knew how to hurt her, and that was to chip away at her image as a mother and her love for the boys.

> You have a duty to pay child support for Jess, Michael and Phillip. . . . Yes, they have suffered, and YES all I want from you is money. I only wish I could give the boys a mother. . . . You have never learned the art of love and caring necessary to be a parent. . . .
>
> Wise up, Sara. . . . Quit trying to punish me for Lynn . . . I never got a chance to tell you this but . . . you are not good at the heterosexual thing – better watch out for Jack before he finds his "Lynn."
>
> . . . Get a life, pay child support. . . . My only goal in life is to raise my boys to be healthy, inspired, adults. . . . Please, Sara, stay healthy, work hard, make lots of money and pay

> all your back taxes . . . so I can . . . subpoena your ass when it is necessary.
>
> . . . I have a good life with the boys. . . . I am also getting incredible sex – you should be so lucky if she would only give you lessons.

The fax was the antithesis of the love letter Brad had once written to Sara begging her to come back to him. Now he hid nothing. As it so often did, his fury ate like acid on the pages of his handiwork.

> . . . I have ventilated all I want to.
> Thanks, I feel better.
> Brad Cunningham c/o Family in Lynnwood

Fortunately, the scurrilous fax was tossed unceremoniously into the wastebaskets of hospital employees who were all too familiar with Sara's problems with her ex-husband. Brad's letter only served as further proof of his genius for projection. Most of the characteristics he attributed to Sara were his own. And the 'newly discovered' Burke Syndrome was, of course, a slap at John Burke, the trustee of Cheryl's estate.

By the spring of 1992, Brad felt he had done as much as he could on his Texas lawsuit and he told Dana that they would be moving north. Although she had never been that fond of Houston and its humid air that was almost too thick to breathe, Dana had become somebody in that city. She was 'Angel,' the most popular dancer at the Men's Club, a kind of celebrity. And now she had to quit her job and trail after Brad.

Still, the pattern of their relationship had long since been established. When Brad and the boys pulled out of Houston, Dana was with them. They moved first to Mill Creek, an affluent area north of Seattle, where Brad rented a quarter-million-dollar house. Dana had to sign the lease. Brad told her he would never have made it past a credit check. His aunt and uncle, Herm and Trudy Dreesen, lived nearby, virtually the last of Brad's relatives to stay in contact with him.

Dana's world with Brad had become akin to living in a velvet and silky prison, and now she was looking for a way out. Before, there had been times when things were bad, but somehow the good times balanced everything out. That was no longer true. 'I couldn't be with Brad any longer,' Dana said later. 'Things were getting too dangerous – too weird. There are things that I'm still afraid to talk about.'

For one thing, Brad was carrying a gun. And he was building up a small arsenal. He was obsessed with guns, with assault weapons, and with paraphernalia like handcuffs and restraining devices. Dana was back in the Northwest, back where she had friends and family. She wanted desperately to leave Brad. It was not that easy. 'He wouldn't let me go,' she remembered. 'He said, "Just be with me. Just live with me, and we can have an open relationship. Just live with me and I'll take care of you. . . ."' What Brad meant by an open relationship was that Dana could date other men, but she could not stay out all night with them. 'If I came home the next day, I got in trouble.'

Why would she even consider an arrangement like that? Dana had been under Brad's thumb for two years. She had lived *his* life in *his* world. She had dressed the way he wanted her to dress; she had even become an exotic dancer because it was what Brad wanted. He had convinced her that she was too uneducated, too dumb, to ever make it on her own. And yet, within her, there still beat the most primitive need that any human has: the need for freedom. Dana didn't have the strength to leave Brad compeltely. She was afraid of him, and she was afraid that she couldn't make it on her own. She took the only bit of freedom he allowed her – he let her date other men. Even so, she sometimes had the feeling that he was nearby with a camcorder, filming her with other men. It wasn't anything she could ever prove. It was just a feeling that made the back of her neck crawl.

Dana met a very handsome, very nice, young professional man who, ironically, had close connections with the judicial system. They dated, and Dana kept her agreement with Brad; she always came home to sleep. But one night, she didn't come home. It was almost two in the afternoon of the next day when she returned to the huge house in Mill Creek.

Brad met her with an accusation. 'You're in love with him, aren't you?' he shouted.

'No, I'm not,' Dana said truthfully. She had come to enjoy spending time with the young man who treated her like a lady with half a brain in her head. She didn't love him yet, but she loved being with him.

Suddenly, Dana witnessed a terrifying transformation. Brad slipped into the blackest rage she had ever seen. 'He started breaking glass and breaking furniture –' As Dana cringed, horrified, he became almost animal-like, crouching and growling. 'I guess maybe when he played football,' she said later, 'they acted like that. He was making terrible grunting, growling noises, and I ran away from him. He came after me until I was trapped, crouched in the bathtub with my back against the wall.'

Dana thought she was going to die. Brad was so infuriated because she had disobeyed him that he was going to come into the tub and kill her. Her thoughts skittered frantically; what could she say to calm him down? 'I told him I loved him. I kept saying I loved him. He left for a few minutes, and then he walked back in and, oh God, he was carrying a loaded .38 in his right hand. But he had both hands closed around the gun and he was pointing it up at the ceiling. Then he said, "You're gonna hurt me, aren't you? You're gonna hurt me like everyone else."'

As far as Dana knew, Brad had done most of the hurting in his relationships with the women who came before her, but she wasn't about to argue that point with him. 'No!' she cried. 'No, Brad. I'm not going to hurt you. I *love* you!'

'No! You're going to hurt me.'

To Dana it seemed that awful scene took hours and hours, but she knew it probably lasted only fifteen minutes from the time Brad erupted into his animalistic rage until it was over. She was trapped in the tub, screaming out that she loved him and wasn't going to leave him. He was aiming the gun alternately at her and at the ceiling. 'And then suddenly Brad just slid down the wall,' Dana said, 'as if his legs were collapsing under him. I went to him, and he took the gun and put it to his head. He was completely relaxed then, with the gun pointed at his own head. I don't know what he did next. I ran. I took the stairs in two leaps and ran to the neighbors.'

She called the police from the neighbors' house. And the local authorities soon discovered that Washington County, Oregon, investigators were very interested in the whereabouts of one Bradly Morris Cunningham. Oregon detectives came north and took Dana back with them to Portland. She was scared enough, and fed up enough, to want to tell them what she knew about Brad. The problem was, she didn't know that much – although she gave her permission for them to go into the Mill Creek house to remove guns and other paraphernalia there.

'I stayed in a hotel in Seattle the first night, and I didn't sleep,' Dana remembered. 'I didn't sleep in Portland either. I finally went back to Seattle because I was tired. Brad found me. He started with the same thing, "You're my *wife*" – but I wasn't his wife – and "I can't live without you." He made promises. Promises, promises.'

Dana went back to live with Brad. She missed the little boys, and she wanted to believe his promises. It didn't last and she knew that if she ran again, she would have to run farther. Her youngest brother, Barney,* who was only twenty, went up to Seattle to help her get away. 'Barney took me to my sister's house in Florida, and I thought I was safe.'

She wasn't. Frustrated, Brad was a force to be reckoned with. He reverted to type. He gathered together all the pictures he had of Dana in lingerie or revealing costumes and had dozens of prints made. He wrote a devastating letter detailing every small slip from grace that she might ever have made. And then he started faxing. 'Brad faxed letters and photos to my parents, the bank in my little hometown, our church, my parents' friends and customers, all my friends. He told everyone that I was a stripper. He told my parents if they didn't tell him where I was, it would get worse.'

It did. Brad put all of his business schemes on hold and drove to the little town in southern Oregon where Dana had grown up. 'He actually *stalked* my father around town, trying to see if he would lead him to me. He contacted my high-school friends and told them lies.'

Dana shuddered, remembering. 'My mother was so horrified by all the letters and pictures and the things Brad was telling people. I told her, "That's not true, Mom!" Sometimes I blamed my parents for even believing the things he was telling them about me. Brad was clever. He knew how to divide a family, and gradually he was tearing our family apart. He thought I was in Oregon, but I wasn't; I was in Florida. It was my family that he was putting through hell.'

Eventually Brad wore Dana down. She couldn't let him destroy everything her parents had worked for, their position in the town that had been their home for decades. He sent her messages through her family and friends, and the message was always the same: 'For every day you stay away, it's going to be that much worse.' It was too much for Dana. Stronger women than she had been broken by Brad's relentless campaigns. He never quit. He never let up. In time, she knew, he would find her, and in the process her family would be destroyed. She remembered the words he had said to her so often: 'I can wait three years if I have to, to get back at the people who have screwed up my life – because I have patience. I can outwait *anyone*. . . .'

Dana knew that Brad had a long list of people he blamed

for 'screwing up his life.' Mike Shinn was on it. John Burke was on it. Just as Brad insisted her own family was infected with 'Malloyism,' he had invented a disease he now called 'Burkeism,' whose symptoms included everything Burke had done to prevent him from dipping into the assets Cheryl had specifically earmarked for her sons.

Brad had bragged about 'stalking' Burke one day as he left the offices of Garvey, Schubert in Seattle, following him down Madison Street and waiting while Burke, unaware, browsed in a bookstore. Later he found out where Burke lived, and Dana had ridden along when Brad located his house on one of the San Juan Islands. He had brazenly driven up Burke's road and taken his time observing his enemy's house.

Dana knew all too well that when Brad wanted to find someone, he would do it. And in early 1992 he wanted to find her. 'I went back to him,' she later said ruefully. 'I'd had it. But this time, *I* had a plan. If I could convince Brad that he had completely alienated me from my parents, then I figured he would stop sending letters and faxes down there. I told him that I blamed my parents – not him. And he believed me. He left them alone. I had no family any longer, but at least they were safe from him.'

53

Brad never stayed long in one place. He moved from state to state, from town to town, even from house to house in the same town. One day in the summer of 1992 he told Dana that they were going to Canada. So once again they packed up. It wasn't a long trip. Brad had selected White Rock, British Columbia, which is a few miles north of the Canadian border beyond Blaine, Washington, and only a two-and-a-half-hour drive from Lynnwood where the Dreesens lived.

Their White Rock rental was just across the railroad tracks from the beach and the endless stretches of the Straits of Georgia leading to the Pacific Ocean. It was a lovely spot, but Dana could see that Brad was becoming increasingly weird. It was difficult for her even to visualize the handsome young executive who had driven a Mercedes and lived in the Dunthorpe mansion. Brad still spent money, all right, but she had no idea where it came from. She assumed it was some kind of advance on a settlement in the Texas lawsuit. He wasn't working, although he bragged about some projects he and his uncle Herm were discussing.

On July 24, 1992, Brad and Dana had gone down to visit the Dreesens. They were in a grocery store, and Brad suddenly started shoplifting small items. He was laughing; it seemed to be a game. The things he was taking weren't worth very much, but he *was* stealing them. The store's security guard followed Brad into the parking lot and they struggled.

'Brad maced the security guard,' Dana remembered. He was carrying Cap-STUN, a powerful pepper spray police use to stop assailants in their tracks, and he used it on the store guard. He was detained and arrested but refused to give his name. Booked into the Everett, Washington, jail as 'John Doe,' he was eventually identified and bailed out, and disappeared. A felony warrant was issued for his arrest on assault and theft charges.

Back in Canada, things were tense that summer. Brad talked a lot about the 'apocalypse' that was coming. He seemed obsessed with natural disasters and what would happen to them if one occurred. Dana didn't know what the apocalypse was, but it made her nervous hearing Brad talk about it all the time.

Sara tried, in vain, to see the boys the summer they were in White Rock. Brad always waited until the last minute to notify her that she had to be in Vancouver or Victoria within twenty-four hours if she wanted to see Jess, Michael, and Phillip. Dana knew he was making it impossible for Sara to get there in time from Portland.

Brad had always been a stern disciplinarian with his sons, but there was one incident that summer that unnerved Dana. He had a puzzle ring, silver links that could be entwined so they looked all of a piece. One day one of the boys was playing with it and lost it. Brad was enraged. 'He asked Jess, Michael, and Phillip which one of them had done it,' Dana recalled. 'And none of them would admit to losing his ring. He got the car and we all went for a drive, and all the while he was trying to get the guilty kid to confess. They were scared, but they wouldn't tell.'

When they came to a lonely place, far from town, Brad opened the car door and ordered the boys out. 'You'll stay here until you decide to tell me the truth,' he growled, and then drove off as Dana watched the three little boys' images grow smaller in the sideview mirror. She pleaded with Brad to go back for them, but he wouldn't. Jess was not yet twelve, Michael was nine, and Phillip was seven. It would be dark soon. What if the boys tried to find their way back and got on the railroad tracks? What if some pervert found them out there alone?

After a long, long time, Brad turned the car around and drove back to where he had left his sons. They were waiting there, huddled together, and Jess quickly confessed to losing the puzzle ring. 'But I don't think he did it. He just confessed to save the others,' Dana said. 'Brad did that often, dumping the kids way out in the tules someplace. I think he always went back because he needed them. He used to tell me, "These children are my assets."'

The strange summer of 1992 passed. They were living in a picturesque paradise, but Dana felt as if she and the three boys were moving through a minefield, never sure what Brad might do next.

In the fall, they went back to Washington and moved into

a much smaller house in Mill Creek, rented again in Dana's name. Dana knew she had to get away from Brad, but this time she was planning her escape carefully. 'I'd cut off my family, so Brad couldn't write to them. I had no contact with them. I *really* had no contact with them, so it wouldn't do him any good to start sending letters and faxes again.'

Dana told Brad she wanted to move out for a little while. She didn't dare give him the impression that she was leaving him for good. 'I told him, "I can't live with you all the time, but I'll still be with you. I won't be out of your life totally. I'll see you on Sundays, and I'll be here for holidays and for the boys' birthdays. You'll all be living with Uncle Herm soon, and I'll be with you a lot."'

Brad watched Dana's face carefully, searching to see if she was telling him the truth. He had always found her transparent and, of course, he considered her vastly inferior to him in intelligence. 'I guess he half believed me,' Dana remembered. 'He let me go, but he stalked the crap out of me. My tires were slashed. There were bullet holes in my bedroom window. Once I found a stack of bills in his room from the Blue Moon Detective Agency. He'd hired them to follow me.'

Dana couldn't support herself cutting hair and selling makeup – or perhaps she could, but Brad had introduced her to a lifestyle that was hard to forget. She found a job dancing at one of the places on the strip north of Seattle. Rainbow's* wasn't nearly as classy as the Men's Club, but 'Angel' was back in business and was soon a favorite with the crowd. She was living the life that Brad had programmed her for.

Dana kept her promise to be with Brad and the boys on weekends, even though she knew that he was either following her himself or paying Blue Moon to do it. She was there for Phillip's ninth birthday party just before Thanksgiving. To this day she can recite Jess's, Michael's, and Phillip's birthdays – date and year – by rote. Like all their 'mothers,' she cared about Brad's sons.

* * *

That fall, Brad talked continually of new building projects and what he would do with all the money he was going to realize from his Texas lawsuit. Herm and Trudy Dreesen were still supportive, but Trudy was terminally ill. Her breast cancer had metastasized to her bones. Even so, she was helping take care of Jess, Michael, and Phillip.

Herm Dreesen listened to Brad talk about the money to be made from multiple-unit construction projects. No one could be more convincing than Brad. He knew real estate, he knew banking, and he knew construction. If he hadn't had a problem with his contractors in Houston, he would have been a rich man by now. But Brad was still only forty-four and he was prepared to share his knowledge with his uncle Herm, who was a dozen years older.

Herm and Trudy Dreesen had been good friends with a couple their own age for a long time. 'Herm approached us about going in together on some property development,' the wife would recall. 'The way it began, Herm was going to put up the money and we were going to put in this piece of property we had. It sounded like a good idea, and Herm introduced us to his nephew, Brad Cunningham. We liked him at first; he was charming and knew the business and it sounded like a great idea. We thought it would be wonderful.'

The Dressens' friends tore down an existing house on their property, a rental, in preparation for the construction of a forty-two-unit apartment complex. 'Right away, we lost our income from the rental,' the wife said. 'And, of course, we had the cost of the demolition and clearing. And *then* this Brad Cunningham, Herm's nephew, wanted us to co-sign for a million-and-a-quarter loan! We had understood that our part was to provide the land.'

It got worse. They also discovered that, if they did agree to sign for the loan, there were clauses stipulating that they would have absolutely no control over how the loan was administered. Brad would handle all the money. 'We pulled out, and there were hard feelings with Herman and we felt bad,' the husband said. 'But we couldn't co-sign on a loan that large and have no say in how it was spent. We lost the house, but we still had the land. . . .'

Brad was furious with them for not having the vision to let him handle their land *and* their money. It clearly was to have been his way back up the ladder of success. Meanwhile the suit in Texas dragged on as Vinson and Elkins continued its work on the case.

Brad had always intimidated Dana and now he scared her. 'By that fall of 1992, I had started carrying a gun for protection,' she said. 'I didn't think much about it at the time, but at Phillip's birthday party, Brad asked to borrow my gun. He just said, "I need your gun," and I said, "Not a problem," and gave it to him. I realized later that he had something planned for me and he wanted to make sure I wasn't armed.'

Dana had made a platonic friend of one of the muscular bouncers at Rainbow's, Denny Johnson.* On December 9 Brad and Dana argued, and she could sense he was working up toward the kind of rage she had seen before. She called Denny and asked him for protection. And then she decided to pack up her things and move to another location where it wouldn't be so easy for Brad to find her.

'I was going to meet Denny at the Fred Meyer [store] parking lot. I tried to put my stuff in the trunk of my car – it was a 1989 Mitsubishi – but the trunk lock seemed to be broken. I couldn't get it to turn. I just threw my stuff in the backseat and headed for Fred Meyer. I waved Denny down, and he stood by while I forced my trunk open.'

There was a body in her trunk. Dana screamed when the 'body' moved, and Denny drew his handgun and shouted, 'Whoever's in there, get out!'

Brad, a phantomlike figure dressed completely in a black spandex body suit, crawled out of Dana's trunk. With Denny Johnson standing by, he had no choice but to leave. 'I called my dad, and he called the Oregon State Police,' Dana said, 'and we both gave reports to them. I think that Brad borrowed my gun deliberately at Phillip's party because it was only two days after that when he was hiding in my trunk, dressed like that. If I'd been alone . . .'

Brad had a ready excuse for hiding in Dana's trunk. 'I was only trying to hook up a listening device,' he told her – as if to say, 'Doesn't everybody?'

A cousin recalled visiting Brad in late 1992 or early 1993. Brad bragged that the previous spring, after Dana called the authorities and they had surrounded his block, he had driven through the police lines five times and they never knew who he was. He was apparently amazed to see them there. 'They tore up my house,' he said plaintively. He told his cousin that Dana had been 'kidnapped' by the Oregon State Police then and that they were keeping her now in Portland against her will. Brad's preoccupation with what law enforcement officials in Oregon were doing was obvious. And, six years after the fact, he gave his cousin yet another version of where he was on the night Cheryl died. 'He started mumbling about how he couldn't have killed Cheryl. He said he wasn't even in Oregon the night she died. He said he was in a laundromat on Bainbridge Island.'

With Dana gone, Brad had become what he had always said he was – the primary parent. His three young sons were now completely at his mercy.

54

Brad might have walked away from his civil judgment, but he had not shrugged off the losses in his life as easily as he pretended. He was growing more and more paranoid. He had every reason to feel paranoid. Since late January 1993, a grand jury in Washington County had been listening to some ninety-one witnesses describe the events leading to Cheryl's murder. For nine weeks the jurors met behind closed doors. And since grand jury proceedings are secret, no one knew if they were close to handing down a criminal indictment of murder against Brad.

When he realized he no longer had Dana under his control, Brad was shocked that she, of all his women, had been able to walk away from him. He had been so busy convincing her that she was dumb that *he* believed it too. And yet she had been able to get away from him by leaving without really leaving. When he finally caught on that he was seeing her less and less, he panicked. Unlike the other women he had let go, he was obsessed with getting Dana back. She was many things to him. She was a meal ticket. She was young, sexy, and extremely beautiful. And she knew things about him that he never wanted her to tell.

Brad wasn't finished with Dana, nor was he finished with Sara. He still needed them both – for different reasons. He had told Sara that he detested her, but he wanted her to 'stay healthy' so he could sue her for child support. He had really been scrambling for money. He had sold the little rental house in Tampico – the house he always referred to as 'the boys' house' – and collected a $40,000 balloon payment. They never saw the money; Brad bought a truck and trailer with it, and a Macintosh computer.

On February 23, 1993, he kept his promise to seek child support from Sara by filing a motion in Multnomah County Circuit Court. In his affidavit Brad said he was unemployed while Sara earned about $350,000 a year. He stated that he was the 'full-time primary care' parent of his sons and was commuting to Yakima, Washington, to work on the 'family home.' No mention was made of the mountain of debts he had saddled Sara with when they divorced.

* * *

District Attorney Scott Upham and his investigators in Washington County were getting antsy. They were more so when they learned from Greg Dallaire at Garvey, Schubert that Judge Sharon Armstrong had received a surprise phone call from Dana Malloy. Mike McKernan called Dana and learned that Brad was getting ready to vanish.

On March 16, 1993, Brad had gone to Dana's house in a rage and accused her of talking to the Oregon State Police. He told her that she had betrayed him and now he was about to be indicted on murder charges. Jess and Michael had been subpoenaed to appear before the Washington County grand jury and Brad was in a panic. 'You can mess with me – but don't mess with my kids,' he warned. He told Dana that he would never, *never* allow his sons to testify before a grand jury again. Dana had been frightened enough to call the Seattle police to have Brad removed from her premises.

Then on Sunday, March 21, Brad had called Dana and talked to her for two hours. He told her that before he allowed his children to go to Oregon to testify before the grand jury, he would leave the country. His voice softened and he urged her to come back to him. She could go with them when they fled America. They would be together, just like old times.

Dana told McKernan she knew that Brad had done thorough research on both Mexico and Chile by going to the library and by talking to people who had lived there. This wasn't something new. Fleeing the country had long been his alternative plan if he ever felt pushed to the wall. Brad had had passports for himself and the boys since May of 1990. Now he told Dana that he planned to take Jess, Michael, and Phillip to Chile; he had already arranged for them to live with a Chilean family.

Dana was ambivalent. Part of her still loved Brad, the other part was afraid of him. She told him that she couldn't be with him because of what had happened to Cheryl. Brad said *he* wasn't the one who had killed Cheryl; he personally believed that the killer was probably someone from Garvey, Schubert – one of the men Brad claimed Cheryl was sleeping with. 'I was going to depose this guy in our divorce,' he said, 'and his wife would have found out and then *he* would have gotten divorced and it would have cost him a lot of money.'

'I want to know, Brad,' Dana pleaded. 'I want you to make me believe you didn't kill Cheryl.'

Brad was quite willing to do that. As Dana later told Mike McKernan, he said he was home with his sons all night, and the only time he left was to do laundry and to put something in his car. 'I wasn't *gone* long enough for them to say I did it.'

Brad went into greater detail with Dana than he had with anyone else, adding the information that 'the police never found blood under my nails.' He talked on and on, certain he was convincing her that he was safe to be with. He told her that Cheryl was involved with cocaine and that she used cocaine with people in her law firm. 'Maybe someone into drugs killed Cheryl Keeton,' he said.

As Dana listened, Brad became more and more specific about names involved in the investigation of Cheryl's murder. She suddenly recalled seeing the name 'Sharon Armstrong' in some police files Brad had once shown her, and she asked him how Judge Armstrong fit into the picture of Cheryl's murder. Brad was instantly upset. He said she must be hiding something from him and he accused her of talking to Judge Armstrong.

Dana hadn't talked to Sharon Armstrong, but now she wanted to. She scribbled that name down as Brad continued to talk. He told her he couldn't let his kids go before a grand jury because it would 'ruin' them. And he asked her again to go with him when they left America. 'If you don't go with me when I leave, Dana – there will be an "apocalypse" and I won't be around to be indicted.'

Dana was beginning to believe that Brad really was going. He had always told her in the past that, if he had to leave, she would know because he would turn off his voice mail. Now he said, 'I have brought you my last gift, and I am turning off my voice mail.'

He did not go. He continued to harass Dana, creeping up to her house late at night and banging on her walls. He shouted at her, 'I want all the information you have, Dana!' And he attached another listening device to her phone, recording her calls. It may well have been that he wanted his 'Angel' dead. And it is just as likely that he was still obsessed with her sexually. 'He always wanted me back,' Dana recalled, bewildered. 'He was very jealous. . . . He phoned me so often in those first months of 1993. He told me that he had consulted a psychic. He said the psychic told him that four men had killed Cheryl and then the psychic said that I was going to commit suicide.'

Dana shivered when she repeated that phrase to Mike McKernan. She knew what it meant. He thought he had enough power over her mind to make her take her own life. Brad had always been able to persuade her to do things she didn't really want to do. It would be very convenient for him now if she *did* commit suicide. Then he could be sure she would never testify before the grand jury in Hillsboro.

But Dana had become obsessed with knowing the truth. She located Judge Sharon Armstrong's number and called her, identifying herself as a former girlfriend of Brad's. Not surprisingly, Sharon was disturbed to hear from anyone connected with Brad. Dana confided that she had information about Brad, but that she was frightened. 'He could have me killed if I came forward.'

Dana had trusted Sharon enough to leave two phone numbers with her. And Sharon had passed them on to OSP Detective Mike McKernan.

The world was closing in around Brad. McKernan was working closely with D.A. Scott Upham's office, helping to tighten the net. It was true that the Washington County grand jury wanted to hear testimony from Jess and Michael

Cunningham. On March 12, the subpoena documents were sent to the Snohomish County Prosecutor's office in Everett, Washington, ordering that Bradly Morris Cunningham be compelled to produce Jess and Michael before the Washington County grand jury on March 25. Snohomish County authorities were hopeful that they could get Brad to come to the courthouse in Everett voluntarily with his sons so they might be served. He responded by saying that he had hired an attorney for his children. McKernan asked to be notified about any hearings in Snohomish County where Brad was expected to appear. He advised the Washington authorities of Dr Herman Dreesen's address. When contacted, Dreesen said it would be up to Brad to bring the children in. He would not override his nephew's decisions.

As he always had, Brad contested every legal document that came his way. Day after day, he had more delaying tactics. Finally Gloria Parker, a legal assistant for the Snohomish County Prosecutor's office, informed McKernan that Brad and his attorney were scheduled to appear in the Everett courtroom at 4 P.M. on March 25 and promised to do so – *if* the court did not require them to bring the children.

Brad knew the authorities were breathing down his neck. They had little doubt that he would, as he had told Dana, flee the country before he would submit himself or his sons to questioning. No way was he going to appear willingly in that courtroom in Everett, and if they didn't move fast, he and the boys would be on a plane to Chile or Mexico.

On Thursday, March 25, 1993, Scott Upham and investigators Jim Carr and Mike McKernan had reason, finally, to smile – and to take a deep breath. Even without hearing Jess and Michael Cunningham's testimony, the grand jury had handed down a secret indictment charging Bradly Morris Cunningham with the murder of his wife Cheryl Keeton on September 21, 1986. The jurors believed the testimony they had heard, and stated their conclusion that Brad had killed his estranged wife by beating her on the head twenty-one times with an unknown blunt instrument.

Now Upham and his team could get their arrest warrant. But their biggest fear was that Brad had somehow learned of the indictment and had already bolted and run, taking Jess, Michael, and Phillip with him. They had done their best to keep a lid on the grand jury proceedings, and there was no news release on the indictment. Brad was aware the police were watching him. But maybe he didn't know they were now ready to move in on him. Brad had always been the stalker. He was now playing a completely different role. He was the one being stalked.

McKernan flew to Washington before dawn to be sure he was in Everett when the arrest warrant arrived. Word was that Brad still had plenty of weapons. When the Mill Creek police checked back at the house where he had collected a virtual arsenal, they found almost every interior wall smashed; they speculated that Brad had been removing additional guns from their hiding places.

Above all, McKernan wanted to facilitate a nonviolent arrest by working with authorities in Snohomish County. He contacted Captain Don Nelson of the Snohomish County Sheriff's office, and Nelson assigned Sergeant Kevin Prentiss to coordinate Brad's apprehension.

It was 2:25 P.M. on March 25, 1993. The no-bail murder warrant – C930434CR – for the arrest of Brad Cunningham was entered into the NCIC (National Crime Information Center) computers. At 3:43 P.M. Jim Carr faxed a copy of the arrest warrant from Scott Upham's office in Hillsboro, Oregon. In the best of all worlds, Brad would show up at the courthouse in Everett at 4:00 P.M. as he had promised.

At 4:20 P.M. Doug Purcell, the boy's attorney, arrived at the Snohomish Courthouse – without Brad. He said Brad had informed him he could not be there. He was in Burien, Washington, picking up items needed for a civil trial in Yakima the next day and said 'he couldn't make' this court appearance.

At 4:45 P.M. McKernan spoke to a records clerk at

Yakima County Superior Court. Brad's civil trial there (which involved his selling of properties that were legally in Cheryl Keeton's estate) had been rescheduled to April 16 – and all parties were informed, Brad included.

At 7:45 P.M. McKernan observed the black Isuzu Trooper that Dana said was Brad's vehicle parked at Herman Dreesen's house.

At 8:05 P.M. the Snohomish County Sheriff's office SWAT team and McKernan gathered near Dreesen's house while Deputy David Vasconi stationed his patrol unit across the street so he could watch the residence. The waiting lawmen observed a Jeep Wagoneer and a new maroon sedan drive away. Mike McKernan couldn't help feeling nervous. What if they were watching Dreesen's house while Brad was boarding a plane for Chile? He knew how adept he was at slipping through police lines.

At 9:31 P.M. Sergeant Tim Shea called the house using his cell phone. All he got was Dreesen's answering machine.

At 9:41 P.M. Shea called the residence and spoke with Dreesen. Brad's uncle confirmed that he was inside the residence. Brad came on the line and was informed that the officers had a warrant for his arrest. 'We request that you exit the house now. If you don't, we will obtain a search warrant and the SWAT team is coming in.' Brad asked for more time. He said he would call the police mobile phone to let them know when he was coming out.

Outside in the dark, officers had completely surrounded the perimeter of the residence. Minutes later, they saw a large white male come out of the back door and look around. Apparently spotting the waiting police, he turned and went back inside.

At 10:03 P.M. Brad came out of the house, accompanied by his uncle. Deputy Vasconi drove his patrol car to the front of the house and watched as Brad obeyed orders to put his hands up and walk slowly toward the patrol car. 'When the suspect reached me,' Vasconi wrote in his report, 'I had him get down on his knees, at which time I placed him into handcuffs.'

Brad's arrest was almost anticlimatic. He had put up no fight at all; he hadn't even tried to run – not when he realized his uncle's property was alive with cops. He was searched for weapons and put into the back of the patrol car. Mike McKernan advised Brad of his rights under Miranda and asked if he would like to explain his side of the story.

Brad looked at McKernan and said flatly, 'I want to talk with my attorney.'

'Does that mean that you don't want to talk to me – *ever*?' McKernan asked.

Brad simply repeated, 'I want to talk to my attorney.'

That was no surprise to McKernan; he knew his prisoner had had almost as many attorneys as a law-school graduating class. Their names and faces changed continually. Brad scarcely went to the bathroom without consulting an attorney.

McKernan asked Dreesen if he might speak with Jess and Michael about what they remembered of the night their mother died, but Dreesen shook his head. 'I would be bitterly opposed to you talking with the kids. If I could grab you by the neck and tell you, "Don't hurt these kids!" I would.'

The last thing in the world McKernan wanted to do was hurt Cheryl Keeton's children. On that matter, he was in complete agreement with Dreesen. But sometime, somehow, there had to be a way for the boys to release whatever was buried in their memories.

Brad was driven to the Snohomish County jail. On the way, he attempted to talk to Vasconi. 'This has been hard on my children,' he said. 'I was going to come to the police department . . .'

'I don't want to talk to you,' Vasconi said.

For once, Brad shut up.

He had plummeted a long, long way down from the successful bank executive and millionaire builder. On his knees, in handcuffs, silhouetted in the lights of police units, he had not made a very prepossessing picture. It had taken six years, six months, four days, and two hours, but he was finally facing criminal charges for Cheryl's vicious murder. The charge he was booked under was 'Fugitive from Justice.'

A bail hearing was held at one the next afternoon. Brad had retained yet another lawyer, James Tweety, to oppose his extradition to Oregon. The hearing was conducted by video linkup between the jail where Brad was being held and Superior Court Judge Richard Thorpe's courtroom. During the course of the hearing, Brad interrupted the proceedings and asked to speak to his attorney.

He then began a lengthy statement in which he essentially blamed the women in his life for his current predicament. He said that Dana Malloy had given him an Uzi as a gift; otherwise he would not have had such a weapon. He said that he had lived with Dana for three years, that she was a stripper, and that he had finally broken up with her. All the charges coming out of Oregon were the fault of one of his former wives, Dr Sara Gordon. Brad suggested that both Dana and Sara had set him up to seek revenge – Dana because he had left her, and Sara because he was suing her for child support.

As Brad watched the television image from his jail cell, Judge Thorpe set his bail. Brad always talked in millions, and his bail fit his lifestyle: $2.5 million. David Wold, a legal assistant in the Snohomish County Prosecutor's office, said that he would have to post cash bail of $250,000 and post a security deposit for the remaining $2,250,000.

Brad didn't have $250,000.

A hearing was set for April 23 when the court expected to review the bail and to consider extradition requests from Oregon. For the first time in his life, Brad was behind bars, dressed in jail issue clothes, treated like a criminal. It is quite possible that he never really considered that such a thing might come to pass.

McKernan made one more effort to talk with Brad before he returned to Oregon. He explained to James Tweety that Brad had said repeatedly in television interviews and to newspaper reporters that all he wanted was a chance to 'tell his side of the story.' McKernan was willing to listen.

Tweety reported back that his client had nothing to say to any representative of the Oregon State Police or the Washington County District Attorney's office. Disappointed, but not particularly surprised, McKernan headed home.

55

Jess, Michael, and Phillip stayed with their father's recently widowed uncle Herman. He had grown to love them, but caring for three young boys was a daunting task for Dreesen, who had a busy medical practice and no woman in the house to help. Moreover, he was still grieving for his kind, beautiful wife. Jess was thirteen, Michael was eleven, and Phillip was nine. Their mother had been dead for six and a half years, they hadn't seen their adoptive mother, Sara, for almost three years, their aunt Trudy was dead too, and their temporary 'mother' Dana was virtually gone from their lives. They had lived in Houston, Portland, Seattle, Lynnwood, and Canada, traveling continually. The central figure in their world was their father – he had seen to that. Now they had watched him kneeling in handcuffs and escorted to a patrol car by uniformed officers. Brad had been correct in his statement to Deputy David Vasconi. His arrest had been 'very hard' on his children.

Even so, Dreesen noticed that the boys were less reclusive and more animated after their father was out of the house.

They had never dared to speak back to him on any subject, but as Dreesen commented to another of Brad's relatives, 'Once Brad was in jail, and calling to talk with the boys, sometimes I've noticed that they actually disagree with him. . . .' Jess, Michael, and Phillip were no longer the obedient automatons that Brad had programmed. They were brilliant young boys, beginning to assert themselves, but they must have been terribly confused.

Sara Gordon read the news of Brad's arrest. The *Oregonian* headlined it 'Jury Indicts Man Six Years After Murder.' It confirmed what she had finally come to believe: that Brad had indeed murdered Cheryl. But she worried constantly about Jess, Michael, and Phillip. She had managed to go on with her life; she had had no choice. Brad was suing her for child support, but he had made it impossible for her to see her sons. They had been little boys when they went away, and now Jess was in his teens.

Sara and Jack Kincaid had renewed their romance. He had been there for her when she needed someone solid – someone who told the truth. They were considering marriage and had purchased a secluded house that fronted on Lake Oswego. ('I loved that house more than any other I've ever had,' she would remember.) They had been in their new home for two months when Brad was arrested.

Brad's indictment meant that Sara would again be in a witness chair for days of testimony. This time, Brad would be in the courtroom, and she knew he would instruct his attorneys to go for her throat. If that had to be, it had to be. But it was something she dreaded. She wasn't alone. Every other woman ever involved with Brad dreaded the thought of once more testifying against him. Their fear wasn't something they could explain – not to someone who hadn't lived through it.

Sara had never had children of her own, and Jack had raised his two. They had planned a life without children, although Sara knew she would always miss the sons she had been allowed to have for only a short time. But now Brad's arrest meant that Jess, Michael, and Phillip, by law, might be returned to her. Sara was their legal mother and she wanted them back. But she wanted to be sure they were comfortable with her. She had no idea what Brad might have told them in the last three years. She had listened to their angry voices yelling at her on the phone, heard Brad coaching them in the background. For all she knew, her sons might be completely brainwashed by now and consider her the ultimate enemy, the real cause of their father's downfall.

Sara got in touch with Herm Dreesen and they talked about what would be best for the boys. The weekend after Brad's arrest, Betty and Marv Troseth and Sara and Jack went up to Dreesen's house to see Jess and Michael and Phillip. They moved very gently and very slowly. They had some idea what the boys had been through. And they knew the boys were seeing relatives they hadn't been allowed any contact with for years – relatives their father had told them were dangerous and evil.

Ever so slowly, the ice melted. Sara had never been anything but loving to her sons, and they began to remember that. They began to remember 'Mom' and they began to remember their grandmother, Betty Troseth. 'Every weekend after that,' Sara said, 'I went up to Lynnwood to spend time with them. Herm and I agreed that they should finish the school year up there, but that it would be best if they came back to live with me and Jack.'

Brad continued to fight extradition to Washington County, Oregon. He was finally transported to Hillsboro and arraigned on murder charges on May 6, 1993, in the county where Cheryl had died. On June 6, Brad pleaded 'not guilty' to murder charges.

If Jess, Michael, and Phillip hadn't gone to live with Sara, they would probably have been placed in a foster home. It was their decision and they picked Sara. But it was not going to be an easy road.

On June 22, 1993, Sara and Jack drove to Lynnwood and brought the boys home to Lake Oswego. By that time they had come to a decision about their relationship. The future they had planned together had to take a backseat to Sara's sons. 'Sara and I had finally gotten to the point where most of the financial messes Brad created were resolved or under control,' Kincaid remembered. 'We had a great life together and it looked even brighter, despite the lingering concern about Brad's continued legal harassment and some issues of personal safety. . . . Bingo! Brad gets arrested. Because I knew it wouldn't work with me living in the same home as Brad's three children, Sara leased a home for herself and the boys . . . where she lives at this time. Obviously, this has taken a toll on our relationship, but not on our friendship. . . .'

Sara had made her choice, the only choice she felt she could make. Jack stayed in the house on the lake for a while, they still saw each other, but it wasn't the same.

Brad was rapidly running out of family to support him – both emotionally and financially. Herm Dreesen finally realized that he was merely expedient to his nephew. That was brought home loud and clear when Brad assumed his uncle would pay for criminal defense lawyers, and referred prospective attorneys to Dr Dreesen. Estimating conservatively, a murder defense was going to cost two hundred thousand dollars. Dreesen had backed Brad for years now, given him and his children a home, advanced money to him, tried to get a building project started, but there was no way he could afford legal fees like that. With his refusal to guarantee Brad's legal expenses, his uncle Herm became another one of Brad's 'enemies.' He told the court that he was indigent. The State of Oregon would have to provide him with an attorney. But as always, he would continue to go through attorneys the way a hot knife cuts through butter.

56

Sara hired a nanny to be with Jess, Michael, and Phillip when she was at the hospital. She was happy to see that they were all accomplished on the Mac computer that Brad had bought them, and that they still loved sports. They began to rebuild their lives together, steadily narrowing the emotional distance that three years had wrought. Sara signed the boys up for tennis, baseball, and basketball, and chauffeured them around herself. She went to every one of their games she could. Jess loved to fish, Michael – who was the image of Cheryl – had a great sense of humor, and Phillip had real talent as a cartoonist. At first, Phillip's drawings were mostly black on black, but gradually he began to use yellow crayons, flooding his work with 'sunshine.'

Meanwhile, as Brad awaited trial, Sara had little sunshine in her life beyond her sons. She was under almost constant siege – by phone and by mail – from the man who gave his return address as 'cunningham dad, Washington County Jail, 146 N.E. Lincoln Street, Hillsboro, OR.' Brad addressed his letters to 'Cunningham' or 'Cunningham Boys/3.' The envelopes were decorated with cartoons demeaning Sara, and with pornographic references to Jack, whom Brad had dubbed 'The Infamous Lake Oswego Weasel – Mr G.Q.'

Brad had always related to his sons in an oddly demarcated manner. He demanded absolute and unquestioning obedience from them because he was their father, and yet he often treated them as peers, as small adults whom he dragged into press conferences and discussions that would be terribly upsetting to any child. Sara was trying to protect them now, but Brad did everything he could to undermine her.

He phoned his sons often and Sara accepted the collect calls. But it was soon obvious that Brad was telling his sons outrageous lies about her. She did not cut off his phone contact with the boys, but she informed Brad in writing that she would be taping his calls and monitoring what was said. It scarcely slowed Brad down. He told the boys they would be better off in a foster home than living with Sara. He said she was a lesbian who hated men, 'and *you* are little men.' He berated them for calling her Mom 'after all she's done.' He suggested to his sons that Sara was giving them drugs.

Sara was trying to follow counselors' advice; she didn't want to cut the boys off completely from their father. But understandably, she didn't want them to listen to a steady stream of propaganda against her either. It was hard to find a middle ground.

Brad's first state-appointed attorney was Timothy Dunn. Dunn was a capable attorney, but he was a mild-mannered man and his client would find fault with almost everything he did. Even in court appearances, it was soon obvious to spectators that Brad intended to run the show. He was always tugging at Dunn's sleeve or whispering in his ear.

The first real skirmish in what would prove to be a long, long road to a criminal verdict took place in Judge Alan C. Bonebrake's courtroom 309-C in the historic Washington County Courthouse on August 24, 1993. Brad was seeking to be released from jail on bail pending his criminal trial. Not surprisingly, Scott Upham wanted Cunningham kept inside the Washington County jail. If ever a defendant had shown a tendency to disappear, it was this one.

Only a handful of spectators waited on benches outside Judge Bonebrake's courtroom. Mike Shinn was there, Betty and Marv Troseth, Jim Karr, Jack Kincaid, a few reporters. It might well have been a simple traffic or domestic dispute hearing for all the interest Brad's bail hearing aroused.

A broad-shouldered man dressed in a dark suit – probably an attorney from the look of him – approached the courtroom door. He was carrying a huge file, and he had to juggle it as he tried to turn the knob. He scrupulously ignored the others waiting to get in. Only on a closer look were the handcuffs on his wrists apparent. It was Brad. He wasn't alone; he was followed by two court officers, J. C. Crossland, a huge man who stood six feet seven and weighed a good 250 pounds, and a slender female security officer. Their eyes never left Brad. He moved into the courtroom easily. If he was embarrassed or felt diminished by his restraints, he didn't show it.

The bail hearing would take more than four days – as long as most trials. Scott Upham gave an overview of his case and presented more than twenty-five witnesses. The small gallery saw a minitrial, the 'Cliff's notes' of the real trial to come. Featuring a parade of witnesses beginning with paramedic Tom Duffy and ending with Oregon State Police criminalist Julia Hinkley, the proceedings were fascinating, intense, and comprehensive.

A handful of attractive women who had once loved Brad took the witness stand. They answered Upham's questions – but almost reluctantly, offering no more than they were asked. One spectator commented later in the hallway, 'You know why they're not talking, don't you? They're scared to death he may be getting out on bail!'

Defense Attorney Tim Dunn argued that the State had no direct evidence linking his client to Cheryl Keeton's murder, and that witnesses' memories had become so faulty with the passage of time that they gave conflicting statements. On Friday, August 27, 1993, however, Judge Bonebrake ruled that Upham had met the State's burden of proof in presenting evidence to show why Brad should be held over for trial without bail.

The first trial date was set for January 1994. But Brad had fired Dunn as his attorney and could not, of course, proceed. He needed time for his new attorneys to get up to speed on his case, and there were voluminous files for them to go through. His new court-appointed attorneys were two of the best criminal defense attorneys in the state of Oregon: Tim Lyons and J. Kevin Hunt. Hunt was an expert on DNA and a superior researcher, and Lyons was smooth, sharp, and quick on his feet. Hunt was an intense young man who rarely smiled; Lyons was more laid back and smiled often.

There was a scheduling problem. In fact, there were to be problems month after month. Hearings would be set and postponed. Lyons was involved with another murder trial in which the victim was a small child. It was impossible for him to know when he could go to trial with Brad. An omnibus hearing was on the docket for June 6, put off until June 14, and then rescheduled for July 5. Omnibus hearings take place before the trial itself to give both sides a chance to bring up issues that concern them and may be ruled on before the trial begins. In many trials, it saves time. No one could yet have any idea how time-consuming Brad's legal manueverings would be.

As the weeks passed, Brad continued to bombard Sara's home with letters and phone calls. He knew that his calls and letters were being monitored and that Sara had informed Judge Bonebrake that she was going to do so to protect the boys. Brad rarely failed to complain about that on the envelopes. One envelope had a cartoon of a rabbit. The balloon over its head read, '. . . and I thought I had *big* ears!' Another cartoon of a child talking into the phone read, 'You mean she's still doing it? . . . Man, she's either a straight up freak, or dominantly stupid!!' Beneath the phone, Brad had printed 'TAP-TAP-TAP.' Most of the envelopes' cartoons had to do with sex, vibrators, batteries, and sexual toys most fathers would not discuss with preadolescent boys.

For years Brad had kept his sons continually on the move to be reassured that they would not testify at a grand jury hearing or in a trial. He was doing his best now to continue influencing them through phone calls and letters. In June 1994, with his trial date scheduled for August, he hand-printed a four-page letter to Jess, Michael, and Phillip – a document full of outrageous lies – that detailed for them how he was being unjustly persecuted by a crooked prosecution team and, of course, by Sara. Brad had once blamed Mike Shinn, John Burke, Betty Troseth, and Sara Gordon for the problems in his life. Now he included Scott Upham as a scheming 'co-conspirator.' Never since her death had Brad referred to Cheryl as the boys' 'mom,' and he didn't in this letter.

Brad wrote to tell his sons to remember that 'Cheryl died clutching a small wad of hair in her hand. It was determined that the hair was *not* my hair, and the hair was not necessarily hers.' *Not true.* 'Scott Upham (Sara's co-conspirator) will not further test the hair and will not let me see it to do a DNA test.' *Not true.*

He told his sons that 'your mother had a date with a policeman (Finch who later investigated her homocide [*sic*]). This is the same police officer who interviewed each of you days after her death, and totally destroyed my life and work career by his actions and statements.' This was also untrue – but the 'affair with Jerry Finch' story would become one of Brad's favorite red herrings in his upcoming trial.

Brad wrote to his sons that their dead mother was a cocaine user, that his attorneys were not permitted to look at bloody handprints in the van, that the crime scene had been deliberately contaminated by Jerry Finch, and that all manner of evidence had been deliberately destroyed – again by Jerry Finch. He discussed his own sexual liaisons quite openly, and accused Sara once again of being a bisexual. That his intended audience was aged thirteen, eleven, and nine didn't cause him to hold anything back.

'We have reason to believe you boys have been "tampered with" too,' he wrote. 'Either drugs or hypnosis. We think Sara and Upham have tried memory alteration or implantation techniques. . . . We think Sara/Upham are using "memory therapy" wherein they, through a hypnotist, are *planting* by suggestion new memories into your minds. Sara will punish me, hurt me, cause me to be found guilty of a crime I had nothing to do with. She wants to inflict great hurt and harm upon your dad in retaliation for my having an affair with Lynn. . . . We have some leads she is paying off people. Jack is involved. AND THERE'S MORE!!'

Dr Ron Turco had described Brad as being a prime example of 'malignant narcissism,' and his messages to his sons seemed to verify that diagnosis. He had always treated them as his possessions and he needed them now to be his alibi witnesses for his movements on the night their mother was murdered. He had finally accepted the fact that whether he wanted to or not, he was going to trial.

57

Brad vacillated between wanting a speedy trial and doing whatever he could to delay it. He was frustrated by his belief that Tim Lyons was not giving him enough time for conferences. He didn't like the Washington County jail and demanded to be moved to another facility. He told Judge Bonebrake that prisoners were hiding cigarettes and matches in the jail ceiling and creating a fire hazard. He feared for his life and asked to be moved to safer quarters. He did not approve of the alternate jails that were suggested, however, and he remained in the Washington County jail.

His betrayal of his fellow prisoners did not go unnoticed. The lowest creature in any penal institution is a 'snitch,' and Brad was a constant snitch. In grade school, he would have been called a 'tattletale.' In jail or prison, the revenge against a snitch may not come swiftly – but it always comes.

William Berrigan was the commander of the Washington County jail and Brad was not one of his favorite prisoners. During Brad's eighteen-month stay, he would be disciplined eleven times and spend six months in lock-down in a six-by-nine-foot cell. He wrote to the FBI and asked for an investigation of the jail because he felt his civil rights were being violated.

At his July 5 omnibus hearing, Brad was represented by Tim Lyons and Kevin Hunt. This time he was dressed in the traditional faded orange pajamalike jail uniform. His hands were cuffed; his legs were shackled. His complexion had taken on the yellowish jail pallor that all longtime prisoners have, but his shoulders and biceps were 'buffed' – he had obviously been working out in his cell. He carried his omnipresent box of files, and his confidence had not diminished at all. This was to be the only time when Tim Lyons could truly act as Brad's attorney, and his expertise was apparent. Since so much of the evidence was circumstantial, it was quite possible that Lyons could win an acquittal, but Brad treated him as he had all his other attorneys. He had to be in charge, and he leaned against Lyons constantly, mouthing directions. He pushed notes across the polished defense table, tapping his finger to get Lyons' attention. Lyons often pulled away from his client.

The defense hit hard at the long delay in issuing the criminal indictment and asked what new evidence the State had. Most of all, they wanted to have any statements Cheryl had made just before her death banned from the criminal trial. They also sought Upham's 'work products' in preparation for the trial and during his investigation. Judge Bonebrake would not allow that and would delay his ruling on whether Cheryl's statements and notes were 'hearsay' or 'excited utterances.' If Upham could get into the trial Cheryl's statements made to her mother minutes before she died and the note she wrote to her brother, he would breathe easier.

There *was* new evidence. DNA analysis had come into its own since 1986, and OSP criminalist Julia Hinkley had retained the hairs found on Cheryl's body. There was more witness testimony, too. But the most important testimony, if Judge Bonebrake would allow it, would be from a woman dead for eight years: the victim.

Brad's next trial date, August 29, 1994, was postponed. Lyons was representing another murder defendant and Brad complained that neither of his attorneys was available for conferences with him when he felt it was necessary. His phone calls were not returned quickly enough. He abruptly fired J. Kevin Hunt and Tim Lyons and announced that he would represent himself.

Brad felt completely capable of handling his own defense. Even though he was not an attorney, he certainly was conversant with the law, with attorneys, with courtrooms, and with all manner of suits. He had had his own office at Vinson and Elkins' law firm in Houston whenever he wanted it during the years his suit in Texas dragged on. But he had no experience with a criminal trial and had never gone to law school. And even if he had, the old saw that almost anyone can quote is, 'He who defends himself has a fool for a client.' But nothing and no one could dissuade him from taking the reins of his own defense.

Once he had dispensed with his lawyers, Brad went after Judge Alan Bonebrake. He couldn't legally fire a judge, but he did the next best thing. He sued him, claiming Bonebrake had violated his civil rights. Now that Bonebrake had personal legal matters pending with the defendant, he felt he could not serve as an impartial judge. He recused himself.

Judge Timothy Alexander replaced him. But if Bonebrake had been an implacable brick wall whom he detested, Brad would soon find that he had unwittingly placed himself in front of a judge who not only had an encyclopedic knowledge of the laws of Oregon but who had almost no patience with defendants' histrionics and diversionary tactics. Alexander would carefully explain pitfalls to the defense, but once he had given his warning, he was not pleased to have to repeat it again and again . . . and again. Outside the courtroom, Tim Alexander had a great sense of humor. Inside, he had virtually none.

With twenty years' experience as a trial lawyer, Scott Upham was confident that, facing even as savvy a layman as Brad Cunningham one-on-one, he could make mincemeat of him. But Upham shuddered at the thought of the circus Brad could create if he was allowed to represent himself. There is an order and a sequence to the law. Brad knew nothing of that. Even law school graduates rarely venture into criminal law until they have been in practice for five years or more. Brad's defending himself was going to be a little like a first-year medical student performing open heart surgery.

Brad didn't know the rules, he didn't know the procedures, he didn't know the language, he didn't know the techniques, and he would probably turn what should be an orderly progression of witnesses, evidence, and arguments into utter chaos. Of all people concerned, Upham hoped that Brad could be dissuaded from being a one-man show, that he would be opposing a real attorney and not a man who had demonstrated throughout his life that he had to be in charge.

But Brad was adamant that he would defend himself, although he grudgingly agreed to allow the State of Oregon to retain Hunt and Lyons as his legal advisors, if not as his attorneys. He himself would select the jury, question witnesses, and present his own arguments. He would be the voice, but he would have Lyons and Hunt next to him to consult on issues where he had ventured out of his depth.

The trial that had been first scheduled for January of 1994 was set over from August to October 24 and then to October 26. Main Street in Hillsboro was decorated for Halloween when the trial began at last – nine months after it was supposed to. Estimates were that it would last two weeks. When it finally ended, the jack-o'-lanterns were long since gone, snow covered the Washington County Courthouse grounds, and Main Street was decorated for Christmas.

Part VII

The Criminal Trial

58

Brad's initial bail hearing fourteen months before had been held in the old section of the Washington County Courthouse. On the fourth floor of the newer addition, two elevators open onto a corridor with a huge woven wall hanging done in peach, orange, and blue tones that greets everyone who emerges with the motto 'Wherever Law Ends, Tyranny Begins' – John Locke. Every spectator heading for the two courtrooms on the fourth floor has to pass through highly sensitive metal detectors. Nothing metal gets through. No pocketknives. No hat pins. No nail files. No 'church keys.' No jokes.

Judge Alexander's courtroom had only three rows of chairs for the gallery, and when Brad's trial began, the back row was almost entirely filled with Cheryl's family. They had been through this too many times before, but this was the trial that might finally give them some closure. It would not be easy for them, but they would commute every day of the trial from Longview in the hours before dawn and after sunset: Betty and Marv Troseth, Susan and Dave Keegan, Bob McNannay, Jim Karr, and Cheryl's cousin Katannah King. Her half sisters and their husbands flew up from California to be present: Debi and Billy Bowen and Kim and Bill Roberts.

So many people had been involved with Cheryl's life – and with her death. Mike Shinn would often be in the courtroom, as would Sara's friend and protector Jack Kincaid (a presence that particularly rankled Brad). There would always be a line at the metal detectors and, except for the media and family, seating would be scarce. Portland network-affiliate cameramen, radio and television field reporters, an occasional syndicated tabloid television producer from Los Angeles, even a reporter from the London *Guardian* would wander in and out. The constant media presences, however, were Fiona Ortiz and Robin Franzen from the *Oregonian*, Laurie Smith from the *Daily News* in Longview, Eric Apalategui from the *Hillsboro Angus*, and this author and her assistant.

Every trial takes on a life of its own, and this one more than any other would have a strangeness and, indeed, the chaotic propulsion that Upham had feared. There was always the sense that, had it not been for Judge Alexander, it might hurtle off the track at any moment. No one could ever really know what the defendant would do next.

As the trial got under way, Upham was as low-key and inscrutable as his opponent was volatile. Brad was once again dressed in a neat dark suit. He had a fresh haircut, combed so that it mostly hid an encroaching bald spot at the crown of his very large head. His handcuffs were always removed outside the courtroom so the jury would not see them. But he wore a brace on his left leg, a bulky anti-escape device that extended from his ankle to well above his knee. Brad had asked that he always be in place at the lectern from which he spoke to the jurors before they came in, so they would not know about the brace. Judge Alexander acceded to that request.

Next, Brad said he needed glasses; he couldn't read all his files, he had headaches, and his eyes blurred. Sighing, Judge Alexander acceded to that request too, but wondered why Brad's attorneys – or rather his legal advisors – hadn't seen to this a long time ago. (Over the weekend, Brad would be taken to the Oregon Health Sciences facilities to get glasses. Because he was escorted there in his orange jail 'scrubs,' he complained when the trial resumed that a potential juror might have seen him there.)

It was startling to hear Brad speak. He had a rather high, almost boyish voice. He did not sound in the least violent. He smiled pleasantly when he said yet again, 'Motion to continue . . .'

'Denied.'

Brad glanced around the courtroom and his eyes fell on Cheryl's family in the back row. He asked that potential witnesses be barred from the courtroom.

'We're not going to play that game,' Alexander said calmly. In Oregon, survivors of crime victims have the right by law to be present in the courtroom, whether they are to be witnesses or not.

It was time to pick a jury. During voir dire, the opposing attorneys could rather informally ask questions of those in the jury pool when they filed into the jury box three at a time. Brad had difficulty asking simple questions and continually lapsed into conversation with potential jurors – almost as if he felt he had to convince them *now* of his innocence. When Judge Alexander chastised him, Brad smiled and said, 'I've never done this before.'

'This is very important to me; it's my life' was another of Brad's frequent comments. As, indeed, it was. He was not facing the death penalty, but the hedonistic freedom he had enjoyed his whole life would end if he lost this most important courtroom battle. Brad's arguments, however, weren't what Judge Alexander wanted to hear on voir dire.

'Mr Cunningham, I haven't heard a question yet,' he said. 'If you don't ask one, I'll move on to Mr Upham.'

Brad was a quick study. He asked the potential jurors questions about their jobs, background, family, children, possible divorces, custody battles. Again and again he asked, 'Do you wonder why I'm defending myself? Does it bother you?'

They all wondered. It bothered none of them.

When Upham asked a question of a potential juror that drew a meaningful response – such as 'Have you heard of *winning* at all costs?' – Brad appropriated that question for the next trio of possible jurors. 'Does it concern you that someone is indigent?' he asked one juror. Upham objected and Alexander sustained.

It became quickly apparent that Brad wanted to begin trying his case with jurors who hadn't even been chosen yet. His voir dire questions centered around 'crooked cops,' 'frame-ups,' the plight of the 'indigent' defendant, the 'loose morals' of the victim, and the length of time between the murder and his trial.

To his credit, Judge Alexander would spend much of the trial giving short lectures to Brad on law. At this point, he explained what voir dire of jurors was supposed to be, adding, 'Mr Cunningham, it takes *years* to understand this sophisticated process.' Alexander likened Brad to a first-year law student and reminded him to ask questions that elicited only the facts of the jurors' lives. Brad had taken two hours on three jurors. 'You have ten minutes to finish, Mr Cunningham,' Alexander warned.

The prospective jurors often seemed intimidated by Brad. He asked them to define 'affidavit' and 'deposition' and other legal terms. Most of them could not. And when they could not answer or the answer was not what he wanted to hear, Brad was unfailingly calm and smiled, saying softly, 'Okay.' He asked about 'vendettas' and 'people who lie to fit the facts' and 'entrepreneurs' and 'poisoning the well' and 'burden of proof.' But his most revealing questions were about what a potential juror might think of him. 'How about someone who blames someone else for all their problems?' he asked one juror. And another, 'How about women who collect men as prizes?'

No way was this trial going to be finished in two weeks. With Brad's tedious questioning of prospective jurors, it took until ten minutes after two on November 8, 1994, for both sides to agree on twelve jurors. Although two alternates would be chosen soon after, thirteen days had passed and opening arguments were still ahead.

Upham was sanguine. His theory on juries was that

almost any combination of personalities would make a functional jury. He was satisfied with this one, balanced equally between males and females, youth and age, professional and blue collar. He had lost some he would have liked – particularly a young paramedic, who he knew would never survive the defense's challenges. All and all, it was a good jury.

But Upham had much more to be confident about. In pre-trial rulings, he had won the most important witness he could possibly have: Cheryl. Her last note to Jim Karr was in. Her last call to her mother was in. The jury would hear about those final, hopeless cries for help. Judge Alexander ruled that they were not 'hearsay' but rather akin to 'deathbed statements.'

Cheryl Keeton, one of the most brilliant young attorneys in the Northwest, dead too soon, would 'testify' in this trial. And if Brad was both the defendant and the defense attorney, then Cheryl would be both the victim and the star witness.

On Monday afternoon, November 14, Judge Alexander's courtroom was packed so tightly that the sacrosanct first row of seats – heretofore kept empty of spectators – was grudgingly opened to the press. Reporters were allowed to sit in the first row *except* for the four seats directly behind the defense table. They all knew why: the premise was that Brad might try to escape and use a reporter seated directly behind him as a hostage – a soap opera scenario, perhaps, but one policy that all courtrooms adhere to. For the same reason, murder defendants never have wheels on their chairs; it would be too easy to spin around and sprint for a door or window.

Brad was certainly no ordinary defendant. He wore his two hats proudly. There were television cameras aimed directly at him, and he almost basked in their strobe lights. He was no longer sleeping in a jail cell. The Washington County jail had provided him with a three-room suite, part of the infirmary, all to himself. He was now housed alone in part so he could study his files late, and in part because he was the least popular prisoner in the jail. He had a television, but he complained that he had no fax. He also complained that his lights were not bright enough.

In addition to his suit against his last judge, Brad was suing the jail. He was as litigious a defendant as most reporters had ever seen – and the most quarrelsome. As the trial began, he objected to Upham's exhibits, maps, and photos. He moved for a mistrial because Judge Alexander walked out of the courtroom before Brad had presented his motion asking to be present at the jury's on-site viewing of the crime scene earlier that morning.

'We ruled on that weeks ago, Mr Cunningham,' Alexander said implacably.

Had Brad realized yet that he had forced one judge to recuse himself only to place himself squarely in the eye of a man as obdurate as he was himself? Apparently not. And even if he had the legal lingo down, he didn't understand much more criminal law than any neophyte. He said that Alexander's rulings were 'arbitrary and capricious.' He moved again for a mistrial. He didn't know that he had to submit such requests in writing. Upham did; Brad didn't.

'We won't spend time retreading old ground,' Alexander said sternly. 'Don't waste my time.'

Brad objected to the microphone on his table. It had no 'kill' button.

'It's a public courtroom, Mr Cunningham.'

Brad had still more complaints. He said that Scott Upham had lied about how long the trial would last, and that Upham had deliberately kept 'good jurors' out by saying that the trial would take so long.

'Sit down, Mr Cunningham,' Judge Alexander said. Brad remained standing. '*Sit down!*'

No one had ever really told Brad what to do. Alexander went further. If there were any more delays, any more 'games,' he would throw Brad out of the courtroom.

'Bring the jury in.'

If ever two men were opposites, it was Scott Upham and Brad Cunningham. Upham was low-key, quietly confident, almost businesslike in his refusal to become emotional in the courtroom. He began his opening arguments at 1:47 P.M. He explained to the jury that they would have evidence to consider in two forms: the sworn testimony of witnesses, and exhibits. He encouraged them to take notes, and to remember that his own opening statement was not evidence. 'What Mr Cunningham says is not evidence.'

Upham detailed the charges against Brad. He stood accused of intentionally causing the death of another human being. The question the jurors must decide was quite simple: 'Did Bradly Morris Cunningham bludgeon Cheryl Keeton to death on September twenty-one, 1986?' Then, in his steady deep voice, Upham told the story – the tragedy, really, of Cheryl's and Brad's lives. All the marriages. All the divorces. The births of their children. Cheryl's steadfast emotional and financial support. Brad's million-dollar projects and the collapse of his financial empire. The faltering of their marriage.

For reporters and witnesses who had committed to memory the horrific end of that marriage, there were no surprises, only admiration for Upham's precise memory of every detail, every date, all the diminishing highs of Cheryl's life and the accelerating lows. For months Upham had sat up late, reviewing literally a roomful of files until he probably knew Cheryl Keeton's life better than he recalled events and dates of his own life.

What were the jurors thinking? Had they ever heard a story of stalking and terror like this one – outside of a movie theater? No one could tell. All jurors quickly develop poker faces. They stare at the prosecution and defense alike without expression. They look at photographs that show horros they could never have imagined and pass them on down the line. Only courtroom amateurs say they know what jurors are thinking. No one knows.

Rarely do opposing sides object during opening statements, but Brad did. With Tim Lyons and Kevin Hunt on either side of him to try to keep him from popping up, he managed to keep silent until Upham began to describe the Saturday before Cheryl died, when she had gone to her son Jess's soccer game, violating, Brad felt, his custodial rights. 'At the soccer game,' Upham said, 'Brad grabbed Michael and Phillip and walked around the field – away from Cheryl. Cheryl told Nancy Davis, an old sorority friend, that Brad had threatened her if she came—'

'I object!' Brad shouted.

'Overruled,' Judge Alexander said.

Upham continued the dreadful recital of the last forty-eight hours of Cheryl's life until he reached Sunday night, shortly after 7 P.M. 'Cheryl calls Betty. Mr Cunningham has just called – he has gas problems. . . . He hung up on her.

'Seven-thirty P.M. Jim Karr called . . .

'Seven fifty-nine P.M. Cheryl calls Betty. She's upset . . . she's stern. "Mother, write this down." Mr Cunningham had just called. "He told me he's at the Mobil station by the IGA." That station is seven-tenths of a mile from her house. She said to her mother, "I know that station's closed."

'Her mother said, *"Don't go—"*

'She said, *"I have to."*'

As often as most of those in the courtroom had heard this awful progression, it never failed to raise gooseflesh. And there was always the fervent wish that somehow the ending might be rewritten. . . .

When Upham began to describe the murder, the muscles in Brad's neck and jaw tightened. 'She was beaten to a pulp,' Upham said, moving to the jury box to show the pictures of the face and head of the once beautiful victim.

'I object,' Brad shouted.

'Overruled.'

'I think the word to describe that is overkill,' Upham

said, 'done by someone who is extremely angry and bent on destruction—'

'*I object!*'

'Overruled.'

Upham moved on to complete his description of the murder and to state his belief that there was only one man who could have committed it. Brad was seething, apparently forgetting that Upham had told the jury that this was not evidence; it was the State's theory.

Then Upham began to talk of the physical evidence he would present. 'In 1992 the Oregon State crime lab became "DNA capable,"' he said. 'In 1993 hairs found on Cheryl Keeton's arm were submitted for DNA analysis. They were Cheryl's – but a contaminant on the hair was cellular material that was consistent with that of Bradly Morris Cunningham. . . . He had motive, opportunity, and the timetable was right,' Upham continued. 'She was too tough. She wasn't going to give up . . . so the defendant destroyed her physically.'

It was 2:45 P.M. and Upham had spoken for only an hour. But his whole case had been laid out for the jury. As the gallery filed out for the afternoon break, no one said a word.

When the trial resumed, Brad was raring to go. He would now have his first chance to plead his case. He was confident that he could explain everything to the jury's satisfaction. Dressed in his neat dark suit, crisp white shirt, and wine-colored tie, he looked like the bank executive he once was – or like an attorney. With whispered instructions from Kevin Hunt, he walked to the lectern before the jury entered so that they would not know about the restraining brace on his leg.

It was 3:09 when Brad began to talk. His technique was to attack, not to defend, and there was no logical order to his remarks. 'Right before you left, the DNA evidence was mentioned,' he said. 'We just got it five minutes before.

It has nothing to do with me. It won't be borne out. He ambushed us with tainted evidence. . . . In 1986, I was not charged. I had alibi witnesses. . . . My children, six, four, and two, told the police I was home all night with them. In 1994 they are fourteen, twelve, and ten, and they don't remember. In 1986 my children told the police to their satisfaction – and now it's been too long. That's very, very important to remember.'

Brad's opening statement had much to do with the conspiracy he believed existed to keep his children from him and to tape his calls. He said that of the fifty thousand relevant documents he needed, only sixteen thousand of them had been paginated. He then gave his own version of the last day of Cheryl's life, telling of his strong suspicions that Cheryl was 'with someone' when he called her Sunday night. 'She was coming for them. I fixed popcorn and I put in a movie. Michael and I went down to pick up their little packs. . . . Lilya saw us. Jess was watching *The Sword in the Stone*. . . .

'Cheryl had a clump of hair in her hand, a cord with a key wrapped around her wrist – not my hair – not my key.'

Brad then launched into his prime defense – his belief that Detective Jerry Finch, who had been dead for six years, was having an affair with Cheryl. 'The Collins Towing driver said Jerry Finch had a date with Cheryl that night. Why didn't they check Finch's house for blood?'

Brad told the jury how *he* had suffered. 'I lost my job. I was kicked out of my apartment. Harassed by the news media. I couldn't pay my rent.' He then moved quickly to Cheryl's seamy childhood. 'Cheryl had had a very, very tough childhood,' he said. 'She had to baby-sit all her younger siblings. She was sexually molested by her mother's men – they were lower middle class—' In the back row, Betty Troseth's mouth dropped open in shocked, silent protest. Brad had set out to throw mud not only on Cheryl, but on her whole family.

In another abrupt change of direction, Brad began listing

his many accomplishments in real estate and construction. He said he had made millions before he was thirty-five. 'We went to Houston and built seven office buildings *and* a warehouse.' But those responsible for completing the project had ruined his and Cheryl's dreams, he said. He then veered off the subject of Cheryl's murder into an extremely complicated explanation of his financial picture. 'In 1983, we had fourteen million dollars in assets and six million in debts. It was a tough time. We were lepers in the financial community. I was earning an income from the warehouse and two office buildings. It was hard for Cheryl to work because she faced the lawyers who were suing us. . . . We eventually lost everything.'

Standing at the lectern, facing the jury, Brad resumed his attack on Cheryl. 'Our life was difficult . . . Cheryl dealt with problems differently. . . . She went to the Jubitz Truck Stop and picked up men. She went to nude beaches. She slept with attorneys. She gave me sexually transmitted diseases.' He dropped his head and half smiled, saying that he wasn't very mad about that. He clearly wanted to be perceived as the ultimately forgiving husband. In the next breath, however, he continued to attack Cheryl's morals, her family's morals, and the police who had investigated her murder.

He offered up many suspects for the jurors to consider. Jerry Finch, of course; a 'persistent' older man who was 'bugging' Cheryl; her many other lovers. He even suggested that her brother, Jim Karr, was not above suspicion. In the days ahead, he promised to reveal more possible killers.

There was missing evidence, Brad suggested, and he listed items he would request continually throughout his trial: a grocery receipt for seventy-seven dollars' worth of groceries allegedly purchased by Cheryl at the IGA on Sunday, September 21, 1986; the groceries; a garage door control; fingernail scrapings from Cheryl; phone records; exterior photos of the Toyota van; a bedroll allegedly given to Jerry Finch; a 'gold ring' found on Cheryl's belt.

* * *

The long Monday finally ended, but Brad was not yet finished with his opening statement. There was more lost evidence to be considered, lost years, the secret lifestyle he insisted that Cheryl lived – with cocaine, illicit lovers, nude beaches, intrigue. All of his innuendos were completely alien to everyone who knew Cheryl. And when they walked out into the autumn afternoon, the trees around the courthouse were aflame with color and it felt good to leave Brad's ugly accusations behind.

59

Judge Alexander warned Brad again the next morning that there were very few attorneys in Oregon qualified to defend a murder case. 'You are way, way off,' he admonished. 'You *have* to follow the same rules they do. If you say something in the opening and then can't prove it, you're opening yourself up for trouble.' He explained once again that Brad was not to try his case during his opening statement; he was only supposed to be outlining what the jurors could expect to hear and see.

Brad stood in place at the lectern as the jury filed in the next morning. He was calm and gracious, speaking often of his financial affairs, but, jarringly, the emotion evoked as he recalled lost business deals seemed greater than when he spoke of his lost wife. In March 1993, he said, he was at his 'nadir' financially. The jurors, none of whom appeared to be millionaires, appeared nonplussed by all his talk of 'million-dollar loans,' 'tax loss carry-forward,' and 'bankruptcy.' They had agreed to sit on a murder jury and the defendant scarcely mentioned the murder.

After he explained his status as an executive with

U.S. Bank, Brad frowned, remembering the period after Cheryl's murder. 'After Cheryl's death, we were all very scared . . . fear that the children would be stolen – by Betty, or by Washington County. . . . I tried to stay available to the police in case they wanted to arrest me.' He said that he and his sons had endured a 'tough' existence in Yakima that fall and winter. In late January he had finished building the barn, and 'at Sara's request, I moved back.'

Then Brad began to talk about Sara Gordon. Aware that she would be a chief witness against him, he also had to impugn her morals. He said a C.P.A. told them that Sara could use his tax loss carry-forward, but only if they were married. This, he claimed, was the main reason for the marriage. 'We weren't real compatible,' he confided to the jury. Again boasting of his accomplishments, he told the jury about the 'dilapidated' building that he turned into the Broadway Bakery, and how he found the formula for Symptovir. 'I'm interested in chemistry and math,' he said. 'I was the guinea pig for Symptovir. I started the FDA process . . .'

From Brad's viewpoint, virtually nothing in his life had been what it seemed to be. He was the fall guy, the patsy, who had always struggled against great odds. He said that he and Sara learned after marriage that the tax loss carry-forward could be used only against *his* income. The reasons for their marriage were gone. Sara was not fair with his children. Yes, he admitted, he had had an affair with Lynn Minero, his bakery manager, but he blamed that too on Sara, because she had moved out of their Dunthorpe home, deserting him.

It was Jim Ayers, the Oregon State Police investigator, who was basically responsible, Brad suggested, for Sara's change of heart about testifying against him. Ayers had encouraged Sara to 'recall' the bruise allegedly present on his arm after the murder. 'Sara and Ayers broke into the house,' Brad said, 'and took pots, pans, bedding, a computer, Cheryl's wedding ring, a necklace that the boys had given Cheryl for Mother's Day.'

In his rambling opening statement Brad pointed his finger at many enemies and spoke of his despair after Sara abandoned him. He and his sons had only an old VW bus that his aunt Trudy gave them. 'We had to have a garage sale to live,' he said, hanging his head. 'We made about five thousand dollars.'

Suddenly, Brad returned to Cheryl's rampant promiscuity and added that she also disposed of assets in their bankruptcy. He seemed about to launch a still longer attack on his dead wife when Alexander warned him that he had far exceeded the time limits and legal parameters of opening statements. When Brad paid no attention to the admonition, Alexander interrupted the verbal torrent. 'That's enough, Mr Cunningham. Please take your seat! Sit down!'

Judge Alexander explained to the jury that they had yet to hear one word of evidence. They were to go back 'to ground zero. Start fresh. Wait until you hear testimony. Listen to what is acceptable. Disregard the vast majority of what you have heard.'

Brad wanted Mike Shinn banned from the courtroom. He might want to call him as a witness.

'I'm going to permit Mr Shinn to stay,' Alexander said.

And so it began, the whole sequence of Cheryl Keeton's life and death passing once again through a courtroom. Sometimes it would rain relentlessly outside the Washington County Courthouse, and sometimes the sky was clear blue. There were unseasonal snow storms, but inside the courtroom, no one knew. Participants and gallery alike were all caught in a window of time, a window that existed not in 1994 but in 1986, when the weather was warm and the sun had just set behind the Coast Range mountains.

Again, Randall Blighton told of finding Cheryl's van crosswise on the Sunset Highway; again Tim Duffy, the paramedic, recalled trying to save Cheryl. Witnesses who once lived on 79th Street returned. Oregon State Police troopers, detectives, sergeants, lieutenants, supervisors. Cops. Medical examiners. Attorneys. Dr Russell Sardo. Most of the gallery knew the witnesses by sight. It was akin to seeing the same movie for the fifth time, only this time the film would have an ending.

Cheryl's family all testified, and Brad cross-examined Betty Troseth savagely. He had begun his character assassination of her during his opening statement, saying that she drank and caroused and that some of the men in her life had sexually abused Cheryl. He asked her again about the alleged abuse, and Betty looked not at him but through him as she said she never heard of it.

'Do you recall making the statement that you wish you'd had four retroactive abortions?' Brad lashed out.

'Mr Cunningham, let's not have any more outbursts like that,' Judge Alexander cut in, telling the jurors to disregard the remark.

Once again, Cheryl's mother had to live through the last conversation she ever had with her oldest child, her pain achingly obvious.

It had not been a good morning for Brad. Karen Aaborg testified about the money he gave her to spirit his sons away, so far away that even he could not find them. Perhaps worse for Brad, she recalled the phone calls she had overheard between Brad and Cheryl, and his saying, 'I'll kill Cheryl. I'll *kill* her.' 'I remember it pretty vividly, because he said it with such passion,' she said. Karen also remembered the time in February of 1986 when Brad returned to Cheryl's home after he had moved out. 'He was trying to make it so miserable for Cheryl that *she'd* leave.'

After the jurors left for lunch, Alexander turned to Brad. 'If you ever had a chance with this jury, you just ruined it,' he said quietly, referring to Brad's attack on Betty Troseth. 'You're so convinced that you're right that you're not listening to the advice I suspect these lawyers [Hunt and Lyons] have given you.'

Any real lawyer knew the cardinal rule of defense attorneys: you do not attack the grieving family of the victim, and you do not portray the victim as a loose woman – no matter what she may have been in life. Brad had made devastating remarks about Cheryl, and several female jurors darted looks at him that were no longer unreadable.

There was a buzz in the courtroom when Scott Upham – not Brad – called Jess Cunningham as a witness that afternoon. Tall and handsome, Jess looked very much like his father – but with a gentler mien. Under Upham's matter-of-fact questioning, Jess explained that he was a freshman in high school, and that he and his three brothers – Michael, Phillip, and Brent – all lived with Sara. He admitted that being in court scared him. He avoided looking at his father. In general, he demonstrated a remarkable memory. He remembered going from first to third grade in Riverdale School and living in Dunthorpe. He remembered the big house, the guest house, and the live-in baby-sitters. He remembered Tampico and the little house on the farm, going to school for a few months there, the moves to Houston, to Canada, to Uncle Herm's.

But he could not recall Bridlemile School where he spent a few short weeks in first grade, or playing soccer then. He remembered living with his mother, and his father's apartment when they were getting divorced.

'Your mother—' Upham began.

'Cheryl?'

'Do you remember the weekend she was killed?'

'Not the weekend – some things,' Jess said.

'Do you remember testifying before the grand jury?'

Before Jess could answer, Brad stood up to request a sidebar. He clearly wanted Jess off the stand. Alexander overruled his objections. Brad seemed to be afraid of what Jess was about to say.

Answering Upham's questions, Jess said he remembered

a long table in a room and a group of people who asked him questions three days after his mother's death. But in 1994, he had only limited memory of the night his mother died. He could remember seeing *The Sword in the Stone* and *Rambo*, and he associated those movies with the night his mother died, but details of that night had faded for him.

'After your mom was killed,' Upham asked, 'where did you stay?'

'In the apartment,' Jess said, but he could not remember how long. It had to have been a terrible, numbing time for a little boy. 'I remember a key tied on a shoelace,' Jess said. 'I think it was flat and white. I tied it on the handle of the door [of the Toyota van] and to my lunch box. . . . Cheryl asked me to untie it and I did, but I left the key in the car, I think.' The shoelace was blue, and it and the key had ended up around Cheryl's arm as she tried desperately to get away from her killer through the passenger door.

One thing that Jess remembered quite clearly was the sound of dishes being washed in the kitchen of his father's apartment after Brad came home from wherever he had been that night. His father was washing something in the kitchen.

'No more questions.' Upham looked toward Brad.

Brad rose to cross-examine his son. He offered him a glass of water and, in a gentle, fatherly fashion, told him not to be nervous. Brad established that he had not seen Jess since early September – approximately two and a half months at that point in the trial. He asked Jess to recall 'the fun things' they had done together, and to describe all the work he had done on the Dunthorpe house. But Brad did most of the talking, reminding Jess of all the good works they had done together, giving out clothes at Christmas. Then he launched into a very long documentary of his idyllic life with his sons, and of the hard times they survived. But he never explained why he himself had not just gone to work.

Upham let Brad ramble on – until he suddenly asked his son, 'Did Jim Karr show you dirty pictures?' Upham's objection was sustained. There was no foundation at all for that question.

Jess agreed that his father told him his mother had died in an accident, and later that she was murdered. But he had not told Michael and Phillip.

'Sara had doctors hypnotize you?' Brad asked quickly.

'Objection!'

'Overruled.'

'I don't remember . . .' Jess was confused by his father's constant switching of questions. He remembered that he had seen a psychologist or a psychiatrist to help him deal with the events of the prior eight years.

'On your birthdays, do I always bring out pictures of your mom?' Brad asked.

'I remember pictures, sometimes.'

Betty Troseth, sitting in the back row, was obviously distressed to see her grandson pinioned to the witness chair, bombarded with questions designed to make Brad look like an ideal father.

'Do you remember your dad telling you how much he missed your mother? Remember people stealing money from us?'

Jess shook his head, confused. At last, his father was done with him – at least for the moment. It was obvious to the gallery that Brad had tried to manipulate his son Jess to his advantage.

Brad had sent out a plethora of subpoenas – but they all bore the same date. If all his witnesses showed up on the date specified, they would be packed in the hallway like sardines. He had subpoenaed virtually the entire Oregon State Police staff and they knew better than to make the trip to Hillsboro without further notification. But Sara brought Brad's three youngest sons as their subpoenas dictated. The boys were nervous, too upset to eat lunch. And Brad allowed Sara and his own sons to wait all day in the corridor. The next day, they were not there. He insisted they were violating their subpoenas; he wanted them available in case he needed them in court.

That was the way the trial was going, just as Upham had feared. There was no order and little continuity. Brad didn't know how to cross-examine witnesses, and belatedly realizing his omissions, he wanted them back after they had left. Certain witnesses – like Betsy Welch, Cheryl's attorney, and Julia Hinkley, the OSP criminalist – would almost wear a path back and forth from their offices to the witness stand.

Time after time Judge Alexander attempted to explain the law to Brad, and even to protect him from his own ignorance. And he warned him that he did not intend to give him a crash course in criminal defense during the trial. 'Mr Cunningham, am I going to have to sit here through the trial and teach you the law?' Alexander asked. 'The vast majority of what you said was improper. You still haven't figured out what your role is here.'

On November 21, Dr Karen Gunson took the stand to testify about the autopsy she performed on Cheryl Keeton's body eight years before, and once more Cheryl's family braced themselves to hear the terrible details. In her soft feminine voice, Dr Gunson described the massive head wounds Cheryl had sustained. She used enlarged photographs to show the jurors the victim's injuries. She pointed out the 'defense wounds' that Cheryl had sustained when she tried in vain to ward off the blows coming, in all probability, through the driver's-side window. Finally, Betty Troseth could not take any more of this. She moved quickly from her seat at the far end of the last row and disappeared through the double doors into the corridor.

Dr Gunson pointed out that the most unusual abrasion was the angry red line across the front of Cheryl's waist. She didn't know what had caused that.

'Death was instantaneous?' Upham asked.

Dr Gunson shook her head slightly. 'No, it probably took several minutes.'

One of Brad's contentions was that Cheryl drove herself onto the Sunset Highway. Upham asked Dr Gunson if Cheryl's wounds would have allowed her to drive.

'No way.'

Upham then asked who usually takes custody of a body after it is released by the Medical Examiner's office. Dr Gunson listed the answers in descending order. 'First, the husband or spouse, then the parents, then children or other family. Finally, a public official.'

Upham asked if Cheryl's husband had claimed her body.

'No.'

Brad remained seated when he cross-examined Dr Gunson. Some of his questions seemed designed to challenge the thoroughness of her postmortem examination of Cheryl's body, others to learn details of her death that he wanted to know. 'Was she ever conscious?' he asked, referring to the period after Cheryl had been attacked.

'Probably she would have gone unconscious and remained so.'

'Part of the time?' Brad pressed. 'Passing out and coming to?'

'Probably not.'

'Was she in close contact with [her attacker]?'

'Probably within arm's length.'

Brad asked if fingernail scrapings had been taken.

'I observed Julia Hinkley attempting to take scrapings.'

'Were her hands bagged?'

'Yes.' There was blood under Cheryl's fingernails – her own blood – but her nails had been too short to retain other material.

'Did you check for semen?' Brad asked.

'I took anal and vaginal swabs.' There had been no evidence of sexual assault.

'Did you estimate time of death?'

'It appeared that she died shortly before her automobile was found.'

Brad sighed suddenly, a dramatic sound full of pathos, as if he were about to break into tears. He looked down at the table in front of him, the very image of a grief-stricken widower. But the dark shadow across his face disappeared in an instant and he continued to question Dr Gunson. He switched his emotions on and off as if he were pulling on the string of a bare lightbulb.

Brad asked Dr Gunson if she had observed petechiae (small blood hemorrhages associated with strangulation) in Cheryl's eyes. Was she wearing glasses? Contacts?

'I didn't see any,' she replied.

Brad was pleased, as if this proved her incompetence. He commented that Cheryl was very nearsighted and should have been wearing either her glasses or contacts.

Scott Upham was aware of Brad's strategy. 'Contact lenses were of no significance to you in this type of situation?' he asked Dr Gunson on re-cross. 'Is that correct?'

'That is correct,' she answered. Given the force of the blows the victim sustained, the transparent slivers of contacts could have been knocked out, hidden in the massive amounts of blood, or lost back in the swollen eyes.

'How do you determine time of death?' Upham wanted to reinforce Dr Gunson's earlier testimony about when Cheryl died.

In reply, she explained that even the best guess of a medical examiner would be 'plus or minus four or five hours.' The very best way to establish time of death, she told the jurors, is by determining when the victim was last seen – or, in Cheryl's case, heard. She had telephoned her mother just before 8 P.M., and Randy Blighton came upon her body less than a half hour later.

'Witnesses and the scene investigation tell far more than anything we can do at autopsy,' Dr Gunson said.

Julia Hinkley testified that afternoon. She and Jim Ayers

had done a reenactment of Cheryl's actual murder, and Brad tried to forestall discussion of it. Judge Alexander denied his motion, and again anger suffused Brad's face with scarlet.

Julia Hinkley was a smiling, cheerful woman. She also knew her stuff. This jury had not yet heard of the evidence she had collected in 1986, and she went through it all for them. Then she offered photos to show the reenactment that she and Ayers had done in 1992 to check out her findings and Dr Gunson's. With Hinkley as 'Cheryl' and Ayers as 'the killer,' the reenactment was only theory, but it was chilling theory. And it was chillingly exact.

All of the forensic evidence indicated that Cheryl had been assaulted while she was sitting in the driver's seat of her Toyota van and had been bludgeoned with a multisurfaced blunt instrument. Hinkley demonstrated the positions of the crime, explaining that she had suffered an injury herself in the reenactment, an injury much like one of Cheryl's. 'Now, she attempts to escape toward the passenger door,' Hinkley said quietly. 'She gets the door partially open.' At this point in the reenactment, Ayers had yanked violently back on the waistband of Hinkley's jeans. In the interest of forensic science, Hinkley had suffered exactly the same linear abrasion that Dr Gunson had found on Cheryl's waist, the deep red mark of the jean material cutting into soft flesh.

All independently, Hinkley and Ayers had come up with almost exactly the same sequence of a violent death struggle that Lieutenant Rod Englert had presented at Brad's civil trial. Blood *will* tell – in more ways than the poets ever knew.

Upham asked Hinkley why the graphic equalizer knobs of the Toyota's radio were broken off.

'It probably was done by her kicking when she was on the console. There were elongated scrapes on the bottom of her shoes that match . . .'

Near the conclusion of her testimony, Upham asked

Hinkley about the hairs she had retrieved from the crime scene. The hairs had been sealed in glass slides in 1986, and in the custody of Oregon State Police investigators since. 'The chain of custody is impeccable,' Hinkley commented. DNA matching was not possible at that time, but she found later that some of the hairs had DNA possibilities, and she gave them to DNA specialist Cecilia Von Beroldingen in 1993 for analysis. 'I was looking for a root – using a stereo zoom scope – for a follicular tag. . . . I found four for DNA,' Hinkley said. Von Beroldingen was scheduled to testify for the State later in the trial – *if* Judge Alexander ruled in favor of the admissibility of DNA evidence.

Every prosecution witness who had faced Brad had managed to present a bland face to him, keeping private feelings hidden. During his testimony, Jim Ayers had accorded him a flat civility that was, somehow, more telling than if he had allowed his disdain to show. Now, Julia Hinkley's eyes bore directly into Brad's as he questioned her interminably on how she retrieved and preserved evidence. Whatever she was feeling, she did not betray it.

Brad wanted to know what 'contaminants' might be on the hairs preserved. 'What is a contaminant?' he asked Hinkley.

'[Something] not expected to be there – foreign,' she replied.

'Trace evidence is invisible to the naked eye?' Brad asked.

'It depends.'

Brad was obsessed with what he considered the missing fingernail scrapings. How did Julia Hinkley take scrapings?

'With a fresh scalpel.'

'With my wife, you did that?'

'That's the only way to do it.'

'There was nothing there?'

'Nothing you could see.'

Brad obviously knew something about trace evidence –

blood, fiber, hairs – and yet it was apparent his knowledge was superficial. He latched onto anything that he deemed 'missing,' including Cheryl's garage door opener.

'I left it for the police,' Hinkley said.

There was no argument from the prosecution. That device *was* missing. What significance it might have had was obscure – but Brad would ask for it again and again.

Cheryl's Toyota van was also gone, sold a long time ago after it had been thoroughly processed and photographed. Brad considered its absence an important point in his favor. But it was of no consequence, nor was the other 'missing' evidence.

'Detective Finch gave you human teeth on October first, 1986?' Brad asked Hinkley.

'No, I went to the van and got them. There were some in the back and some in the front.'

Brad asked about the missing 'gold ring.'

'I don't know where that is,' Hinkley said, explaining that she had kept only those items that were 'forensically important' to her. The ring and the teeth were not, nor were the buttons kicked off the radio.

'You are married to Sergeant Hinkley?' Brad asked.

'Yes.'

'He was first on the scene,' Brad said, suggesting that the Hinkleys had collaborated on their recitation of events.

'We have not discussed the case,' Hinkley said firmly, and most believably.

The reenactment of the crime still rankled Brad. 'This re-creation is your scenario?' he asked.

'That is correct.'

'And there could be many other scenarios,' Brad stated confidently. 'Is that correct?'

Hinkley shrugged. 'There could be. That is correct.'

60

As in the civil trial three years earlier, only one of Brad's former wives agreed to testify. Upham and Carr made numerous out-of-state trips to speak with Loni Ann, Lauren, and Cynthia. The women were all cooperative – but not to the point that they felt they could face Brad in court.

Sara Gordon would. This trial was drawing more media attention than the last, and what she had to tell was personally embarrassing. It didn't matter. She had Brad's sons to think about, and that *did* matter. The boys were in limbo; she could not guarantee them anything about their future. If Brad was acquitted, she knew he would come for them and she would have to give them back to him. If he was convicted, she had pledged to raise them to adulthood.

As Sara took the stand for the prosecution on November 22, she was the third witness of the day. Cheryl's secretary, Florence Murrell, and Sergeant James Hinkley had preceded her. Sara was very pale and terribly thin. She wore a black suit and a white blouse, making her look even smaller than she already was. She was so pretty that the jurors must have wondered why Brad had described his marriage to her as one of financial convenience only. Sara was apprehensive – not of direct testimony but of cross-examination. She spent hours on the stand answering Upham's questions about her relationship with Brad, from their first meeting to their marriage and her discovery of his infidelity. Four years.

With the jury out of the room, Upham asked Sara about Brad's veiled threat as their relationship finally disintegrated. 'Brad told me that the person who killed Cheryl might kill me,' Sara said. 'He said, "Never be alone. Make sure you have someone with you. . . ."'

Brad, of course, objected on the grounds of 'marital privilege.' In a blow to the prosecution, Judge Alexander concurred. Sara was still legally married to Brad when he alluded to the danger in her life – even though she was living in fear of him.

To counter Sara's testimony about his infidelity, Brad wanted to introduce evidence that he felt would show she was 'plotting' against him with Lynn Minero's husband, and that she had talked about this from an operating room phone – even while she administered anesthesia. Judge Alexander would not permit it, again protecting Brad from his own ignorance. 'That testimony would be so damaging to your case . . . I can't allow you to keep doing this to yourself.'

The jury filed back in and Sara's direct testimony continued until the lunch break. When court reconvened at 1:37, the moment Sara feared most was at hand. She was about to be cross-examined by her ex-husband.

Brad looked at Sara dispassionately. 'You currently have a lawsuit pending against me based on what the children and I own?' he asked. The property in contention in the 'lawsuit' Brad mentioned was in a storage locker in Snohomish County. As always, he seemed preoccupied with possessions that had been taken away from him. But then, he may have just been trying to establish prejudice against him.

'The trustee put a hold on the children's property,' Sara replied. 'The children are living with me, and I'm their guardian *ad litem*. To get their toys and stuff – I plan to leave it alone right where it is – until the end of this trial and then I will get the children's things. . . .'

Brad continued his cross-examination, only on financial matters. But when he had not made many positive points with that line of questioning, he tried another tack. He moved to the bakery acquisition and attempted to get Sara to say that he had done a great deal of work in remodeling it. No, Sara countered, he had *hired* a contractor to do the work.

'The equipment for the bakery?' Brad asked. 'Did I buy it?'

'You chose. I paid.'

Brad was still getting nowhere. He was trying to establish how hard he had worked during all the years of their marriage – when he had no real job – but Sara would not validate that. All of the remodeling on the Dunthorpe house and on the bakery/bistro had been, in her opinion, done by hired labor. Nor would she support his recall of his pitiful circumstances after Cheryl's murder.

Sara sighed with relief when the afternoon break interrupted Brad's rambling cross-examination, but she had held her own. And he had obviously not expected that.

When the trial resumed later that afternoon, Brad at last asked a question that had some relevance to the case. 'Did you say your third call to me was at eight-fifty P.M. [on September twenty-first]?'

'Yes.'

'Could it have been even earlier?'

'No.'

'The answering machine was only on when I was away?'

Sara had no reply to that, other than that she knew it had not been on that night.

Brad asked only a few more questions and they seemed pointless: when they met, where they lived, when she met the boys, what they had eaten on the night Cheryl was killed. The jury had already heard this information.

'No more questions,' Brad finally said.

Incredulous with relief, Sara smiled broadly for the first time during her testimony. Her ordeal was over. She stepped down from the witness chair. Except for the unalterable fact that Brad was the father of her sons, he was for all intents and purposes out of her life.

61

Upham continued his case for the prosecution. Eric Lindenauer, the young lawyer whom Cheryl had mentored at Garvey, Schubert and who had been with her the day she enrolled Jess in Bridlemile School, testified that she had been terrified of Brad. He said he had learned that Cheryl had been murdered at 11:30 on September 21, the night she died. Betty Troseth had called him and he was 'absolutely devastated.' He then called the Oregon State Police to give them information about her fear of her estranged husband.

'When did you last talk to Brad?' Upham asked.

'On the phone – on September twenty-fifth. [My secretary] said that a Mr Ballaster was calling. I knew no one by that name. I picked up the phone and it was Brad. . . . He asked if I was probating Cheryl's will. I said, "No," and I directed him to Brian Whipp.'

When Brad cross-examined Lindenauer, he insisted that he had called a full *week* after Cheryl's death, not three days later, to ask about her will. To suggest that Lindenauer and Cheryl might have been having an affair, Brad asked him how close he and Cheryl had been.

'We were close friends.'

'Didn't you have keys to each other's houses?'

'No,' Lindenauer said flatly.

Then Brad tried out another of his alternate-suspect theories. He asked Lindenauer if Garvey, Schubert and Barer had 'key man' insurance.

'I don't know.'

'Anything that pays benefits to Garvey, Schubert if [a partner dies]?' Brad pressed.

'I don't know.'

'Was the firm having financial problems in 1986?' Brad asked.

This was a new motive. Brad was suggesting that Garvey, Schubert and Barer might have insured Cheryl as a 'key man' and then had her killed so they could bail the firm out of financial problems. That made five entities Brad had suggested were far more likely to murder his estranged wife than he: Jerry Finch, the OSP detective who investigated her murder; some unknown pick-up from Jubitz Truck Stop; Cheryl's own half brother, Jim Karr; one of her 'many lovers' from her law firm; and, now, the law firm itself.

Brad listed names and Lindenauer identified them as partners at Garvey, Schubert and Barer.

'Were you aware that Cheryl was having affairs with these men?' Brad asked quickly.

'I object!' Upham barked.

'Sustained.'

A disgusted Eric Lindenauer stepped down.

Oregon State Police Detective Mike McKernan took the stand to give the jury a sense of the distances involved on the Sunday night of September 21, 1986. He had driven the route on a Sunday night, at the speed limit. From the American Dream Pizza restaurant to Brad's apartment was six miles. 'It took me fifteen minutes.' From Cheryl's house to the Madison Tower, the time elapsed on a Sunday evening was nine minutes and forty-eight seconds. The distance from Cheryl's house on the West Slope to the Sunset Highway where her body was found was three-tenths of a mile. The distance from her house to the Mobil station was seven-tenths of a mile. A man with an hour and twenty minutes of time unaccounted for could have made the drive to the Sunset Highway and back with relative ease.

The next big hurdle for the State was to get into evidence the DNA analysis of hairs removed from Cheryl Keeton's body. Ray Grimsbo, formally a criminalist with the Oregon State Police crime lab, would observe the tests done by Dr Cecilia Von Beroldingen. Judge Alexander ruled that he would allow the DNA results in. But Dr Von Beroldingen's testimony would have to wait. She had been called from California, but Brad was throwing the court schedule into such chaos that she could not testify. Now, she would not be able to return from California again until the fifth or sixth of December. Perhaps even later.

62

The tension in the courtroom was building by the day, chiefly because of Brad's incompetence as a defense attorney and his ignorance of criminal procedures. He continually asked the D.A.'s office to produce the items of 'missing' evidence.

'Every bit of this has been available for a year and a half,' Scott Upham said finally in exasperation.

'Let's get the whole batch up here,' Judge Alexander said with equal exasperation.

The D.A.'s chief investigator, Jim Carr, a man known for his pleasant – if inscrutable – expression, had sat next to the courtroom door throughout the trial. Obligingly, he went to get the evidence that Brad thought would be so important. Some of it, in fact, had been missing for years. Some – like Cheryl's checkbook with her West Slope address imprinted on the checks – was more *dangerous* than helpful to Brad. The rest wasn't relevant to his case.

The witness list that Brad had held so close to his vest proved to be almost identical to the prosecution's. He planned to question Upham's witnesses, apparently to bring out testimony about some massive coverup by the Oregon State Police, the D.A.'s office, and the firm of Garvey, Schubert and Barer. Perhaps that was also the reason behind his continual demand for 'missing' evidence. But Brad's witnesses were seldom on hand. The court clerk, Gwen Lipske, would step out into the hall and call out a name. Once. Twice. When no one answered, she would step back into the courtroom to say that the witness was not there. That wasn't really surprising, since Brad's subpoenas were all dated on the same day, and that day was now long past.

Whether he would admit it or not, Brad was finding that the law was far more intricate than he was prepared for. Much of the testimony that he wanted to elicit was closed off to him. Again and again, Judge Alexander reminded him that his questions centered on areas that he should have handled when he was cross-examining Upham's witnesses. Alexander saw – if Brad could not – that many of his proposed witnesses would damage his case. But Brad refused to listen to most of Alexander's warnings. 'At some point I can't protect him from all his choices,' Alexander said with resignation. 'I've tried to do that through this whole trial.'

Overriding Judge Alexander's warning, Brad called Phil Margolin, his first attorney after the murder, and tried to get him to say that the Washington County D.A.'s office had 'kidnapped' his sons to testify before the grand jury. Margolin denied it. The objections flew so fast that the only information that came from this witness was that Sara was the one who had paid for Brad's consultations with Margolin – not a particularly positive point for his case.

Often Judge Alexander had to remind Brad that he had run out of proper questions. 'You're done, Mr Cunningham. The witness may step down.'

Brad called the tow truck driver who allegedly had told him that Cheryl had made a date with Jerry Finch for later on the night she was killed. He wanted to reinforce his contention that Finch deliberately destroyed evidence that would link him to Cheryl.

'What did it matter, [assuming] that Finch allegedly said he had a date *later* with Cheryl?' Alexander asked wearily.

Undeterred, Brad suggested that the missing garage door opener might have been to Finch's garage. 'Evidence was destroyed,' he said again. 'I'm not saying that Mr Finch was the murderer. . . .'

Brad seemed to be writing a Perry Mason script and Judge Tim Alexander wasn't buying it. Jerry Finch had been a happily married bridegroom. There was no evidence whatsoever to show that he had ever seen Cheryl before he viewed her body the night she died. Alexander would not admit testimony regarding Detective Finch from the tow truck driver, or any testimony on 'the Finch connection.' It was all hearsay.

Nevertheless, Brad tried again when he questioned Harley James Collins Jr., the tow truck driver who hauled away Cheryl's van.

'Was Finch upset?' he asked.

'Objection!' Upham said.

'Sustained.'

'Was he emotionally disturbed?'

'*Objection!*'

'Sustained.'

Once more, Judge Alexander sent the jury out. He pinioned Brad with his stare and told him that he could be held in contempt of court for asking questions he had been repeatedly warned about. 'I can sentence you to jail for six months each time you do that,' Alexander said. 'You could stay in jail longer than you might if you were convicted in this trial.'

'I'm walking just on the edge,' Brad countered defiantly. 'And you're stumbling over—'

Brad had always argued with anyone who did not agree with him. Stubbornly he was arguing now with Judge Alexander.

'This is why we go to law school, Mr Cunningham,' the judge said. 'It's a sophisticated concept.'

Brad's witnesses remained elusive and he volunteered to fill the time until someone showed up. Was it an act of pure bravura? Perhaps not. He had longed to get on the stand. Hadn't he always been able to talk his way out of anything?

Judge Alexander warned Brad of the dangers of taking the witness stand himself. The defendant in a criminal trial does not have to testify, but if he does, he opens himself to cross-examination and to questions from the prosecution whose answers might totally destroy him. 'Carefully consider the risk you place yourself in if you take the stand,' Alexander said.

Brad barely nodded, anxious to talk directly to the jury. 'I want the jury to know that this will just be a portion of my testimony,' he said, adding that he would have much more to say.

'Okay. If other witnesses show up, we'll take them.'

Brad was smiling broadly and he shook his head when Alexander suggested that he have Kevin Hunt or Tim Lyons question him on the stand. No, he was determined to go it alone. As he limped to the witness chair, hampered ever so slightly by the brace on his left leg, he was totally in his element. He sat, poised and supremely confident, waiting for the jury to file into the courtroom.

It was 2:45 P.M. on Thursday, December 1, 1994, and suddenly the witness was Brad Cunningham himself. There *was* no one else – at least not on that day. He was the only witness he had, but he seemed quite comfortable to be testifying.

Brad began with a brief autobiography of the years before he met and married Cheryl. He made no mention of his three previous wives. And oddly, in his description of his life with Cheryl, almost all he talked about was his financial empire. The jurors' eyes glazed over as he told them in a friendly, confidentially soft voice about the huge amounts of money he had made – and lost. 'Debts of four million nine hundred thousand dollars – but *assets* of fourteen million seven hundred sixteen thousand . . .' He spoke of banks, venture partners, his construction equipment, his apartment complexes, his office buildings, his laundromat, the homes in Tampico that he and Cheryl had bought, the hay crop he had harvested. The figures he tossed around were more than most people made in three lifetimes.

During his first hour as a witness in his own defense, Brad didn't even mention Cheryl's murder, but he talked in a mournful voice about having to sell 'the boys' house' in 1992. 'I got a court order in Yakima and a fair price of fifty-nine thousand nine hundred dollars, but the boys and I only realized six or seven hundred dollars. We sold because we were behind in our taxes.'

Brad's testimony was a litany of his own financial misfortunes caused, always, by someone else – Bob McNannay, Sara – never through his own actions. But after he had declared bankruptcy and everything seemed lost, he told the jury, his and Cheryl's suit in Houston had finally been settled in 1991. In a settlement, the contractor would pay Brad $380,000, and the bonding insurer Brad had sued lost in court and was ordered to pay $609,700 – plus interest. The award ended up to be $1,765,537.49. But all that was virtually wiped out by what Brad owed Vinson and Elkins and other creditors. 'It took eight years,' he said proudly, 'but we won.'

A wave of what seemed to be genuine pain and loss swept across Brad's face as he ended his testimony by saying, 'It was very sad. It wasn't something that should have happened. . . .' The courtroom was hushed and those listening expected Brad to say how sad it was that Cheryl hadn't lived to realize they had finally won their suit. Instead, he repeated, 'It was very sad. We didn't have to declare bankruptcy at all.'

* * *

Judge Alexander had ruled that he would allow DNA testimony into the trial, and Scott Upham would not rest his case until Dr Cecilia Von Beroldingen had presented the DNA analysis for the prosecution. Dr Von Beroldingen had been left legally blind after surgery for a brain tumor. But she remained one of the outstanding experts on DNA in the country, and she was able to testify with the use of magnifying devices. She was presently in California training with a guide dog. She had already flown back to Portland once to testify, and she would have to fly back again because of the incompetent way Brad was handling his defense.

The trial, expected to be finished by Thanksgiving, was headed toward Christmas with no sure end in sight. In mid-trial, in an unusual move, Judge Alexander ordered that Brad be examined by psychologists – one chosen by the State, and one by Alexander himself – to see if he was indeed competent to conduct his own defense. By Monday, December 5, it would be decided whether the trial would continue with Brad acting as the sole defense 'attorney,' or if there might even be a mistrial. The question made for a glum weekend. The Christmas lights were up all along Main Street in Hillsboro and on the giant fir on the courthouse lawn. Nobody involved in this case seemed to have noticed.

On Monday, Judge Alexander excluded everyone but the principals and the press from the courtroom. Brad, as usual, had a number of issues to take up with the judge, issues concerning the unfair way he felt he was being treated. With Kevin Hunt attempting to run interference for him, Brad began to speak. 'My position—'

Hunt quickly explained that the first issue Brad was about to bring up had already been ruled upon. Brad wanted a DNA report from *his* expert. But that was not all. He said he couldn't get his out-of-state witnesses to court. He felt he could not count on his attorneys to find them. 'I can't get time with Lyons,' he complained. 'I had other expectations of what would happen. . . . I just got the DNA reports . . . My experts aren't here. Mr Upham surprised me. . . .'

What had happened, quite obviously, was that Brad had begun to see the consequences of his inept attempts to defend himself. 'I need to talk to witnesses one-on-one before they testify,' he said, harried and angry now. 'I need – I need to have access to my attorney. I need an order to be with my expert witnesses.'

Brad now requested *more* attorneys. He wanted attorneys who would seek and subpoena witnesses in Washington and California. 'I need new lawyers to advise me – who will *be* there.'

Alexander looked at Brad, perplexed. 'Your lawyers have done an excellent job,' he commented. 'I'm not going to hire different ones. . . . You may be the only person in the history of Oregon who has had *two* lawyers advising you. I'm not going to give you *three*.'

The question of just how many attorneys Brad was going to have might very well have been moot. It looked as if the trial was about to evaporate. Both Lyons and Hunt had filed documents expressing their concerns about the way Brad was handling his defense. He had ignored their advice; he had brushed aside the judge's warnings. They sincerely questioned his mental competence.

The two psychologists who had been observing Brad's behavior were in the courtroom and ready to offer their opinions as to whether he should be allowed to continue. Judge Alexander had selected Dr Donald True to observe and examine Brad, and Scott Upham had chosen Dr Richard Hulteng. The question on everyone's mind was: Is this a man of monumental ego and almost suicidal arrogance who is, nevertheless, sane – or is Brad Cunningham psychotic? The jury was not present in the courtroom while the two psychologists presented their findings.

Dr Donald True testified first. He had observed Brad for five hours, watching him in the courtroom and on a one-to-one basis. But he had given him only one test –

the Rorschach ink-blot test. It was True's opinion tha
was diagnosable, according to the guidelines in the DS
(*Diagnostic and Statistical Manual*, the bible of psychologists and psychiatrists), as suffering from 'severe delusional disorder.' He felt that Brad was 'depressive, borderline suicidal,' and had 'paranoid type ideation. . . . His mental disorder,' True said, 'is such that he's defeating his defense – fighting his own attorneys. . . . In my opinion, he's not able to accurately perceive – or aid – himself.'

Although Dr True believed that his mental problems were major, he said that Brad was probably delusional and paranoid only in certain areas. He could, for instance, go on with his life otherwise. 'It's not paranoid schizophrenia; he can function adequately – even brilliantly – in other areas.'

Brad did not care for Dr True's diagnosis. He asked to have an independent advisor, another psychologist, to evaluate him, someone to contest True's findings. Alexander would not grant him another psychologist.

Kevin Hunt rose to tell Alexander that he was concerned about having Brad cross-examine Dr True. Lyons and Hunt had now made full disclosure of their adversarial position with their client. Hunt wondered if he and Lyons could even continue. But they did agree to continue, and Upham's chosen psychologist took the stand to give his opinion on Brad's competence.

Dr Richard Hulteng, director of evaluation and treatment at the Oregon State Hospital, a Ph.D. in clinical psychology who was also an attorney, said he had observed Brad, held a structured clinical interview with him for four hours, administered the MMPI test, and reviewed some five hundred pages of documents, police reports, and other test results. His diagnosis was diametrically opposed to that of Dr True. Hulteng had found Brad a little depressed, not surprising given his current situation, and said that Brad did have a personality disorder – a 'depressive maladaptive personality.' Hulteng found him 'antisocial, paranoid, and narcissistic.' But none of these – or *any* personality disorder

– indicated that a subject was 'crazy.' They were, rather, an integral part of the way some people relate to the world.

'He wants to do the case *his* way?' Upham asked Dr Hulteng. 'Is that accurate?'

'Yes . . . at some point, he asked me not to talk to his attorneys. . . . Within a reality-based way, he cited individuals who may be against him – there were many. . . .'

'Is he competent to act as his own attorney?'

'I concluded that within the framework of understanding the nature of the procedure, he's perfectly rational,' Dr Hulteng replied. 'He's at least of high-average intelligence. . . . As defined by Oregon law, he has the capacity to assist in his own defense.'

Oddly, even though this testimony had the potential to damage him more than Dr True's, Brad was happy with Dr Hulteng's diagnosis. Odder still, clearly seeing this as an opportunity to get many of his complaints into the record, he proceeded to demonstrate his paranoid personality disorder. He complained to Dr Hulteng that Judge Alexander wasn't being fair, that he gave Scott Upham favorable treatment. As Alexander listened without expression, Brad told Hulteng that the judge was prosecutorial and more interested in 'getting me convicted than conducting a fair trial.'

'Yes – you told me that,' Hulteng said calmly.

Judge Alexander had a question for Dr Hulteng. 'Did you observe Mr Cunningham going ahead even when I was concerned it was dangerous for him? Doesn't that concern you?'

'Yes,' Hulteng agreed, 'but that's more maladaptive, narcissistic behavior. He isn't delusional.'

'What about his inability or failure to recognize danger?' Alexander pressed.

'That's just his poor judgment.'

Brad continued to complain about several of Judge Alexander's rulings that he felt were unfair, and patiently Dr Hulteng tried to explain to him what the crux of the matter was. 'You and the judge were clearly having a difference of opinion. From where I sit, your view is distorted, but it doesn't fall into "crazy" because you're *not* saying the judge is ruling against you because he's receiving messages from Mars. *Then* I'd be concerned.'

For the first time in a very long time, there were smiles in the courtroom.

Dr Hulteng's opinion would prevail and the trial would go on. Brad, poor judgment and all, would continue to conduct his own defense. Lyons and Hunt would continue to try to advise him. And he, in all likelihood, would continue to ignore their advice.

63

DNA evidence is an esoteric and recent addition to a criminalist's already impressive knowledge of things seen and not seen by the naked eye at a crime scene. And Cecilia Von Beroldingen was one of the outstanding DNA experts in America. She was a pretty, slender young woman whose self-confident movements belied the fact that she was legally blind. She took the stand just after lunch on December 12, and her seeing-eye dog, a golden retriever, waited for her at the far end of the press row next to investigator Jim Carr, its eyes never leaving its mistress.

It took several minutes for Scott Upham to elicit the plethora of credentials that Von Beroldingen possessed. She gave the jurors a crash course in DNA, explaining that humans normally inherit twenty-three chromosomes from the male parent and the same number from the female. DNA, the stuff of life, is found in these chromosomes. Although there are three basic methods, namely RLFP,

PCR, and DQ Alpha, used to extract, amplify, and evaluate DNA, she told the jury that she had used the DQ Alpha typing process on the hairs preserved as evidence after Cheryl's murder.

With blood samples taken from both Brad and Cheryl, Von Beroldingen was able to establish that they had different DQ Alpha profiles. Cheryl's was '1.3,3,' while Brad's was '1.2,4,' she said.

The only thing that Von Beroldingen had had to work with were the hair follicles. Two hairs had been found on Cheryl's arm and blouse, hairs that still had the root or follicle attached. The hair shaft itself cannot be tested for DNA components but the 'tag' or follicle can. The hair found on Cheryl's forearm was consistent with Cheryl's 1.3,3 DQ Alpha profile, but the human cellular contaminant on it was Brad's type: 1.2,4. This contaminant could be anything from sweat to blood to mucus to semen, or any other bodily secretion. That would indicate that someone with a 1.2,4 DQ Alpha profile had been in contact with the hair found on Cheryl's body.

It would be essential for the defense to establish what percentage of the population had 1.2,4 DQ Alpha profiles, and Kevin Hunt had planned to cross-examine Von Beroldingen. Judge Alexander ruled that he could not. Brad had chosen to defend himself and he could not have it both ways. Hunt would be allowed only to whisper questions, while Brad himself cross-examined Dr Von Beroldingen. With his first question, however, an interesting phenomenon took place. Although his voice was as soft and conciliatory as it usually was when he questioned witnesses, there was apparently something in it that raised the hairs on the back of Cecilia Von Beroldingen's dog. The perfectly trained animal leaned forward and growled deep in its throat, a sound that no one in the courtroom missed.

Brad had always been a quick study, and he had apparently boned up on DNA. The DNA pattern revealed during Von Beroldingen's tests, he submitted, was not that unique.

In fact, he managed to establish that approximately one out of ten Caucasians in the greater Portland area also had the same DQ Alpha genotype that Brad did. It was not as if he had left a fingerprint on Cheryl's flesh, a fingerprint that was absolutely unique to him. Von Beroldingen could only say that he was among the 10 percent of the population who *could* have left the contaminants on the retrieved hairs, as opposed to the 90 percent with other DQ Alpha genotypes who could *not*. This was physical evidence to be considered with the circumstantial evidence that pointed to Brad, but it was not conclusive.

There were fireworks later in the day when the defense's DNA expert, Randell Libby, testified. Brad's questions and Libby's answers seemed to meld too well, and a suspicious Upham raised an objection. It turned out that Libby had prepared seven and a half pages of questions – including many of the answers he planned to give – for Brad to use. Upham said that the list should have been shared with the prosecutor, and that the fact that it was not was a violation of discovery.

Judge Alexander sent the jury out, and when they were gone, he ruled that Libby's testimony and the list that Upham called 'crib notes' were indeed a violation of discovery. Randell Libby and his testimony disappeared from the trial. When the jury returned, he was gone and no explanation for his absence was given.

Brad moved once again for a mistrial.

'Motion denied.'

Brad took the witness stand for a second time on December 14. He was once again both witness and defense attorney as he continued his direct examination of himself. He spoke for more than two hours, focusing on the good times and bad times of his marriage to Cheryl. On a number of occasions he choked up and seemed about to burst into tears as he remembered his love for Cheryl. His emotions were still evanescent, however – gone in an instant. Strangely, his grief did not prevent him from harping on Cheryl's promiscuity. Again and again he told the jury that she was having sexual relationships with seven or eight men at the time of her death. 'That didn't make her a bad person,' he said generously. 'It didn't bother me.' With a half smile of sad acceptance, he said only that he had worried because he didn't think Cheryl's affairs left her much time to care for their three sons.

Brad insisted that he was home with his sons all the Sunday evening in question, except for two quick runs with Michael to the parking garage. He estimated he hadn't been out of his apartment for more than ten minutes total. 'I was trying to run off his energy,' he said of Michael. 'He was very hyper that evening.'

He denied that he gave conflicting stories of his whereabouts and activities to a number of different people. 'I am telling you today,' he said earnestly to the jurors, his voice quavering, 'I did not kill Cheryl.'

Just as Judge Alexander had warned him, Brad was now fair game for the prosecution. Scott Upham had memorized the convoluted transfers of homes, land, building materials, heavy equipment, guns, and vehicles that Brad had accomplished. He had already been relentless in questioning some of Brad's attorneys and accountants, and now he was harder on Brad himself. Many of Brad's holdings had never been disclosed to the bankruptcy court. This, Upham maintained, was one of Brad's reasons to want Cheryl dead: she had been about to expose his financial machinations. Now, Upham did what Cheryl had been unable to do – he held those transactions up to the light.

Brad had a hard time explaining how trucks and trailers and guns changed hands on paper but, apparently, not in reality. The Prowler trailer that had eventually been purchased by Sara had bounced all over Washington State without ever once actually moving. Paperwork showed that Brad had given it to a law firm to pay for attorneys' fees, then bought it back, then given it to his father. It seemed to have been the same with Brad's guns and expensive cameras. He fumbled when he tried to remember where they had all gone. 'We had fifty guns. . . .' Some went to a gun shop on consignment, some to his law firm. He wasn't quite sure.

When Upham pointed out bankruptcy report irregularities, Brad had a ready answer. 'Cheryl filled those out,' he said.

Upham was also fascinated with Brad's tax returns, returns that Brad seemed to have forgotten. During the years when he had brought in virtually no income, he had taken huge deductions for business expenses. Cheryl had also threatened to expose his tax dodges to the IRS – heightening his motive for murder.

Brad's face glistened with sweat as he tried to answer Upham's increasingly intricate questions. At the same time, he took notes to help him with his own re-direct testimony.

Brad wasn't concerned with questions about his sex life. He readily admitted to having affairs with his baby-sitter Marnie and with Lilya Saarnen. As for his other coworker, Karen Aaborg, he was disdainful. 'She would come to my apartment and she was a date I couldn't get to go home. . . . She wanted sex so I did. . . . I only slept with her so she'd go home.'

'You have a facetious sense of humor?' Upham asked suddenly, changing the subject.

'Yes,' Brad said warily.

'The "poison plot" was a joke?' Upham asked incredulously.

'Cheryl and I thought it was a joke,' he said, then added, 'But it was like Betty – to poison me and take the kids to Arkansas and hide them so Cheryl could live the kind of life she wanted until she wanted them back.'

It was obvious to everyone watching that Brad was not only in deep water, he was way over his head. Upham hit him again and again with questions that demanded precise answers. And Brad could no longer tailor his answers to fit the facts and make them sound like anything but fiction. Even so, he would not show that he was in the least rattled. He continued to write down each question Upham asked him. He was alternately insolent and bored. He ignored Upham as much as anyone on the witness stand could ignore the attorney who was verbally pummeling him up one side of the courtroom and down the other.

Brad choked up as he said he had cried when he learned how Cheryl had died. 'Finch said she had been bludgeoned. . . . You understand my state of mind,' he said. 'I was nauseous. I was actually weaving. I threw up a little in my hand and ran for the bathroom.' Had he forgotten Jim Ayers' testimony that he had shown virtually no emotion upon learning that Cheryl was dead, and that neither he nor Finch had told Brad how Cheryl died?

Again and again, Upham tripped Brad up. On times. On whom he had talked to the night of the murder and when. Even on what snacks he fed his children and what was on television. Brad was angry, but controlled.

'You were wearing a yellow-and-orange vest when Jess opened the door?' Upham asked.

'No.'

'You didn't tell Jess you'd been jogging around Sara's hospital?'

'No.'

'You washed up in the kitchen?'

'No.' Brad said he had put an old pair of shoes and pants in Sara's car because he had to test soil on land in Tigard the next day. He had planned to pick up his Suburban at Providence Hospital early the next morning.

Upham asked a question that surprised Brad. 'Who was going to take care of Phillip?'

Brad looked puzzled.

'You didn't call anyone Sunday night to take care of Phillip Monday morning?'

He had not. The inference was, of course, that Brad knew

that this Monday morning would be different, that there would be no need for routine baby-sitting.

Brad wanted to talk instead about the many loads of laundry he had done in his apartment Sunday night. 'I did a lot of wash. I was staying busy,' he said. 'I was having a good time with my sons.'

Brad's answers were making less and less sense. Now in response to many of Upham's questions, he evaded answering and talked instead of the destruction of his life by everyone. He could count on no one. He had been fired after Cheryl's murder. Yes, Sara had paid some of his legal fees – but he had paid her back. Bob McNannay withheld trust funds from the boys, so he had had to borrow from the Colville tribe. He had had no choice but to let Sara adopt his sons so Betty wouldn't get them. Sara didn't want children. 'I wish I hadn't done it.'

Upham showed Brad the letter in which he begged Sara not to divorce him. 'I wasn't going to talk about certain things,' Brad said, 'but it looks like I'll have to.' He smiled. 'It appeared she was seeing other men. Want to hear about it?'

Brad had slipped into a familiar refrain, but Upham didn't encourage it. Instead, he asked if there was another reason for his divorce from Sara, and Brad said that his marriage began to disintegrate when the 'tax thing' started to fall apart.

'In 1990?' Upham asked.

'Before,' Brad replied. 'We had tax problems. There were certain accusations. Certain disclosures.'

Upham asked Brad if he recalled a stipulated money judgment and dissolution-of-marriage document he had signed on September 21, 1991 – ironically on the fifth anniversary of Cheryl's murder. In that document, Brad had admitted to most of Sara's accusations and agreed to pay her a fifty-thousand-dollar judgment against him. 'The boys got the farm,' Brad said vaguely. 'I don't remember the fifty-thousand-dollar judgment. I can't remember certain events taking place . . . can't remember denying Sara visits and phone calls with the children. . . . I just wanted out. I wanted nothing to do with her.'

Upham remarked that Brad's divorce from Sara was 'eerily reminiscent' of the last days of his marriage to Cheryl. Brad didn't get it. He said that he suspected Sara of drugging his children to control them. 'I still do. They're like Stepford children. . . . My boys have one mother – *Cheryl*.'

Upham had cross-examined Brad for three hours. He was unruffled, but Brad looked exhausted, stress tightening his face into a deeply lined mask.

When the letters that he had been sending to his sons while they were living with Sara were admitted into evidence, Brad panicked. He didn't want the envelopes in evidence. Anyone who had seen those envelopes understood why. Judge Alexander allowed Brad to hold back the envelopes with their vicious and suggestive cartoons. And when court recessed, he grabbed for the stack of letters and hurriedly ripped the envelope off each one.

On re-direct, Brad took the stand to try to patch up the huge rents Upham had torn in his case. His own explanations were really all he had; the witnesses from his long list never materialized. Now, to refute the prosecution's witnesses, he launched another tirade against the women in his life. He hinted that Sara was a lesbian who was using her money to keep his sons from him. 'It's been the boys and me, and now Sara has the children. . . . We're going to sue Sara and get our farm back together. . . . the boys and I will be back together.'

Judge Alexander warned Brad that he was sliding toward closing argument rather than giving testimony.

Ignoring the warning, Brad again listed the faults of Loni Ann, Cynthia, Lauren, and of course Cheryl. He covered old territory, oblivious to the damage he was inflicting on his case as, once again, the details about his whereabouts and activities on the night of the murder changed slightly. Brad apparently feared that the jury had noticed his security leg brace, because he explained to them that he had a bad leg and wore a brace. 'I had cancer of the bone when I was little, but it got better so I could play football in high school and college. . . .'

He was rambling and Alexander was running out of patience. He warned Brad to finish up. 'I've done a lot of depositions,' Brad said. 'I've always tried to be honest.'

Judge Alexander warned him again.

When Brad veered back into his financial affairs and once again began to quote dollar figures, Alexander told him that there was no need to re-cover old ground. He looked at Upham and said, 'Any request for recross will be viewed with great disfavor.'

'No questions,' Upham said wisely.

Brad wanted to call Judge Alexander as a witness, and Alexander explained that the judge of a trial cannot be called to the stand.

'I'm not sure that's your call,' Brad said rudely.

'Well, in my courtroom, it is. You've rested your case,' Alexander said flatly.

'I move for a judgment of acquittal,' Brad said.

'Denied.'

Only Alexander had managed to keep the trial from becoming a 'Keystone Kourt,' and he tried again to save Brad from his own ferocious ego. He offered him one more chance to change his plea from 'not guilty' to 'manslaughter in the first degree.'

'This would be your last chance,' Alexander said. 'Murder is life in the penitentiary with various minimums.'

Brad huddled with Kevin Hunt, who obviously was urging him to take the judge's advice. But Brad would have none of it. He was going for a straight 'not guilty' verdict.

64

It was 3:27 P.M., three days before Christmas Eve, and at last the time had come for final arguments.

Although few knew it, Scott Upham was suffering from a violent case of forty-eight-hour flu that day. But his voice never betrayed his queasy stomach and pounding headache, and when a wave of dizziness hit him, he managed to make holding on to the lectern look like a strong posture rather than a need for support. He had not come this far to back off now.

Upham told the jury that their job was to decide what was worthy of belief and what was not, what was relevant and what was not. They must consider 'direct evidence' such as eyewitness testimony and 'circumstantial evidence' – a chain of circumstances pointing to an obvious conclusion. 'Murder is the intentional taking of the life of a human being,' he said. 'I'm here to tell you the defendant is guilty of murder.'

It would take twelve jurors to convict, and only ten to acquit. With flawless memory, Upham went over the story of the lives of Brad and Cheryl. He had done so back in October when the trial began, and now the story was familiar and the jury had a chance to judge for themselves who was telling the truth.

'Cheryl was scared,' Upham said. 'She changed her will, the beneficiary of her life insurance.' Gesturing toward Brad, he said, 'This is the public Mr Cunningham. Cheryl knew the private Mr Cunningham . . . the temper, selfish, no empathy, competitive. He's willing to act on his propensity to destroy . . . feels very comfortable, very at ease, in hurting other people. "The kids are my possessions." Cheryl wanted peace. What an enemy he was! Relentless. He has staying power, and he'll do *anything* to get his way.'

What a horror Cheryl had lived through. This jury had never – and would never – hear about what Brad had done to his first three wives, not in a criminal case, but they had come to know Cheryl, and their eyes moved from Upham to Brad as Upham spoke. 'The note [Cheryl left] and her conversation with Betty were sufficient to convict,' he said, 'but there's more.' He listed the strongest points of an already strong case: Brad's threatening and obsessive behavior before Cheryl's murder, his inconsistent alibis for the time of her death, his flight to evade questioning. 'He told Sara on Monday evening,' Upham said, '"I'd better not answer – I'm digging too many holes, and I've got too many holes to fill now."'

Upham recalled all the people Brad had accused of lying: Karen Aaborg, Jim Ayers, Dr Sardo, Jess, Jim Karr, Sara. 'Finally, he says Cheryl lied to her mother and her brother in her last note. . . . The innocent do not behave like that. The innocent don't have to lie to that degree. He viciously murdered Cheryl Keeton, and he's lied. . . . He lured Cheryl Keeton from the safety of her home. Because of her love for those children, she went. Cheryl has told us what the truth is in her conversation with her mother and in her note. "Bradly Morris Cunningham murdered me."'

Brad and Upham had been allotted a total of two hours each for final arguments. Upham could speak once more; Brad could speak only once, and he was clearly nervous. But he had now formulated a timetable for the night of the murder that warred with that established by the Oregon State Police, and Mike Shinn, and Upham and his staff. By adding a few minutes here and shaving a few there, he set out to prove the prosecution wrong.

As he spoke, Brad warmed to his subject and became animated. He insisted that, had he been the killer, there would have been a window of only nine minutes and forty-eight seconds in which he could have driven from the death site back to the Madison Tower, disposed of his bloody clothing, driven through the gate, parked, gone up the elevator, and unlocked the door 'with a four-year-old boy in tow.' He asked, 'How could you get back to the Mobil station that fast? I don't run four-minute miles. It would take at least seven minutes to run back. . . .'

No, he insisted, his Sunday evening had not been spent the way Upham said. He could account for every minute of the time between 7:30 and 10:00. 'I made popcorn. Michael and I had to leave the room because he couldn't settle down. I left to get blankets out of the car. We'd race like that. Zip here. Zip there.' He said he had changed into shorts and a T-shirt because that was comfortable 'and I felt I looked good. Cheryl was coming over to see my apartment.'

There were no dishes to wash, Brad said, but Michael had helped him wash three or four loads of laundry. 'He'd pour in the soap and I'd throw the clothes in the dryer.' Female jurors exchanged glances. Three or four loads of laundry would have taken at least four hours. But Brad was on a roll now and seemed to be enjoying himself. He became magnanimous as he smiled at the jurors. 'All you wonderful people had to sit here so long because I didn't know they'd bring in income tax fraud and bankruptcy. I thought we had a five-to-ten-day case. . . . Ninety-eight percent of the time, I'm happy with court decisions, because it's fair. I *am* litigious. . . .'

He talked of items that Cheryl and her brother had hidden from the bankruptcy court. 'She was committing bankruptcy fraud by giving away the bronze moose head, my Rolex, the stereo, the Nikon camera . . . and I was about to depose some of her partners. It was the right time to paint me black. . . . Cheryl wasn't a little wallflower. She was fully apprised of everything we did.'

The transformation that took place in Judge Alexander's courtroom was fascinating as Brad obviously felt he had the jury in the palm of his hand. He was alternately sarcastic and expansive. 'I wanted custody so I killed my wife,' he said almost laughing. 'That's ludicrous. . . . I wasn't interested in full custody. You had to go for the whole enchilada? I didn't want it. I was president of a seventeen-million-dollar company. My life was good. All I wanted to show the judge was that Cheryl couldn't be the *primary* parent. She had to spend time with Mr Sloane,* Mr Miller,* Mr Thomas,* Mr Green,* et cetera. She didn't have *time* to be the primary parent.'

Brad smiled winningly. 'I tend to be too analytical. I tend to be too practical,' he said. 'I'm not a day at the beach, sometimes. Today, I stand before you only ten percent of the man I was two or three years ago. I'm more introspective. Cheryl was a good mother. She was going through a cycle. I was too. I was coming out. She got her licks in with her affairs with guys at the office. . . . My life was back on track in September 1986 . . . I was on a career track, my kids were happy, I was making eighty thousand a year, and I was dating Dr Gordon. . . . I'm a person who has fiscal responsibility. I always have been.'

Suddenly, Brad's charismatic smile faded as he talked of the pictures of Cheryl after she was dead. 'I never saw those pictures before,' he said. 'They do that to shock you and upset you. It bothers me. They have no right to take pictures of Cheryl and show them like that. It's a stunt.' His voice faltered and he began to cry. 'Believe me, the police officers have a set too. . . . You have to find me not guilty. You have to look at the facts.'

Brad continued to sob. 'I loved Cheryl. I loved her in August of 1986.' His tears caught in his throat. 'I loved her in September of 1986.' His voice dropped dramatically. 'I can still hear her say, "Possession is nine points of the law." . . . I'm also a little naive – I always have been – I'm always a little shocked. . . . Cheryl lied in her deposition.'

Spectators were transfixed by his performance. 'I don't have to prove anything,' Brad said softly. 'But I tried to.

This was not a life experience I want, but I had a duty to my children. This was incredible. I had no idea it would be like this technically. I'm not very proficient and Judge Alexander got mad at me.'

Brad spoke of 'depraved indifference' as he stood before the jury, but Judge Alexander called it a day for him. He would have the rest of his two hours in the morning. And when he resumed his final argument, Brad explained that he had only wanted to put Michael on the stand, his alibi witness, but the judge hadn't allowed it. He said that he had just begun to understand the way the trial should go when it was all over. And once again he went down the list of those he blamed.

'Your time is up,' Judge Alexander interrupted. 'Make some concluding remarks.'

'Think about Cheryl's life,' Brad said earnestly. 'Strange stuff. *I* had no motive. This was Mom. This is Mom. I can tell you on the health of my children, I would never have killed their mom.'

Scott Upham rose to give the prosecution's final argument. He looked at the jurors whose faces were as impassive as all jurors' are. Had they believed any of Brad's histrionics? There was always the danger of finding out that one or two jurors had bought a story that seemed, to Upham, patently false. He never quit until it was *really* all over. Still a little pale around the gills, he began, 'This isn't about theories. This is about truth. . . .'

Upham commented that real people didn't have stop watches as they went about their lives. All of Brad's careful manipulation of times was not enough to change the facts. There was no question, he said, that Cheryl was terribly upset when she called her mother shortly after seven on Sunday night. 'The month of September had been especially brutal for her – all the incidents added to her fear and apprehension.' Even changing times slightly, Upham said, 'the defendant clearly had the opportunity to do what Cheryl said he would do – that's sufficient to find him guilty of murder.'

Brad had deliberately staged a car wreck, he said. Hadn't his first question to Jim Ayers been, Did she die in a traffic accident?

No, Ayers had said.

Upham speculated about what Brad must have thought: *Damn! Now what do I do?*

'To believe he didn't do this [crime],' Upham said, 'Cheryl's note would have had to be a lie. Her call to Betty would have to be a lie. She'd have to lie to Jim Karr at seven-thirty. She deliberately lied three times?' And then, Upham pointed out, Sara had, of course, lied about her calls to Brad that went unanswered. Marv Troseth's calls weren't answered either, so that would make him a liar too. 'The last lie was when Jess unlocked the door and Brad said, "I've been jogging around Sara's hospital." That makes nine lies told by four different people,' Upham said. 'Jess, Cheryl, Marv, and Sara. I believe Mr Cunningham is unworthy of your attention.'

Brad's furious objection was sustained.

'Brad's lie,' Upham continued undeterred, 'was "I'm excited about showing her [Cheryl] my digs – even though I'm destroying her in the divorce, with the kids, and ruining her partners' reputation.' He listed all the people who had to be wrong for Brad to be right, and the list encompassed almost everyone he had been in contact with – or who had seen him when he hadn't wanted to be seen – on the night Cheryl died. 'Mr Cunningham is willing to say anything under any circumstances to suit his convenience.

'Cheryl's note, the phone calls, the time-line witnesses, his behavior after Cheryl's murder, and his contradictory statements all point to guilt,' Upham said. 'The autopsy shows that Cheryl Keeton was savagely murdered. . . . But there was no sexual attack, and it was not robbery. The motive was pure hatred.

'And he left his calling card,' Upham added. 'His DNA.'

Upham said that the only person who hated Cheryl was Bradly Morris Cunningham. Brad objected and was overruled. Upham's final argument was getting to Brad, and he objected constantly until Judge Alexander reminded him, '*This* is closing argument.'

'Everybody's out to get Mr Cunningham,' Upham said wearily. 'He consistently and relentlessly lies. It just wears me out to think of them all. I'm not going to try.'

Upham picked up a handful of the letters that Brad had sent to Jess, Michael, and Phillip from jail. While Sara cared for his children, he had clearly tried to destroy their trust in her. As Upham read excerpts, the jurors' faces and body language reflected shock for the first time in the trial.

'I worry about you. . . . Sara's destroying our father and son relationship. . . . Her sick black soul . . . controls you with money.'

'Dearest Sons, Things are going really well. . . . Maybe her reign is nearing the end.'

'Dear Sons, She is sweating her butt off. She is praying to her black God, her devil master. I think her condition is becoming critical and terminal. . . .'

Brad slouched in his chair, quietly enraged, his jaw working as Upham wound up his remarks. 'He's a master of trickery and deceit. He has special talents. It's okay for him to lie, to violate court rules, to destroy her family, to destroy Cheryl's memory – okay to destroy innocent motorists on Highway 26 to cover his tracks, but he can't overcome all the witnesses and evidence.

'You do not need to be afraid,' Upham told the jury. 'Cheryl Keeton has told us what the truth is. "I went to meet Brad Cunningham on September 21, 1986, to get my kids but he tricked me and savagely beat me. . . ."'

65

Brad had changed his mind, probably with Kevin Hunt's urging, and allowed Judge Alexander to include the criteria for a finding of manslaughter in the first degree as well as for murder as he read the instructions to the jury. He was, perhaps, not as confident as he had been before Upham's final argument. He slouched deeper in his chair and leaned to one side with his jaw resting on splayed fingers. Listening had always been difficult for him. He seemed to have felt his words were convincing, but now he appeared apprehensive.

The two alternate jurors, not needed, were dismissed and the jurors filed out to deliberate. It was so close to the noon break that no one expected they would begin to discuss the case until early afternoon. The 'regulars' in the courtroom walked out into the chilly air and headed toward the Copper Stone Restaurant. For an hour or two, the tension would be gone. Too early to worry about a verdict. Seated at tables were Betty and Marv Troseth, Susan and Dave Keegan, Bob McNannay, Jack Kincaid, Debi and Billy Bowen, Kim and Bill Roberts, Mike Shinn, Katannah King, Donna Anders, and myself. Sara Gordon was too nervous to be present – and, besides, she wanted to be with her sons when the verdict came in.

Nobody ate much and conversation was determinedly cheerful, while Christmas songs played on the Muzak and Hillsboro shoppers passed by outside, intent on finding last-minute gifts. Most of the trial-goers had yet to buy a first present for anyone. It was as if their lives had been suspended until they knew if Brad would be convicted or walk free. If he *did* walk free, there would be no Christmas for Sara. The first thing Brad would do was come and take his sons away from her. She had no doubt about that.

There wasn't much happening on the fourth floor of the Washington County Courthouse when we all returned. A few days before, there had been two murder trials – Brad Cunningham's and Cesar Barone's. Now Barone, a suspected serial killer, had been convicted of the murder of nurse-midwife Martha Browning Bryant, and Brad waited in his jail suite for the verdict in his case. The only courtroom that wasn't 'dark' that long Friday afternoon handled civil cases, and the complainants and witnesses came and went as a score or more of people waited for the Cunningham jury to return.

Experienced court watchers say a quick verdict is a guilty verdict; the longer the time that passes, the more likely an acquittal. The afternoon dragged on. When the clock over the public phone read two, and then three, we all began to grow nervous. How long did it take to poll twelve jurors? What were they doing in there?

The most nervous paced the circular route past the elevators, the wall hanging, the civil courtroom, the waiting room, the phones, the water fountain, and around again. Of them all, Jack Kincaid was the steadiest pacer – stopping only long enough to call Sara every hour and, with great acting ability, reassure her that it looked great for a conviction.

Did it? Nobody knew. To pass the time, everyone put up a dollar and guessed an exact time the jury would come back. The 'pot' held more than twenty dollars. Cheryl's sister Susan, happily pregnant with her first child, was designated the most reliable person to hold the money. At four o'clock, the jury had been out for five hours. Allowing even an hour and a half for lunch, that still left them more than three hours to deliberate.

Nerves began to fray. Kincaid was joined on his circular pacing route by a half dozen others, and stern court guards stepped out of the civil courtroom and shushed them. The word was that the jury would not stay after six to deliberate, and the thought of having to wait overnight was agonizing. Cheryl's California relatives had small children who were looking forward to Christmas and they would have to leave. But somehow everyone felt that it was essential to wait, that being there in the hallway was the last thing they could do for Cheryl, even knowing that it couldn't really matter. The jury was locked in its own cocoon behind so many doors.

It didn't look good. It was almost five, and all the pool guessers had long since passed the time they had picked – all but Marv Troseth.

And then Jerry Wells, the courtroom deputy who had always been full of jokes and irreverent remarks, walked back to where Cheryl's family and a few reporters waited. For once, he was entirely serious and he looked worried. 'Whenever the jury comes back,' he said slowly, 'I want you all to know that there are to be no demonstrations, no remarks, no noise. I'll have to ask you to leave the courtroom if you can't live by those rules.'

'*Is* the jury coming back?' somebody asked.

'I didn't say that,' Wells said carefully. 'When it does, I'm telling you that I mean that I don't care how much I like you, anybody who acts up is out.' He looked straight at Billy Bowen, Cheryl's tall, husky brother-in-law, as he spoke. Billy grew emotional whenever he thought that Cheryl had had no one to help her. Now he looked back at Jerry and nodded slightly. He wouldn't cause any trouble.

Something was happening. The elevator doors opened and Kevin Hunt and Tim Lyons stepped out and hurried into Suzie Dudy's office. Word was that Scott Upham and Jim Carr were on their way up the back stairs from the D.A.'s office.

The short corridor outside Judge Alexander's courtroom where spectators had lined up every day for two months was suddenly full of people, some leaning against the wall, others sitting on the floor. Waiting. It was 5:15 P.M. on

Thursday, December 22, 1994, and everyone sensed there would be no overnight wait.

At 5:24, a bell began to ding in Suzie's office. The jury was back. The jury had a verdict.

At 5:40, Cheryl's family sat together in the back row of the courtroom and held hands as they fought to contain their emotions. Brad was sitting at the defense table with Hunt and Lyons, Upham at his table. Judge Alexander glanced at the gallery and repeated the warning that Jerry Wells had given. There were to be no outbursts when the verdict was read. Either way it went, it would be difficult to keep silent after eight years of waiting.

The jury filed in silently and took their seats.

'Have you reached a verdict?' Judge Alexander asked.

'We have, Your Honor,' jury foreman Robert Wilcoxen said, and handed the findings to bailiff Suzie Dudy. She handed it to Judge Alexander who read it without expression and returned it to Suzie.

Silently and quickly, court security officers Jerry Wells, Trish DeLand, and J. C. Crossland had moved to stand behind Brad, creating a barrier between him and the first row of the gallery where reporters waited, pens poised.

'We find the defendant, Bradly Morris Cunningham,' she read, 'guilty of murder. . . .'

Brad sat slouched in his chair, his face turned away from the spectators, but he shook his head very slowly back and forth as if to say, This is all a terrible mistake.

Upham didn't ask for a poll of the jurors, but Brad wanted it done. One by one they looked at him as they repeated 'guilty' until the twelfth 'guilty' hung on the air.

'It was over so quickly,' Susan Keegan remembered. 'After all those years, it was over. When I walked out of the courtroom, Jim Carr grabbed me and took me over to Scott. Scott had tears in his eyes and I hugged him. I just kept saying to him, "You never gave up. You never gave up!"'

While television cameras focused on Cheryl's family,

Jerry Wells and Trish DeLand waited to lead Brad back to jail. Betty Troseth cried too as she told reporters, 'Cheryl believed in the justice system and now I know it works.'

For the first time in his life, perhaps, Brad Cunningham had lost and lost big. Jerry Wells observed that he could barely stand, his legs turned to rubber by shock. To no one in particular, Brad asked, 'Has anyone ever come back here on appeal?'

Wells looked away, but Trish DeLand said, 'Yeah, a woman did – and she got convicted the second time too.'

Jack Kincaid rushed to the phone to tell Sara that she would have her sons with her for Christmas, that, in all likelihood, she would have her sons with her until they grew to be men.

While everyone outside was agonizing about what they were doing, the jurors had taken a quick vote when they first retired to deliberate. That vote was eight for guilty and four undecided. They didn't vote again until forty-five minutes before they returned with their verdict. At that point, just as everyone waiting was beginning to panic, Wilcoxen counted eleven guilties and tore up the twelfth, his own – he knew he had voted guilty. It had been a long hard afternoon for them, and many of the women had cried because of the tremendous responsibility they felt. For all of Upham's research into Brad's checkered financial background, he later learned that the jurors 'didn't give a hoot about all the bankruptcy stuff and they weren't impressed by the DNA.' None of them had cared for Brad, but they knew they couldn't render a verdict on whether they liked him or not. What had really made up their minds was the testimony from the silent witness. Cheryl's last note and her conversation with her mother right before she left the house to go to meet her killer were the two pieces of evidence that the jurors had found totally convincing.

In five hours, it would be the day before Christmas Eve. The snow had all disappeared and the air was cold and smoky with fog. Cheryl's family headed toward Longview for their eighth Christmas without her but, somehow, it would not be so bad now. Celebrants wandered back to the Copper Stone, still almost stunned that it was over and that it was okay. Scott Upham, Mike McKernan, and Jim Carr had a beer, and Upham enjoyed a good cigar. Mike Shinn and Upham shook hands as Shinn complimented Upham on his remarkably convincing final arguments.

By tomorrow, everyone who had been together daily for months would be scattered, off to their real lives in three states.

On January 6, 1995, the group reassembled for the last time. Brad was to be sentenced that afternoon for the crime of murder. Now that he had been convicted, Upham could present witnesses about prior bad acts he had committed and reveal incidents and behavior that might affect the length of his sentence. Two women from his past, women Brad had not expected, were in the courtroom. Dana Malloy took the witness stand, a glamorous figure with masses of long blond hair, dressed in what looked to be a thousand-dollar outfit.

She was so frightened to be there, less than a dozen feet from Brad, that her voice was barely audible. Even the sound of a reporter's pen on paper drowned out her words. Brad's life with Dana had been a secret thing and the jurors had never heard about how he indoctrinated her into the world of topless dancing. Now, with Upham's gentle urging, she told it all. The nights in Houston, the times the little boys were left alone, and Brad's bizarre actions and threats, how he had told her that a psychic had predicted she would commit suicide.

When Brad rose to cross-examine his former mistress, Dana looked at him with apprehension. She had reason to. He immediately set out to characterize her as working for the 'Seattle Mafia.'

'I tried to set you and your mother up in your own

business space as cosmetologists – didn't I?' he asked. 'I was concerned for your safety?'

She stared back at him. 'No.'

Brad reminded her that he had found her and her lover, Nick Ronzini, having sex and he had thrown them out of his apartment.

'You're twisting everything around,' Dana said.

'And I put your things down the hall—?'

'No. You took everything I owned and put it in the Dumpster,' she said.

In the back of the courtroom, a new spectator, a very tall, slender young woman with black hair and round European-style black sunglasses, leaned forward, listening intently.

Brad insisted that Dana had been told exactly what to say by the Oregon State Police and the D.A.'s office, and she would not agree. Nor would she agree that he had hired the Blue Moon Detective Agency to find her only because he was worried about her and thought something had happened to her. Brad was determined to show that Dana was a prostitute, but Judge Alexander stopped him, saying that her job had nothing to do with her credibility.

'You make over two hundred thousand dollars a year, don't you?' Brad pushed on.

'I don't know what you're talking about,' Dana said.

Finally Dana's voice rose to a pitch everyone in the courtroom could hear. 'Brad, do you *really* want to get into this?'

Apparently he did not. Dana looked at Brad with an almost unreadable expression. 'I thought you were God,' she said quietly. It was obvious she no longer did.

Scott Upham asked Dana about the times Brad had followed John Burke, Cheryl's old friend and the administrator of her estate. 'Did he say he wanted to kill John Burke?'

After a long hesitation, Dana said, 'Yes.'

* * *

Upham wanted to be sure that Brad stayed in prison as long as possible under the guidelines that were extant for the crime of murder in Oregon in 1986. He had another surprise witness, Ronald O. Marracci, a private investigator whom Brad had hired in the summer of 1994, only months before his trial for murder. He testified that Brad had paid him two thousand dollars at forty dollars an hour, and paid by check.

'What did he want you to do for him?' Upham asked.

Marracci said that Brad had hired him to buy a truck, a camper, a .30–.30 rifle, and some handguns. He said he would need all those things when he was acquitted of murder and got out of jail. He planned to pick up his three sons and travel with them, and, of course, they would need the truck and the weapons. It was Sara's worst nightmare, although she had not known that Brad was actually making preparations to disappear with the boys.

Upham rose to ask for the stiffest sentence possible. 'The pattern started early in his life,' he said. 'He has very little regard for other people or rules. He will do anything he has to to get what he wants. . . . He should not ever be allowed to be free. As he sits here, he has no family. He has no friends. He has a character disorder and it can't be fixed.'

Brad also made a brief statement, 'I would not benefit from long-term incarceration,' he said, 'because I am a caring person.'

Unfortunately, Judge Alexander was bound by statute and he could not be sure that Brad would never be free. He could sentence him to life in prison, but the only discretion he had was to raise the mandated ten-year minimum to twenty-five years. He set the minimum at twenty-two years. Brad would not be eligible for parole until 2014, and if he was still alive, he would be sixty-eight at that time.

'That the attack was premeditated and carefully planned, the viciousness of the attack, Mr Cunningham's total lack of remorse, and repeated false statements by Mr Cunningham' were all factors Alexander took into account. The only mitigating factor he found was that Brad had no prior criminal record.

Brad assured the judge that he would appeal his sentence within thirty days.

As the spectators filed out, the tall young woman in the back row moved out into the hall. The mention of Dana's possessions being thrown into a Dumpster had been all too familiar to her. It was Kait Cunningham, who was now twenty-five. Despite her father's predictions in Houston that she would never amount to anything, Kait had grown up to be a willowy beauty, a model in Paris. She had come back to witness her father's downfall and to tell him in person – adult to adult – what she thought of him and his treatment of the frightened little girl she had once been.

As she had with all Brad's children, Sara had opened up her home and Kait was staying with her. Later, she visited Brad in the visitor's area of the jail and blasted him with the pent-up emotion of many years.

Brad asked not to stay in the Washington County jail any longer than necessary. He was anxious to move down to Salem to the Oregon State Penitentiary.

That request was granted.

AFTERWORD

Sara wanted to buy something happy to celebrate the fact that she and her sons would no longer have to be afraid. When she learned of the guilty verdict, she chose a figure of Santa Claus in his workshop, executed to precise scale with toys and ornaments and sugarplums. It was a symbolic purchase that meant they would be together not just for the Christmas of 1994 but forever. And as the months passed, the rift between Sara and Jack Kincaid narrowed and it was obvious that they too would be together when the time was right.

Sara still works in the anesthesiology department at Providence Hospital. On weekends, she usually attends baseball games and other events the boys are involved in. Brent Cunningham lives with her and his brothers and goes to school. When Sara cannot be there, he is with Jess, Michael, and Phillip.

Scott Upham is involved in another convoluted murder case, but he and Mary Ann Upham finally managed to break ground on their new house in May 1995.

Jim Carr was involved in a horrendous accident in February 1995, when a felon speeding from a police chase slammed broadside into the driver's-side door of his car. He is recovering after emergency surgery.

Mike Shinn is back out on the Columbia River sail-boarding. He bought some hilltop property in Hawaii where he plans, one day, to build a house. In the meantime, he has more cases than he can handle and he presents trial seminars with criminal defense attorney Gerry Spence.

Susan McNannay Keegan gave birth to a baby girl, Ann Marie Keegan, in May 1995. She would have loved to share Anna Marie with Cheryl and she had always believed that accidents of birth had hastened her sister's death. 'The thing that killed Cheryl,' she said, 'was that she gave Brad three boy children, and she tried to keep them. If she had only had one child – a girl – she'd be here today. If Loni Ann had had two boys, instead of a boy and a girl, she'd be dead now. If Lauren had had a boy instead of Amy, she'd be dead. But Cheryl had three boys. . . .'

Bob McNannay still lives in Longview and he dotes on the only child of his only child.

Marv and Betty Troseth have moved away from Longview. Betty still works as a therapist for the mentally ill.

Loni Ann Cunningham is hoping to move back to the Northwest, now that she no longer has to hide from Brad.

Rosemary Cunningham Kinney died in 1993 in Washington. To the end of her long illness, she hoped that Brad might call her. One cousin says, 'I think he did call – but she was already gone.' Kait Cunningham stood at her grandmother's grave and gave a eulogy, after telling the minister, 'You didn't know my grandmother. How can you speak of her?'

Brad Cunningham found that the Oregon State Penitentiary was not much more to his liking than the Washington County jail. Two longtimers who had been in the jail at the same time he was remembered that he had 'snitched them off' about their secret places for hiding cigarettes. A few weeks after he got to the Salem prison, he was eating lunch in the chow hall when a convict walking down the row popped him in the face and broke his nose. He will probably be transferred to an eastern Oregon prison for his own protection.

Brad has appealed his conviction.

In the spring of 1995, the proceeds from Brad's Houston suit were disbursed. After his legal fees, he had something more than six hundred thousand dollars left. Secured creditors and others in his bankruptcy got all but two hundred thousand. Garvey, Schubert and Barer, Cheryl's law firm, had spent twice that amount to sue him civilly. 'We split what was left with Cheryl's sons,' Greg Dallaire said. 'We'll hold it in trust for them.' Brad got nothing at all.

The taxpayers of the State of Oregon took a heavy hit from the cost of Brad's defense. The enterpreneur (now indigent) defendant's attorneys-*cum*-'legal advisors' and his private investigator cost the state $261,435. That amount did not include the general costs of his lengthy trial.

Sara Gordon wants her sons to remember the mother they lost. She has asked all of Cheryl's family to write down their memories of Cheryl, and to send pictures and videos so that Jess, Michael, and Phillip will know what a wonderful woman their mother was and how very much she loved them.

ACKNOWLEDGMENTS

The case that is the center of *Dead by Sunset* didn't receive much media coverage when it began. Had it not been for a dozen letters and phone calls from people I had never met, I probably never would have looked into it. What I discovered is the stuff of nightmares. Quite frankly, I almost walked away from it. In the end, I stayed. Once I began to peel away the first layers of a bizarre and dangerous personality, I found that I needed the recall and experience of dozens of people to help me reveal the truth. Because in some cases they feared for their lives, it took a great deal of courage for many of them to approach me. It took even more for them to tell me secrets that had been hidden for years. Some of them didn't want their names mentioned at all, and in other instances I have changed names.

For their trust in me and their willingness to discuss tragic memories, I am grateful, in particular, to Betty and Marv Troseth, Susan McNannay Keegan, Bob McNannay, Jim Karr, Debi and Billy Bowen, Kim and Bill Roberts, and Katannah King.

I could never have written this book if it had not been for Michael Shinn, Diane Bakker, and the late Connie Capato. They literally risked their lives to expose an evil man who still walked free. The professional insight I got from Detective Jim Ayers of the Oregon State Police was invaluable. Even though I never had the chance to meet him, the work of the late Detective Jerry Finch on this murder investigation also helped me a great deal. Thanks too to Oregon State Police Sergeant Greg Baxter, Detective Mike McKernan, Sergeant James Hinkley, Criminalist Julia Hinkley, Dr Cecilia von Beroldingen, and Portland police officers Rick Olsen and Craig Ward.

Washington County District Attorney Scott Upham and his staff – particularly Investigator Jim Carr and Juanita Carey – shared their perceptions and their recall of a very long investigation and a grueling trial. Scott and Jim were especially helpful.

The Washington County Court Security staff, under the command of Sergeant Mel Leutwyler, became friends, and I forgive them for all the times they searched my purse for alleged contraband. Although they were dealing with *two* major trials, they always kept their sense of humor. Thanks especially to Jerry Wells, J. C. Crossland, Scott Barnes, Larry Watts, and Trish DeLand. I know it wasn't easy – ever.

And my thanks go to Judge Alan Bonebrake, his judicial assistant Linda Campbell-Peachy, Judge Tim Alexander, his judicial assistant Suzie Dudy, and his court clerk Gwen Lipske. And to Judge Ancer Haggerty.

In a case such as this, people often don't want to be specifically identified for the part they played, but I still want to thank them: Gwen Elkin, Kay Hicks, April Arwood, Janet Haines, Alice Baldwin, 'Duke' Wells, Kari Morando, Betty Pautsche, Mary Hilfer, Michele Hinz, Halle Sadle, Kate Ayers, Jeanne Hermens, Jack Livengood, John Burke, Clyde Gideon, Jr., Sharlene Mastrandrea, Arlene Reynolds, Craig Anderson, Wesley Bishop, Doreen McIness, Kalen Thomas, and Amy Lowin.

In this complicated legal marathon, it helped to have fellow journalists to compare notes with, and we covered for each other when one of us couldn't be in court: Fiona Ortiz, Margie Ramirez, and Robin Franzen of the *Oregonian*, Laurie Smith, Bill Wagner, and Greg Ebersole of Longview, Washington's *Daily News*, and Eric Apalategui of *The Hillsboro Argus*.

The law firm of Garvey, Schubert and Barer refused to

let the murder of their senior partner, Cheryl Keeton, go unpunished. I commend them, and I thank especially Greg Dallaire, Eric Lindenauer, and Kerry Radcliffe for their memories of Cheryl and their fight to avenge her.

Dr Ron Turco helped me a great deal with his psychological profile of the kind of killer who would have carried out the brutal murder in September 1986. And to my old friend and mentor, Retired Deputy Chief Rod Englert of the Multnomah Sheriff's office, thanks again for your expertise on the more arcane aspects of crime-scene investigation.

Although I do all my own research, I always seek backup and second opinions on how I have perceived the events as they occurred, *and* on the way I wrote it all down. Thanks for a tremendous amount of wisdom and sensitivity go to Donna Anders, Ozzie Carlson, and Gerry Brittingham.

My gratitude to Neil Wilburn of Limelight Video for providing tapes of legal proceedings that took place when I could not be present.

I am grateful to the Commons at Creekside and the Hallmark Inn in Hillsboro, and to the people of Hillsboro and Washington County, Oregon, who were such gracious hosts for the months I lived there.

I am a lucky woman to have the continuing support of a solid foundation of friends: Anne Jaeger, Haleigh Jaeger, Jim Bosley, Mary Starrett, Sue and Joe Beckner, Verne Carver, Maureen and Bill Woodcock, Bill and Shirley Hickman, Ione and Jack Kniskern, Hank Gruber, Bill Hoppe, Jim Stovall, Verne Shangle, Joyce and Pierce Brooks, Austin and Charlotte Seth, Barbara Easton, Clarene Shelley, Millie Yoacham, Mike O'Donnell, Vern and Ruth Cornelius, Peter Modde, Jennifer and Siebrand Heimstra, Ginger and Julian Carlson, Cheri Luxa, Bill and Ginger Clinton, Hope Yenko, Bill and Joyce Johnson, Bill and Connie Meloy, Jim Byrnes, Nils and Judith Seth, Erik Seth and Denise Watson. To my children, Laura, Leslie, Andy, Mike, and Bruce, and my grandchildren, Rebecca and Matthew. And to my brother and sister of the heart, Luke and Nancy Fiorante, and, of course, Lucas Saverio Fiorante.

As always, I thank my literary agents, Joan and Joe Foley, and my theatrical agents, Mary Alice Kier and Anna Cottle of Cine/Lit. Without them, there would *be* no books and no movies!

The best is last. I am an author who really *likes* her editors, Fred Hills and Burton Beals, and their enthusiastic assistant, Hilary Black. They absolutely refused to allow me the luxury of writer's block, and even as they were cracking the whip, they were also cheering me on. No author could ask for more. Thanks too to Leslie Ellen and Ann Marlowe, and, as always, my vigilant literary lawyer, Emily Remes.